RENEWALS 458-4574.
DATE DUE

WITHDRAWN
UTSA Libraries

Economic Policy under Uncertainty

Economic Policy under Uncertainty

The Role of Truth and Accountability in Policy Advice

Edited by

Peter Mooslechner

Helene Schuberth

Martin Schürz

Oesterreichische Nationalbank, Austria

Edward Elgar
Cheltenham, UK • Northampton, MA, USA

© Peter Mooslechner, Martin Schürz and Helene Schuberth 2004

All rights reserved. No part of this publication may be reproduced, stored in a retrieval system or transmitted in any form or by any means, electronic, mechanical or photocopying, recording, or otherwise without the prior permission of the publisher.

Published by
Edward Elgar Publishing Limited
Glensanda House
Montpellier Parade
Cheltenham
Glos GL50 1UA
UK

Edward Elgar Publishing, Inc.
136 West Street
Suite 202
Northampton
Massachusetts 01060
USA

A catalogue record for this book
is available from the British Library

ISBN 1 84376 485 7

Library
University of Texas
at San Antonio

Printed & Bound in Great Britain by MPG Books Ltd, Bodmin Cornwall

Contents

v

Contributors

Roger E. Backhouse is Professor of the History and Philosophy of Economics at the University of Birmingham in the UK. He is the author of *The Ordinary Business of Life*, published as *The Penguin History of Economics* in the UK (Princeton University Press/Penguin Books, 2002) and *Truth and Progress in Economic Knowledge* (Edward Elgar, 1997), and the co-editor of *Macroeconomics and the Real World* (Oxford University Press, 2000) with Andrea Salanti, and *Toward a History of Applied Economics* (Duke University Press, 2000) with Jeff Biddle. He is also an associate editor of the *Journal of the History of Economic Thought*.

James Bohman is Danforth Professor of Philosophy at Saint Louis University, US, and the author of *Public Deliberation: Pluralism, Complexity and Democracy* (MIT Press, 1996) and *New Philosophy of Social Science: Problems of Indeterminacy* (MIT Press, 1991). He has also recently edited *Deliberative Democracy: Essays on Reason and Politics* (with William Rehg) and *Perpetual Peace: Essays on Kant's Cosmopolitan Ideal* (with Matthias Lutz-Bachmann), both with MIT Press. He is currently writing a book on cosmopolitan democracy. His other interests include philosophy of social science, critical social theory and pragmatism.

Nancy Cartwright is Professor of Philosophy at the London School of Economics and at the University of California, San Diego, US. She is the author of *How the Laws of Physics Lie* (Oxford University Press, 1983), *Nature's Capacities and Their Measurement* (Oxford University Press, 1989), *Otto Neurath: Philosophy between Science and Politics* (with Jordi Cat, Thomas Uebel and Lola Fleck, Cambridge University Press, 1996) and *The Dappled World: A Study of the Boundaries of Science* (Cambridge University Press, 2000). Her current research interests are causal inference, objectivity, modeling and concept formation in social science.

Paul Davidson is Editor of the Journal of Post Keynesian Economics. He is currently a Visiting Scholar at the New School University. He has authored, edited or cooauthered over 20 books and more than 200 professional articles. His latest book is *Financial Markets, Money and the Real World* (2002).

Sheila C. Dow is Professor of Economics at the University of Stirling, UK and the author of *The Methodology of Macroeconomic Thought* (Edward Elgar, 1996) and *Economic Methodology: An Inquiry* (Oxford University Press, 2002). She is also the co-editor of *Money, Macroeconomics and Keynes* (Routledge, 2002) and *Keynes, Uncertainty and the Global Economy* (Edward Elgar, 2002). Her current research interests include uncertainty and monetary policy, the regional impact of monetary policy, open systems, pluralism and the work of Hume, Smith and Keynes.

Gebhard Kirchgässner is Professor of Economics and Econometrics at the University of St. Gallen, Switzerland and Director of the Swiss Institute for International Economics and Applied Economic Research (SIAW-HSG). He has been a member of the German Academy of Natural Scientists, Leopoldina, Section for Economics and Empirical Social Sciences and a Research Fellow of the CESifo Network since 2001. He is the author of *Homo Oeconomicus* (Mohr Siebeck, 2001) and the co-editor, with Bruno S. Frey, of *Demokratische Wirtschaftspolitik: Theorie und Anwendung* (Vahlen, 2002). His current research interests include applied econometrics, public choice and public finance, as well as methodological foundations of the social sciences.

Uskali Mäki is Professor of Philosophy at the Erasmus University of Rotterdam and Academic Director of the Erasmus Institute for Philosophy and Economics, The Netherlands. He has authored articles on topics relating to the philosophy of economics, such as realism and realisticness, idealizations, causation, explanation, rhetoric, the sociology and economics of economics and the foundations of New Institutional and Austrian economics, which were published in journals such as the *Journal of Economic Literature, Philosophy of the Social Sciences, Studies in the History and Philosophy of Science, Perspectives on Science, Kyklos*, the *Journal of Economic Methodology, History of Political Economy, Economics and Philosophy* or the *Cambridge Journal of Economics*. He is the editor of *The Economic World View: Studies in the Ontology of Economics* (Cambridge University Press, 2001), *Fact and Fiction in Economics: Models, Realism, and Social Construction* (Cambridge University Press, 2002) and a co-editor of *The Handbook of Economic Methodology* (Edward Elgar, 1998), *Economics and Methodology. Crossing Boundaries* (Macmillan, 1998) and *Rationality,*

Institutions and Economic Methodology (Routledge, 1993). He is also an editor of the *Journal of Economic Methodology*.

Peter Mooslechner is Director for Economic Analysis and Research at Oesterreichische Nationalbank and Lecturer in Economic Policy at the University of Economics, Vienna, Austria. His research interests concentrate on monetary and fiscal policy, financial markets and institutions, EU enlargement as well as on the history of economic development and economic thought. He has recently co-edited *Institutional Conflicts and Complementarities* (Kluwer Academic Publishers, 2004), *Structural Challenges for Europe* (Edward Elgar, 2003) and *Economic Convergence and Divergence in Europe* (Edward Elgar, 2003).

William Rehg is Associate Professor of Philosophy at Saint Louis University, US. He is the author of *Insight and Solidarity: The Discourse Ethics of Jürgen Habermas* (University of California Press, 1994), the translator of Habermas's *Between Facts and Norms* (MIT Press, 1996), and co-editor, with James Bohman, of *Deliberative Democracy* (MIT Press, 1997) and *Pluralism and the Pragmatic Turn* (MIT Press, 2001). His current research interests include science and technology studies, argumentation theory and ethics.

Julian Reiss is a post-doctoral researcher on the project *Causality: Metaphysics and Methods* at the Centre for Philosophy of Natural and Social Science at the London School of Economics, UK. He has published various articles on the scientific method and the history and philosophy of economics in academic journals and books. His specific research interests include experimentation, concept formation, econometric method and the mathematization of economics.

Kurt W. Rothschild is Professor Emeritus of the University of Linz, Austria. He is mainly interested in macroeconomic theory and methodology and in questions of the labor market and unemployment. He has written books on economic forecasting, disequilibrium, wage theory, unemployment theories, ethics and economic theory.

Helene Schuberth is economist at the Austrian National Bank. She studied history, political science and economics. Her current research interests include monetary policy, macroeconomic coordination and financial governance. She has published articles on monetary transmission, monetary policy strategy and optimal currency areas.

Martin Schürz is economist at the Austrian National Bank. He studied philosophy, political science and economics. His research interests include democratic theory and monetary policy. He has published as a co-editor two books on economic policy coordination in EMU.

James R. Wible is Professor of Economics and Associate Dean at the Whittemore School of Business and Economics, University of New Hampshire, in Durham, New Hampshire, US. He is the author of the *The Economics of Science: Methodology and Epistemology as if Economics Really Mattered* (Routledge, 1998) and many articles on macroeconomics and philosophy of science, the economics of science and the economic contributions of the pragmatist philosopher C.S. Peirce. His current research interests include a monograph in progress, titled *The Cambridge Scientific Club and the Mathematical Political Economy of Charles Sanders Peirce: Economic and Evolutionary Complexity as an Algebra and Applied Calculus of Qualitative and Quantitative Relations.*

Preface

At an international workshop organized by the Oesterreichische Nationalbank (OeNB) in the fall of 2002, economists, economic policy-makers and philosophers, among them Uskali Mäli and Sheila Dow, discussed issues related to 'Truth in economics.' One of the conclusions we arrived at during the workshop was that deliberations among philosophers, economists and economic policymakers are difficult mainly because of different theoretical perspectives, divergent research interests and heterogeneous terminologies. Thus, we decided to continue our project by focusing in particular on the question as to whether the request for truth may provide a relevant link between these three fields.

Truth has not been a topic in economics for decades. While in the 1960s Keynesian economics seemed to provide the theoretical basis for an adequate economic policy approach, the decline of Keynesianism actually undermined these certainties without explicitly raising the issue of truth. In fact, the question of truth and accountability has not received particular attention in the literature on economic methodology either.

This situation might change with the renaissance of pragmatism in social sciences. Pragmatism seems to provide a way out of the dichotomy between foundationalist epistemology and relativism. Pragmatic theories relate concepts of truth to human concerns, such as beliefs, thoughts and intentional actions, and blur the relationship between theory and practice. Pragmatism does not start from the epistemic question of how beliefs reflect the world but relates the truth of beliefs to social processes. Thus, it focuses on the practical context of scientific inquiry. As even well-justified economic assertions are fallible, discursive truth-seeking procedures help ensure that relevant contributions are not suppressed and that any available information is considered.

Reflections on truth and accountability in economic policy advice under uncertainty may be of interest to academics who reflect on the stance of their discipline, philosophers dealing with economic issues as well as economic policymakers wishing to reflect on the quality of the policy advice they receive.

We want to acknowledge the help of Brigitte Alizadeh-Gruber, Michaela Beichtbuchner and Ronald Heinz.

Peter Mooslechner, Helene Schuberth, Martin Schürz, Vienna, May 2004

1. Economic Policy under Uncertainty: The Role of Truth and Accountability in Policy Advice

Peter Mooslechner, Helene Schuberth and Martin Schürz

Many of the most interesting economic phenomena are characterized by uncertainty as they involve situations in which individuals cannot anticipate the outcome of their decisions. While the notion of risk would allow assigning probabilities to the outcome, it is not easy to account for uncertainty as it is such a fundamental issue. Consequently, uncertainty involves characteristics that transcend scientific disciplinary barriers.

What can economists and philosophers learn from each other? They do not share the same texts and are unlikely to suspend strong beliefs about each other. However, if they are prepared for a reflexive turn on their beliefs both groups might gain new perspectives of their own topics. The issue at heart is what economists actually do when they act as economic policy advisers and what philosophers believe that economic policy advisers shall and can do.

When politicians formulate economic policy measures they explicitly or implicitly refer to the advice of economic experts. The community of economists includes academics, business-economists and media-economists. As the discipline of economics is, among other things, concerned with social actions and structures, some economists aim at acquiring knowledge about social kinds. Others consider their discipline to be applied mathematics. While the kind of economics that focuses on self-defined problems may not take into consideration social problems, the kind of economics that is part of applied mathematics can only be of limited relevance for economic policy. Generally, economic science can be idealized as a framework for the search for truth. But science is social, interest-laden, situated and contextual. Thus, opinions on what economists can and will contribute to economic policy differ necessarily.

When perspectives and beliefs differ and the knowledge of economists is insufficient, on what should economic policy be grounded? What justifies economic policy actions when the outcome is uncertain but expectations are high? If politicians want to evaluate policy advice as good, true, false or other they need a standard of evaluation. This standard has to be based on something other than the evaluation of policy advice.

But what is truth? According to classical metaphysics, truth is correspondence with reality, that is, a statement is true only if it corresponds to mind-independent facts. The alternative approach considers thoughts, ideologies and scientific theories as subjective and puts forward a relativist view of truth.

Against this background, this book focuses on the conditions that make it possible to consider an economic policy statement a reliable basis for action and at the same time justifiable in a broad public discourse. It examines the kind of economic policy advice which could facilitate the distinction between true policy statements and wrong ones. After all, passing for true does not make an economic claim true. Moreover, scientific inquiry (working on an economic model) and rational discourse (trying to convince someone with arguments) do not follow the same pattern of logic.

The book starts out with a chapter by Uskali Mäki on the different concepts of truth. According to Mäki the ambiguousness of economists about the concept of truth does not play a major role. What does matter is a lack of clarity about the identity of relevant truth-bearers (something that may be either true or false) and truth-makers (things that make a truth-bearer actually true). Thus an economic model (a truth-bearer) would be made true by the actual state of the economy (a truth-maker). To provide an example: the assumption of efficient financial markets would be made false by market anomalies.

However, this does not mean that the economic discourse attempts to truly represent the world, even if we can never be sure whether our representations are true. Mäki advances the following proposition: 'It is not the whole and nothing but the truth'. The assumptions of models can be false. But despite false assumptions, views of economics do not necessarily have to be unrealistic. According to Deirde McCloskey all we know is rhetoric and not truth, that is, the legitimacy of economic knowledge hinges on the accountability to peers. Mäki opposes this view. He says that false assumptions can be incorporated into realism. Models are used to describe how the economy functions and even models with false assumptions can be true about the causal constitution of the economy. However, this does not mean that the correspondence theory of truth does not apply. Indeed, the coherence theory of justification can be combined with the correspondence theory of truth.

Is it sufficient, for instance, to ground the financial markets efficiency hypothesis on the fact that it is instrumentally useful and widely accepted? Or do we need to know that it is true? Paul Davidson examines a truth-maker as defined by Mäki and raises the question whether financial markets are really as efficient as assumed by orthodox economics, either the New Classical or the New Keynesian School. He concludes that the primary function of financial markets is to provide liquidity and that liquid markets can never be efficient. In the real world people are fallible and the future is uncertain. As people make forecasting errors, they conclude contracts at non-equilibrium prices but re-contracting with a view to correcting those errors would come at a price.

But what if the key issue in economic policy advice is only persuasion? Also Kurt Rothschild believes that 'it is not the whole and nothing but the truth'. Rothschild maintains that one should be sceptical about truthfulness in an economic policy advisory process. He identifies a few tendencies not to tell the truth in practice. Scientific standards will be violated by compliant experts. Dishonest politicians will not look for truth. Thus, in the process of economic policy advice there are unavoidable shortcomings, and things might change only if one cared about the limitations of the advisory process and if efforts to improve it were undertaken.

In this volume a number of authors adhere to a pragmatic notion of truth. The pragmatist tradition going back to Peirce and Dewey undermines the approaches of Popper and Lakatos. Positivism concentrates on factual truth and objectivity, that is, it is sceptical about values that cannot clearly be distinguished from facts. Pragmatism questions the positivist ideals of methodology and formal idealizations. A justification based on a formal and ideal method cannot be sufficient for economic policy advice.

James Bohman argues that deliberative democratic models are best suited for resolving truth-based disputes. Globalization has led to new forms of domination and political authority resulting in deficient accountability to the democratic public. Democracy requires a multi-perspective polity. A decentred form of democratic inquiry is necessary. Democracy is decentred along two dimensions: the micro-dimension of the sort of processes that constitute decision making and the macro-dimension of the scale of interlocking levels of governance from cities to regions to global society. The first one involves the recognition of the role of social perspectives in just and wise democratic decision making; the second one requires smaller units embedded in larger units whenever the actions and interactions of people constitute a common world.

Under the current circumstances of pluralism and globalization, Bohman favours multi-perspective institutions and deliberations. With a thorough decentralization of the underlying norms and concepts of democratic theory along these pragmatic lines, a deliberative democracy would be better equipped to take up what is correct in some of the forceful criticisms of its ideal, yet at the same time preserve its normative core.

But pragmatism also contributes to a certain kind of theoretical modesty that might stem from abandoning some of the strong metaphysical assumptions that still dominate our idea of democracy. It also seems that no democratic institution could be comprehensive enough to solve problems effectively. With the concept of consensus and representative institutions we seem to have reached the limits of democratic control.

Bohman proposes a concept of democratic inquiry which is capable of taking multiple perspectives in expressive practices that, as Dewey puts it, produce an enriched and enlarged experience among participants. Pragmatism considers democratic institutions experiments in which deliberation and publicity are crucial for testing validity and acceptability to citizens. Democracy is a multi-perspective practice, as it is an institutionalized discourse that takes up problematic situations and their reflexive justification. Pragmatism suggests a normative basis for learning and testing.

Thus, if economic policy-makers claim their economic policy advice to be true, then this should hold up also in a discourse that is as open as possible. Is the idealized character of such an understanding troublesome? William Rehg criticizes the formal character of Habermas's approach – acceptability before a universal audience – as a far too formal criterion. The truth claims of economic policy advisors have to be evaluated in a contextually sensitive way. As an ethnomethodologist, Rehg focuses on contextualizability and relevance across a range of interested practical domains. Participants must consider their social practices reasonable and non-coercive. Ethnomethodology focuses on the methods the participants themselves use and does not judge the adequacy or importance of these procedures. In other words, it neither takes the participant view as an objective one nor does it believe that a scientific researcher can separate subjectivity and objectivity. Actors treat each other as accountable and accountability is not only about words but also about the situational appropriate interpretation of words. All scientific claims are indexical.

James R. Wible argues that economic science has not fulfilled the standards of positivism. The context of controversy in the academic world refutes the simplification of the ideals of scientific methods. But the conception of science in positive economics methodology has changed. An alternative approach is the pragmatist one. Peirce viewed the world as characterized by indeterminism and evolutionary complexity. Agents have only incomplete and imperfect knowledge. If policy-makers want to fulfil the standards of the pragmatist concept of science, they should be aware that there are multiple economic theories and explanations.

Are methodologists in the position to judge these differences from an epistemic point of view? Methodologists do not remain outsiders to the practice of economics, as they would have no chance to judge from an epistemically privileged position. However this does not imply that they must take the viable standards of the community of economists as sacrosanct. Economic methodology can be considered a part of philosophy. Although Roger Backhouse is rather sceptical about the contribution of methodology in this context he identifies a task for science theory. First, it would be necessary to consider the heterogeneous field of economics comprising academic economics and applied economics. Academic economists assume a hierarchy ranging from abstract theory to policy. As the general equilibrium theory or the non-cooperative game theory are too abstract they are used as a basis for more specialised applied models. Because this hierarchy may be wrong, one should also study economic practice more intensively. The theoretical challenge is to better understand the processes by which economic ideas are applied on policy.

Peter Mooslechner doubts that Thomas Kuhn has considerably influenced economic research. He argues that it is more important to study the social context of the individual practices of economics. The influence of Karl Popper on economics is a rather loose interpretation of his falsificationism, given that econometrics has become the major tool for examining the truth claim of various economic hypotheses in a very specific form. In this sense, economists seem to have been very successful in creating their own methodological basis of economics and economic policy advice. Yet this has contributed to a situation where a widening of the gap between economics and real world problems seems to be clearly visible. For the sake of effectiveness, that is to ensure that this gap narrows again, it is important to realize that economics and economic policy are embedded into a reality that is very much characterized by an essential historical dimension as well as considerable uncertainties, instead of concentrating on rather abstract models and self-defined questions within them.

What drives economists in providing policy advice? One may argue that science is the search for truth and that policy advice is distorted by ideology biases and values. Gebhard Kirchgässner provides a classic economic answer assuming that the values of economists are the values derived from their models, which would mean that they are driven by self-interest. In other words, policy advisors may follow incentives that will distort the process.

The role of economists can also be studied from an epistemologically different point of view. Martin Schürz tries to answer the question whether and how philosophical concepts of truth may play a role in justifying economic claims. He traces implications truth concepts have for the way economic policy advisors present their arguments to economic policy-makers. One has to investigate more closely how economists argue. If economist argumentation has a philosophical basis then the world view and the non-scientific values can be made explicit to the politicians quite easily. If economists use only a common sense argument, that is if they talk about 'obvious plausibility', then hidden concepts of truth will have to be made explicit. These explicated concepts of truth would allow politicians to broaden their view on real world policy actions. The methodological principle of epistemic reflexivity stresses the importance of deconstructing socially effective constructions that are broadly held to be legitimate. Reflections on the practice of economic policy advice will help challenge underlying and often hidden ideologies of hegemonic economic arguments.

Orthodox economists tend to look for optimal policy rules as a kind of substitute for the search for truth. Thus, economic orthodoxy appears to have problems understanding the need of accountability of economic politicians. Let us suppose, though, that academic economists come up with *optimal rules* for economic policy. This would mean that it is only the economists coming up with the rules who could be made responsible. Policy-makers would function like machines, and machines cannot be made accountable. In such a setting, the rules either fulfil their tasks or they have to be fixed.

Economic policy rules such as inflation targeting have been advocated as a means by which independent economic agencies can be made accountable to the general public and herewith alleviate the democratic deficit of insufficient democratically legitimized institutions. For the monetary and fiscal policy case, Helene Schuberth points out that this concept of accountability breaks down in the case of Knightian uncertainty. Policy rules can be considered substitutes for democracy. The notion of 'optimal' rules applied by independent institutions spreads illusions about the optimality of technocratic decision making processes that supposedly best serve the welfare of society. Given Knightian uncertainty, delegating policy to independent agencies is thus associated with high agency losses that cannot be reduced by policy rules, as the respective agent will – with or without a rule – act according to the wise men's belief.

Julian Reiss and Nancy Cartwright study the use of counterfactuals in policy advice. Their proposal of how to deal with epistemic uncertainty is to use our best guess to the probability of each possible implementation and weigh the results accordingly. The suggestion to make the underlying assumptions as transparent as possible brings them quite close to pragmatist presuppositions.

Sheila Dow examines how uncertainty affects the foundations of economic policy-making. Although the real world is uncertain, the economics profession provides models that entail incomplete connectedness to reality and rule out uncertainty. As economic policy requires action, neither complete open-system models (which imply rejection of mathematical formalisation and impede action) nor closed-system models in a fixed way (which impede learning) provide useful ways to proceed. Instead it is suggested to consider the middle ground: some closures should be introduced in the models in order to reduce uncertainty. This implies a form of pluralism where a recourse to a range of methods suited to the problem at hand takes place.

The epistemological framework of the positivist tradition is not adequate for answering the question for truth in economic policy advice. It attaches legitimacy of scientific knowledge to epistemological standards that economists have to fulfil. It prescribes clearly specified methodological rules for the proper conduct of economic science. Privileged and unquestioned epistemic foundations form the basis for economic research. The pragmatist tradition provides an alternative as it focuses on democratic inquiry.

Actual policy advice is largely restricted to experts and not open to any person capable of making a relevant contribution. Yet arguments by economists giving policy advice should not be challenged only by other economists on a purely scientific basis; an adequate justification of scientific claims requires a broad debate in extra-scientific settings. Workers can easily challenge them by asking questions related to the impact of policy decisions on their life world. How large are the costs of an interest rate increase? When the monetary policy experts cannot answer these questions, their truth claim is rather weak and their accountability has to be strengthened. A greater plurality of perspectives is facilitated by strengthened requirements for accountability.

But do we have arguments regarding the range of perspectives that should be included? Is there a guideline that helps us decide when to accept and when to reject a piece of economic advice? When policy advice is given, the lines of argumentation have to meet numerous pragmatist presuppositions ranging from publicity, inclusiveness, equality for all participants, exclusion of deception to a sincere weighting of arguments.

Taking the arguments put forth in this volume for pluralism and multi-perspectives serious, divergent contributions have been included in this book. However, pluralism does not mean that the editors refrained from judgement about the value of truth and accountability for economic policy-making under uncertainty. With this volume we do not intend to contend that there is some compromise that should be searched for; this book rather examines the truth about the Truth. Readers will find contributions with a positivist notion of truth but also advocates of an instrumental notion of truth, with the authors not even sharing the same understanding of accountability. But what they do agree on is the importance of uncertainty for policy-making.

Therefore, many authors in this volume construct science differently. They avoid dualistic alternatives between truth-oriented academic theory and economic policy practice and remove the epistemic privilege for academic economists. Pragmatism rejects economic science as a method of acquiring true representations of the world. In a pragmatist conception good science requires respect and discourse ethics. In this line of thinking, science requires the democratization of inquiry.

The topic of truth and accountability leads to issues of democratic policy. Economic policy advice has to be embedded into a broader social discourse. Otherwise it may follow ideologies and degenerate. Only far-reaching deliberations may ensure that policy advice is truth-oriented and accountable to the democratic public.

2. Some Truths about Truth for Economists and their Critics and Clients

Uskali Mäki[*]

1. INTRODUCTION

Economics appears to have a somewhat troublesome relationship with truth. Undergraduate students of economics, other social scientists, policy-makers, journalists, and others often express doubts about economics insofar as its veristic ambitions and achievements are concerned. The charge levelled against economics by a critic may be that economists are not interested in seeking the truth about some significant phenomena, or that the models they build tend to be false, or that the predictions their models yield systematically fail to be true. The clients or consumers of economics – such as governments and businesses and other organizations – characteristically expect economics to deliver truthful information about the world, about the changing economic conditions of their activities. A critic – a sociologist or psychologist, say – may blame economics for building its models upon utterly false assumptions. A client – say a government or an investment bank – may be disappointed in its expectations of being supplied true (conditional or unconditional) predictions. Critics and clients feel that what is at issue is the accountability of economists for the performance of economics and that truth-seeking and truth-acquisition have a great deal to do with accountability.

In response to such criticisms and such expectations, economists may defend their models by claiming that truth is unattainable in principle; or that their models (or at least the 'assumptions' of their models) are false,

[*] Erasmus Institute for Philosophy and Economics, umaki@fwb.eur.nl, October 2003. Earlier version presented at the Methodology Workshop on 'Truth in economics: How does economics relate to social reality?' hosted by Oesterreichische Nationalbank, Vienna, 18 October 2002.

yet their falsehood does not matter; or that somehow the best of them are true after all; or at any rate they are closer to the truth than any available alternative; or that if their predictions fail to be sufficiently close to the truth, they are to be improved, and so on. If nothing else helps, then the claim may be that economics at any rate is better off than the various sorts of snake-oil prescribed by uninformed economic witch doctors who make their appearances in the media.

When ascribing truth or falsehood to anything, one implies some concept of truth. Such concepts of truth are given by 'theories' or 'accounts' of truth examined and developed by philosophers. What about economists and their critics and clients? What theories of truth do economists and others (often just implicitly) hold when theorizing and modelling the economy, when making remarks about economic theories and models, when forecasting future developments, and when offering policy advice? What theories of truth would economists and others be advised to hold, and what truth-related comments would they be advised to make about their theories and models and policy recommendations? What parts of, or claims about, their models and theories would they be advised to consider as candidates for truth, thus to be true or false, and on what grounds?

Why would an attempt to answer such questions be a worthwhile project? The simple reason is that it seems obvious that both economists and their critics and clients hold rather unsophisticated ideas about truth, as well as about the issue of truth in economics. This is both understandable and excusable. Yet, improved clarity around the issue, including clarity about the key concepts of truth and falsehood themselves, is required to enhance the communication and debate between the various parties with an interest in how what economists say relates to the world.

More particularly, in response to the charges that theirs is not a truth-seeking or truth-acquiring discipline, and in response to the disappointments of the clients, economists had better be in possession of conceptual tools that will help them avoid agreeing with their critics for wrong reasons and that will help them adjust their truth claims so as to minimize the disappointments of their clients. Insofar as the clients' expectations are concerned, economists should adjust their promises so as to make them match with their capabilities: disappointments in expectations are best avoided by making sure the expectations are in line with what economics is able to deliver. But economists should not go too far in lowering their ambitions. They should not too easily settle in low-ambition or skeptical attitudes by claiming that all models are false anyway, that truth is in principle unattainable, that truths can be made attainable by making them dependent on our judgment, or that considerations related to truth should play no role in driving economic research and debate and policy advice.

Among other things, the chapter attempts to deliver the following limited services: clarifications of some of the key concepts that relate to truth-talk in general; a brief overview of theories of truth and of theories of theories; sketches of versions of the argument to the effect that for an economic model to be true, it can be allowed to involve a number of genuine or apparent falsehoods; an outline of the argument that economists had better not adopt the notion of truth as persuasiveness, but rather stick to what they mostly seem to hold, namely some sort of non-epistemic correspondence notion of truth.

2. ECONOMISTS AND THE VOCABULARY OF TRUTH

In their daily business of research and communication, economists much of the time are rather parsimonious in their use of the vocabulary of veracity. Surely, there are many ordinary conversational situations in which the term 'true' is used. 'It seems we failed in our prediction of the third quarter' to which another research team member may respond, 'That's true'. In response to a questionnaire inquiring about economists' opinions and attitudes they do not hesitate to check the 'true' box (or 'false' box) next to claims such as 'Friedman's monetary rule is an effective tool of controlling inflation'. Such apparent truth ascriptions do not necessarily imply any serious thoughts about truth as a substantive property of statements, they may rather just signal agreement or other such attitudes. Yet, at other times, when using words such as 'true' and 'false' economists do seem to attribute the properties of truth and falsehood to some of the statements and models they work with. In particular, they do not seem to have a difficulty with saying of a model or assumption or prediction that it is false.

Perhaps emancipated by Milton Friedman's 1953 essay, economists usually openly and without any sense of guilt admit that the assumptions of their models are false. When pressed, economists often say that their models are false. The reason they would give for this judgment is that models are simple, while reality is complex – and therefore economic models are just like models in general: false. In such judgments economists imply a correspondence idea of truth: a sentence, model, or whatever, is true just in case it represents things in the world as they are – and false just in case things in the world are not as they are represented. On the other hand, if they say a model cannot be true just because it has not been tested and confirmed by the data, they thereby depart from the correspondence account.

Much of the time, economists avoid any attribution of truth or falsehood to their models. They rather say that a model is 'useful' (or useless) or that a model 'provides insight into the phenomenon' (or fails to do so). These idioms are compatible with a number of different theories of what truth is as well as a number of claims about whether models are true or false in the senses determined by those theories of truth.

Economists may sometimes say that a claim they derive is 'true in the model' but is not a true claim about the world. This leaves open the question of how exactly, if at all, the model is supposed to relate to the world. One may settle on the easy and unambitious view that the only truths available are true in models and that truths about the real world are unattainable. Or one may take truths in a model as indicative of, or as guidelines towards, truths about the real world. It is this latter view that requires a lot of elaboration to be defensible.

While it is obvious that these scattered observations have missed some interesting uses (and non-uses) of 'true' and 'false' by economists, those listed provide some flavor of the complex issues and invite us to engage ourselves in a closer scrutiny of the conceptual foundations of what is going on.

3. SOME PRELIMINARY DISTINCTIONS

The above brief and casual remarks about the linguistic practices of economists involve several actual or potential unclarities and ambiguities. Let us get some of them out of the way.

Truth and True

It is one thing to ask, *What is truth?* It is quite another thing to ask, *What is true?* In order to answer the second question, we need to have answered the first. In seeking an answer to the question, say, *Is sentence P true?*, we need to be clear about what we take truth (of any sentence) to be, and what we mean when we say something is or is not true. If an economist is asked to explain what he means by 'the quantity theory is true (or false)', it is not enough for him to explain what he means by the quantity theory: he also needs to explain what he means by 'is true' and 'is false'.

Truth Bearers and Truth Makers

Truth bearers are those things that may be true or may be false: they possess the properties of truth and falsehood, and they can be properly ascribed such properties (even though this ascription is bound to be fallible). Philosophers have suggested a number of different candidates for proper truth bearers, such as beliefs, sentences (both sentence tokens and sentence types), utterances, and propositions. In economics, the relevant truth bearers include models as well as their assumptions and predictions; I think we can take them as mainly propositional entities.

Truth makers are those things that make truth bearers true: a truth bearer is true in virtue of a truth maker making it so. Truth makers may have the character of facts, causal relations, states of affairs, and so on. The efficient market assumption in finance theory would be made true by the actual efficiency of the financial markets. The actual inflation rate in some country this year would make the last year's prediction about it true (or false). Depending on one's philosophical outlook, one may also take truth makers to consist in properties such as coherence (of the statement with other statements), consensus (of a community of people about the acceptability of the statement), or instrumental usefulness (of believing the statement).

True and What Counts as True

Most of us are intuitively inclined to take truth to be something objective, in the sense that true statements (or whatever one takes to serve as truth bearers) are true independently of what people believe about them. It is then one thing for a statement to be true, and quite another for it to count as true, to be taken as true, to pass for true, to be believed to be true, to be accepted as true. While being true is objective, passing for true is non-objective – and is moreover relative to persons, cultures, schools of thought, stages of scientific development, and other such things. The wages fund doctrine counted as true in the early 19th century for many economists, but it no longer passes for true amongst economists. Regardless of any changes in its believability, the doctrine was – and is – either true or false. What is generally agreed to be true may not in fact be true.

Some philosophers refuse to accept this distinction, holding instead that what passes for true (subject to some qualifications) is all there is to truth. Others believe that this distinction may help us understand things such as the way in which social mechanisms of consensus formation shape what counts as true without shaping truth itself; or the way in which truth and power are connected: what passes for truth is a function of social power, while truth is not. What counts as true is a proper subject for investigation by the sociology of knowledge and the social studies of science.

A piece of policy advice given by an economist will be more easily adopted by policy-makers if its factual components are considered true, if they count as true. And they are more likely to count as true in case the economist enjoys the status of a credible scientist. However, the recommended policy is more likely to succeed if those factual components are true – not just considered true, but true.

Truth and Justification

Truth is one thing. Our concept of truth is another yet closely related thing. Our criteria of identifying what is true and of distinguishing it from what is false is something quite different. A truth bearer being true in virtue of being made so by a truth maker is one thing. Our ways of justifying claims or beliefs that, indeed, that truth bearer is true, is another thing. In other words, the concept of truth and the criteria of truth are to be kept distinct. This means that our means and results of testing, justifying, or confirming a hypothesis have no implications for whether the hypothesis is or is not true. They only have implications for whether we are advised to take it to be true – for whether it is rational for us to believe it is true. Collecting additional evidence in support of a hypothesis does not make it more true: it is true or false (or more or less so) independently of any evidence for or against it. This is to say that no body of evidence is among the truth makers of a statement. 'Hans killed Hannelore' is true or false depending on whether Hans killed Hannelore; its truth is independent of any amount of evidence that is or can be presented for or against the charge (it is only dependent on whether the truth maker of the statement – the fact that Hans killed Hannelore – is there). Likewise, no econometric or other test will have any implications for the truth of the efficient market hypothesis: such tests only have implications for the rational believability of the hypothesis.

The above claims suggest that truth is non-epistemic: what is true (in contrast to what counts as true) is independent of our means of finding out about it, of justifying any beliefs in it. Not surprisingly perhaps, there are those who deny this and take truth to be epistemic. In the pragmatist tradition, this is put variously by suggesting that truth amounts to properties such as warranted assertability or ideal acceptability.

Truth Ascription and Truth Nomination

There is a difference between truth ascription and what I call truth nomination. When we ascribe truth or falsehood to some truth bearer, we do it, or should do it, on the basis of evidential considerations, based on empirical testing or theoretical argument. When we nominate a proposition (or whatever) for truth, we decide to treat it as a candidate for truth that has a fair chance of being true (even though it may turn out to be false). Truth (and falsity) ascription is a stronger act that presupposes the weaker act of truth nomination. Truth nomination turns a proposition into a hypothesis that will be considered for its truth, while truth ascription turns it into a confirmed hypothesis that will be considered true.

Truth and Skepticism

Skeptical attitudes in regard to truth come in different kinds and degrees. The most radical form of skepticism is to reject the very notion of truth as nonsensical or inapplicable to anything. Not only truth ascription but also truth nomination are out of the question. There are no truth bearers, and there is no such property as truth, thus nothing can bear the properties of truth or falsehood. Therefore, other (characteristically pragmatic) properties of statements and theories enter the center stage: usefulness, convenience, simplicity, fruitfulness, etc. Another form of skepticism will suggest that even though truth bearers are true or false, we can never find out about this; we will always remain in the dark regarding matters of truth and falsehood. Truth nominations are in principle sensible, but they are useless since truth ascription will always remain ungrounded. Here, too, pragmatic properties may adopt the main role in assessing theories and statements. Yet another (Popperian) version suggests that we will never be in a position to justify any claim as true, even though we are able to refute claims as false. Finally, a weak and healthy form of skepticism is to recommend a cautious attitude: theories are true or false (or more or less so), but whenever evidence is insufficient, one is advised to suspend any firm and final judgment as to the truth-value of a theory. In general, in order to make one's beliefs rational, one is advised to adjust the intensity of one's belief in a hypothesis so as to make it match with the strength of evidential support to it. This last form of epistemic caution seems quite popular in economics regarding individual hypotheses. It is a combination of permitting both truth nomination and postponed or cautious truth ascription.

The Whole Truth and Nothing But the Truth

Especially when thinking of systems of statements, such as certain kinds of theories and models, one is tempted to conflate violations of the whole truth and violations of nothing but the truth. From the unsurprising fact that a model is incomplete or partial, that it does not deliver the whole or comprehensive truth as it misses a lot of facts and factors in economic reality, one may conclude that the model is just false, and inescapably so. In the case of individual statements, such as 'One third of the unemployed in Austria this year are women', the problem is less difficult: the claim is about the female proportion of unemployment, and supposing there is a fact of the matter about it, the statement is (nothing-but) true or false about it – it does not have to be about anything else. Models and theories are a bit more challenging from this point of view, since it is often less obvious what exactly they are used to claim about economic reality (an issue that will be taken up in later sections below).

4. THE SHORTEST POSSIBLE SUMMARY OF THEORIES OF TRUTH, AND OF THEORIES OF SCIENTIFIC THEORIES INSOFAR AS THEIR TRUTH IS CONCERNED

Theories of Truth

What are often called 'theories' of truth (or 'accounts' of truth) provide definitions of truth: accounts of what it is for a truth bearer to be true, of what truth consists in. They do not as such provide criteria of truth.

Correspondence theories
Truth consists in a correspondence of a statement (or whatever truth bearer) with what the statement is about. For a statement to be true, the world must be like what it is claimed to be in the statement. A statement that corresponds to the facts, 'gets the facts right'. This is the commonsense notion of truth, much of the time also implied in economists' linguistic practices. 'We have now reached the bottom of the business cycle' is true just in case we have, as a matter of fact, reached the bottom. 'Business cycles are primarily caused by monetary shocks' is true just in case business cycles are, as a matter of fact, primarily caused by monetary shocks – if they were primarily caused, say, by technology shocks, the statement would be false. There are many ways to elaborate the details of the correspondence idea of truth, depending on what one

takes the relata to be and what one takes their relationship of correspondence to be like.

Coherence theories

Truth consists in the coherence of a belief or statement with a larger system of beliefs or statements. The property of coherence can be defined variously, such as in terms of entailment (between statements) or consistency (of a system as a whole). The first and second welfare theorems are true in the sense that they are logically entailed by the axioms of the theory of general equilibrium. The law of demand is true in the sense that it is consistent with utility maximization at one end, and statistical market data at the other. In general, truth is defined as coherence: coherence is all there is to truth.

Consensus theories

Truth consists in an agreement to a statement (or whatever truth bearer) by a relevant group of people. Usually it is required that the consensus defining truth is global rather than local, and stable rather than temporary. The law of demand is true in the sense that all economists, regardless of their other doctrinal affiliations, are in agreement on it. In many cases, determining the criteria of membership in the relevant group is a special empirical problem for consensus accounts. The truth status of the macro model currently used by the Austrian Central Bank is not to be decided by its builders, users, critics and clients alike, is it? Do heretic or deviant minority views ever have a chance of being true? Did Copernicus and Galileo hold false beliefs just because there was no consensus in support of them? The method or path by way of which the consensus is reached is usually not taken to matter – but one may as well impose requirements concerning the mechanisms of consensus formation for the outcome to qualify (just think of the difference between forcing and indoctrination as opposed to open and honest conversation). Consensus accounts are often strongly idealized by assumptions such as equality of power and limitless availability of time. In general, consensus gives us a concept of truth rather than a criterion of truth.

Usefulness theories

Truth consists in a belief (or whatever truth bearer) being useful for some purpose. Versions of this account vary depending on specifications of the relevant purposes that the belief is supposed to serve; on whether usefulness is relative to individuals, some local groups, or humankind as a whole; on whether short-term or long-term usefulness is required. The law of demand is true in the sense that it is profitable for price setters to believe it and to act on it. In general, truth is defined in terms of instrumental usefulness: this gives us a concept rather than a criterion of truth. To be true is to be useful.

Theories of epistemic justification

These are not theories of what it is to be true; these are about criteria of identifying or recognizing what is true. Of the above theories of truth, all but the correspondence theory can be turned into theories of justification. We may invoke coherence, consensus, and instrumental usefulness as criteria of truth. Indeed, those who endorse some correspondence account of truth often cite one or more of those three properties as being among the criteria of truth, while correspondence itself cannot serve as a criterion. Naturally, all three can provide the basis for both defining what truth is and for recognizing what is true. Thus, one may take coherence to constitute both the criterion and the essence of truth. In other words, not only is coherence a means of measuring the extent to which truth has been attained, it also constitutes what is measured, it *is* truth. In such cases, we say truth is taken to be epistemic: the very concept of truth is defined in terms that refer to our ways of recognizing truths. The correspondence account uncompromisingly takes truth to be a non-epistemic matter: truths are independent of how we proceed to discover them and justify our beliefs in them.

Practicing economists and their clients characteristically have a high regard for coherence, consensus, and usefulness. They may appeal to the coherence between the explanatory and predictive accounts of a large variety of phenomena, to a situation of consensus amongst economists, or to the usefulness of a given model, as somehow related to truth. However, this does not necessarily imply a subscription to the consensus (or coherence or usefulness) notion of truth, it is rather to take, say, a situation of consensus as an indication that there are good grounds for believing the theory to be true – thus there is less need for further testing and search for alternatives. Whenever members of the economics profession address an external audience (their clients, say), a situation of consensus, or at least an appearance or pretension of consensus amongst economists, helps raise the credibility of the claims they make and of advice they provide – without, by that token, increasing their truthlikeness.

Redundancy accounts

There is no such thing as truth as a property of truth bearers: there is no truth for truth bearers to bear, thus there are no truth bearers either. When we say, 'The sentence "Inflation is a monetary phenomenon" is true' we do not say anything in addition to saying, 'Inflation is a monetary phenomenon': we do not say anything about that sentence, what we say is rather about inflation. Thus all apparent ascriptions of truth (and falsehood) are redundant: anything that can be said with them can be said without them. Much of the linguistic behavior of economists does without explicit truth ascriptions, but this alone is not sufficient for attributing a redundancy view to them. It is natural that truth ascriptions become explicit only in special circumstances.

Performative theory

Speaking is acting: one accomplishes acts by uttering strings of words. Utterances of sentences including the words 'is true' or 'is it true' are performances or gestures: they express an attitude or mental state. When one says, 'It is true that the inflation rates in Europe are lower today than they were twenty years ago', one thereby signals agreement on the proposition, 'The inflation rates in Europe are lower today than they were twenty years ago'. When saying 'it is true that p' one appears to ascribe truth to sentence p – but as a matter of fact one does not do that, but rather something else, namely one signals consent just like in nodding one's head up and down. Raising questions of the form, 'Is it true that the unemployment rate in Austria is so-and-so?' express surprise, doubt, or disbelief (see Strawson 1950). No doubt 'is true' appears in economists' linguistic behavior also in these ways.

Theories of Theories

Realism

Scientific theories are truth-valued: they are either true or false, or more or less close to the truth. These properties are possessed by scientific theories in virtue of how *what they say about the way the world is* relates to *the way the world is*. Good scientific theories are true, or close to the truth, or capable of helping us get closer to the truth. Scientists are prescribed to ultimately aim at creating true theories. (For more on versions of realism, see Mäki 2001c.) A challenge to realism is to accommodate the fact that the best theories characteristically appear to contain false elements. To deal with this requires providing an account of the structure of theories: it is only within such a structure that truth and falsity nominations and ascriptions can be appropriately located.

Instrumentalism: Two Versions

a)   Scientific theories are not truth-valued: they are neither true or false, nor anywhere in the neighborhood of truth. They are not about anything real, thus cannot be true or false in virtue of how they relate to what they might appear to be about. No truth nomination, therefore no truth ascription. This version is suited for interpreting physical theories that postulate unobservable entities. For example, electrons and electromagnetic fields are not observable, hence not real but rather imaginary fictions, therefore theories apparently referring to them are not true or false about them (note that a correspondence notion of truth is presupposed here). Theories are instruments for some purpose(s) or other (such as prediction or generally systematization of the data, or provision of solutions to practical problems), and are not to be assessed for their (semantic property of) truth but instead for their usefulness, convenience, fruitfulness, and other such pragmatic properties that relate theories to such purposes.

b)   Scientific theories are false, thus truth-valued (in some correspondence sense). However, their (semantic property of) falsehood plays no role in their assessment: theories are false instruments that are to be assessed in terms of their pragmatic properties such as usefulness, convenience, etc. (again, a correspondence notion of truth is implied here). This version is better suited for interpreting economic theories that deal with what I have called 'commonsensibles' (such as goods and their prices, firms and households, preferences and expectations, employment and inflation, costs and contracts) rather than unobservables in the sense familiar from discussions about fundamental physics (such as quarks and black holes). (See Mäki 1992b, 1996b, 1998a, 1998b.)

Constructive empiricism
Theories are about real things (whether observable or unobservable) and are truth-valued, thus either true or false (roughly in some correspondence sense). But there is no way to determine whether the unobservable posits of scientific theories are real, and whether those theories are true or false. This is based on epistemological skepticism that denies access to unobservables. Theories are just empirically more or less adequate, based on how their observational consequences relate to empirical data (see van Fraassen 1980). If economics is (mainly) about commonsensibles, then the details of, and motivation behind, the

constructive empiricist position do not seem to apply very well to the case of economics.

The next few sections briefly outline and discuss some ways in which one can defend the relevance and reasonableness of truth nominations and truth ascriptions in economics. It appears that economists most of the time implicitly subscribe to some rough correspondence notion of truth and that the uncertainties and confusions around truth ascriptions largely originate from difficulties with identifying the relevant truth bearers within theories and models. It has been a prominent theme in my work to argue that what appears false may, after all, be true or conducive to truth.

5. JUSTIFYING APPARENTLY FALSE ASSUMPTIONS BY PARAPHRASING THEM AS TRUE ASSERTIONS

Almost by definition, models violate the whole truth. Models also appear to involve false elements, ones that violate nothing-but-the-truth. At the same time, good models are expected to yield true representations of some real features of the economy – not just true predictions, but true descriptions of the structures and processes in the economy. This section outlines one possible way of reconciling truth and falsehood. It is based on Alan Musgrave's contribution (Musgrave 1981) and my suggested modifications and elaborations (Mäki 2000a). The trick is to relocate truth claims by paraphrasing assumptions. The lesson here is: one should not criticize what appears as a false assumption without understanding what assertion is intended when using it.

Suppose an economic model involves assumption [B]:

[B] The government budget is in balance.

If one considers this as a factual assertion, it may turn out that it is never exactly true; indeed, sometimes it is very far from the truth. The key move in the present argument is to refrain from considering [B] and other such assumptions as factual assertions but rather to paraphrase them so as to turn them into other sentences that are then used to make factual assertions about the world. In other words, truth-values are not ascribed to 'assumptions' like [B] but rather to their paraphrases that are treated as the genuine truth bearers. There are several such paraphrases. A very important one turns an assumption into a claim about the negligibility of a factor, given one's purposes. Thus, [B] would be paraphrased as:

[NB] The imbalance of the government budget has negligible effects – effects that are negligibly small, given our purposes.

Now the crucial payoff of this move is that while [B], if considered as a factual assertion, would be false, paraphrased as [NB] it may well be true. [B] would be a claim about the government budget having a property, while [NB] is a claim about the negligibility of the budget not having that property. These are claims about two very different things, thus it is not surprising that their truth-values have little to do with one another: one may be utterly false while the other may be true. Thus 'assumptions' like [B] are not to be taken as candidates of truth at all, hence they cannot fail as such candidates either. Given that they are not treated as such candidates, as worthy of truth nomination – that is, as factual assertions – it is not sensible to ascribe them truth-values at all: because they are not taken to make any claims about the world, they are not regarded as true or as false. It is their paraphrased forms such as [NB] that are candidates for truth, and it is these assertions that are to be ascribed truth-values. And such ascriptions, to be successful, require factual inquiries into the world. Finally, one hopes that claims about negligibility such as [NB] are true.

Another paraphrase of [B] amounts to turning it into a claim about a property of a theory or model in relation to a relevant domain of phenomena. Such a claim would be a claim about the applicability of the theory:

[AB] Theory T only applies to domains in which the government budget is balanced – or more precisely, domains where any budget imbalance has negligible effects.

Again, what appeared to be a false assumption – namely [B] – is not treated as making any factual claims whatsoever, hence is not nominated for truth. It is rather paraphrased as a claim about applicability, a property that is jointly determined by the theory in question and some domain of phenomena. Considered as such a claim, [AB] is worthy of truth nomination: it may be true or may be false. Again, ascribing a truth-value to claims such as [AB] requires factual inquiries into the real world. One hopes such claims to be true. (One may also hope that the domain covered by the theory be as large as possible in order to make the theory as testable as possible.)

Yet another paraphrase of assumptions such as [B] turns it into an early-step assumption: an assumption, that is, that is supposed to be relaxed at some later step or stage of the modeling exercise. The need for its relaxation is based on the recognition that the effects of the factor identified and excluded by the assumption are not negligible.

[ESB] [B] is an element of an early-step version of theory T and will be
relaxed in its later-step versions.

Now the propositional identity of [ESB] is not as clear as that of [NB]
and [AB]. In case one takes 'will be relaxed' as a prediction or some
other kind of descriptive claim about the fact that [B] will be relaxed,
then [ESB] is properly treated as a candidate for truth, and one hopes it
indeed is true. An easy case is an article or book that begins with a closed
economy model and at a later step relaxes the assumption and ends up
with an open economy model. A harder case is one where a research field
is predicted to move towards putting together later-generation models
that are able to relax some of the key assumptions in earlier-generation
models. But 'will be relaxed' may be taken to mean also something else,
such as involving a promise or a hope: it is promised or hoped that the
assumption in question indeed will be just an early-step assumption and
will be relaxed at a later step. Now promises and hopes are things that are
slightly different from predictions or other descriptive claims in that they
cannot as obviously be taken as truth-valued propositions, thus not
clearly worthy of truth nomination.

There are many other possible paraphrases that are able to turn
apparently false 'assumptions' into true assertions. Consider the
following:

[TractB] The use of [B] improves the tractability of modeling.
[PedB] The use of [B] serves useful pedagogical purposes.
[AesB] The use of [B] yields aesthetically pleasing models.
[EntrB] The use of [B] is a prerequisite of getting one's paper accepted.

All such claims may be true even though [B] were false. In this respect
they are similar to paraphrases [NB] and [AB]. At least occasionally,
economists utter claims of these last four forms. Yet it is not at all
obvious that one is justified in using these paraphrases for justifying
assumptions such as [B]. The reason for this is obvious: these four
paraphrases make no appeal to any facts about the real world 'external' to
academic economics itself. Their possible truth lies in facts about some
'internal' characteristics of the discipline of economics – and one rightly
takes this to weaken their capacity to justify the assumptions they are
about. This means there are limits to the art of paraphrase in legitimizing
apparently false assumptions.

6. ISOLATION AND IDEALIZATION: THE ROLE OF FALSE ASSUMPTIONS

Economists (and others) often have difficulties with thinking of models as potentially true. Here is a statement by David Hendry:

> I take it as self-evident that economic behaviour is sufficiently complex and evolutionary that it is not helpful to talk about economic theories being 'true' or of inferences yielding the 'correct' results. . . . By their very nature, models are inherently simplifications and inevitably false. (Hendry 1986, pp. 30–31)

One reason why it may be hard to consider models as candidates for truth is that they violate the whole truth: models are incomplete, they necessarily leave out a lot. If one is inclined to conflate the whole truth and nothing but the truth, or to miss the distinction between the two, then one easily takes the violation of the whole truth to imply the violation of truth *simpliciter*.

Milton Friedman's 1953 essay gives an illuminating example of this conflation. He sets out to block the charge that the profit maximization assumption is illegitimately false, namely 'the recent criticisms of the maximization-of-returns hypothesis on the grounds that businessmen do not and indeed cannot behave as the theory "assumes" they do' (1953, p. 31). This is a judgment about nothing but the truth in the correspondence sense. Friedman then proceeds by imagining 'a completely "realistic" theory of the wheat market' that would cite the color of the traders' and farmers' eyes and hair, their antecedents and education, the physical and chemical characteristics of the soil on which the wheat was grown, the weather prevailing during the growing season, and so on and so forth (1953, p. 32). Making rhetorical use of the fact that everybody would agree that an insistence on such a 'theory' would be unreasonable, Friedman invites the reader to conclude that it is equally unreasonable to be critical of the assumption of profit assumption. This flawed argument exemplifies a conflation of the whole truth and nothing but the truth (see Mäki 1992b, 2003).

Another reason why it may be difficult to treat models as potentially true is the presence of recognizably false elements in them. When interpreted literally as truth-valued statements, many assumptions of economic models appear to be flatly false; just think of perfect information, perfect divisibility and substitutability of goods and factors, closed economy, complete contracting, zero transaction costs. These are among the idealizations of economic models.

It would be a mistake to conclude, without further reasons, from the falsehood of the idealizing assumptions to the falsehood of the models that use them. The assumptions of a model are not the main claims that the model is used to make about the world. In the basic version of Galileo's law of freely falling bodies (an example popular in economics and its methodology at least since Friedman's 1953 essay), it is assumed that the body falls freely in a vacuum, that no forces other than the earth's gravity (such as the pull of all other bodies in the universe, magnetic forces, etc.) make an impact on it, that the radius of the earth is infinitely large. Such idealizations, in physics as well as economics, are based on assuming that the value of a variable is zero, infinity, or some fixed value such as one. The lesson here is: one should not criticize a false assumption without understanding the function it is intended to serve.

The point of making such idealizing assumptions is clear enough. They are made to create imagined conditions in which the influence of a number of potentially relevant factors is removed or neutralized in order to examine the impact of another selected set of factors. The analogy with experimental research is obvious: economic models are 'thought experiments' that have the structure and purpose of material experiments. In both, the aim is to isolate a small set of interactions from the influence of the rest of the universe. The disanalogy lies in the way in which the isolation is accomplished: while material experiments in laboratories purport to causally isolate some dependencies of interest from other influences by way of materially effective controls, the thought experiments of theoretical economic models do the same by way of just assuming that those other influences are not there. Theoretical models are the laboratories of economic modelers within which isolated conditions are created to examine a small set of key dependencies (see Mäki 1992a, 1994, 2001b).

Just as Galileo's law is not false simply because it employs idealizing assumptions that are false of real situations, an economic model is not false just because its idealizing assumptions are false. Galileo's law makes a claim about the way in which the force of gravity influences freely falling bodies, regardless of whether the conditions in which they fall are ideal ones. Conceived as such a claim about the impact of one isolated force, it is either true or false. Likewise, an economic model may be taken to make a claim about the existence of a major causal mechanism and about the impact it makes, isolated from other causes and conditions, on some phenomenon. As such a claim, it may be true or it may be false even though the idealizing assumptions that effected the isolation are false.

This is not so with the predictive or retrodictive implications of such isolative models about phenomena occurring in non-isolated conditions. In such conditions phenomena emerge as mixtures of the influences of multiple causes. Even though a model might get the facts about some major causal mechanism right, it also might get some facts about its actual effects wrong. The model would yield the truth about those consequences only subject to the proviso that there are no 'disturbing' causes. The important point is that the falsehood of its predictive implications alone does not render a model itself false. (The situation would be different in the case of certain kinds of forecasting models that are uninterested in the mechanisms by way of which the phenomena to be predicted are brought about.)

7. 'TRUE IN A MODEL' AND THE MODEL-BASED VIEW OF THEORIES

Many observers of science argue that contemporary science is largely a matter of building and examining models. There are important ambiguities about the term 'model' that are related to the issue of truth. One may take a model to be linguistic, or a set of equations. One may also view a model as an abstract entity, a 'model world' or an idealized system, isolated from external influences, whose structure and behavior is characterized by a set of 'assumptions' or equations or by some other linguistic or other means. In economics, such an idea is inviting – economists construe, make reference to, make claims and reason about closed economies, 2·2·2 worlds, one- and two-sector worlds, overlapping generations worlds, representative-agent worlds, stateless economies, zero-transaction-cost economies.

Indeed, because the equations define the model world as an abstract entity, the equations are exactly true about the model. 'The equations truly describe the model because the model is defined as something that exactly satisfies the equations' (Giere 1988, p. 79). Yet this does not mean they are true about the real world, since they are not claims about any real system but about an abstract model world. On this view, models themselves are not true or false of anything: in particular, model systems are abstract objects and make no claims about real systems, thus should not be nominated for truth as they are neither true nor false about any real systems. In Giere's account, models are linked to the real world by hypotheses. A theoretical hypothesis is a truth-valued statement about the relationship of similarity between a model and a real system. The truth of a hypothesis depends on whether it gets the respects and degrees of similarity between a model world and the real world right. Yet, in the spirit of the redundancy view, Giere thinks that we can do as well without truth ascriptions:

That theoretical hypotheses can be true or false turns out to be of little consequence. To claim a hypothesis is true is to claim no more or less than that an indicated type and degree of similarity exists between a model and a real system. We can therefore forget about truth and focus on the details of the similarity. A 'theory of truth' is not a prerequisite for an adequate theory of science (Giere 1988, p. 81).

Giere's conclusions are a bit quick. Let us take a step back and consider the relationship of similarity which Giere thinks is crucial for linking model to reality: 'The relationship that does the heavy representational work is not one of truth between a linguistic entity and a real object, but of similarity between two objects, one abstract and one real' (1988, p. 82). Giere believes that models are not true or false about the real world just because models are abstract rather than linguistic entities. The premise here is that only linguistic entities (such as theoretical hypotheses in Giere's account) can be nominated for truth and ascribed truth-values. An obvious comment is that truth does not require one of the relata being linguistic: theoretical models conceived as abstract objects can serve as truth bearers – in particular since models are understood as representations (Mäki 2001b). Similarity can be viewed as a species of correspondence. What we need are notions of partial truth (truth about respects or aspects of a real object) and approximate truth (accuracy or degree of truth about those aspects).

In an account of economic theories that draws on Giere's account, Daniel Hausman (1992) has argued that economists use models for what he calls 'conceptual exploration'. This is based on the notion of model as a definition of a predicate that has no truth-value (or else is trivially true by definition). Models thus are bundles of assumptions that define predicates such as 'is a general equilibrium system' or 'is a Keynesian system'. The study of models is then a matter of 'conceptual exploration' into the properties of the predicate with no claims made or implied about economic reality. What Hausman calls theoretical hypotheses are truth-valued statements about the applicability of models-as-predicates to real economic systems, such as 'The Dutch economy is a GE system'.

In my view, this does not help very much. It seems theoretical hypotheses would regularly come out as flatly false. It does not seem to matter whether one directly views models as truth-valued (and false) representations of the real world, or whether one takes theoretical hypotheses to be the relevant truth bearers (and false). Of course, much depends on further specifications of what exactly any given theoretical hypothesis says about how certain aspects of a model relate to certain aspects of the real world. It seems 'The Dutch economy is a GE system' has a form that lacks these details and is therefore unhelpful for sustaining optimism about the acquisition of truths by way of modeling.

Another remark is that Hausman's account of models as serving the purposes of truth-valueless conceptual exploration does not seem to do full justice to theoretical modelling in economics (Mäki 1996a). Theoretical modelling is characteristically constrained by empirical considerations of the sort that one could expect in much of social sciences. In their roles as participants and observers of social processes economists hold empirical beliefs that are brought to bear on their theoretical work in an unsystematic – or at any rate formally uncontrolled – manner. Economists will not leave those beliefs behind when they set out to build and modify theoretical models. Empirical beliefs about many things, such as plausible behavioral dispositions and responses, play a role in constraining modelling choices.

Even though theoretical models are relatively unresponsive to empirical data – or at any rate unresponsive in a fully systematic or formally controlled fashion – they are responsive to economists' beliefs about human behavior and social structure, about the way the world works (www). It is generally understood that models have to be such that the imaginary worlds they depict are really possible worlds in the sense that what happens in those imaginary worlds is plausible given the beliefs we have about the constituent components and their causal properties. Such beliefs, or ontological convictions, constrain the range of possible models that economists agree to consider. This is the 'www constraint' on modelling (Mäki 2001a). Sugden's (2002) idea of models as 'credible worlds' is in line with this notion. A credible world is one that meets the relevant www constraints.

8. FROM TRUTH IN THE MODEL TO TRUTH ABOUT THE WORLD: THE RELEVANT TRUTHS AS TRUTHS ABOUT REAL MECHANISMS

It was suggested above that economic models often represent mechanisms, and that as such representations, models may be true or false. Thomas Schelling's famous checkerboard models of segregation serve as an example (Schelling 1978). Schelling's models are concerned with the processes of sorting and mixing in populations whose members respond to certain characteristics of the population itself or its part, such as some ratio or average or percentage of the total or its part. The models specify a dynamic process of interactive responses that yield an aggregate outcome. This outcome serves as the explanandum of Schelling's models: what is to be explained is the generic aggregate phenomenon of segregation in the social lives of people. Such segregation occurs between men and women, young and old, black and white, smokers and non-smokers, swimmers and surfers, students and faculty, to cite some of Schelling's examples.

The dynamics of the checkerboard model can be generated by very simple means, using a roll of pennies, a roll of dimes, and a ruled sheet of paper divided into sixty-four squares. One starts by distributing the coins on some of the squares of the board, at random for example. One makes assumptions about the 'preferences' of the dimes and pennies, for example that every dime wants a third of its neighbors to be dimes and that every penny wants at least half of its neighbors to be pennies. If these preferences are not met, any penny or dime will get up and move to a square where they are met. One keeps moving the coins until a pattern has emerged where every coin is settled such that there is no reason for further moves. The aggregate outcome will be a segregated one.

The important thing about all this is that the outcome is not dependent on many of the specifics of the exercise, such as the initial distribution of the coins, the order in which they are moved, the ratio of dimes to pennies, and their exact preferences (this last one provided the coins are not completely indifferent about their neighbors). The point is that most preferences, even of the mildest kind, result in segregation provided the process is determined 'from within' – that is, based just on the independent decisions of the occupants of the squares of the checkerboard. From the set of conclusions based on particular sets of initial conditions we can infer to the inductive generalization that segregation emerges in all checkerboard cities with any set of initial conditions (Sugden 2002).

The epistemic ambitions behind these sorts of models are an interesting issue. Schelling is explicit about the rationale of his models. It is not the ambitious one of serving as 'first approximations that can be elaborated to simulate with higher fidelity the real situations we want to examine'; it is rather the modest purpose of illustrating 'the kind of analysis that is needed, some of the phenomena to be anticipated, and some of the questions worth asking' (Schelling 1979, p. 183). To use a popular philosophical expression, the model does not permit 'inference to the best explanation'. It only permits inference to a possible explanation: it articulates a possible mechanism that could have produced the aggregate outcome that is observed.

Let us consider the possibility that Schelling-type models represent social reality – a purpose that seems more ambitious than Schelling's own modest one. Let us consider the checkerboard models as models of racial segregation in the housing market in US American cities. The study of the models shows that racial segregation emerges in checkerboard cities. The question we need to ask is: which fact or facts about real cities could checkerboard cities represent? A negative answer is that they do not represent the shape of real cities (suggesting that they consist of squares in a checkerboard-like structure). A positive answer is that the checkerboard models represent a causal mechanism that is also present in real cities. It is this causal mechanism that produces racial segregation in the housing markets of model cities as well as of real cities. Checkerboard models help isolate this causal mechanism as the one responsible for actually observed patterns of racial segregation.

Strong racial segregation emerges in Schelling's imaginary checkerboard cities. Strong racial segregation is also a fact about many large industrial cities in the North East of the USA. Robert Sugden (2002) suggests an analogy between inductive inference from real cities and one from imaginary model cities. From the fact that there is racial segregation in Baltimore, Philadelphia, Detroit, and Pittsburgh we can inductively infer to the statement that it also occurs in Cleveland due to the presence and efficacy of the same causal mechanisms. Similarly, we can infer from the truth that racial segregation emerges in checkerboard cities to the likely truth that it emerges in all cities, whether imaginary or real, due to the same causal mechanisms. Both imaginary checkerboard cities and the real cities in North-East USA serve as models – theoretical models and natural models – that represent the responsible causal forces, the same in all cases. Checkerboard models welcome truth nomination and truth ascription with truth as non-epistemic.

9.   TRUTH AS EPISTEMIC. PRESUMING TO ENSURE THE ATTAINMENT OF TRUTH BY SACRIFICING CORRESPONDENCE: THE RHETORIC OF ECONOMICS

The accounts discussed in sections 5 through 8 above all implicitly employ some sort of non-epistemic (or even correspondence) notion of truth. In such accounts, truth is taken to be a property of models and their assumptions that is objective and independent of our ways of recognizing it, or of assuring ourselves and others about its presence or absence. Such an idea of recognition-transcendent truth seems to be much in use also in economists' occasional commentaries about their theoretical endeavors.

There are many possible ways to go with the general idea that truth is epistemic – that truth itself is dependent on how or whether we recognize it, on how we decide whether we have reached it. One may say that if the evidence strongly confirms a hypothesis, this is all there is to the truth of the hypothesis – truth just consists in being strongly supported by the evidence. Or one may say that if the scientific community is in agreement on whether to judge a theory as true, there is nothing else to the truth of it – truth simply consists in consensus. On such accounts, truth bearers are not true or false independently of our ways of attempting to determine whether they are true or false. People determine those truth-values, not in the sense of discovering them, but in the sense of creating them by means such as collecting evidence and testing, and participating in other processes of consensus formation. Truth-values are made by people who are in the business of assessing truth claims for their truth status. In consequence, truth-values may change as these activities evolve: what was false may become true, and what was true may become false – not just because the world may change but because our judgments change.

A special version of the epistemic notion of truth is one that takes truth to consist in persuasiveness: a statement is true in case it is found persuasive by some audience. Some such idea is a major component in Deirdre McCloskey's view of economics as rhetorical persuasion. Economists put forth arguments in their ongoing conversations in order to persuade one another and other audiences (McCloskey 1985, 1990, 1994).

Many economists seem to have welcome McCloskey's message – that economics is rhetorical – as offering grounds for a relaxed attitude, liberating them from stringent demands of accountability. In this respect, McCloskey's contribution seems to have been similar to that of Friedman 1953. I am less sure that McCloskey's ideas about truth would have played a powerful role in all this. Economists do not seem to have adopted the notion of truth as persuasiveness as a vehicle of their rhetorical emancipation: they are not keen on claiming that their models are true in the special McCloskeyan sense of persuasiveness. If this is a correct picture, I think what it describes is welcome: economists would do wisely by not adopting this (or any other) epistemic notion of truth. In order to see why, we need to give a somewhat elaborate reconstruction to the otherwise somewhat obscure idea (see Mäki 1995; for McCloskey's reply, see McCloskey 1995, 2002 and Mäki 2000b).

McCloskey entertains a distinction (or, in fact a number of distinctions) between small-t truth and capital-T Truth. Small-t truths are attainable by humans, while capital-T Truths are not. Both of these are coherence concepts of truth.

[*truth*]   The truth (with a small t) of a statement consists in its coherence with a certain set of beliefs that humans end up with

in an ongoing persuasive conversation before the ideal limit of all conversation.

[*Truth*] The Truth (with a capital T) of a statement consists in its coherence with a set of human beliefs reached as an outcome of persuasive conversation taken to its final, ideal limit.

Economists are capable of attaining small-t truths in the above sense, but capital-T truths will escape them forever, since there is no way to know what economics will look like when it will have finished its job, at the imaginary end of all conversations between economists. Therefore, Truths should not be pursued. McCloskey believes correspondence truths are just like her Truths: unattainable, inoperational, therefore not worth pursuing.

Now, it would violate some of our central intuitions to permit all statements that cohere with some system of beliefs to be true. Otherwise we would have to accept both Keynesian and Monetarist theories (of, say, the efficiency of fiscal and monetary policies) as well as both Austrian and Marxian theories (of, say, the causation of interest) as true at the same time. What any coherence account of truth needs is a set of constraints that the relevant system is required to meet: such constraints help exclude some statements from the family of true ones. I have suggested there are two kinds of constraint in McCloskey's account: social and moral. Here is evidence for the social constraint:

> The very idea of Truth – with a capital T, *something beyond what is merely persuasive to all concerned* – is a fifth wheel, inoperative except that it occasionally comes loose and hits a bystander. If we decide that the quantity theory of money or the marginal productivity theory of distribution is persuasive, interesting, useful, reasonable, appealing, acceptable, we do not also need to know that it is True. Its persuasiveness, interest, usefulness, and so forth come from particular arguments: 'Marginal productivity theory, for one thing, is a consequence of rationality in the hiring of inputs' (and we think highly of rationality). 'The quantity equation, for one thing, is a simple framework for macroeconomics' (and we think highly of simplicity). (McCloskey 1985, pp. 46–47; emphasis added)

Given what 'we' are supposed to believe and value, it seems obvious that the relevant group of people whose beliefs matter consists of something like the majority of the present economics profession. For a statement to be true in the sense of [truth], it has to cohere with the beliefs held by this conversationally privileged group. That this constraint is social and that it works in excluding other beliefs is evident in McCloskey's (somewhat anti-postmodern) explanation for why there are dilettantes in the market for economic ideas whose claims are wrong but yet found persuasive:

'Stories can go wrong, which is hardly news. We swim all day in wrong stories told by liars, incompetents, and the self-deluded. . . . Economic snake oil sells . . . because the public wants it' (McCloskey 1990, p. 3). Economic snake oil is persuasive yet false because its claims do not cohere with the beliefs held by the majority of professional economists – and 'the public' is no part of the economics profession. Economic snake oil does not meet the social constraint, thus is false. I have dubbed this the 'elite theory of truth' – a combination of the ideas of coherence and (limited) consensus:

[*E-truth*] The truth (with a small t) of a statement consists in its coherence with a certain set of beliefs that an elite group of people ends up with in an ongoing conversation before the ideal limit of all conversation.

This means that truth cannot be equated with persuasiveness *simpliciter*. Not all persuasive ideas are true; some persuasive ideas are false. Only those that satisfy the social constraint are true: what matters is coherence with the beliefs of those whose beliefs matter. The first sentence of the following passage cites a social constraint and thus contradicts the second sentence that bans any attempt to go 'beyond persuasive reasoning' in the account of truth: 'We believe and act on what persuades us – not what persuades a majority of a *badly chosen* jury, but what persuades *well-educated* participants in the conversations of our civilization and of our field. To attempt to go beyond persuasive reasoning is to let epistemology limit reasonable persuasion' (McCloskey 1985, p. 46; emphasis added).

One then wonders what is behind this sort of epistemic discrimination: what justifies privileging the beliefs of the elite. One possible justification of invoking the social constraint lies in the second constraint on coherence: the moral one. Not any conversation matters in determining small-t truths. Only 'honest' conversation does. Honest conversation is defined in terms of the notion of *Sprachethik*, the ethics of conversation. Here are some of the prescriptions of *Sprachethik*:

Don't lie; pay attention; don't sneer; cooperate; don't shout; let other people talk; be open-minded; explain yourself when asked; don't resort to violence or conspiracy in aid of your ideas. We cannot imagine good conversation or good intellectual life deficient in these. They are the rules adopted by the act of joining a good conversation . . . (1988, p. 251; McCloskey 1985, p. 24)

Honest conversation and persuasion observes these norms that together constitute a moral constraint on coherence. Given that abiding to the *Sprachethik* is somewhat demanding, I have dubbed the ensuing notion of truth as the 'angel theory of truth'.

[*A-truth*] The truth (with a small t) of a statement consists in its coherence with a certain set of beliefs that an elite group of people, obeying the canons of *Sprachethik*, end up with in an ongoing honest conversation before the ideal limit of all conversation.

Honest conversation for McCloskey is an exemplification of the liberal market order in the realm of ideas. The *Sprachethik* is 'liberalism incarnate' (McCloskey 1988, p. 251), and there is a competitive market of conversation where 'all writers are . . . competing minute-by-minute with other writers in an atomistic market of ideas' (McCloskey 1985, p. 189). Rather than methodological control, laissez faire is the right policy: the 'free market – not the central planning proposed by official methodologies – gives the only promise worth having that the economy of intellect will continue to run as well as can be expected' (McCloskey 1988, p. 252). McCloskey must be supposed to follow Adam Smith in thinking that the proper functioning of the market order requires that the agents – economists in our case – are equipped with the right moral sentiments.

On this account, truth emerges as socially and morally constrained coherence. Let us consider this account from the point of view of the major problem that McCloskey said plagues the correspondence account: correspondence truths are not attainable, or at any rate we cannot know if we have attained them, thus this notion of truth is 'inoperational'. Are truths conceived as socially and morally constrained coherence radically different in that they are attainable? To answer this question, we may raise another two questions: does the moral constraint actually hold; and are we able to determine the degree of approximation to which it does hold?

As to the first question, McCloskey's own writings are at times rather harsh about the economics profession: Economists are inclined towards 'fanaticism and intolerance' (1985, p. 4); 'the war among economists should stop, . . . we should start treating each other with fairness' (1987, p. 88); '[t]he violence with which economists outside the main stream [are] excluded from the conversation' (1989, p. 235); and citing a physicist who made observations about economists at a conference: 'I used to think physicists were the most arrogant people in the world. The economists were, if anything, more arrogant' (1991, 16n2). All this seems to suggest that economists do not behave quite like angels, and that therefore the moral constraint does not hold. As a result, economists have not been able to produce any A-truths, truths as socially and morally constrained coherence.

But perhaps economics is evolving towards a morally elevated stage – maybe thanks partly to McCloskey's own admirable campaign to raise the moral standards of the profession. McCloskey would then have to withdraw the judgment that many small-t truths have been delivered by economics already. Another possibility is to relax the requirement of strict adherence to the *Sprachethik*: a close enough approximation to angel-like behavior will do. But this solution runs into its own problems. This brings us to the second question concerning whether we are able to determine the degree of approximation to which the moral constraint holds.

The problem is one of infinite regress. The task of determining the degree of approximation to which the moral constraint holds is the task of assigning a truth-value to second order statements about such degrees of approximation. The truth of any such second order statement requires that the moral constraint be met at that second order level. But the truth of any statement about the degree to which the moral constraint holds at that second order level itself requires that a third order moral constraint holds. And so on and so forth, ad infinitum. Due to this infinite regress, there is no way that A-truths would be free from the problem that McCloskey claims plagues correspondence truths: inoperationality. If correspondence truths are inoperational, so are angel-truths. McCloskey's thoughts about truth in economics fail to deliver what they promise.

My proposed cure is simple. In your theory of truth, retain some sort of non-epistemic correspondence notion of what truth is: it is independent of our ways of finding out about it, it is independent of conversations, persuasions, elites, and angels. In your theory of justification and discovery, include whatever ideas promise to serve the purpose of successful and reliable truth-acquisition, such as, possibly, persuasiveness in an honest conversation in a forum with relatively free entry. Honest conversation does not constitute truth, but may help discover truths.

10. CONCLUSION

While it is obvious that economists (just like the rest of us) use the vocabulary of veracity in a number of meanings and for a number of purposes, for the most part, they at least implicitly seem to subscribe to some simple correspondence notion of truth, or at any rate some general idea of truth being non-epistemic. Surely, economists regard things such as coherence, consensus and persuasiveness as important, but they don't in general take them to constitute truth, or so it seems.

How does one then explain the observation that economists appear to have a major difficulty with claiming their models to be true? Is it because their models systematically fail so miserably? Or is it because correspondence truth is an all too ambitious goal for ordinary mortals to reach anyway? Whatever one thinks of these explanations, I believe a major role is played, not primarily by any big unclarity about the concept of truth, but by an unclarity about the identity of the relevant truth bearers and truth makers. What I mean is that the difficulties with ascribing truth (as well as falsehood) to entities such as models are at least partly due to a deep unclarity about what sensible truth claims one can make when using models to talk about the world: in other words, the problem is with truth nomination. One manifestation of this is the statement that no model can be true, this statement being based on the conflation of the whole truth and nothing but the truth; in fact a model can be true about what it is used to capture without giving us the whole truth. Another is the conclusion that a model is false from the observation that its assumptions are false; in fact the assumptions of a model are not among its main claims that should be taken as its prime candidates for truth; and assumptions can often be paraphrased so as to turn them into potentially true claims.

The key to understanding the identity of relevant truth bearers in connection to economic modeling is to see what major claim is being made about the causal constitution of the economy when using the model. That claim is not given by the assumptions of the model nor by the predictions it yields. What fact or facts about the economy is the model used to capture? Much of the time, models are used to describe a 'mechanism' that is believed to be functioning in the economy. Does the model offer a description that is true of some real mechanism? On this, the model may fail – and its failure is not implied by the plain falsehood of its assumptions, nor by the partiality of its coverage of causes, nor by the falsehood of its predictive implications. Naturally, the model may fail because of the way in which some of its assumptions are false and because of some causally indispensable factors that it fails to capture.

Whatever the value of the foregoing discussions, their underlying motives are rather clear to myself. The motivation behind them can be formulated in terms of two normative principles:

1. Economists should not attribute falsehood to their theories and models for wrong reasons. (For if they do, one easy conclusion would be that all models are false, therefore there is nothing

particularly blameworthy about this or that particular economic model.)

2. Economists should not abstain from attributing truth-values (true or false) to their theories and models and their constituents for wrong reasons. (For if they do, one easy conclusion would be that economics is not accountable for its intellectual products in terms of their truth contents or veristic value.)

Indeed, these principles have implications for the terms of research and debate in and about economics. They have implications for the ambitions of economic research and policy advice as well as for the terms in which we should judge the degree to which those ambitions are being fulfilled. One may consider them as vehicles in any 'anti-complacency campaign' anyone might wish to run in economics (what follows the two principles between parentheses are descriptions of complacent attitudes that are to be resisted). Neither economists themselves nor their critics or disappointed clients should debunk economics too easily by claiming, for wrong reasons, that it is a discipline that is neither truth-seeking nor truth-acquiring. It is quite another thing, and perhaps more difficult, to make that sort of charge for the right reasons.

REFERENCES

Friedman, Milton (1953), 'The Methodology of Positive Economics', in *Essays in Positive Economics,* Chicago: University of Chicago Press, pp. 3–43.

Giere, Ronald (1988), *Explaining Science*, Chicago: University of Chicago Press.

Hausman, Daniel M. (1992), *The Inexact and Separate Science of Economics,* Cambridge: Cambridge University Press.

Hendry, David (1986), 'Econometric Methodology: A Personal Perspective', in T.F. Bewley (ed.), *Advances in Econometrics,* Cambridge: Cambridge University Press, pp. 29–48.

McCloskey, D.N. (1985), *The Rhetoric of Economics*, Madison: University of Wisconsin Press.

McCloskey, D.N. (1987), 'Reply', Review of Radical Political Economy, **19** (3), 87–91.

McCloskey, D.N. (1988), 'Thick and thin methodologies in the history of economic thought' in Neil de Marchi (ed.), *The Popperian Legacy in Economics,* Cambridge: Cambridge University Press, pp. 245–58.

McCloskey, D.N. (1989) 'Why I am no longer a positivist', *Review of Social Economy*, **47** (3), 225–38.

McCloskey, D.N. (1990), *If You're So Smart. The Narrative of Economic Expertise*, Chicago: University of Chicago Press.

McCloskey, D.N. (1991), 'Economic science: a search through the hyperspace of assumptions?', *Methodus*, **3** (1), 6–16.

McCloskey, D.N. (1994), *Knowledge and Persuasion in Economics*, Cambridge: Cambridge University Press.

McCloskey, D.N. (1995), 'Modern epistemology against analytic philosophy: A reply to Mäki', *Journal of Economic Literature*, **33** (3), 1319–23.

McCloskey, D.N. (2002), 'You Shouldn't Want a Realism if You Have a Rhetoric', in U. Mäki (ed.), *Fact and Fiction in Economics. Models, Realism, and Social Construction*, Cambridge: Cambridge University Press, pp. 329–40.

Mäki, Uskali (1992a), 'On the method of isolation in economics', in Craig Dilworth (ed.), *Idealization IV: Intelligibility in Science*, special issue of *Poznan Studies in the Philosophy of the Sciences and the Humanities*, **26**, 319–54.

Mäki, Uskali (1992b), 'Friedman and realism', *Research in the History of Economic Thought and Methodology*, **10**, 171–95.

Mäki, Uskali (1994), 'Isolation, idealization and truth in economics', in Bert Hamminga and Neil de Marchi (eds), *Idealization in Economics*, special issue of *Poznan Studies in the Philosophy of the Sciences and the Humanities*, 38, 147–68.

Mäki, Uskali (1995), 'Diagnosing McCloskey', *Journal of Economic Literature*, **33** (3), 1300–1318.

Mäki, Uskali (1996a), 'Two portraits of economics', *Journal of Economic Methodology*, **3** (1), 1–38.

Mäki, Uskali (1996b), 'Scientific Realism and Some Peculiarities of Economics', in R.S. Cohen et al. (ed.), *Realism and Anti-Realism in the Philosophy of Science*, Boston Studies in the Philosophy of Science, Vol. 169, Dordrecht: Kluwer, pp. 425–45.

Mäki, Uskali (1998a), 'Aspects of realism about economics', *Theoria*, **13** (2), 301–19.

Mäki, Uskali (1998b), 'Instrumentalism', in J. Davis, W. Hands and U. Mäki (eds), *The Handbook of Economic Methodology*, Cheltenham, UK and Northampton, MA, USA: Edward Elgar, pp. 253–56.

Mäki, Uskali (2000a), 'Kinds of assumptions and their truth: Shaking an untwisted F-twist', *Kyklos,* **53** (3), 303–22.

Mäki, Uskali (2000b), 'Performance against dialogue, or answering and really answering: A participant observer's reflections on the McCloskey conversation', *Journal of Economic Issues*, **34** (1), 43–59.

Mäki, Uskali (2001a), 'The Way the World Works (www): Towards an Ontology of Theory Choice', in U. Mäki (ed.), *The Economic World View. Studies in the Ontology of Economics*, Cambridge: Cambridge University Press, pp. 369–89.

Mäki, Uskali (2001b), 'Models', in *International Encyclopedia of the Social and Behavioral Sciences*, Volume 15, pp. 9931–37, Amsterdam: Elsevier.

Mäki, Uskali (2001c), 'Realisms and Their Opponents', in *International Encyclopedia of the Social and Behavioral Sciences*, Volume 19, pp. 12815–21, Amsterdam: Elsevier.

Mäki, Uskali (2003), '"The Methodology of Positive Economics" (1953) does not give us *the* methodology of positive economics', *Journal of Economic Methodology,* **10** (4), 495–505.

Musgrave, Alan (1981), '"Unreal" assumptions in economic theory: the F-twist untwisted', *Kyklos,* **34** (3), 377–87.

Schelling, Thomas (1978), *Micromotives and Macrobehavior*, New York: Norton.

Strawson, P.F. (1950), 'Truth', *Proceedings of the Aristotelian Society*, **24**, 129–56.

Sugden, Robert (2002), 'Credible worlds. The Status of Theoretical Models in Economics', in U. Mäki (ed.), *Fact and Fiction in Economics. Models, Realism and Social Construction,* Cambridge: Cambridge UP, pp. 107–36.
van Fraassen, Bas (1980), *The Scientific Image*, Oxford: Clarendon Press.

3. Deliberative Democracy as an Institutional Mode of Inquiry: Pragmatism, Social Facts and Normative Theory

James Bohman[*]

When compared to alternative theories, deliberative democracy is a particularly demanding ideal. There are many versions of deliberative democracy, with some more liberal and oriented to the institutions of the constitutional state and others more participatory and oriented to affording citizens more direct opportunities to influence decisions. All share the common demand that democracy is the rule by citizens of their common affairs through the public use of reason. Deliberative democracy, broadly defined, is thus any one of a family of views according to which the public deliberation of free and equal citizens is the core of legitimate political decision making and self-government. Behind this fundamental agreement, each of the terms of this definition is hotly debated among deliberative democrats, who have put forth a variety of conceptions of the deliberative process and its normative constraints. Various institutional and non-institutional locations for deliberation have been proposed and debated, as well as various attempts to determine its conditions of feasibility. The answer that I propose here is that it is a public form of social inquiry.

Any ideal as demanding as deliberative democracy is open to criticism, as the chorus of critics now grows louder and sometimes even strident. Some argue that its ideal is by nature elitist and exclusionary, in that it seems to leave out relevant power differences and pervasive asymmetries of race, gender and class.[1] Others see it as based upon an

---

* Saint Louis University.

[1] See Sanders (1997), also Young (2002), Chapter 2. Both emphasize alternative forms of communication such as testimony and story telling as opposed to argumentation. For a cogent reply, see Dryzek (2000, p. 68). Dryzek emphasizes that all forms of communication

inadequate conception of politics, reducing democracy to seminar discussion or so infeasible and idealized as to be unrealizable and unable to guide reform.[2] More sympathetic critics have raised serious internal difficulties, including the need for fundamental revisions in order for the ideal to be practicable.[3] One such difficulty suggests a dilemma at the very heart of any attempt to institutionalize deliberation: either deliberation is confined to the institutions of liberal democracy and thus inherits all their problems of legitimacy; or it proposes its own institutions and decision procedures, at the cost of making its own democratic legitimacy infeasible. Consider the problem of who deliberates. While including everyone makes the ideal impractical, limiting participation and opportunities for influence makes it potentially elitist. In the first case, the critic can show that under actual institutional conditions the space for deliberation is rather small. In the second case, the gap between actual empirical conditions and the rationalist ideal of inclusive deliberation seems too large to bridge.

While some of these criticisms have already been accepted and incorporated into deliberative theories, the discussion of objections raised by skeptics has lacked any clear sense of what constitutes a decisive criticism in the first place, much less one that is fatal to deliberative theory rather than to democracy as such. The purpose of this chapter is to address this question and to show that the answer hinges, perhaps surprisingly, on the philosophy of social science; that is, on how empirical and descriptive statements that have a social scientific status can inform and criticize normative political theory. In order to evaluate the force of most skeptical criticisms of deliberative democracy, it is necessary to clarify the status of empirical or factual claims in arguments for or against a normative political theory. Skepticism about democracy more often than not trades on the idea that there is only one form of social facts. One of the great achievements of pragmatism is to show that this is not the only or even the most significant use of 'social facts' in critical, normative theories of democracy.

---

are admitted conditionally because they can produce exclusions. For each of these objections, I will cite quite cogent replies that extend deliberative democracy. My task here is not to give such a reply to each objection, but to reconstruct deliberative democracy in a pragmatic fashion.

[2] See, for example, Walzer (1999), and Shapiro (1999). For a cogent response to this criticism that sees the adversarial dimension of deliberation as unavoidable in certain contexts, see Christiano (1996, p. 91).

[3] See Dryzek (2001). Dryzek raises powerful objections to formulations that require the 'deliberation of all' See also Valadez (2001, p. 63). Valadez raises related objections to the standard idea of agreement as based on 'reasons that all can accept'. For a response to this sort of objection, see Benhabib (2002, p. 145ff.).

Guided by a pragmatic conception of social inquiry, theories of deliberative democracy take a reflexive step beyond some of its impasses. According to a pragmatic account, democracy itself is a form of inquiry typical of problem solving in cooperative social activity. A mode of inquiry is democratic not only if it fulfils the basic conditions of freedom and equality; if it does so, it is *eo ipso* 'multiperspectival'. In contrast to the single perspective of the social scientific observer, a mode of inquiry is multiperspectival to the extent that it seeks to take into account the positive and negative dimensions of current social conditions as well as to incorporate the various perspectives of relevant social actors in attempting to solve a problem. According to Dewey, such a multiplicity of perspectives distinguishes a 'public' from 'mass' opinion. Deliberative democracy is a particular way of organizing and institutionalizing multiperspectival inquiry, for which social facts are descriptions of problematic situations. From this pragmatic perspective, current problematic situations from pluralism to globalization uncover deep normative assumptions concerning democracy that deliberative democracy tacitly inherits but need not endorse. In such a case, pragmatism suggests that the ideal of democracy needs to be 'reconstructed' and thus transformed so as to save its normative core while making it an effective form of governance and problem solving in the current open field of possibilities. Such a reconstruction shows how pragmatism provides the basic framework in which to 'decenter' deliberative democracy, that is, an account that does not take the goal of deliberative democracy to have all the citizens discuss and decide by their collective will how best to order and to control their society as a whole. It will also require decentering experts from their role as those who engage in institutionalized social inquiry by making them one among many participants in 'multiperspectival' inquiry.

1. PRAGMATISM, SOCIAL FACTS AND DEMOCRACY

Consider a normative democratic theory that did not respect social facts. Such a theory might argue in the following way: democracy is the principle that defines the legitimacy of any political association; since deliberative democracy is the best version of such a principle, all legitimate political associations must be governed by the ideal of deliberative democracy. We might call this the principle of 'pure' democratic association. There is something right about this sort of theory, in that it does not accept that politics consists of a delimited domain that is fixed in advance. Instead, it seeks to apply democratic principles broadly to many forms of social organization and institutions and thus to extend freedom and equality to all areas of social life. But is this form of democracy feasible? Such a theory seems to have forgotten that democracy itself has enabling and constraining conditions that make it possible, something no less true of deliberative democracy in particular. Certain conditions make democratic deliberation possible, and in their absence it would be hard to call the deliberation in various institutional locations public or democratic. These seem to include the existence of formal institutions of some kind or another to organize opportunities for influence over decisions, the autonomy and openness of civil society as the domain of social activity, and a public sphere that permits communication across these various spheres. In societies that are differentiated in this way, certain social facts seem generally applicable: pluralism, complexity, globalization, the social and epistemic division of labor, the necessity of mediated communication, and so on. These facts act as constraints on the realizability and feasibility of a purely democratic association.

Democracy requires some framework of voluntary constraints on action, such as commitments to basic rights and the constitutional limits on political power that make it possible. Social facts can be seen as nonvoluntary constraints, that is, as constraints that condition the scope of the application of democratic principles. When taken up in a practical social theory oriented to suggesting actions that might realize some ideal, social facts may operate as constraints, but not only constraints. For Rawls, 'the fact of pluralism' (or the diversity of moral doctrines in modern societies) is just one such permanent feature of modern society that is directly relevant to political order because its conditions 'profoundly affect the requirements of a workable conception of justice' (Rawls 1999, p. 424). Such facts become permanent in that modern institutions and ideals developed after the Wars of Religion, including constitutional democracy and freedom of expression, promote rather than inhibit the development of further pluralism. This fact of pluralism thus alters how we are to think of the *feasibility* of justice and 'a stable and unified order' (Rawls 1999, p. 425). Thus, for Rawls, whether facts are regarded in terms of possibility or feasibility, they are only considered as *constraints*, as restricting what is politically possible or what can be brought about by political action and power.

If this were the only role of facts, then political liberalism would not be a case of a full practical theory in the sense that I am using the terms. Rawls also wants to add that the relevant social facts such as the fact of pluralism are 'permanent' and not merely to be considered functionally in terms of stability. Social facts related to stability may indeed constrain feasibility without being limits on the possibility or realizability of an ideal; in this case, for example, political ideals other than liberalism might be possible. Without a necessary connection between feasibility and possibility, describing a social fact as permanent is not exactly apt. It is better instead to think of such facts as 'institutional facts' that are deeply entrenched in some historically contingent, specific social order rather than as general normative constraints of democratic institutions. What Rawls calls 'permanent' facts about modern societies are rather those features that are embedded in relatively long-term social processes, the consequences of which cannot be undone in a short period of time such as a generation. Practical theories thus have to consider the connection of facts and norms in processes of 'generative entrenchment' (see Wimstatt 1972). By 'entrenchment of social facts' I mean that the relevant democratic institutions further promote the very conditions that make some social fact possible. When the processes at work in the social fact begin to outstrip particular institutional feedback mechanisms that maintain it, then the institution must be transformed if it is to stand in the appropriate relation to the facts that make it feasible and realizable.

Consider Habermas's similar use of social facts. For Habermas, as for Rawls, pluralism and the need for coercive political power make the constitutional state necessary, so that the democratic process of law making is governed by a system of personal, social and civil rights. Habermas introduces a third and more fundamental social fact for the possibility and feasibility of democracy: the fact of complexity. Complex societies for Habermas are 'polycentric', with a variety of forms of order including nonintentional market coordination. This fact changes the nature of democratic institutions and limits political participation. Indeed, these facts make it such that the principles of democratic self-rule and the criteria of public agreement cannot be asserted simply as the proper norms for all social and political institutions. As Habermas puts it, 'unavoidable social complexity makes it impossible to apply the criteria [of democratic legitimacy] in an undifferentiated way' (Habermas 1996, p. 305). This fact makes a certain kind of structure ineluctable; since complexity means that democracy can 'no longer control the conditions under which it is realized'. In this case, the social fact has become 'unavoidable', and certain institutions, for which there is 'no feasible alternative' (Habermas 2001, p. 122), become necessary for social integration. Taken as a macro-sociological fact about modern societies, complexity may indeed make impossible any direct realization of democracy as a single organizing principle for all social institutions. This fact says little about the wide field of indirect and institutionally mediated forms that are still possible and feasible, which in turn would also affect the conditions that produce social complexity itself. Some ideals of democracy may rightly seek to preserve aspects of complexity, such as the ways in which the epistemic division of labor may promote wider and more collaborative problem solving and deliberation on ends.

When seen in light of the requirement of entrenching facts and conditions, institutions are necessary for maintaining the conditions for the realization of norms and ideals. An important contribution of pragmatism to understanding institutions in this way is precisely its practical interpretation of the status of social facts. Dewey sees social facts always related to 'problematic situations', even if these problems are more felt or suffered than fully recognized as such. The way to avoid such an empirical-normative dilemma is, as Dewey suggests, to see facts themselves as practical: 'Facts are such in a logical sense only as they serve to delimit a problem in a way that affords indication and test of proposed solutions' (Dewey 1986, p. 499). They may serve this practical role only if they are seen in interaction with our understanding of the ideals that guide the practices in which such problems emerge and for which neither fact nor ideal is fixed and stands in judgment over the other. In response to Lippmann's insistence on the fact of expertise, Dewey criticized the possibilities inherent in 'existing political practice, by completely ignoring occupational groups and the organized knowledge and purposes that are involved in the existence of such groups'. To use some contemporary vocabulary, Dewey is here arguing that epistemic interdependence of the division of labor 'decenters' democracy away from its voluntarist metaphysical roots. With its implicit reliance on the unified will of the people or the face-to-face model of the forum, such an understanding of democracy sees obstacles in current social circumstances.

By not taking due account of such social interdependence, the understanding of democracy becomes 'centered' and finds the division of labor to be a problem because it 'manifests a dependence upon a summation of individuals quantitatively' (Dewey 1991, pp. 50–51). In response to Lippmann's elitist view of majority rule, Dewey held on to the possibility and feasibility of democratic participation by the well-informed citizen no longer based on the aggregation of individuals into a collective will. However, current institutions have become obstacles to the emergence of such a form of democracy in an era when 'the machine age has enormously expanded, multiplied, intensified and complicated the scope of indirect consequences' of collective action and where the collectives so affected by actions of such scope are so large and diverse 'that the resultant public cannot identify and distinguish itself' (Dewey 1988b, p. 255 and p. 314). Our democratic ideals have been shaped by outdated 'local town meeting practices and ideals', even as we live in a 'continental nation state' whose political structures encourage the formation of 'a scattered, mobile and manifold public' and interdependent communities, a public that has yet to recognize itself as such and to form its own distinct common interests. Thus, the solution is a transformation of the public and of the institutions with which the public interacts. Such an interaction will provide the basis for new forms of political organization, the nature and scope of which is 'something to be critically and experimentally determined' (Dewey 1988b, p. 281). As an experimental form of practical inquiry, democracy is about finding new ways to entrench institutions and publics in new social facts.

Pragmatism suggests an understanding of social facts for a social scientific praxeology, as a way to realize various norms and ends. It is better to think of social facts as creating a new space of democratic possibilities, opening up some while foreclosing others. In certain cases, problematic situations lead to judgments about the need for structural transformation of democracy. 'Given the limits and possibilities of our world,' Dahl asks, 'is a third transformation of democracy a realistic possibility?' (Dahl 1989, p. 224). How can we determine such limits and possibilities? Pragmatism argues that this is itself a democratic question, and not just an institutional one. In so far as it is a democratic question it concerns not just specific arrangements such as constitutional or parliamentary democracy, but the fundamental self-understanding of democracy and its basic concepts of self-rule. Various problematic situations or social facts thus go deeper, and challenge such fundamental assumptions that inform democratic practices, such as the common fate of all citizens, the possibility of a unified collective will, or a common public sphere. Some deliberative democrats have challenged these assumptions and have called for the 'decentering' of democracy. With its emphasis on innovation as crucial to a vital democracy in the new situation at the turn of the last century, pragmatism already faced such questions regarding the emergence of large-scale industrial society and the epistemic division of labor and called for democracy as a method of experimentation and testing in response. What is needed, in Dewey's terms, is a 'reconstruction' of these ideals, to 'transfer the attention of theory from the preoccupation with general conceptions to the problem of developing effective methods of inquiry' (Dewey 1983, p. 177).

How might democracy be decentered? The answer as expressed by Habermas is to rid democratic theory of some of the metaphysical assumptions that it inherited from eighteenth century voluntarism, which saw democracies as constituting a 'people' whose 'collective will' was expressed to the extent that democracy was genuine and democratic norms were lived up to in practice.[4] In many conceptions of deliberative democracy, an assumption of the same sort is made by favoring face-to-face interaction in a single forum, so that such a deliberative body could take society as a whole as the object of a singular and orderly process of deliberation about what is best and just. Such a concept finds little application in large-scale, complex and pluralistic societies. According to the decentered view, democratic politics must be embedded in the 'context of large and complex social processes the whole of which cannot come into view, let alone under decision-making control' (Young 2002, p. 46).

The decentered approach has several advantages. It does not see democracy as the expression of a collective unified will, nor as tied to a special set of institutions or communal locations. In his response to Lippmann, Dewey decenters democracy in a similarly twofold way. He denies that the aggregate opinion of the actual body of citizens is as important as the multiple publics formed by the indirect consequences of institutions. He also decenters the state as a given institutional form, since under the conditions of the expert division of labor the state is not the only institution whose decisions are potentially authoritative. Without assuming the state as a given institutional form, the scope and nature of politics is yet to be publicly and experimentally determined.

Next I turn to the discussion of a specific social fact, the 'fact of globalization' and show how it raises such fundamental democratic questions. The issue concerns not just territoriality but the ways in which globalization is not a uniform process but as just such a problematic situation that is experienced in different and even contradictory ways and assessed quite differently by rival theories of democracy. This sort of problematic situation requires 'creative democracy' in Dewey's terms, where deliberation is about transforming both the means and ends of democratic institutions. The problems and social fragmentation wrought by the supporting institutions of globalization suggests that such a 'decentering' and deepening of democracy is now not merely possible but also necessary if democracy is to solve these problems.

---

[4] On the concept of decentering, see Habermas (1996, pp. 296–307). Also Frug (1999), Part Two. I take Dewey's attempt to reconstruct the subject of purposive, teleological action to have this same result, since it undermines the idea that there is some preconceived way to conceive of decision making and intentional, cooperative action. See, for example, Dewey (1986, p. 229). On why democracy lends itself to decentering, see Bohman (forthcoming).

2. DEMOCRACY AND THE FACT OF GLOBALIZATION

For some proponents of the need to transform democracy, the fact of increasing global interdependence permits a direct inference to the need for new and more cosmopolitan forms of democracy and citizenship. Whatever the specific form it takes, the usual arguments for political cosmopolitanism have a relatively simple form despite the fact that the social scientific analyses employed in them are highly complex and empirically differentiated in their factual claims. The fact of global interdependence discussed in theories of globalization refers to the unprecedented extent, intensity and speed of social interactions that now occur along many dimensions across borders, from trade and cultural exchange to migration.[5] The inference from these facts of interdependence is that existing forms of democracy within the nation state must be transformed and that institutions ought to be established at the scale of problems that escape national boundaries.[6] Here globalization is taken to be a macrosociological, aggregative fact that constrains the realization of democracy without further political integration and congruence, much in the same way that Habermas sees the fact of social complexity as constraining the possible realizations of democratic principles. The Deweyan alternative is to see that facts 'have to be determined in their dual function as obstacles and as resources', as problems that also hold out the conditions that make the transformation of the situation possible (Dewey 1986, pp. 499–500). The 'mere' fact of the wider scale of interaction (such as the increased extensiveness and intensity of social and economic interaction across borders) is thus inadequate on its own and does not capture what role globalization may play as a problematic situation for the emergence of new democratic possibilities.

On the pragmatic interpretation of social facts, globalization is both a resource and an obstacle for democracy. Even the notion of 'interdependence' can be misleading insofar as it suggests the *telos* of an increasingly integrated world or an increasingly homogeneous culture or political community.[7] Instead of using such terms that suggest a single rather than a multidimensional process, a pragmatic analysis is better

---

[5] On the various positions in the controversies over globalization, see David Held et al. (1999).

[6] See, for example, Held (1995, p. 98ff.). Held emphasizes the scope of interconnections and its effects on the realization of autonomy as the key problem for democratic governments.

[7] On complex interdependence, see Keohane (2000, p. 117).

served by a concept such as interconnectedness. Taken as an aggregative social fact on the model of the complexity of modern societies, globalization appears to be a convergent social fact for all modern societies. Rather, it is important here, as in the case of the fact of pluralism, to see that this process can be experienced in different ways by different peoples or political communities, given that it is a multifaceted and multidimensional process that produces 'differential interconnectedness in different domains' (Held et al. 1999, p. 27). In some domains such as global financial markets, globalization is consistent with hierarchy to the extent that it is profoundly uneven and deeply stratified in the distribution of its benefits and burdens. These inequalities of access to and control over aspects of globalizing processes may reflect older patterns of subordination and hierarchy, even while it produces new ones with some communities shut out of financial markets and makes others more vulnerable to its increased volatility (see Held et al. 1999, p. 213).[8] The fact of globalization is thus a new sort of social fact the dispersed effects of which can be disaggregated into indirect consequences that differ across various domains and at various locations.

Given the sort of fact that globalization is, there are a number of possible democratic responses to it. The lack of effective global institutions suggests that many of its practical consequences can be seen as suboptimal outcomes of a coordination problem, solved to the mutual benefit of all by the appropriate application of technical knowledge or expertise. This understanding of the fact of globalization leads to greater authority being invested in international financial institutions in which experts are guided by economic theories of proper market functioning that suggest the policies necessary to avoid instability and volatility in increasingly global financial markets. While such theoretical knowledge has a role to play, it assumes that the fact of globalization is to be taken as a coordination problem. Only by having methods that ensure that the full range of perspectives are available for inquiry can institutions manage the problems in ways that consider the interests of everyone concerned. In this case, it requires a kind of second-order testing and accountability not yet available in international financial institutions, the standards of which do not yet fully consider the social disintegration that globalization may bring. [9] How can we understand its practical significance in a normative theory concerned with the feasibility and realization of the democratic ideal?

---

[8] For various dimensions of this issue, see Hurrell and Woods (1999).

[9] Rodrik (1994); also Woods (2001).

The example of global financial markets and their governing institutions raises the question of the sort of practical knowledge to be employed in institutions and how the method of inquiry in them may promote or inhibit democratic alternatives. The practical alternative to such a solution through *techne* must be 'multiperspectival', in that it considers the many different perspectives of those caught up in webs of social interaction. If it is profoundly uneven, then the more interconnected locations and domains of the global structure may be enabled in a variety of ways to achieve various political and economic ends and thus to dominate the less interconnected. In this way, the increased scale and extent of interconnectedness across borders increases the possibilities of domination, and for this reason requires some process of democratization in which the freedom of all may become possible.

One further question about the 'fact' of globalization must be raised in order to understand the possibilities inherent in it for democracy. Is globalization a 'permanent' fact for democracy in the way that Rawls described the fact of pluralism for liberalism in that it is deeply embedded in its possible realizations? As many social theorists have argued, globalization is part of long-term social processes beginning in early modernity; as Giddens put it, 'modernity is inherently globalizing'. If this is true, then undoing such processes is possible, although not feasible in any short time span and under the normative constraints of democracy. That is, so long as globalizing societies are democratic, we can expect such processes and their impacts to continue, since to attempt to stop them would make such societies less rather than more democratic by undoing some institutionally entrenched facts.

This is not to say that globalization in its current form is somehow permanent or unalterable. Indeed, just how globalization will continue and under what legitimate normative constraints become the proper questions for democratic politics. In political activity around issues related to globalization, the currently existing and overly weak normative constraints will be reconstituted along with the institutions themselves. Rather than a 'permanent constraint', the social fact of globalization is open to democratic reconstruction, should creative reinterpretation of 'deeply entrenched' democracy come about. In the face of this task, the normative emphasis on democracy as a form of political nondomination brings out new features of its ideal. We could call this ideal that of a multiperspectival polity. Contrary to some interpretations of cosmopolitan democracy, such a polity is not oriented to an ideal according to which democracy is the self-determination of citizens who 'should be able to freely choose the conditions of their own association'. [10] Certainly many experience the scheme of global co-operation as having been imposed upon them. This is better described as an issue of domination. Under conditions of pervasive interdependence, it is difficult to see how it is possible that any body of citizens exert control sufficient to choose the conditions of their association. Given that the circumstances of politics now apply globally, we cannot voluntarily choose with whom we cooperate and associate. Nonetheless, the terms of cooperation are still matters for democratic politics. While no less demanding than self-determination, nondomination captures democratic norms of accountability and public influence without the now questionable features of democratic voluntarism. Instead of trying to capture the global will of humanity, a more decentered approach that calls into question the normative desirability of these notions is more fruitful for reinterpreting democracy so as to solve the new potential for domination in international institutions. More importantly, these conceptions that seem to many to be necessary conditions of democracy cannot organize the ends of inquiry for transnational institutions and their publics.

3. THE IDEAL OF A MULTIPERSPECTIVAL DEMOCRACY

The analysis thus far has held a robust deliberative ideal constant, taking it more or less for granted as consisting of self-rule by the public deliberation of free and equal citizens. Given the uneven and potentially contradictory consequences of globalization, current democratic institutions at the fundamentally national scale do not seem able to be responsive to all the dimensions of domination and subordination that are possible given the scale and intensity of global interconnectedness. This prospect raises the difficulty of organizing the deliberation of all in a unified public sphere and single set of institutions in its most extreme form. What are the alternatives? Here it is not just a matter of exercising an institutional imagination in coming up with innovative designs. Properly informed by democratic ideals of nondomination, the prior question is to identify the practical knowledge and methods of inquiry needed to promote the democratization of uneven and hierarchical social

---

[10] Here I am rejecting Held's formulation of how the norms of democracy ought to be rethought in light of globalization. See Held (1995, p. 145).

relations. Such inquiry necessarily considers alternative possibilities of social organization. The democratic ideal of autonomy leads Held and others to emphasize the emerging structures of international law that produce a kind of binding power of collective decisions.[11] Others look to ways of extending current international institutions through reforms of their structures of representation. Still others look to the emergence of various institutions in the European Union to discuss the trend towards international constitutionalism or supranational deliberation. I will not here solve the problem of the proper design of such institutions, but only discuss some general features of the multiperspectival practices that might bring any of them about and make them potentially deliberative.[12]

Theories of cosmopolitan democracy usually select one or another institution such as Courts or identify some current institution such as the United Nations as the basis for extending democracy beyond the nation state. However, they do not face an important, reflexive question about the practical character of theoretical knowledge about democracy: Is the relevant practical knowledge needed to make such institutions responsive to publics not also transformed under current conditions? How might a theory of international relations and politics capture the new epistemological perplexities of any current attempt to realize a normative ideal such as democracy? Here we return to the question of how pragmatism might contribute to the reconstruction of deliberative democracy in Dewey's sense. Rather than follow the paths of institutions meant to solve a different set of problems in a different historical situation, democracy must now 'achieve new ends with new means'. The situation now places demands on democracy in the form of pluralism and interconnectedness among communities that it can no longer solve by the previous methods of inquiry. 'Social experimentation' must emerge that permits those who suffer the consequences to have access to influence in the decision-making process.[13] As a second-order, reflexive form of inquiry and testing, deliberative democracy can be reconstructed as a means of inquiry for creating and testing new ends.

According to the sort of plurality of perspectives that is endorsed in a pragmatist philosophy of social science, an observer's point of view on the growth of institutions may be fruitful in producing knowledge of practical knowledge. In Gerald Ruggie's masterful analysis of the

---

[11] Held (1995) and Habermas (2001) have argued for such a legal interpretation of cosmopolitan democracy.

[12] That is not to say that a multiperspectival polity does not have better or worse institutional forms. For the best discussion of a feasible institutionalization of multiperspectival inquiry (without using the term), see Cohen and Sabel (forthcoming).

[13] See West (1989, p. 213), also Dewey (1986, p. 99).

organizational shifts that produced the territorial state and new forms of organization beyond it, he shows that the modern sovereign state and the social empowerment of citizens emerged within the same epistemic order as single fixed-point perspective in painting, cartography, or optics. 'The concept of sovereignty then represented merely the doctrinal counterpart of the application of single point perspective to the organization of political space' (Ruggie 2000, p. 186).[14] Unbundling sovereignty would lead to new political possibilities, including the re-articulation of international political space in a new way that could not be anticipated in dominant theories of international relations. Focusing on the shifts in the authority of states and the development of the European Union, Ruggie sees the 'EU as the first multiperspectival polity to emerge in the modern era' and thus the emergence of a new political form. The concept of 'the multiperspectival form' not only offers 'a lens through which to view other possible instances of international transformation today' (Ruggie 2000, p. 196); it also provides a lens for reflection on the methods of inquiry that would open up and extend the possibilities of democracy.

One possibility for a more comprehensive practical theory of democratization has been suggested by Alexander Wendt as a theory of the 'steering' of the evolution of the international system, with states as the only viable actors to be the democratic subjects under current constraints.[15] This way of thinking about the problem continues the theoretical project of a less pragmatically oriented social science. As such, these evolutionary accounts may also provide 'general interpretive frameworks' on which it is possible to construct 'critical histories of the present' (McCarthy and Hoy 1994, pp. 229–230).[16] In contrast, a pragmatic conception of social facts allows for a more modest account of critical inquiry that no longer sees general theories as comprehensive. Rather, they are interpretations that are validated by the extent to which they introduce new perspectives and open up new possibilities of action that are themselves to be verified in democratic inquiry. A more empirical and less state-centric way to raise the problem would be to ask the pragmatist question of the possibility of transforming the form of

---

[14] Besides its ultimate origins in George Herbert Mead, multiperspectival inquiry is common in feminist and other critical social inquiry in transnational contexts. See for example, Brooke Ackerly's conception of 'the multisited critic' in Ackerly (2000). See also Bunch (1990). For a general account of multiperspectival inquiry as essential to practical and critical social science, see Bohman (2002).

[15] See Wendt (2001, p. 208ff.). In an interesting contrast, Habermas speaks of the role of democracy as 'countersteering' rather than 'steering'. The issue seems to be one of degrees of control over large social processes of learning and change. See Habermas (1996), Chapters 8 and 9.

inquiry operative in various international and transnational institutions. In many cases the 'mode of inquiry' involved in solving problems and making decisions is justified by the *techne* of experts who are not subject to sufficient democratic accountability or potential contestation.

Consider the most clearly contested domain of international administration, the policies adopted by the hierarchical authorities of international financial institutions that, broadly speaking, function as agents for various member state principals (including the World Trade Organization, World Bank, International Monetary Fund or the various organizations that set international technological standards). The problem lies in the specific character of the agent/principal relationship of delegation that has replaced formal political authority. As the performance criteria on which the World Bank and the International Monetary Funds base creditworthiness have expanded, 'the new conditionality is dramatically deepening and broadening the purview of the functions of international financial institutions within countries' (Woods 2000, p. 393). Challenges to expert authority may be seen as leading to the implementation of 'delegative democracy' (see O'Donnell 1999) that aims at undoing the reversal of agency that accountability to such institutions and their fiscal policies produces. At the very least this authority creates new 'circumstances of politics' in which the linkages between authoritative decisions and the publics affected have not yet been created. This framework should include social and institutional conditions for accountability through deliberative inquiry. The problematic situation here in need of second-order testing is the increased potential for domination in many international institutions.

This form of political domination has been challenged by the efforts of NGOs in forming transnational civil society. The European Union has also developed a novel form of inquiry in its new form of decision via committees, where the implementation of legislative acts is assisted by hundreds of committees from member states.[17] Much more dispersed than the broader authority invested in experts in the World Bank or the IMF, 'commitology' is broadly subject to the epistemic norms of experts and their transnational epistemic communities. Such committees work through argumentation in which each seeks to change the standpoints and interests of others in the committee, while being open to the same sort of influence of others. Joerges and Neyer (1997) argue that such committees tend towards such a communicative and deliberative form of interaction rather than mere bargaining or negotiation. Such a mode of inquiry is

---

[17] For two contrasting views, see Joerges and Everson (2000) and Eriksen (2000).

much more deliberative than that of international financial institutions, in that the latter seek only to permit the public to influence rather than shape their policies. The one is multiperspectival and the other is not.

Multiperspectival inquiry could be taken a step further in the EU in creatively employing its 'Open Method of Coordination'. Such deliberative processes provide a space for ongoing reflection on agendas and problems, as well as an interest in inclusiveness and diversity of perspectives. These enabling conditions for democracy can take advantage of the intensified interaction across borders that are byproducts of processes of the thickening of the communicative infrastructure across state borders. Regulatory, but still decentralized federalism provides for modes of accountability in this process itself, even while allowing for local variations that go beyond the assumption of the uniformity of policy over a single bounded territory typical of nation state regulation. Sabel and Cohen argue that the European Union already has features of a directly deliberative polyarchy in the implementation of the OMC in its economic, industrial and educational standards.[18] The advantage of such deliberative methods is that interaction at different levels of decision making promotes robust accountability; accountability operates upwards and downwards and in this way cuts across the typical distinction of vertical and horizontal accountability (see O'Donnell 1994, p. 61). Thus, directly deliberative polyarchy describes a method of decision making in institutions across various levels and with plural authority structures.

Unlike attempts to exert public influence upon representative institutions, this sort of institutionalized method is more directly rather than indirectly deliberative. Indirectly deliberative institutions hold out the promise of democratic legitimacy to the extent that their formal institutions are connected to the various public spheres in which all citizens participate (although not necessarily all in the same ones). Directly deliberative institutions might at the level of fixing general goals and standards that guide such a process require a similar sort of connection to the European public sphere at large, which in turn may be mediated through a more effective European parliament. Given various linguistic and mass media limitations, this public sphere would not be a unified one, but a public of publics in which various linguistic public spheres debate common issues and through intermediaries translate across linguistic and cultural boundaries the results of deliberative processes in other publics. Just what *is* the public at large at the level of implementation and democratic experimentation in directly deliberative

---

[18] See Sabel and Cohen (1998). For a fuller account of polycentric deliberation in the EU, see Cohen and Sabel (forthcoming).

processes? Sabel provides no answer to this question, asserting only that the process must be transparent and public (see Sabel and Cohen 1998, p. 29). Without a clear account of the interaction between publics and the various levels of the institutional decision-making process, it is hard to see why the process does not simply reduce to a more open form of commitology, of expert deliberation at various levels governed by various interests which attempt to influence their decisions. In this case, such deliberation may have a certain epistemic quality, but its sole claim to be democratic is that committees are internally pluralistic across national identity and are governed by some conception of the common European good. Direct deliberation must be kept institutionally distinct from commitology, precisely with respect to its particular disaggregated form of publicity. What is needed here to go beyond commitology is not a new method, but rather a Europe that is a public of publics. The problem for institutional design of directly deliberative democracy is to create precisely the appropriate feedback relation between disaggregated publics and such a polycentric decision-making process.

Whether or not such a structure of deliberation could close the gap between citizens and experts remains an open question for further democratic inquiry. But it at least shows the emergence of newly possible forms of inquiry in supranational deliberation. In good pragmatist fashion, it suggests the transformation of some of the epistemological problems into the practical question of how to make their forms of inquiry and research open to public testing and public accountability. The institutions in which such public deliberation takes place should then seek to become explicitly multiperspectival, not only in their internal organization but also in their vertical accountability to citizens and transnational civil society. The positive conditions for such an extension of current political possibilities already exist in the fact of increased interconnectedness: the emergence of greater social interaction among citizens who participate in vibrant transnational civil societies and in emerging global public spheres. On this basis, the conditions for extending norms of inquiry beyond epistemic communities to more egalitarian and ultimately multiperspectival forms of accountability is at least a possibility that follows from the fact of increased interconnectedness: here Dewey's conception of the interaction of public and institutions that is responsible not only for their democratic character, but is also the mechanism for their structural transformation into a decentered form.

How might new forms of inquiry emerge that are able to accommodate a greater number of perspectives than either of the expert forms? Here we need to distinguish between first- and second-order forms of deliberation, where the latter emerges in order to accommodate an emergent public with new perspectives and interests. Dewey sees the normal, problem-solving functioning of democratic institutions as based on robust interaction between publics and institutions within a set of constrained alternatives. When the institutional alternatives implicitly address a different public than is currently constituted by evolving institutional practice and its consequences, the public may act indirectly and self-referentially by forming a new public with which the institutions must interact. This interaction initiates a process of democratic renewal in which publics organize and are organized by new emerging institutions with a different alternative set of political possibilities as a new political form. This is a difficult process: 'To form itself the public has to break existing political forms; this is hard to do because these forms are themselves the regular means for instituting political change' (Dewey 1988b, p. 255). This sort of process of innovation describes the emergence of those transnational publics that are indirectly affected by the new sorts of authoritative institutions brought about by managing 'deregulation' and globalization.

In keeping with Dewey's admonition that facts are both 'obstacles and resources', inquiry into the transformation of democracy should consider various positive or enabling conditions for deliberation. For a nation state to be democratic, it requires a certain sort of public sphere sufficient to create a strong public via its connections to parliamentary debate. For a transnational and thus polycentric and pluralist community, such as the European Union, it requires a different sort of public sphere in order to promote sufficient democratic deliberation. Whatever institutions could promote and protect such a dispersed and disaggregated public sphere will represent a novel political possibility that does not, as Garnham argues, 'merely replicate on a larger scale the typical modern political form' (Ruggie 2000, p. 195). The difference is between a unified public sphere that gathers together the citizens of a state and a distributive public sphere that disperses opportunities for influence among a wider group of those affected, with alternative linkages between publics and formal institutions.

With the emergence of new public spheres and the proliferation of NGOs and other forms of transnational civil society organization, it is plausible to expect that two different levels of multiperspectival innovation may emerge: in new institutions such as the European Union which are more adapted to multiple jurisdictions and levels of governance; and with the emergence of a vibrant transnational civil society as an agent for producing public spheres around various institutions with the goal of making their forms of inquiry more transparent, accessible and open to a greater variety of actors and perspectives. This approach does not limit the sources of the democratic impulse to transnational civil society and its discourses and thus is still a deliberative model (see Dryzek 2000, p. 133ff). With its emphasis on transforming institutions and on interactions among institutions and publics at various levels, some of the structural limitations and imperatives of states as a single-perspective institution may be overcome (or at least suggests ways that these problems may be obviated). Rather, the better alternative is to reject both bottom-up civil society and top-down statist approaches in favor of vigorous interaction between publics and institutions as the ongoing source of democratic change and institutional innovation. Once a transnational and post-territorial polity rejects the assumption that it must be what Rawls calls 'a single cooperative scheme in perpetuity', a more fluid and negotiable order might emerge with plural authority structures along a number of different dimensions rather than a single location for public authority and power. Without a single location of public power, the dependence of inquiry on a unified public sphere becomes an impediment to democracy rather than an enabling condition for mass participation in decisions at a single location of authority. Instead, inquiry at the transnational level requires dispersed sites of deliberation that do not assume uniform policies over an entire territory but differential solutions that aim at the end of nondomination rather than the unified will of the global demos.

4. CONCLUSION: PRAGMATISM AND DECENTERED DELIBERATIVE DEMOCRACY

The pluralizing impact of various social facts of modern societies dominates much of both philosophical and social scientific discussions of the future of democracy. Such pluralism has a variety of forms: the epistemic pluralism that results from expertise and the division of labor, cultural pluralism that is produced by old and new migrations and conquests of peoples, the value pluralism of various social conflicts surrounding religion and identity politics, and so on. Sometimes these forms of pluralism intersect with one another, producing the possibility of wider and more pervasive disagreements and political conflicts. Such societies manifest a 'new' pluralism. The fact of complexity gives rise to various integrative institutions outside of politics, potentially exercising power without the influence of democratic inquiry. Similarly, the fact of globalization leads to new potential and actual forms of domination and political authority that are not yet fully accountable to any democratic public. It increases both complexity and pluralism of any potential form of democratic politics. In all these cases, democracy requires the new structural connections between deliberation and institutions that reflect the practices of inquiry in a multiperspectival polity. Indeed, all of these facts together suggest that a new and ultimately decentered form of democratic inquiry and deliberation is necessary.

If we follow pragmatism, democracy is then decentered along two dimensions: the micro-dimension of the sort of processes that constitute decision making, and the macro-dimension of the scale of interlocking levels of governance from cities to regions to global society. The first involves the recognition of the place of social perspectives in just and wise democratic decision making; the latter requires having smaller units embedded in larger units whenever people's actions and interaction constitute a common world. So understood, the genuine requirements of democratic communication and political unity come into view. I have argued that under current circumstances of pluralism and globalization, the appropriate institutions and forms of deliberation already are and should be more fully 'multiperspectival'. A thorough decentering of the underlying norms and concepts of democratic theory along these pragmatic lines would put deliberative democracy in a better position to take up what is correct in some of the forceful criticisms of its ideal, yet at the same time preserving its normative core. The Dewey/Lippmann debate about the public sphere is a good model not only for the need for decentering but also of how further debates about deliberative democracy might be conducted.

Pragmatism also contributes a certain kind of theoretical modesty that might come from abandoning some of the strong metaphysical assumptions that continue to guide our thinking about democracy. It also seems that no democratic institutions could be comprehensive enough to produce effective problem solving. We seem to have run up against the limits of democratic control based on consensus and representative institutions. What is the alternative? I have proposed a conception of democratic inquiry based on the capability to take multiple perspectives in expressive practices that produce 'enriched and enlarged experience' among participants in Dewey's terms. Pragmatism sees democratic institutions as experiments, in which deliberation and publicity are crucial to testing the validity and acceptability to citizens. As an institutionalized discourse taking up problematic situations and their reflexive justification, democracy is a multiperspectival practice. Those democratic societies that have already embraced wider pluralism as a resource have already transformed themselves from within and have models in their innovative practices for transnational experimentation. Size is not the issue as much as multiperspectival inquiry into innovative democratization.

Furthermore, pragmatism suggests a further normative basis for such an account of learning and testing. One of the virtues of Mead's account of the generalized other is that it can be applied to testing and inquiry in a variety of political institutions and to just these new forms of democracy. Certainly, Mead saw the issue of the scope of the political community as one of adopting the relevant second person perspective. As he put it: 'The question whether we belong to a larger community is answered in terms of whether our own actions call out a response in this wider community, and whether its response is reflected back into our own conduct.' This sort of mutual responsiveness and interdependence is the basis for a potential democratic community, and this in turn depends on the expressive freedom available to social actors in cases of conflict. To the question of the applicability of such norms and institutions internationally, Mead continues with an optimistic answer: 'Could a conversation be conducted internationally? The question is a question of social organization' (Mead 1934, p. 271). This is not merely a question of size, since many societies characterized by wide pluralism have also been decentered from within and creatively embraced more decentered ways to organize deliberation and decision making. Deliberative democracy can be an impetus for the reform of existing democracy institutions. But it can also do more in more deeply problematic situations, especially if democracy today includes a mode of creative deliberative inquiry into new possibilities for social cooperation and democratic organization at many different levels and dispersed locations.

REFERENCES

Ackerly, Brooke (2000), *Political Theory and Feminist Social Criticism*, Cambridge: Cambridge University Press.

Benhabib, Seyla (2002), *The Claims of Culture*, Princeton: Princeton University Press.

Bohman, James (forthcoming), *Decentering Democracy*, Cambridge: Polity Press.

Bohman, James (2002), 'Critical Theory as Practical Knowledge', in P. Roth and S. Turner (eds), *Blackwell Companion to the Philosophy of Social Sciences*, London: Blackwell, pp. 91–109.

Bunch, Charlotte (1990), 'Women's rights as human rights: towards a revision of human rights', *Human Rights Quarterly*, 489–90.

Christiano, Thomas (1996), *The Rule of the Many: fundamental issues in democratic theory*, Boulder: Westview Press.

Cohen, Joshua and Charles Sabel (forthcoming), 'Sovereignty and Solidarity: EU and US', in J. Zeitlin and D. Trubeck (eds), *Governing Work and Welfare in a New Economy: European and American Experiments*, Oxford: Oxford University Press.

Dahl, Robert (1989), *Democracy and Its Critics*, New Haven: Yale University Press.

Dewey, John (1981), 'Experience and nature', in Jo Ann Boydston (ed.), *John Dewey: The Later Works,* Volume 1, Carbondale: Illinois University Press.

Dewey, John (1983), 'Reconstruction in philosophy', in Jo Ann Boydston (ed.), *John Dewey: The Middle Works*, Volume 12, Carbondale: Illinois University Press.

Dewey, John (1986), 'Logic: the theory of inquiry', in Jo Ann Boydston (ed.), *John Dewey: The Later Works*, Volume 19, Carbondale: Illinois University Press.

Dewey, John (1988a), 'Creative democracy – the task before us', in Jo Ann Boydston (ed.), *John Dewey: The Later Works*, Volume 14, Carbondale: Illinois University Press, 224–230.

Dewey, John (1988b), 'The public and its problems', in Jo Ann Boydston (ed.), *John Dewey: The Later Works*, Volume 2, Carbondale: Illinois University Press, 235–373.

Dewey, John (1991), 'Liberalism and social action', in Jo Ann Boydston (ed.), *John Dewey: The Later Works*, Volume 11, Carbondale: Illinois University Press.

Dryzek, John (2000), *Deliberative Democracy and Beyond*, Oxford: Oxford University Press.

Dryzek, John (2001), 'Legitimacy and economy in deliberative democracy', *Political Theory* **29** (5), 651–69.

Eriksen, Erik (2000), 'Deliberative Supranationalism', in E. Eriksen and J. Fossum (eds), *Democracy in the European Union*, London: Routledge, pp. 42–64.

Frug, Gerald (1999), *City Making*, Princeton: Princeton University Press.

Habermas, Jurgen (1996), *Between Facts and Norms*, Cambridge: MIT Press.

Habermas, Jurgen (2001), *The Postnational Constellation*, Cambridge: MIT Press.

Held, David (1995), *Democracy and the Global Order· From the Modern State to Cosmopolitan Governance*, Stanford: Stanford University Press.

Held, David, Anthony McGrew, David Goldblatt and Jonathan Perraton (eds) (1999), *Global Transformations: Politics, Economics, and Culture*, Stanford: Stanford University Press.

Hurrell, Andrew and Ngaire Woods (eds) (1999), *Inequality, Globalization and World Politics*, Oxford: Oxford University Press.

Joerges, Christian and Jürgen Neyer (1997), 'From intergovernmental bargaining to deliberative political processes: the constitutionalisation of comitology', *European Law Journal* 3(3), 274–300.

Joerges, Christian and Michelle Everson (2000), 'Challenging the Bureaucratic Challenge', in E. Eriksen and J. Fossum (eds), *Democracy in the European Union*, London: Routledge, pp. 164–99.

Keohane, Robert (2000), 'Sovereignty in International Society', in D. Held and A. McGrew (eds), *Global Transformations Reader*, Cambridge: Polity Press.

Lippmann, Walter (1925), *The Phantom Public*, New York: Harcourt Brace.

McCarthy, Thomas and David Hoy (1994), *Critical Theory*, London: Blackwell.

Mead, George Herbert (1934), *Mind, Self, and Society*, Chicago: University of Chicago Press.

O'Donnell, Guillermo (1994), 'Delegative democracy', *Journal of Democracy*, **5** (1), 55–69.

O'Donnell, Guillermo (1999), 'Delegative Democracy', in *Counterpoints*, Notre Dame: Notre Dame University Press, pp. 175–94.

Rawls, John (1999), 'The Idea of an Overlapping Consensus', in Samuel Freeman (ed.), *Collected Papers*, Cambridge: Cambridge University Press, pp. 421–48.

Rodrik, Dani (1994), *Has Globalization Gone Too Far?*, Washington, DC: Foreign Affairs Press.

Ruggie, Gerald (2000), *Constructing the World Polity*, London: Routledge.

Sabel, Charles and Joshua Cohen (1998), 'Directly Deliberative Polyarchy', in *Private Governance, Democratic Constitutionalism and Supranationalism*, Florence: European Commission, pp. 3–30.

Sanders, Lynn (1997), 'Against deliberation', *Political Theory* **25** (3), 347–76.

Shapiro, Ian (1999), 'Enough of Deliberation', in S. Macedo (ed.), *Deliberative Politics*, New York: Oxford University Press, pp. 28–38.

Valadez, Jorge (2001), *Deliberative Democracy, Political Legitimacy and Self-Determination*, Boulder: Westview Press.

Walzer, Michael (1999), 'Deliberation and What Else?', in S. Macedo (ed.), *Deliberative Politics*, New York: Oxford University Press, pp. 58–69.

Wendt, Alexander (2001), 'What is International Relations for?' in R. Wyn Jones (ed.), *Critical Theory and World Politics*, Boulder: Lyn Rienner Publishers, pp. 205–24.

West, Cornel (1989), *The American Evasion of Philosophy*, Madison: University of Wisconsin Press.

Wimstatt, William (1972), 'Complexity and Organization', in *Proceedings of the Philosophy of Science Association*, pp. 67–86.

Woods, Ngaire (2000), 'Order, Globalization and Inequality in World Politics', in D. Held and A. McGrew (eds), *The Global Transformations Reader*, Cambridge: Polity Press, pp. 387–400.

Woods, Ngaire (2001), 'Making the IMF and the World Bank more accountable', *International Affairs* **77** (1), 83–100.

Young, Iris (2002), *Inclusion and Democracy*, Oxford: Oxford University Press.

4. Communicative Rationality as the Basis of Economic Science: Contextualist Implications of the Pragmatic Turn in Critical Social Theory[1]

William Rehg

INTRODUCTION

The critical social theory that was originally associated with the Institute of Social Research in Frankfurt took a significant turn in the mid-twentieth century. Whereas the founders of the Frankfurt School drew their inspiration from theorists such as Karl Marx and Max Weber, second-generation critical theorists such as Karl-Otto Apel and Jürgen Habermas turned to American pragmatism, hermeneutics and the Anglo-American philosophy of language. The pragmatic critical theory developed by these and similar thinkers relied on a normative, universalistic conception of communication and argument, which stood in marked contrast to the postmodern, relativistic versions of pragmatism (e.g. Rorty 1991). In the ensuing debates, however, it became clear to many critical theorists that strongly universalistic approaches required contextualist modifications that stopped short of relativism.

In this chapter I present a contextualist model of discourse as a possible framework for the critical assessment of scientific claims, including those of economists. By critical assessment I do not mean the skeptical dismissal of science. Rather, the proposed model provides a non-relativistic but contextually sensitive way of evaluating the argumentative cogency of scientific claims both within the science

[1] This chapter is a heavily revised version of Rehg (2001). I am grateful for feedback from a number of perspectives: that of ethnomethodologist David Bogen, critical theorists Michael Barber and James Bohman, philosopher Scott Berman and economist Douglas Marcouiller.

community and in broader policy-making contexts. To achieve contextual sensitivity, the model enlists the aid of a heterodox branch of sociology known as 'ethnomethodology'. By way of background, I begin by sketching Habermas's universalistic approach to critical social theory (Section 1) and the difficulties raised by the relation to context (Section 2). I then sketch the radical ethnomethodological version of the contextualist challenge (Section 3). We can then examine what it would mean for argumentation theory to take those difficulties seriously. To this end, I elaborate a pragmatic notion of truth that incorporates important features of ethnomethodology and thus contextualizes the argumentative cogency of scientific claims in a non-relativistic manner (Section 4).

1. HABERMAS'S TURN TO THE PRAGMATICS OF LANGUAGE IN CRITICAL THEORY

When Max Horkheimer formulated the tasks of the Institute for Social Research in 1931, he conceived of critical theory as an interdisciplinary endeavor in which social philosophy and the empirical sciences mutually informed one another. In line with their Marxist heritage, first-generation Frankfurt School theorists such as Horkheimer assumed that political economy would play an important role in this project (Horkheimer [1931] 1993; Bonß 1993). Influenced by Max Weber, these theorists situated questions of political economy in the broader context of problems connected with societal rationalization (the growth of science and technology, bureaucracies, etc.). As Europe descended into the depths of totalitarianism, however, economic analysis gave way to the pressing need to rethink the concept of rationalization on which critical theory relied. Second-generation theorists such as Habermas also saw a need for a more adequate theory of democratic politics. To carry out this project, Habermas followed Apel's lead and turned not to Marx but to Kant, American pragmatism and the philosophy of language (Habermas 1979; Apel 1980).

We can understand Habermas's approach as a species of the broader 'linguistic turn', which we may understand here negatively as a turn away from both the premoderns' metaphysical concerns with the structures of being and the moderns' epistemological focus on the possibility of a subject's access to an objective world. Positively, the turn focuses on the conditions of language use as the unavoidable context and medium for philosophical inquiry. Habermas gave the linguistic turn a specifically pragmatic emphasis by arguing that an adequate theory of linguistic meaning must go beyond the analysis of syntax and semantics, inasmuch as these do not fully account for the ability of competent speakers to *use* grammatically well-formed sentences in ways that are appropriate for social interaction. Habermas proposed that this pragmatic know-how could be captured by a set of basic linguistic structures that underlay all language use – thus a 'formal' or 'universal pragmatics' (Habermas 1979, Chap. 1).

In his effort to rework the rational basis for social critique, Habermas argued at length that the conception of rationality dominant in the social sciences (and in earlier critical theory) in fact captured only one aspect of the richer communicative rationality on which social integration depends (Habermas 1984). According to the dominant model, reason operates above all in fact-stating forms of theoretical discourse, as exemplified in the empirical sciences. In the practical domain, the positivist emphasis on factual truth translates into an exclusive focus on means–end reasoning: with ultimate ends assumed as given, the task of reason consists in the comparison and choice of efficient means for achieving those ends. Action based on this conception of practical reason is instrumentally rational (*zweckrational*) or, in social contexts, 'strategic': one approaches the choice situation, including other actors, as a set of conditions that must be controlled (as means) for the sake of the rational pursuit of one's own ends.

To get beyond these truncated conceptions of rationality, Habermas elaborated a broader conception of reason as it operates in everyday social interaction. The key to his analysis lies in the concept of 'communicative action', which he contrasts with strategic action. If actor A interacts with actor B strategically, then A tries to influence B's behavior in a manner favorable to A's goals by appealing to B's desires and fears (preference orderings) – which, as 'reasons' for B's cooperating with A, are only arbitrarily related to A's goals. In communicative action, by contrast, A presents B with 'validity claims' to factual truth, moral rightness and evaluative authenticity that B is free to accept or reject on the merits.[2] Thus if B cooperates with A, then B does so on the basis of claims that A and B both accept as deserving *intersubjective* recognition on the basis of good reasons. Such reasons are inherently related to A's goals and freely accepted by the cooperating parties.

Although Habermas argues that communicative action enjoys a kind of priority in social interaction, the two types of action typically

---

[2] Habermas's analysis of the third type of validity claim has developed over the years to include not simply the sincere expression of subjective feelings but, more broadly, the evaluation of personal life choices as authentic from an individual's (particular) 'ethical-existential' perspective, as distinct from the (universal) moral perspective (Habermas 1984, pp. 15–18; 1993, Chap. 1).

intertwine. Moreover, in certain social domains, such as economic markets, more efficient social coordination is possible if we give greater play to strategic motivations (within limits). Economists should have no trouble noticing the affinities with neoclassical assumptions about the behavior of economic actors. What concerns us at this point, however, is the contrast between strategic rationality and the richer conception of communicative rationality, which responds not simply to facts but also to moral and evaluative claims.

To defend the rational character of the full range of validity claims against the value-skepticism engendered by the dominant factual-instrumental model of reason, Habermas turned to argumentation theory (Habermas 1984, pp. 15–42; Rehg 1997). From that standpoint, claims to truth, rightness and authenticity are rational because they can be supported, if necessary, by good reasons that would hold up in rational argumentation, or what Habermas calls 'discourse'. Adopting a multi-dimensional account of argumentation, Habermas proposed that good reasons have argumentative cogency insofar as (a) from a logical perspective, they are validly related to the claims they support; (b) from a dialectical perspective, they hold up to relevant questions, objections and counterarguments; and (c) from a rhetorical, or 'process', perspective, reasonable audiences find them convincing.

Habermas places particular emphasis on process standards, according to which cogent arguments are those that would hold up under conditions such as the following:

1. The discourse is open to any person capable of making a relevant contribution.
2. Participants have equal opportunities to participate within the discourse.
3. Participants are free of any socio-institutional constraints that would prevent them from introducing or questioning any relevant assertion (including the expression of attitudes, desires and needs).
4. Participants are sincere and thus are not prevented by psychological pressures from free and equal participation (Habermas 1998, p. 44; 1999, p. 289; Alexy 1990).

Such process conditions are supposed to ensure a persuasive, high-quality discursive exchange of information and arguments – an exchange motivated solely by the search for the better argument – such that participants can identify and agree on the arguments that prove more cogent from logical, dialectical and rhetorical perspectives.

It should not be hard to see that process conditions have a highly idealized character; in fact, it is doubtful that any real discourse could ever satisfy them. They are, therefore, 'counterfactual', but Habermas insists that participants must presuppose they have at least approximated such conditions if they are to consider the outcome of a discourse reasonable (Habermas 1993, pp. 54–59). That is, if we consider some truth-claim as justified, then we must at least presume it *could* hold up in a discourse in which the assessment of the available information and arguments was as open, thorough and rational as it could ever be. Even if no actual discourse can achieve such a degree of rational assessment, under favorable circumstances our experience of an actual discourse should be sufficiently impressive to warrant such a counterfactual presumption, at least provisionally. However, it is precisely the idealized character of such rules that invites contextual criticisms, to which we now turn.

2. DIFFICULTIES IN CONTEXTUALIZING FORMAL PRAGMATICS

Not surprisingly, Habermas's transcendental, decontextualized account of argumentation has drawn critical fire from postmodern pragmatists such as Rorty, whose 'frankly ethnocentric' approach rejects such universalistic arguments (Rorty 1987, 1991). More telling is the fact that even sympathetic theorists working in the Frankfurt School tradition have found problems with Habermas's emphasis on idealized consensus (McCarthy 1991, Chap. 7; Benhabib 1992; Blaug 1999).

From a contextualist perspective, the root difficulty with Habermas's approach lies in its excessively formal character. Habermas assumes that the messy details of actual conversational practices – their rhetorical elements, innuendo, ungrammatical short-cuts, and the like – can ultimately be reduced to standard sentential forms that incorporate the various validity claims described in Section 1 above (Habermas 1979, Chap. 1). Motivating this formal approach is the fear that critical analysis will go astray without the guidance provided by a formal pragmatics, with its idealized system of validity claims and the corresponding argumentation theory. One must then link these abstractions with 'empirical pragmatics' through a rather tortuous program of contextualization (Habermas 1984, pp. 327–8).

The idealized process rules described above carry on this formalist propensity at the level of argumentation theory. Habermas assumes one can derive these rules through transcendental arguments that demonstrate performative self-contradictions in skeptical attempts to reject them (Habermas 1990, pp. 86–94). However, difficulties arise as soon as one attempts to link these idealized rules to actual processes of controversy and argument. Because actual discourses of any scope or complexity cannot satisfy the idealized rules, contextualizing adjustments become necessary – for example decisions about who may participate, or when to consider evidence sufficient to warrant a policy decision – that are not themselves directly based on the rules. Consider, for example, the rule that everyone is free to question any assertion whatever (provided one gives grounds for the questioning). In scientific discourse, this rule is problematic: even with justifications one cannot plausibly question just any assertion in science; rather, a sense of what claims are open to contest partly defines disciplinary competence (cf. Polanyi [1966] 1983, Chap. 3).

To be sure, Habermas is quite aware of this: the ideal rules should not be confused with the limited procedures that structure actual discourses (Habermas 1990, p. 91). Nonetheless, as I explained above the participants' experience in an actual limited discourse should, under favorable circumstances, give them confidence that any outcomes on which they agree would continue to hold up if the assessment of the available evidence and arguments were as open, thorough and reasonable as possible. As pragmatic presuppositions that undergird actual discourse, the ideal rules in effect define the reasonableness or cogency we provisionally attribute to claims we consider justified in light of our participation in actual discourse. But what features of the actual discourse warrant our confidence in making such a counterfactual projection? The question has bite insofar as an actual discourse can sometimes give participants such confidence *without* satisfying the ideal. Consider the various scientific discourses that take place at conferences, in professional journals, between scientists and funding agencies, and so on. It is far from clear that scientists regard all the limitations on such discourses as undermining their confidence in scientific consensus. For example, competition for prestige arguably plays an important role in the functioning of *successful* science. This motivation would seem to introduce a strategic element into discourse, whose participants should, according to the idealized conception, be motivated solely by the force of the better argument.

In reply, one might say that confidence in a discursive outcome emerges insofar as participants perceive one another as displaying features of, or approximating, the ideal audience described by the process standards. Though no doubt partly correct, this answer fails to address the problem that the various process standards cannot be simultaneously optimized, especially when discursive resources – time, patience, knowledge, etc. – are scarce. For example, the openness requirement may conflict with thoroughness and competence standards (cf. Blaug 1999, pp. 48–9; Webler et al., 2001). On what basis, then, do participants decide which aspects of good process to emphasize in cases of conflicting demands?

A second answer holds that in accepting certain limitations in actual discourse, participants tacitly presume that the limitations could be justified under conditions approximating the ideal – an idealized methodological discourse, as it were. According to this answer, then, the criticism and defense of contextual restrictions tacitly presume the idealized court of appeal in which such rules apply. But given the impossibility of an ideal discourse, these rules are too vague to help us understand and criticize actual cases of scientific argumentation. Such criticism, to be effective, must be appropriately contextualized. But on what basis?

3.   THE ETHNOMETHODOLOGICAL CHALLENGE: CONTEXTUALIZED ACCOUNTABILITY AND INDEXICALITY

The foregoing difficulties indicate the need for a better account of the contextualizing rationalities that participants employ in actual discourses. To address this need, Thomas McCarthy (1994, Chap. 3) cautiously enlisted the heterodox brand of sociology developed by Harold Garfinkel and co-workers (1963, 1967; Heritage 1984). Ethnomethodology (EM) distinguishes itself from mainstream sociology by paying close attention to the messy, largely non-generalizable details of social interaction in local contexts. In contrast to Parsonian sociology, which accounted for social order in terms of norms internalized and applied by compliant members of the group, EM emphasizes the agency that members exercise in actively constructing orderly social interaction in concrete situations. Social order arises not from the mechanical application of rules to situations whose intelligibility is given ahead of time, but as an ongoing, occasioned accomplishment in which members actively constitute – and ongoingly transform – the sense of their situations. Shared normative expectations and general interpretive schemas certainly play a role in social interaction, but members employ them creatively, engaging a vast array of ad hoc mechanisms for weaving them together in an orderly interaction that continually adjusts to and reconstitutes changing circumstances.

To get at this creative process of ongoing sense-making, one must attend very closely to the concrete, locally situated details of social interaction and language use. In fact, starting with a set of abstract formal structures as the presupposed basis of rational interaction – the approach taken by Habermas's formal pragmatics – can lead the theorist to miss the concrete 'rationalities' or 'endogenous logic' of actual social practices (Bogen 1999, Chap. 2). Consequently, the more radical versions of EM reject a priori methodologies and theories as a basis for analysis in favor of 'ethnomethodological indifference', the policy of 'abstaining from all judgments of [the] adequacy, value, importance, necessity, practicality, success, or consequentiality' of the local practices being studied (Garfinkel and Sacks 1970, p. 345). According to Michael Lynch (1997, pp. 371–2), this policy 'assigns epistemic privilege to no single version of social affairs, including sociology's own professionally authorized versions'. As a result, one's own ideas about rationality are set aside in order to attend more closely to the situated 'methods' or 'procedures' that members themselves use to produce social order. Indifference thus forbids criticism based on the investigator's own moral, political, or epistemological beliefs. This poses a potentially serious obstacle to the appropriation of EM by critical theorists, an issue I take up below.

As a research policy, ethnomethodological indifference is supposed to keep the sociologist maximally open to the full range of rational agency as a contextualizing capacity that actors employ in their ongoing production of meaningful social interaction. One should not confuse this policy with a disinterested 'pure empiricism' or positivism that would rely on presuppositionless inductive generalizations. On the contrary, EM presupposes its practitioners can formulate the a priori's or 'rational intuitions' they share with their subjects of study as competent language users (Coulter 1983; cf. Lynch 1993, Chap. 6). For example: without a tacit grasp of the adjacency-pair structure, ethnomethodologists would be at a loss to follow a conversation in which answers count as answers precisely because they follow questions as a matter of convention. At the same time, the explicit formulation of such structures results, not from armchair speculation, but from 'a great deal of study of actual transcribed materials' (Coulter 1983, p. 366). One thus strives to notice and perspicuously describe the tacit structures of sense-making that are visible in the transcribed material. Descriptive adequacy is achieved insofar as the investigator has described members' methods in such a way that 'anyone' can 'replicate the observations described' (Lynch 1993, p. 208).

By employing this method of perspicuous description, EM makes at least two important contributions toward a more contextualized pragmatics. The first is that actors make sense of their situations and interactions precisely by treating each other as accountable agents – they hold one another mutually accountable for their sayings and doings. Accountability is displayed by the various moves that members use for continuing intelligible interaction. The situated use of this repertoire of interactive competences involves normatively laden expectations – which Garfinkel once glossed as 'trust' – that others will appropriately contextualize and thereby give a definite sense to actions or utterances that by themselves are indefinite and vague. Garfinkel (1963) famously demonstrated the reality of these expectations precisely by challenging them in 'breaching experiments' in which the experimenter (Garfinkel's student) demanded full explicitness in conversation from unwitting counterparts (often other family members). The moral indignation provoked by such noncooperation reveals, as the flip-side of the accountability displayed in the active mastery of behavioral moves, a corresponding receptive accountability for taking those moves in the appropriate way. Actors hold one another accountable not only for their words and deeds but also for the situationally appropriate interpretation of words and deeds.

The second contribution concerns the ideas of indexicality and reflexivity. The notion of accountability as an active, contextualizing capacity means that the full sense or meaning of any expression or behavior as a *social* action – as a move in social interaction – requires the exercise of creative, contextually appropriate and mutually recognizable agency on the part of participants. The abstract or literal meaning of any sentence, rule, or action remains socially indeterminate and thus vague until it is used by a particular individual before particular others who can recognize it (perhaps only after questioning the user) as a meaningful display of agency on a concrete occasion with all its circumstances – the shared histories of those involved, their particular interests and goals on the occasion and other background assumptions. This contextualized use can even involve the violation of norms, as when an acquaintance refuses to return a greeting to indicate indignation over a previous slight (see Heritage 1984, p. 117).

Thus EM holds that all language, and not just the standard indexical expressions ('this', 'I', 'you', 'now', etc.), acquires a definite sense only in the concrete situation – expressions are 'reflexively tied' to the occasions of their use. This holds even for attempts to translate indexical expressions into fully explicit, context-free 'objective' statements. Not only do such explications always contain further ambiguities, in some cases they actually *lose* the situated meaning of the original utterance by eliminating elisions that hearers depend on and expect as ordinary. For example, making a child's cry 'Mommy!' more explicit as 'My mommy!' changes its situated sense (Bittner 1977, p. 87). Garfinkel considers the irremediable indexicality of language to be empirically demonstrated by a number of studies (see Heritage 1984, pp. 92–7, 144–57). Even scientific texts and representation (figures, graphs, etc.) are not exempt: 'The organization, sense, value, and adequacy of any representation is "reflexive" to the settings in which it is constituted and used' (Lynch and Woolgar 1988, 109; cf. Button 1991; Widmer 1986).

To claim that scientific claims or texts are irremediably indexical flies in the face of the standard conception of scientific objectivity and universality. Thus Eric Livingston's study of mathematical practices of proving offers a good illustration of the idea, inasmuch as mathematical proofs appear most universal, objective and anonymous – a point Livingston does not deny.[3] Rather, he insists that the ability of a proof to travel beyond the context of origin does not reside in the formulated proof alone, the written or diagrammatic 'proof-account'. Such accounts are partial descriptions that have their intelligibility only in relation to the practices of a particular culture of proving and the actual 'lived work' of proving. An effective proof-account supplies just those relevant concrete details that allow other members of the mathematical culture to contextualize the account and 'do' the work of proving. In analogy to one's grasp of a gestalt figure in a set of lines and shapes, appropriately contextualized material cues allow members to make just those embodied, spatiotemporal moves required to 'see' the 'gestalt of reasoning' – and thus grasp the ideal object and its properties – that the proof-account describes.

However, the appropriate contextualizing methods are so ordinary – for example, knowing the sequence of physical actions involved in the construction of a diagram – that competent members take them for granted as 'essentially uninteresting' (Garfinkel 1967, pp. 7–9). Concrete methods do not deserve explicit comment; indeed such commentary would only distract and might even mislead competent practitioners. These practical moves are seen but unnoticed, they are 'witnessed but ignored' (Livingston 1987, p. 56). Ethnomethodologists strive to notice just these moves – to describe the concrete, mundane details of practice *through which alone* general accounts, as 'glosses' that leave out the details, acquire their local, definite sense and relevance for actual scientific practice (Garfinkel and Sacks 1970, pp. 343–5, 362–6). This is not to deny the objective, general character of mathematical and scientific results, but rather to ground objectivity in the corporeal, social practices through which it is achieved.

Nonetheless, EM rests on a radical idea, what Garfinkel terms its 'central recommendation', namely 'that the activities whereby members produce and manage settings of organized everyday affairs are identical with members' procedures for making those settings "account-

---

[3] The following summarizes Livingston (1987, 1999; cf. also 1986, 1995).

able"'(Garfinkel 1967, p. 1). That is, in everyday practices members do and say things that they can observe, and they continually contextualize and update these sayings and doings so that their interaction makes sense. Just these ongoing contextualizing activities or 'procedures' make their sayings and doings 'reportable' in formulations and thus 'account-able'. It follows that formulated accounts are 'reflexively tied' to the concrete occasion of their production, and have a rational character only in the concrete context:

> . . *recognizable* sense, or fact, or methodic character, or impersonality, or objectivity of accounts are not independent of the socially organized occasions of their use. Their rational features *consist* of what members do with, what they 'make of' the accounts in the socially organized actual occasions of their use. Members' accounts are reflexively and essentially tied for their rational features to the socially organized occasions of their use for they are *features* of the socially organized occasions of their use. (ibid., pp. 3–4)

This text could serve as a summary for any number of EM studies of science. However, it poses a difficult challenge for a contextually sensitive critical theory.

The challenge is this: although EM does not deny the generality of scientific accounts *for scientists,* its central recommendation prohibits any generalizing theory *about science,* whether the theory involves a general sociological explanation of science or a traditional epistemology that provides general definitions of 'representation', 'observation', 'truth', and so on. Such theories are, after all, accounts, but accounts that either forget or pretend to overcome the methodological obstacles posed by an irremediable indexicality. The honest alternative to grand theory, according to Lynch, is a deflationary descriptive approach that 'respecifies' traditional concepts as 'epistopics'. The investigator simply notices and describes the variety of situated ways in which actors actually *do* such things as represent, observe, and so on – but resists 'all efforts to build general models and to develop normative standards that hold across situations' (Lynch 1993, p. 306).

Applying this point to argumentation, we should say that its rationality lies in the practical, local achievement of cogent arguments. As glosses, formulated rules of argument and idealizations such as Habermas's pragmatic presuppositions acquire their intelligibility and relevance only in relation to the situated rationalities, the practical know-hows of local practices. Competent arguers must discover each time the concrete methods, the situated rhetorics, by which they can argue reasonably. Consequently, one cannot simply invoke formal structures or idealizations to account for the rationality of argumentation. Herein lies a demanding challenge for critical theorists who look to argumentation theory for their normative standards. Although critical theory involves much more than argumentation theory, the nonarbitrariness of its critical analyses crucially depends on a normative theory whose rules or idealizations supply standards for assessing actual cases of controversy and consensus formation. But critical theorists can employ such standards, it seems, only if they believe their idealizations properly account for the rationality of argumentation – just what deflationary EM prohibits, given its doctrine of indexicality. This poses a dilemma for critical theorists: on the one hand, the project of emancipatory critique seems to require a conceptual framework that, precisely because of its formality, provides a stable platform for critical assessment. On the other hand, if indexicality applies to such ideas, then no such platform exists that could set critical theorists above the social fray. One can, to be sure, formulate such ideas, to which engaged arguers might then appeal. Arguers can invoke these, however, only as glosses that they must contextualize in the much richer local rationalities of practice – whereupon the ideas of reason take on all the local interpretive contingencies the theorist hoped to avoid.

4. INCORPORATING THE RADICAL CHALLENGE

Critical theorists can respond to the above dilemma, I argue, if they can synthesize the attentiveness of ethnomethodologists with the engaged stance of participants. In this last Section I develop this synthesis in a series of steps. First, I shift the critical starting point from formal rules of argumentation to the pragmatic idealizations of objectivity and truth, which find more support from EM. I then show how critical theorists can learn from EM without adopting its policy of indifference. What results, finally, is a more radically contextualized approach that retains a non-relativistic critical potential.

Objectivity and Truth

From an EM standpoint, Habermas's discursive process idealizations represent an abstract theoretical formulation or 'account' of the intersubjective accountability by which participants – in this context, scientists, including economists – make ongoing sense of their discourses as rational affairs. To arrive at a more contextualized model, it helps if we start with the notions of objectivity and truth. Indeed, critical theory and EM both accept a pragmatic understanding of factual objectivity. Drawing on the work of Melvin Pollner, McCarthy points out that in their everyday interaction actors operate with the presupposition that they share the same objective world accessible to all (McCarthy 1994, Chap. 3; cf. Habermas 1984, pp. 12–15). Objectivity thus represents a specific mode of accountability: 'We are held accountable, and in turn hold our interaction partners accountable, for the transcendent objectivity of the world as invariant to discrepant reports' (McCarthy 1991, pp. 31–32). This presupposition underlies the use of 'error accounts'. In order to maintain the world's objectivity in the face of conflicting reports, we must account for differences by revoking one or another ceteris paribus assumption about the 'community of observers' and the conditions of reliable observation (Pollner [1974] 1990, p. 153). The objectivity of the world, in the sense of its intersubjective accessibility, is thus an unfalsifiable presupposition by virtue of which actors anticipate that, 'all other things being equal', competent observers should be able to reach unanimity in their factual reports (ibid., pp. 143, 150–51). Without this presupposition, neither the problem of discrepancy nor the means used to resolve it are intelligible (ibid., p. 142).

The notion of truth further develops the idea of objectivity. As a pragmatic presupposition of interaction – as a mode of accountability – truth involves the tacit recognition that what we take to be true at one point we might later recognize as false in the light of new information. This sense of fallibilism points to the context- and discourse-transcending force of truth claims as resisting reduction to what-we-take-as-true-now (McCarthy 1991, pp. 33–4). Consequently, in claiming truth for a statement we presuppose that future advances in knowledge should not lead us to reject the statement, which, if true, should remain defensible in future contexts and before wider audiences.[4] Thus the notion of truth simply draws the implications of objectivity for assertions about the world: if the unitary objective world is intersubjectively accessible, then true reports and assertions should be intersubjectively acceptable.

How do the ideas of objectivity and truth function pragmatically in science? EM studies of science suggest that these are indexical ideas, reflexively tied to their particular subdisciplinary contexts. That is, scientists typically operate with tacit, *subdiscipline-specific* assumptions about objectivity and truth in light of which standards of argumentative accountability are specified as contextually relevant for the given subdiscipline. At the local level that means that scientists frame their arguments so that these will find acceptance not only by other members

---

[4] Breaking with his earlier consensus theory of truth (Habermas 1973), Habermas (1999) now holds a pragmatic conception of truth that appears close to McCarthy's view: taking a statement as true means we are ready to take the statement (a) as a reliable guide for action and (b) as defensible in discourse.

of their research team or problem area but also before broader subdisciplinary audiences for which those claims have some relevance or applicability. On the one hand, then, scientists strive to make publishable, *locality*-transcendent claims that hold up among peers working in similar or overlapping areas of research (Garfinkel et al. 1981; Lynch 1985; Livingston 1995). In grasping the accountable cogencies of their lived work, scientists in a particular laboratory observe and grasp the reportability of their findings for other members of their subdiscipline – thus its objectivity or independence from the local laboratory. The published article formulates just this recognition for the broader community.

On the other hand, we can distinguish such locality-transcendence, which extends only to those further sites of reproduction that share the background assumptions of the particular subspecialty, from the broader *context*-transcendence exhibited insofar as local findings are taken up by scientists in other areas and by nonscientists. Context-transcendence is possible because scientists work in the awareness of numerous contexts and practices simultaneously – the broader science community, the immediate institutional setting (university, corporation, government lab), funding agencies, technologists and numerous other interested lay publics. Each of these contexts enters into the lived work of scientists and shapes their local practice and methods of accountability. Because these different contexts involve different practices of argumentation, with different notions of relevance and cogency – in a word, different practices of accountability – the context-*transcendence* of scientific findings first proves itself in these broader extra-disciplinary spheres. Consequently, any adequate attempt to formulate idealizations or rules of argumentation must first of all attend to the obvious and not-so-obvious differences in how members in different settings actually employ such idealizations in their production of order.

For example, the idealization of a unitary objective world appears in experimental physics, for example, primarily as a *uniformity supposition,* the idea that the basic laws and make-up of the universe are the same for all times and places. The locality-transcending truth of such claims is understood accordingly: anyone anywhere who reproduces the asserted conditions should arrive at the same observations, and if despite their best efforts they do not, then the truth of the claim is in doubt. These inflected suppositions of objectivity and truth in turn define accountability among physicists: if other laboratories repeatedly fail to replicate one's findings, then one's own competence eventually comes into question. In geology, by contrast, objectivity involves not so much spatiotemporal uniformity as the supposition of a single earth history. Whether an established finding at one site (for example anomalous iridium deposits at the K/T boundary layer in Italy) also holds in corresponding strata elsewhere is not a supposition but an open research question.

In the economic disciplines the question of objectivity appears to be more contested, at least if one examines the methodological debates and various positions taken over the decades by economists themselves (Hands 2001). Although debates among philosophers of science generally do not affect the pragmatic notions of objectivity and truth operative among practicing natural scientists, the situation appears to be more complicated among economists, whose various approaches partly depend on tacit philosophical commitments.[5] Unfortunately, to settle this issue we cannot look to a developed ethnomethodological literature on the economic sciences.[6] Given the importance of abstract mathematical modeling in theoretical economics, Livingston's study of proving practices is suggestive – at least in a broad sense, we should expect that theorists subscribe to a notion of objectivity similar to the one connected with mathematical proof-accounts. Broad similarity, however, does not mean that the mathematical practices of economists exactly match those of mathematicians; rather, we should expect economists to produce proof-accounts that have some descriptive economic sense or interpretability, even if the formal assumptions are not realistic (cf. Livingston 1986, Appendix; Friedman 1953). Exactly what empirical notion of objectivity economists accept remains open to question.[7] However, once economics enters the sphere of policy and becomes applied economics, testable predictions become crucial for its context-transcendent relevance. The kind of objectivity in these domains appears to be primarily of the sort associated with the statistical measurement of quantifiable objects, actions and events that are causally or statistically interrelated within an economic system. An econometric model usable for forecasting, for example, should presumably pick out the statistically significant variables and parameters (disposable income, interest rates,

---

[5] For example, the tradition of economic methodology stemming from J.S. Mill started with assumptions (for example about rational agency) it took as self-evidently true, an approach that was famously challenged by Milton Friedman's instrumentalist or pragmatic approach (Friedman 1953; Hirsch and De Marchi 1990). According to Boland (1989, p. 17), most economists today are in practice instrumentalists.

[6] Other types of sociology have tackled economics as a set of scientific practices (for example Evans 1999); one can find some EM literature on business practices (Anderson et al., 1989).

[7] Key issues concern the status of economic idealizations and role of falsifiability in economic modeling (see De Marchi and Kim 1988; Boland 1989; Blaug 1992, Chap. 16; Mäki 1994; Hands 2001, Chap. 7). From a pragmatic standpoint, the question depends on how the display of competence (accountability) among theorists depends on demonstrating out-of-sample fit between their abstract models and the world.

etc.) that allow one to make reliable predictions of how an economy – as a part of the objective world representable in a particular economic vocabulary of endogenous and exogenous variables – will actually perform (Boland 1989, Chap. 1; Evans 1999).

In sum, the supposition that the reality we apprehend and understand here and now, in a particular local practice, is the same reality for everyone has a different sense that varies with context and practice. The same goes for the ideas of truth and rational accountability: what counts as 'true enough' for the purposes at hand, and what adequacy requirements one must meet before a claim is taken seriously, will vary according to context. If the above observations hold true within science, we should expect them to hold a fortiori for contexts in which scientists must interface with nonscientists. The conflict of background expectations and modes of accountability that can arise in such situations – for example, situations in which scientific experts appear in court, or participate in popular media presentations – have been well documented (Goldstein 1986; Jasanoff 1995). The context-transcendence of a truth claim assumes that such obstacles can be overcome. Thus a scientific truth claim assumes not so much the counterfactual assent of an ideal audience, but rather the potential relevance and contextualizability of that claim in an indefinite range of scientific and extra-scientific contexts.

Engaged Participation: Avoiding Indifference

Can critical theorists appropriate the above findings without forfeiting critical purchase? To answer this we must first determine whether critical theorists can acknowledge the indexicality of objectivity, truth and other argumentative idealizations without adopting a full-blown ethnomethodological indifference. I suggest they can insofar as they combine the substantive findings of EM with the engaged attitude of the participants – an attitude that EM itself takes seriously, albeit without taking sides. As EM itself reveals, scientists engaged in discursive interaction are anything but indifferent chroniclers of their situated methods, which they normally fail to notice (cf. Gilbert and Mulkay 1984). Like ethnomethodologists, critical (argumentation) theorists strive to notice such situated details; like scientists, however, they take the standpoint of participants who are interested in the correct assessment of potentially controversial scientific arguments. This does not mean that critical theorists must become scientists or public intellectuals and engage directly in this or that controversy. Although they may (and at least some should) do that, there is also an indirect mode of engagement available to critical theorists working in academic settings (see Rehg 2002, pp. 32–7). This indirect engagement is evident in those controversies in which participants explicitly invoke argumentative ideals as part of their advocacy. Scientists themselves are observed to invoke such ideals, particularly in interdisciplinary controversies (for example Officer and Page 1996), when they appeal to ideal models of method and cogency in order to make sense of their discursive practices, to produce an orderliness in the controversy, and to persuade – in sum, as an accountability procedure. Argumentation theorists are indirectly involved in these debates insofar as directly engaged participants draw upon formulated ideals of argumentation. Scientists may acquire such ideas in a number of ways – in undergraduate philosophy or critical thinking courses, through contact with philosophers of science, from science textbooks, works by public intellectuals and science journalists, and so forth.

These observations suggest that the context for argumentation theory arises from a dialectic of indirect, more or less disengaged theorizing that characterizes academic practices, on the one hand, and the directly engaged uses of formulated argumentative ideals by participants in controversy, on the other. By formulating indexically sensitive idealizations that participants find relevant to their situated accounting procedures, academic theorists avoid a disconnected top-down approach. But they meet the more radical contextualist challenge only when they recognize formulations as no more than potential accounting procedures that acquire a definite sense only insofar as they inform members' situated assessments of cogency in actual controversies. One thereby avoids mistaking them for foundations or rules with free-standing jurisdictional force over actual argumentative practices (cf. Lynch 1993, p. 187). Argumentatively effective ideals enjoy not transcendental necessity, but a situated practical necessity that is defeasibly acknowledged by actual participants who are committed to the reasonable resolution of disputes.

The Critical Potential of Contextualized Pragmatics

To incorporate the radical contextualist challenge, we must address the worry of relativism, as expressed by the question: can contextually indexed ideas of reason as described above provide sufficient critical leverage, or must they fall captive, finally, to the status quo precisely because they depend so heavily on participants' situated – and often ad hoc – methods? Here I can only provide a preliminary reply by noting some of the possible modes of critique enabled by EM – modes that ultimately point to a larger issue. Some of these modes of criticism hark back to earlier days of critical theory, with its use of immanent critique,

critique of technocracy, and the like. Thus EM helps to reinvigorate older areas of critical theory.

Probably the most obvious critical targets in the area of economics are positivist ideals of method and formal idealizations. Thus the critic might attempt dialectically to undermine or refute simplistic ideals of scientific method, 'Cartesian economics', and so on, which are invoked by experts (cf. Lynch 1999, pp. 227–9; Anderson et al. 1988). The relevant critical moves should not be difficult to imagine, at least in broad outline: essentially the critic adduces more detailed descriptions of situated methods as a counterargument against justifications based on formal ideals of method (for example Evans 1999). Exactly how such counterarguments work depends on the particular context. One can, for example, imagine science-based policy debates in which descriptively enriched critique undermines official policy justifications that assume positivistic models of scientific objectivity.

One can also employ this dialectic ironically. Here the critic challenges appeals to economic modeling as failing to meet ideals of scientific method. I call this move ironic because the critic's real aim is to elicit justifications that elaborate the situated rationalities and local discretionary judgments that the justification did not at first attend to. The critique thus has the maieutic function of eliciting from the participants themselves (1) the recognition of the insufficiency of formal ideals and (2) a further articulation of the actual, concrete reasonableness of their practices. Of course, it may turn out that the articulation lacks plausibility – but then that too would constitute a critical advance in the controversy.

Each of these critical methods trades on the indexicality of the standards and ideals that inform our notions of the 'reasonable'. At the same time, these moves do not specify any particular critical agenda. Thus the larger question remains of how critical theorists justify their specific critical orientation – that is, their commitment to ideals of emancipatory democracy, social equality, economic justice, and the like.

We can approach a possible answer to this question by noting a still further mode of critique, one that shows that a radical indexicality need not leave us entirely at the mercy of local rationality assumptions. Recall that the indexicality of argumentative idealizations is constituted, even at the local level, as a complex social reality. The interleaving-and-nesting of contexts harbors the possibility of criticizing and revising local assumptions in light of broader social demands. This permeability of scientific practices makes possible the public scrutiny of scientific findings, goals and institutional structures. Indeed, the Frankfurt School critique of science has traditionally been concerned primarily with this socially encompassing level of sociopolitical criticism. At this level, the context-transcending force of scientific truth claims must pass its severest test – not as acceptability before a universal audience but as contextualizability and relevance across a range of interested practical domains.

The possibility of critically scrutinizing the economic models and methods used in legal and political decision-making arises precisely from the indexicality of such ideas as truth and objectivity. In adducing scientific findings as justification for policy, one insists on the probable truth and practical relevance of the findings for settings beyond the contexts of origin in a given discourse of economists. Consequently, an adequate justification requires one to make the economic science plausible in extra-scientific contexts. Here disciplinary expertise alone cannot guarantee the expert's authoritative status *for legal decisions and policy-making*. Again, the context determines exactly how this issue is framed. The most straightforward example of this is the situation in which the extra-scientific context involves various complicating factors that the economists' models ignore. One of the most prominent examples is the current debate over the neoliberal economic assumptions guiding the IMF and the World Bank.

The justification of the critical theory project must be developed at this more complex level of political discourse and decision-making. Although I cannot give the full argument here, its point of departure lies in the various kinds of social problems confronting pluralistic societies (in global economic environments) and the requirements such problems impose on legitimate solutions, which must be reached through processes of social argumentation and dialogue that participants consider reasonable and noncoercive. The justification of critical theory thus relies on (1) the practical political need to settle conflicts and resolve truth-based policy disputes in order to maintain social order, and (2) the claim that deliberative democratic models are best suited for this task (and can somehow be realized even at an international level without a world government; see Habermas 2001). To be sure, terms such as 'reasonable' and 'noncoercive' are highly indexical and contestable. But notice that, by starting with specific problems in need of resolution, this approach builds context into the normative ideals from the outset (see Rehg 1999). To this extent, the critique is 'grounded' in practice itself, so that formulated idealizations gain their effectiveness in virtue of *their local relations* to the exigencies of the specific contexts in which the critique is embedded. As a result, critical theory outperforms rival approaches insofar as it attends more carefully to practices and their realities, a task for which ethnomethodology can provide considerable assistance.

REFERENCES

Alexy, R. (1990), 'A Theory of Practical Discourse', in S. Benhabib and F. Dallmayr (eds), *The Communicative Ethics Controversy*, trans. D. Frisby, Cambridge, US, and London, UK: MIT Press, pp. 151–90.

Anderson, R.J., J.A. Hughes and W.W. Sharrock (1988), 'The methodology of Cartesian economics: Some thoughts on the nature of economic theorising', *Journal of Interdisciplinary Economics*, 2, 307–20.

Anderson, R.J., J.A. Hughes and W.W. Sharrock (1989), *Working for Profit*, Aldershot, UK: Avebury.

Apel, K.-O. (1980), *Towards a Transformation of Philosophy*, trans. G. Adey and D. Frisby, London, UK, and Boston, US: Routledge.

Benhabib, S. (1992), *Situating the Self*, New York, US: Routledge, and UK: Polity.

Benhabib, S., W. Bonß and J. McCole (eds) (1993), *On Max Horkheimer*, Cambridge, US, and London, UK: MIT Press.

Bittner, E. (1977), 'Must We Say What We Mean?' in P.F. Ostwald (ed.), *Communication and Social Interaction*, New York: Grune and Stratton-Harcourt Brace, pp. 83–97.

Blaug, M. (1992), *The Methodology of Economics, or How Economists Explain*, 2nd ed., Cambridge, UK, and New York, US: Cambridge University Press.

Blaug, R. (1999), *Democracy, Real and Ideal*, Albany: SUNY Press.

Bogen, D. (1999), *Order without Rules*, Albany: SUNY Press.

Boland, L.A. (1989), *The Methodology of Economic Model Building*, London, UK, and New York, US: Routledge.

Bonß, W. (1993), 'The Program of Interdisciplinary Research and the Beginnings of Critical Theory', in S. Benhabib, W., Bonß and J. McCole, pp. 99–125.

Button, G. (ed.) (1991), *Ethnomethodology and the Human Sciences*, Cambridge, UK, and New York, US: Cambridge University Press.

Coulter, J. (1983), 'Contingent and *a priori* structures in sequential analysis', *Human Studies*, **6** (4), 361–76.

De Marchi, N. and J. Kim (1988), 'Ceteris paribus conditions as prior knowledge: A view from economics', *Philosophy of Science Association Proceedings* 1988, No. 2, 317–25.

Evans, R. (1999), *Macroeconomic Forecasting*, London, UK, and New York, US: Routledge.

Friedman, M. (1953), 'The Methodology of Positive Economics', in M. Friedman, *Essays in Positive Economics*, Chicago: University of Chicago Press, and London, UK: Cambridge University Press, pp. 3–43.

Garfinkel, H. (1963), 'A Conception of, and Experiments with, "Trust" as a Condition of Stable Concerted Actions', in O.J. Harvey (ed.), *Motivation and Social Interaction*, New York: Ronald, pp. 187–238.

Garfinkel, H. (1967), 'What is Ethnomethodology?' in H. Garfinkel, *Studies in Ethnomethodology*, Englewood Cliffs, NJ: Prentice-Hall.

Garfinkel, H. and H. Sacks (1970), 'On Formal Structures of Practical Action', in J.C. McKinney and E.A. Tiryakian (eds), *Theoretical Sociology*, New York: Meredith-Appleton, pp. 337–66.

Garfinkel, H., M. Lynch and E. Livingston (1981), 'The work of a discovering science construed with materials from the optically discovered pulsar', *Philosophy of the Social Sciences*, **11** (2), 131–58.

Gilbert, G.N. and M. Mulkay (1984), *Opening Pandora's Box*, Cambridge, UK, and New York, US: Cambridge University Press.

Goldstein, J.H. (ed.) (1986), *Reporting Science*, Hillsdale, NJ: Erlbaum.

Habermas, J. (1973), 'Wahrheitstheorien', in H. Fahrenbach (ed.), *Wirklichkeit und Reflexion,* Pfülligen: Neske, pp. 211-65.

Habermas, J. (1979), *Communication and the Evolution of Society*, trans. T. McCarthy, Boston: Beacon.

Habermas, J. (1984), *The Theory of Communicative Action,* Vol. 1, trans. T. McCarthy, Boston, US: Beacon.

Habermas, J. (1990), 'Discourse Ethics: Notes on a Program of Philosophical Justification', in J. Habermas, *Moral Consciousness and Communicative Action*, trans. C. Lenhardt and S.W. Nicholsen, Cambridge, US, and London, UK: MIT Press, pp. 43–115.

Habermas, J. (1993), *Justification and Application*, trans. C.P. Cronin, Cambridge, US and London, UK: MIT Press.

Habermas, J. (1998), *The Inclusion of the Other*, ed. C. Cronin and P. DeGreiff, Cambridge, US, and London, UK: MIT Press.

Habermas, J. (1999), 'Richtigkeit versus Wahrheit: Zum Sinn der Sollgeltung Moralischer Urteile und Normen', in J. Habermas, *Wahrheit und Rechtfertigung*, Frankfurt am Main: Suhrkamp, pp. 271–318.

Habermas, J. (2001), 'The Postnational Constellation and the Future of Democracy', in J. Habermas, *The Postnational Constellation,* trans. M. Pensky, Cambridge, US: MIT Press, and London, UK: Polity, pp. 58–112.

Hands, D.W. (2001), *Reflection without Rules*, Cambridge, UK, and New York, US: Cambridge University Press.

Heritage, J. (1984), *Garfinkel and Ethnomethodology,* Cambridge, UK: Polity.

Hirsch, A. and N. de Marchi (1990), *Milton Friedman,* Ann Arbor: University of Michigan Press.

Horkheimer, M. (1993), 'The Present Situation of Social Philosophy and the Tasks of an Institute for Social Research', in M. Horkheimer, *Between Philosophy and the Social Sciences*, Cambridge, US, and London, UK: MIT Press, pp. 1–14.

Jasanoff, S. (1995), *Science at the Bar,* Cambridge, US, and London, UK: Harvard University Press.

Livingston, E. (1986), *The Ethnomethodological Foundations of Mathematics*, London, UK, and Boston, US: Routledge.

Livingston, E. (1987), *Making Sense of Ethnomethodology*, London, UK, and New York, US: Routledge.

Livingston, E. (1995), 'The idiosyncratic specificity of the methods of physical experimentation', *Australian and New Zealand Journal of Sociology*, **31** (3), 1–22.

Livingston, E. (1999), 'Cultures of proving', *Social Studies of Science*, **29** (6), 867–88.

Lynch, M. (1985), *Art and Artifact in Laboratory Science*, London, UK, and New York, US: Routledge.

Lynch, M. (1993), *Scientific Practice and Ordinary Action*, Cambridge, UK, and New York, US: Cambridge University Press.

Lynch, M. (1997), 'Ethnomethodology without indifference', *Human Studies*, **20** (3), 371–6.

Lynch, M. (1999), 'Silence in context: ethnomethodology and social theory', *Human Studies*, **22** (2), 211–33.

Lynch, M. and S. Woolgar (1988), 'Introduction: sociological orientations to representational practice in science', *Human Studies,* **11** (2), 99–116.

Mäki, U. (1994), 'Isolation, Idealization and Truth in Economics', in B. Hamminga and N.B. de Marchi (eds), *Idealization VI: Idealization in Economics,* Atlanta, US, and Amsterdam, Netherlands: Rodopi, pp. 147–68.

McCarthy, T. (1991), *Ideals and Illusions,* Cambridge, US and London, UK: MIT Press.

McCarthy, T. (1994), *Critical Theory,* Oxford, UK and Cambridge, US: Blackwell. Chaps. 1–3; other chaps. by D.C. Hoy.

Officer, C. and J. Page, (1996), *The Great Dinosaur Extinction Controversy,* Reading, MA: Helix Books, Addison-Wesley.

Polanyi, M. (1966), *The Tacit Dimension,* New York: Doubleday, reprinted (1983), Gloucester, US: Peter Smith.

Pollner, M. (1974), 'Mundane Reasoning', *Philosophy of the Social Sciences,* **4**, pp. 35–54; reprinted in Coulter, J. (ed.) (1990), *Ethnomethodological Sociology,* Camberley, UK, and Brookfield, US: Edward Elgar, pp. 138–57.

Rehg, W. (1997), 'Reason and Rhetoric in Habermas's theory of argumentation'. in W. Jost and M.J. Hyde (eds), *Rhetoric and Hermeneutics in Our Time,* New Haven: Yale University Press, pp. 358–77.

Rehg, W. (1999), 'Intractable conflicts and moral objectivity: a dialogical, problem-based approach', *Inquiry,* **42** (2), 229–58.

Rehg, W. (2001), 'Adjusting the Pragmatic Turn: Ethnomethodology and Critical Argumentation Theory', in W. Rehg and J. Bohman (eds), *Pluralism and the Pragmatic Turn,* Cambridge, US, and London, UK: MIT Press, pp. 115–43.

Rehg, W. (2002), 'The argumentation theorist in deliberative democracy', *Controversia,* **1** (1), 18–42.

Rorty, R. (1987), 'Pragmatism and Philosophy', in K. Baynes, J. Bohman and T. McCarthy (eds), *After Philosophy,* Cambridge, US, and London, UK: MIT Press, pp. 26–66.

Rorty, R. (1991), *Objectivity, Relativism, and Truth,* Cambridge, UK, and New York, US: Cambridge University Press.

Webler, T., S. Tuler and R. Krueger (2001), 'What is a good public participation process? Five perspectives from the public', *Environmental Management,* **27** (3), 435–50.

Widmer, J. (1986), 'Wörtliche Bedeutung und reflexiver Sinn', *Zeitschrift für Semiotik,* 8, 63–9.

5. The Role of Truth in Economic Policy Advice

Gebhard Kirchgässner

The final objective of science is to develop 'true theories' about the world we live in, despite the fact that we can never be sure that a certain theory is really true. On the contrary, we are almost sure that every known scientific theory is (literally taken) wrong, as, to state a famous citation of Feyerabend (1975, p. 39), there is 'an "ocean of anomalies" that surrounds every single theory'. Thus, certainty and truth of a theory can never be given at the same time. Nevertheless, the objective to develop true theories remains.

Economics is (or at least should be) a social science; that is the view most economists and also most other people share at any rate. Thus, its objective is to develop true theories about the social world. Economic policy advice, seen as the application of economic theories to solve practical (economic and other) problems should – correspondingly – provide politicians with true statements about the world, be it statements about the actual situation or statements (hypotheses) about causal relations which can be exploited for policy purposes. In this view, the economist as policy advisor is like a social engineer who can tell politicians what they can do to reach their objectives but sometimes also why it might be impossible to reach certain objectives.

This picture of the economist as policy advisor might seem to be too idealistic and – taken as an image of reality – it really is too idealistic, and this for several reasons. First, economists often have strong opinions what should be done by the politicians, and these opinions are not only based on their scientific knowledge but also (and sometimes even more so) on their personal value judgments. This is not astonishing because, secondly, economists are the same self-interested, rationally acting individuals as all other human beings, too. Despite the fact that they tend to deny this, it also holds when they give policy advice. The money they earn when they produce reports in order to be used by their clients to strive for their objectives is not necessarily a sign of corruption. But it can hardly be denied that scientists are often paid for producing exactly the statements their clients want to hear, and that they know about this and put up with it.[1] It does not help to argue – often mainly for the pacification of their own conscience – that this money is spent on scientific research and, therefore, (according to their opinion) for a good purpose. In addition, economists often do not want to be reminded later of what they wrote in earlier reports.

While economists often believe in this ideal picture,[2] the general public has a more negative but also somewhat more realistic picture of economists as policy advisors. The same economic agents, who in modern economic theory are usually assumed to have rational expectations, which implies that their expectations are on average correct, accuse economists who are policy advisors to be biased and sometimes even to be corruptible. They certainly have a point and are not totally wrong. Today it is possible to find a professor of economics willing to write a scientific report in support of nearly every political position.[3]

When asked, economists who are engaged in political debates nearly always claim that their statements are purely scientific and that their clients did not influence their results at all. This may be true in many cases. However, it would be just the opposite of the usual economic procedure if we strongly believed in such affirmations. Economists usually take into account the behavior of economic agents and not their verbal statements, and they try to draw conclusions for the preferences of the individuals from their *actual* behavior.[4] The reason for this is that talk is in many cases cheap, but acting is costly. Thus, in general, individuals are more honest when acting than when talking. This holds for economists as for all other human beings. If we judge by behavior and not by verbal statements, the impression of bias can, however, not be put aside easily.

One might try to distinguish between two kinds of policy advice. The first kind is on behalf of (political) parties and interest groups or directly on behalf of the government. The second kind is done by 'independent'

---

[1] It often does not take very much to induce economists (and other scientists) to act in the interest even of organizations having nothing to do with economics as a science at all. For example, conferences organized as well as books edited by and with contributions of prominent economists have been financed by the 'Professors World Peace Association', an organization financed by the Mun Church, and whose main purpose it is to improve the public image of this organization. For this, also see Blankart (1987, p. 669)

[2] For an – admittedly – extreme example of this position, see, for example, Hesse (1994, p. 18).

[3] See, for example, the examples given in Kirchgässner (1996, 1999).

[4] The basic paper (with respect to the theory of consumer behavior) is Samuelson (1948).

institutions, like (scientific) institutes for economic policy research, the 'Sachverständigenrat' (Council of Economic Experts) in the Federal Republic of Germany, the scientific councils of the different departments of the government or several 'Enquete-Committees' (Enquete-Kommissionen) of the parliament in the Federal Republic of Germany, or the 'Kommission für Konjunkturfragen' (Committee for Business Cycle Questions) of the Swiss Federal Government (Bundesrat). Despite the fact that this is only a (small) part of policy advice activities of economists, the statements and reports of these institutions are often highly debated. In the Federal Republic of Germany (and elsewhere) it is possible to link formally independent economic research institutes to specific political positions. It was not by chance that the German Institute of Economic Research in Berlin (Deutsches Institut für Wirtschaftsforschung) produced in 1994 a report on the economic consequences of an ecological tax reform on behalf of Greenpeace and not the Kiel Institute of World Economics (Institut für Weltwirtschaft an der Universität Kiel). If this report had been produced by Kiel, the study would probably have predicted a reduction of employment as a consequence of such a reform.[5] The German Institute of Economic Research, however, predicted an increase of 800 000 jobs.[6] Moreover, the reports of the Sachverständigenrat are often not uncontested as well. This is made clear not only by numerous deviating statements by the member nominated by the trade unions, but also by 'anti-reports' which are sometimes produced (privately) and, last but not least, by the scientific discussion about these reports.

A closure of this apparent discrepancy between the self-assessment of many economists who are in the business of policy advice and their assessment by the general public can only take place if we dissociate from the picture of the ideal scientist and apply the economic model of behavior to ourselves as well.[7] That is to say that we must assume that economists are self-interested, rationally acting utility maximizers, too. Economic theory supposes that this is a useful assumption for analyzing human behavior. Thus, there is no reason to except economists from this

---

[5] See, for example, Scholz and Stähler (1999). Although they do not answer the exact same question, they make it very clear that it needs – according to their results – extremely restrictive assumptions for unilateral environmental policy measures to have positive economic effects.

[6] See Bonus (1981) for a description of the positions of these two institutes, which he links with 'supply theory' and 'demand theory' and the perspectives and experience associated with these.

[7] For a description of the economic model of behavior, see Kirchgässner (1991).

assumption.[8] This implies not only that their information is limited as well, but also (and more importantly) that strong monetary incentives can cause economists to defend (nearly) any, even arbitrary political positions.

Taking this into account, does economic policy advice make sense at all then? Or does everything go down in the battle of the interest groups, as Krelle (1979) suspects? The fact that there is a demand for scientific advice in the political process does not necessarily imply that there is also a demand for something like 'scientific truth' or 'objective knowledge'. It cannot be ruled out that the only purpose of enrolling economists as policy advisors is to serve the political positions of political parties or various interest groups.

In this chapter an answer to these questions is attempted. First, we ask about the role of the scientist in this process (Section 1). This is done on the basis of a specific position of the philosophy of science, Critical Rationalism. Section 2 shows that economic theory is in many relevant cases so weak that it is possible for different economists to defend pretty contrary positions with the claim of scientific truth. This makes empirical research necessary. However, researchers can often obtain their 'desired' empirical result by manipulating the econometric estimates, without (obvious) violations of the rules of scientific work. To detect such manipulations, a critical discussion of theoretical approaches and empirical econometric results is necessary. Thus, in Section 3 we discuss how it is possible that despite all these problems the process of policy advice may lead to something like 'objectivity' or 'truth' and why even economists who are not corrupt in most cases promote the objectives of their clients. One of the basic preconditions to come closer to 'true' statements in political debate is to have an open public discourse about the reports of the advisors. In Section 4 we finally discuss the (non-trivial) question why scientific policy advice is at all demanded.

---

[8] There is also empirical evidence that economists behave more in accordance with this model than the average individual, especially that economists are more self-interested and less altruistic than others. Experiments with the ultimatum game show, for example, that students of economics show much stronger free-rider behavior (as predicted by economic theory) than other students. For this, see Carter and Irons (1991). Frey and Meier (2003) explain this by a selection effect.

1. SOME REMARKS FROM PHILOSOPHY OF SCIENCE

Despite the fact that their reports are often criticized as being biased, the prestige economists as well as other (social) scientists enjoy in the public is higher than the prestige of ordinary people. Economists benefit from the reputation of others, especially natural scientists. These are seen to be (at least in comparison to others) objective and to feel an obligation to produce 'objective knowledge' more than others. That this reputation spills over to social scientists is one of the main reasons for the demand for reports of (social) scientists from special interest groups trying to pursue their goals in the political process. If a certain position is presented by a scientist, there is usually a greater acceptance in the general public than if it is only presented by a special interest group. Behind this widely held opinion is the image of the ideal scientist who is only striving for truth. This ideal image which has been brought to us (besides others) by Max Weber (1919) is hardly compatible with politically acting scientists. This does not imply that scientists are not allowed to make political statements, but when they act as citizens they should not enjoy special privileges from their status as scientists.

How is this picture compatible with scientists giving contradictory answers to specific factual questions? For example, the question as to which political measures should be taken to reduce high unemployment in the Federal Republic of Germany has in the past been answered quite differently by the Kiel Institute of World Economy and by the German Institute for Economic Research in Berlin. Because of the complexity of this problem and the theories we have to apply if we want to answer this question, obtaining different answers might be understandable. Quite generally, univocal statements seem to be more difficult to obtain in social than in natural sciences. This excuse is, however, not valid if two professors of economics make quite different statements with respect to the question whether the cantonal monopolies or the private insurance companies in Switzerland had lower rates for fire and natural damages insurance in the past.[9] It should be possible to give a univocal answer to such a factual question.

The differentiation between facts and standards, which lies behind this argumentation, and the request for 'freedom from value judgments' (Wertfreiheit) regarding the (social) sciences, which is based on this

---

[9] See Kirchgässner (1996) for an analysis of the discussion between two Swiss economists, Thomas von Ungern-Sternberg and Bernd Schips, who wrote reports for the cantonal insurance monopolies and the private insurance companies, respectively.

differentiation, are largely undisputed in economics as well as in large parts of philosophy of science today. Thus, even if the reality is different, striving for objectivity might nevertheless be seen as a (moral) claim on the individual scientist. Max Weber (1919) at least suggests this. However, it is always possible to make nearly arbitrary moral claims on individuals or groups. What is relevant is the foundation of such claims, but (in a liberal society) everybody can decide for him/herself whether (s)he intends to follow it.

One might argue that this is not a problem of individual attitudes of scientists but that this is a 'systemic request': objectivity of individual scientists might be seen as a necessary condition for scientific progress. However, Karl R. Popper (1962, p. 95) has quite a different opinion:

> It is a mistake to assume that the objectivity of a science depends on the objectivity of the scientist. And it is a mistake to believe that the attitude of the natural scientist is more objective than that of the social scientist. ... [T]he objectivity of science is not a matter of the individual scientists but rather the social result of their mutual criticisms, of the friendly-hostile division of labour among scientists, of their co-operation and also of their competition.

Does this thesis not contradict, however, the position of Albert (1956, 1963), who claims that 'freedom from value judgements' of the sciences is a 'methodological principle'? Is it not necessary that scientists strive for objectivity at least in their internal scientific discourse, even if they attempt to influence political decisions (for example by producing scientific reports) according to their individual preferences?

To get a satisfactory answer to this question, it is necessary to take into account, as Karl Popper emphasizes, that science is not the business of separate individuals but that it is a social process, in which some scientists make conjectures and others criticize these. Some of these conjectures will (at least temporarily) survive the criticism and be taken as approved hypotheses, while others will be refuted because of logical deficiencies or incompatibility with the available empirical data. It is not decisive whether the individual scientist is objective or not, but that the scientific discourse takes place in a climate where criticism is not only allowed but even desired. Only criticism of our conjectures enables us to detect their weaknesses and to proceed to better conjectures. In this respect, there is no difference between natural and social scientists. If we had to rely on the objectivity of the individual scientist to reach scientific progress, then the possibilities for progress would be rather limited, because scientists – like all other human beings – are generally biased in favor of their own ideas. Whether scientific progress is possible or not in a society depends much more on the (rational) organization of the scientific process than on the intentions of the individual scientists.

Nevertheless, in an open discourse scientists have strong incentives to strive for objectivity in order not to be refuted (too swiftly) by other participants. This is the only way to build a reputation and – in this way – also to pursue their other (individual) objectives.[10]

Thus, for the concept of critical rationalism it is less important that individual researchers try to reject their own hypotheses and theories, but that the scientific process is organized in a way that such rejections are possible and even probable. Actually, no scientist has any interest in having his/her hypotheses and theories rejected. Usually, scientists attempt just the opposite: they collect all evidence in favor of their theories, and sometimes they even suppress contradictory evidence. If there is no other way left, they 'extend' their theories to make them compatible with empirical evidence which previously seemed to be in contradiction.

Because scientists behave this way, it is important that the scientific discourse is organized so as to make rejections of hypotheses possible and to provide incentives that such discourses take place. For this we need 'theoretical pluralism'. In such a discourse, it might even be desirable if individual scientists defend their theories as vehemently as possible. This way, the capacity of the theories can be judged. Lakatos (1970) has pointed out the fact that it might be harmful for scientific progress if theories are drawn back 'too fast' whenever empirical evidence against them has been presented. The best conditions for scientific progress are given when both refutation *and* defense of theoretical propositions are possible.

By the way, scientists also try to test their theories and hypotheses. Before they present a hypothesis to the scientific community, they usually try to minimize the probability that this hypothesis will be rejected by others. Therefore, they themselves ask for possible objections against their work. They will, for example, conduct experiments, perform statistical analyses or collect additional data. Just because they want to defend their ideas, they are forced to first perform strong tests in order not to be refuted (too easily). The motivation for this behavior, however, again depends on the organization of the scientific process.

If objective results are due for discussion and mutual criticism already in the internal scientific process and evolve only to a much lesser extent

---

[10] This is in analogy with the role of the (self-interested) entrepreneur in the market and his contribution to the social result. As Adam Smith wrote 'It is not from the benevolence of the butcher, the brewer, or the baker, that we expect our dinner, but from their regard to their own interest. We address ourselves, not to their humanity but to their self-love, and never talk to them of our own necessities but of their advantages' (1776, p. 27).

out of the scientists' quest for truth, why should this be different when science becomes 'political', that is in the realm of scientific policy advice? Scientists (largely) behave according to the economic model of behavior just as everybody else; their scientific work is one (and often a very important) possibility to pursue their personal interests. In this process, they make mistakes, try to manipulate results or at least to present their results in a way which is compatible with their personal interests. Limits to this behavior arise predominantly from public discussion, and only to a lesser extent from their own conscience. In most situations it is (at least implicitly) accepted that they primarily present evidence which is in favor of their own political intentions. But manipulations which are detected can strongly damage an economist's reputation. In the worst case (for themselves) they might even become intolerable as advisors for those interest groups which are politically close to them. Thus, quite independent of whether an intrinsic motivation is present, they have a self-interest to keep up the scientific standards of their profession when they act as policy advisors as well.

But even if economists keep up these standards, the examples given above indicate that it is possible to have totally different opinions with respect to economic policy questions. How can this be the case if economists have (at least in principle) a theoretical common ground? Economic theory does not seem to be as strong as we would like it to be. Thus, the question has to be addressed how strong the propositions are which can be derived from economic theorizing.

2. ON THE POWER OF ECONOMIC THEORY AND OF EMPIRICAL ECONOMIC RESEARCH

Whenever economists give advice on how to solve actual economic problems, they typically give answers which imply changes in relative prices. To reduce unemployment it is demanded that trade unions make moderate wage claims and that taxes and charges on labor are reduced in order to reduce the price of and increase the demand for labor.[11] And to reduce air and water pollution ecological taxes and/or tradable permits are the usual prescription in order to impose a positive price on environmental media.

There are two basic assumptions behind such proposals:

---

[11] See, for example, Sachverständigenrat (1996, pp. 180ff.).

i   *Stability:* The economic system is stable in the following sense: small changes in policy instruments lead only to small changes in the economic objectives.

ii *Substitution:* Increases (reductions) of the (relative) price of a good lead to reductions (increases) in the (relative) demand for this good and increases (reductions) in the demand for other goods: the good which is now (relatively) more expensive will be (partially) substituted by goods which are now (relatively) cheaper.

Whether the economic system is stable in this sense is quite independent of the question whether this system tends to reach full employment or not. Equilibria with (involuntary) unemployment can be stable in this sense as well. The assumption of stability stated above is much weaker, it only excludes chaotic behavior of the economic system. If we had to take into account chaotic behavior, economic policy would be a gamble: small changes of government expenditure or even an infinitesimally small change of a single tax rate could lead to a massive recession, but also to a strong economic upswing.[12]

The assumption of substitutability implies that the (aggregate) demand functions for individual goods have a negative slope: an increase (reduction) of the price leads to a reduction (increase) of the quantity demanded. This assumption is so fundamental for economic theorizing that von Weizsäcker speaks of 'confidence in the working of the substitution principle' as the basic common conviction of economists (1976, p. 69, own translation).

Is this basic common conviction covered by economic theory? This question might sound ridiculous. One should assume that economists who give policy advice take into account the relevant results of economic theory. Until about 30 years ago, it was possible to assume (with more or less of a bad conscience) that these assumptions were without problems. Since then, however, it has been shown that these assumptions are not necessarily covered by economic theory. Thus, the question whether it is possible to give economic policy advice based on economic theory is no longer trivial.

Let us first ask whether aggregate demand functions have a negative slope. Somewhat more precisely, the question is whether we get aggregate demand functions for individual goods with a negative slope if all economic agents behave 'rationally' in the sense of the economic model of behavior. A general answer to this question cannot be derived

---

[12] For the relevance of chaos theory for economics, see, for example, Baumol and Benhabib (1989).

from partial analyses but, if the feedback of the actions of individual actors is to be taken into account, by the theory of general equilibrium. This was the question Sonnenschein (1972, 1973) asked in the early 1970s. He showed that, when employing the usual assumptions about individual preferences in an exchange economy, the demand function for an individual good can (locally) have any slope. [13] To exclude this possibility, rather restrictive assumptions about individual preferences are necessary. This also holds if one tries, as Hildenbrand (1983) did, to impose restrictions on the possible distributions of preferences (and initial endowments).

With respect to the assumption of stability it has been shown that such economies can have multiple equilibria. If such multiple equilibria exist they cannot be globally stable, and some equilibria are not even locally stable: small deviations from one equilibrium can lead to a totally different new equilibrium. [14] This implies, however, that the two basic assumptions about the structure of the economic system which are typically employed whenever policy advice is given are not covered by general equilibrium theory.

Thus, the attempt to derive univocal results about the basic structure of exchange economies which extend the existence and optimality conditions of equilibria but are only based on the general primitives of economic analysis has failed. If one takes into account these 'non-results', then it is no surprise that it is possible to derive nearly any result by employing the corresponding assumptions. [15] Thus, despite the factual consensus between most economists, economic theory is unable to provide a robust theoretical foundation for policy advice. [16] Economic theory seems to be, at best, of limited help for economic policy. This even holds for microeconomics, where there is a large consensus among economists: the validity of the dominating theory is hardly disputed. How much less help can we expect from macroeconomics where the basic consensus which lasted up to the beginning of the 1970s has long ago broken apart? [17]

But even if it is assumed that stability is given and the substitution principle holds, we are still far from an ideal situation. Many economic policy measures have income and substitution effects which go in

---

[13] For this, see Ingrao and Israel (1987, pp. 315ff.) as well as Balasko (1988, pp. 120ff.). Further work in this area and generalizations of the results of Sonnenschein are given by Mantel (1974), Debreu (1974) and Mas-Colell (1977).

[14] For this, see Ingrao and Israel (1987, pp. 329ff.).

[15] For some examples, see Kirchgässner (1999).

[16] Thus claims, for example, Friedman (1985, p. 3).

[17] The situation of macroeconomics is described, for example, by Blanchard (2000).

opposite directions. The overall effect is theoretically open. In such a situation economists – following the statement of von Weizsäcker (1976) – usually argue for the dominance of the substitution effect. There are, for instance, two effects to be considered with respect to the impact of wage increases on unemployment in Europe today. One of the reasons for low employment might be the weakness of domestic demand. [18] The income effect of a wage increase strengthens domestic demand which leads – *ceteris paribus* – to an increase in employment. On the other hand, a wage increase raises labor costs, which leads to a (partial) substitution of labor by other production inputs. At the same time, the costs of domestic compared to foreign production increase, which also leads to a substitution process. These two processes cause a reduction of demand for labor and, therefore, also a reduction in employment. Thus, the overall effect of a wage increase on employment is theoretically open. If one believes in the disposable income argument of wages usually employed by trade unions, the income effect dominates, employment increases and unemployment is reduced. Most economists, however, believe (as the employer organizations do) that the substitution effect dominates: a wage increase raises – *ceteris paribus* – unemployment.

Thus, whenever the income and the substitution effects go in opposite directions it is possible that different economists make opposite statements without violating the rules of the scientific game. Because it is theoretically open which effect dominates, we need empirical research. But how much can we rely on the empirical (econometric) results which are presented?

The traditional approach of econometrics consists of three steps. First, the economic theoretician has to present the 'true' model. Second, the statistician has to provide the appropriate estimation and testing methods. Additionally, the data needed are to be collected. Finally, and most important, the statistical methods have to be applied to the data to get an empirical representation of the theoretical model. [19] If there are conflicting theories, it is supposed that it is possible to find out the 'true' theory by applying statistical test procedures or at least to discriminate between 'better' and 'worse' theories. The most prominent initiator of this 'scientific research program' was Jan Tinbergen who received the

---

[18] See for this, for example, OECD (1997, pp. 20ff.).

[19] For such a description, see, for example, Brinkmann (1970). Moreover, this closely corresponds to the definition of econometrics which – after the Econometric Society had been founded – was given in Issue 1 of *Econometrica* (1933, p. 1). See for this also Hendry (1980, pp. 388ff.).

first Nobel Price in Economics (together with Ragnar Frisch) in 1969 for this enterprise.

That this traditional approach is not without problems became clear (at the latest) when it became obvious that the prediction record of the estimated (large) econometric models was in many cases poorer than that of univariate time series models which did not rely on economic theory (which had been seen as an indispensable basis of the econometric models).[20] In addition, Lucas (1976) formulated principle doubts with respect to the possibility to base effective economic policy on estimated econometric models, and the practical results of actual policies which have been based on such models have at least partially failed.

But even if we employ methods which are not subject to the Lucas critique,[21] there are also other serious problems if we use econometric estimates for economic policy advice. One is the problem of statistical inference in the presence of repeated testing.[22] Another one is 'Data-Mining' or 'Data-Fishing' which makes it possible to produce nearly any empirical result which is demanded. The basic problem behind this results stems from the fact that (at least outside of experimental economics and especially if we use macro data) we cannot perform real tests. The different steps of econometric estimation and test procedures cannot actually simulate a real test.[23] It is more or less open to the researcher which (of the many regressions he performs) he is presenting as *the* empirical evidence. Thus, taking into account the self-interest of the researcher (and his political convictions) it is to be expected that whenever he presents empirical results he will – without violating the usual scientific standards – select those which are mostly coherent with his own political conviction. This is even more true if he is engaged in policy advice. Then, the interests of the customer can play a role as well.[24]

---

[20] For this, see Granger and Newbold (1975).

[21] The empirical relevance of the Lucas critique is, however, disputed. See, for example, Ericsson and Irons (1995).

[22] See, for example, Cooley and LeRoy (1981, 1986), Denton (1985) or Kirchgässner (2001).

[23] This might sometimes be different in microeconometrics if control groups were available or could be artificially generated as is done, for example, in the econometric evaluation of active labor market policies. See, for example, Lechner (1998).

[24] An example which demonstrates how specific results are (or at least can be) selected to produce the desired result is given in Kirchgässner (2001).

3. ON THE PROCESS OF POLICY ADVICE

Thus, we are in a situation where we can find economists providing scientific (and empirical) support for nearly every political position. Apart from other factors, this is possible because economic theory is compatible with nearly all (factual) statements and because the necessary empirical research can result in rather different results. Given this situation, can we expect that (besides ideology) information is transmitted in the process of economic policy advice, or do we have to assume that (most) economists in this business are corrupt, because they deliver the results demanded by their clients?

If information is to be transmitted in the process of policy advice (as well) it must be ensured that the discussion is public and that the respective material is publicly available. As to empirical questions this includes the exact specification of the data employed as well as their sources.[25] Only under these circumstances do competing interest groups as well as the general public have the opportunity to critically discuss different statements. This discussion, however, is necessary to enable participants in political discourse to distinguish between factual statements and political (ideological) positions. Of course, both have their legitimate place in this discourse, but it should always be possible to differentiate between them, irrespective of how difficult this might seem to be in a concrete situation. In this sense, the concept which assumes that public discourse and not the individual motivation of scientists is crucial to get 'objective' information is fully based on the principle of 'freedom from value judgements' as proposed by Max Weber, Hans Albert and others.

With respect to economic policy recommendations it is safe to say that in most cases experts have a personal interest to obtain (almost) exactly those results they actually achieve, which implies that they are biased in favor of their clients. This contradicts the notion of the ideal scientist presented above, whose only objective is to find 'truth'. It is a fact, however, that the clients (often very carefully) look for (potential) experts who can be expected to produce exactly those results desired by the clients themselves. Because experts know these expectations it can be assumed that the results sought by the customer are at least not completely contrary to the experts' own ideological views. In the end, they have to identify themselves with these positions if their report is published.

---

[25] The specific problem that data from surveys are not reproducible (for technical or financial reasons) is not discussed here.

That experts come to different conclusions does, on the other hand, not imply that the results are casual or arbitrary. Even if the statements of experts are quite different a critical discussion is still possible which uncovers mistakes and tricks of individual experts and, therefore, allows a more objective evaluation of the situation from the outside. The main purpose of such a discussion is to show how the different arguments are related to specific interests even if they are garnished with the rhetoric of social welfare. Such a clarifying discussion is certainly not for the benefit of all participants but it can help other independent people or the political authorities to make 'reasonable' political decisions. This holds true to a greater extent in a direct than in a (purely) representative democracy, because public political discourse is of greater importance if people have (the possibility of) the final decision.[26]

Moreover, it can even be helpful for political discourse and the following decision if the experts on both sides try to make their points very strong. In the same way as it can be detrimental for the scientific progress if a theory is withdrawn 'too fast' in a scientific discourse, it makes sense that in a political discourse both sides present all their arguments. Only then do voters (and their representatives in the parliament) really know what they have to decide about.

It might be taken for granted, but it can nevertheless be objected that in many cases scientists strive for truth and that this is their only motivation. Moreover, economists as experts do not always write what their clients expect. This can hardly be denied, just as we can hardly deny the observation that, besides truth, scientists often strive for quite other objectives and that their reports made on behalf of special interest groups usually reflect what those groups expect. What does this mean for the concept which is presented here?

First, it has to be taken into account that the incentives of scientists depend on the environment in which they operate. Conditions in the 'scientific game' are different from those in the 'political game' or in the 'policy advice game'. Generally, the scientific game is more transparent and has a more long-run perspective. Thus, the strive for objectivity is stronger in (purely) scientific activities than in the policy advice game, but it can exist in the latter as well. Moreover, there are many arguments in the utility functions; (monetary) income is a very important one, but only one among many arguments.

Reputation in the scientific community certainly plays an important role for scientists, and they are usually not willing to risk this reputation

---

[26] For this, see Kirchgässner, Feld and Savioz (1999, Chapter 3).

because of negligible financial rewards. Thus, it would not be rational even for self-interested scientists to be corruptible for small amounts of money and to produce results which can easily be rejected.[27] This applies all the more, the greater the intensity at which information spills over from the political to the scientific area, that is the easier other scientific colleagues get knowledge of political advice statements which are scientifically not sound. Thus, striving for objectivity can be generated by self-interest, even if it might appear or be interpreted differently: as intrinsic motivation. On the other hand, among scientists there is also genuinely non-self-interested (altruistic, intrinsically motivated) behavior. In some situations, such behavior can even be very relevant for society.[28]

Nevertheless, in order to find answers to the question of how the process of policy advice has to be organized so that not only ideology but also information is transmitted, it makes sense to follow the concept of constitutional economics and assume self-interested behavior of all participants. This holds even if the majority of scientists were purely intrinsically motivated and solely striving for objective knowledge.[29] In analogy to the constitutional considerations of Popper (1945, p. 121), the relevant question is this: how can we organize the institutions of scientific policy advice in such a way that bad or incompetent experts can be prevented from doing too much damage? A somewhat nicer formulation for this is: the rules of the policy advice game should be built in a way that even those scientific experts who are more interested in their own (monetary) income than in truth will produce objective knowledge. As shown above, a precondition for this is the open discussion of research methods and results: A critical discussion has to be possible.

In (non-experimental) empirical economic research this implies, for instance, that equations from published papers should more often be re-estimated by others than it is done today.[30] To be able to do this, it is necessary that the data which are employed are available for others. In this sense, even today there are some journals which demand that the data which are used in the papers published in the journal are made publicly

---

[27] On the other hand, it is really astonishing how little money is often necessary to make economists (but also other scientists as well as politicians) risk their reputation (and their future careers).

[28] See Kirchgässner (2001a).

[29] On the position of constitutional economics see, for example, Buchanan (1987, 1987a).

[30] As the results of the *Journal of Money, Credit, and Banking* Project show, it is very often impossible to replicate the results exactly. For this, see Dewald, Thursby and Anderson (1986) as well as Anderson and Dewald (1994).

available (for example via the Internet).[31] This should cause no problems as long as only data are used which are provided by public institutions. Problems could arise if the data are collected by private firms for commercial reasons. Similarly, if scientists have collected their own data they will hardly be willing to make them publicly available as long as they have not made full use of them. In both cases, however, it can be demanded that the data are made available to the public after a certain period of time.[32]

The process of economic policy advice, however, often lacks the necessary openness and transparency. This can hardly be changed as long as reports are paid by interest groups. But, at least in the Federal Republic of Germany, openness and transparency are also missing in many cases if the advisor is paid by a public institution. There are rules which allow the politicians to withhold a report at least for a rather long period, and which make some kind of publications impossible. Because these reports are financed by taxes paid by the German citizens, not only do the latter have an interest, but also a right that such reports are made fully available to the public and without changes introduced by third parties. Under this perspective, the rules which exist in Germany are ridiculous.

This is somewhat different in Switzerland. On the one hand, the contracts between public institutions and private advisors are less restrictive. On the other hand, at least partially competing reports are financed and made publicly available in order to make a public discussion possible.

An example for this is the debate about the effectiveness of active labor market policy measures. Five different (groups of) researchers were asked for reports. The results were partly contradictory. After the reports had been finished at the end of 1999 they were presented to the public in April 2000.[33] At the same time, short versions of the reports were published in Issue 4/2000 of the journal *Die Volkswirtschaft*. Thus, the whole process was very much transparent, and the politicians have not been suspended from their responsibility to finally make a political decision.

---

[31] This holds true, for example, for the *Journal of Applied Econometrics*, the *Journal of Human Resources*, or the *Journal of Business and Economic Statistics*, as long as there are no problems of data protection.

[32] An additional problem arises if opinion poll data are used which can – for technical or financial reasons – not be reproduced. For this, see Kirchgässner (1992, pp. 16f).

[33] See for this: 'Aktive Hilfe für Arbeitslose – aber bitte effizient: Bedingt positive Noten für die Schweizer Arbeitsmarktpolitik', *Neue Zürcher Zeitung* No. 80 of April 4, 2000, p. 23. There, the names of the research teams are listed as well.

This example shows that – given the political intention – it is possible to make the process of policy advice transparent in a way that the empirical results which are presented to support a specific political argumentation can be comprehended and criticized by others. The competition of the different interests to influence the political decision will generally give rise to such a critique.

With respect to the question of the objectivity of scientific reports it additionally has to be taken into account that scientific experts who get their mandate from interest groups are in many cases neither able nor willing to do anything else than to support the political objectives of their clients. This applies even if they are in no way corrupt. First, a report which is not in support of the political objectives of the client will – with high probability – never be presented to the general public. This alone ensures that the published reports are (largely) supportive of the objectives of the clients. Second, an expert who presents results which contradict the objectives of his/her client might get no further mandate. Consequently, the selection of the experts by clients leads to a substantial convergence of interests of clients and experts. We observe a similar process in the market for scientific reports as, following Adam Smith (1776), it has already been described by Alchian (1950) and Friedman (1953). (i) The self-interest of the experts provides incentives for them to help their clients to reach their political objectives. (ii) Even if all experts only support those political objectives of which they are personally convinced and which they believe to be justified (in a moral way), the selection mechanism generates an assignment between clients and experts so that, in the end, the political objectives of clients and experts are largely overlapping. In this game all experts may survive, but only under the protection of specific clients. 'Objectivity' in this game can only be reached approximately and only by a public discourse.

4. CONCLUDING REMARKS

The fact that economists as policy advisors usually produce those results which are expected from their clients does, therefore, not necessarily show that economic experts (or at least a large part of them) are corrupt. They might be no more (but also no less) corruptible than other citizens. This fact is also compatible with their striving for objective knowledge, as long as it is seen that economists (like all other citizens) have political objectives and that it is legitimate that they attempt to pursue these political objectives with their scientific work as well. Thus, it always has to be taken into account that their (scientific) statements are biased because, for example, they only have a selective perception of reality and the selection is influenced by their political objectives. From this it follows that objectivity can hardly be expected to be generated by (isolated) individuals. It has to be produced in an open political discourse. And it may evolve out of this discourse because of the countervailing interests which are represented in this discourse. What holds for the scientific process holds for the political process *a fortiori*. The better and more open the discourse is organized, the larger is the probability that it helps to find some truth and that we get 'better' political decisions. And because this process is much more general and open in direct than in (purely) representative democracies, we can assume that – on average – the decisions are better in a direct than in a representative democracy. Truth and objectivity do not necessarily disappear in the struggle of interests in the process of economic policy advice, but they are also not as easily reached as the traditional theory of economic policy advice believed and as many economists engaged in this process still want to make us believe today.

Why, however, is economic policy advice demanded after all? Why are reports needed, and what does an interest group gain, for example when it presents such a report to the general public, if it takes into account that by paying enough money a 'scientific' foundation for nearly every political claim can be obtained? If, as the economic theory assumes, citizens have rational expectations, they will see through this game and hardly be impressed by such reports. If, however, such reports have no effect, why are interest groups (and political parties) paying for them? If they also have rational expectations, should they not waive such reports?

The possibility discussed above that public discourse might lead to (socially) 'better' solutions does not provide a reason for this, because the question of the production of a public good is at stake, and self-interested individuals will – under 'normal' conditions – hardly be willing to make a voluntary contribution to such a good. This is not contradicted by the fact that individuals sometimes make such voluntary contributions, as these are in most cases small contributions in 'low-cost situations'.[34] Moreover, it is hard to believe that especially (economic) interest groups exhibit such 'altruistic' behavior when paying economists for writing reports. After all, the only reason why such groups are organized is to gain political influence in order to promote the (special) interests of their members (and leaders). But then, at first glance, it seems incompatible with rational expectations that these groups spend money for economic

---

[34] See Kirchgässner (1992a, 2001a) for the concept of low-cost situations.

policy advice. This holds for at least as long as the corresponding reports are not only technical ones but as long as their main purpose is to influence public opinion and/or the opinion of the citizens' representatives to make them more inclined to meet the demands of this interest group.

However, such an argument overlooks the fact that those interest groups – especially in a direct democracy – strongly depend on convincing arguments. A rational, enlightened public takes into account *cui bono* a certain argument is presented and it also knows that arguments which are presented by scientists are weapons in the struggle of interests, but it can nevertheless distinguish between 'good' and 'bad' arguments. It might (perhaps) be convinced by the former, whereas the latter might hardly have any impact. Scientists, however, are (or are at least seen as) specialists who are able to produce 'good' arguments. Thus, it makes sense that interest groups and political parties have a demand for scientific policy advice. And if the rival presents such a report, an interest group hardly has any other chance than to also present a scientific report, even if its only purpose is to disprove the other side's arguments.

This also implies that the customers have an interest in high-quality advice: the arguments which are provided by the scientists have to be convincing in the political debate. Thus, when political parties and interest groups select their advisors, they will take not only their (presumed) political conviction into account, but also their reputation. The latter does not only depend on their experience in giving policy advice but also on their scientific reputation. Thus, the self-interest of customers leads them to demand 'good' reports, and if this is done by all participants of a political discourse, the chances for 'good' solutions rise.

Let me conclude: this chapter started with an ideal (idealized) description of the process of scientific political advice. It is obvious that the actual discourse does not meet this description (and even less so the criteria demanded by the proponents of the theory of 'discourse ethics' like Habermas (1983)). Nevertheless, competition between advisors and an open discourse might promote truth despite all acknowledged obstacles.

REFERENCES

Albert, Hans (1956), 'Werturteil und Wertbasis: Das Werturteilsproblem im Lichte der logischen Analyse', *Zeitschrift für die gesamte Staatswissenschaft*, **112**, 410–39.

Albert, Hans (1963), 'Wertfreiheit als Methodisches Prinzip', in Erwin von Beckerath, Herbert Giersch and H. Lampert (eds), *Probleme der Normativen*

Ökonomik und der Wirtschaftspolitischen Beratung, Berlin: Duncker und Humblot, pp. 32–63.

Alchian, Armen A. (1950), 'Uncertainty, evolution, and economic theory', *Journal of Political Economy*, **58**, 211–21.

Anderson, Richard G. and William G. Dewald (1994), 'Replication and scientific standards in applied economics a decade after the Journal of Money, Credit, and Banking Project', *Federal Reserve Bank of St. Louis Review*, **76** (6), 79–83.

Balasko, Yves (1988), *Foundations of the Theory of General Equilibrium*, Orlando: Academic Press.

Baumol, William J. and Jess Benhabib (1989), 'Chaos: Significance, mechanism, and economic applications', *Journal of Economic Perspectives*, **3** (1), 77–105.

Blanchard, Olivier (2000), 'What do we know about macroeconomics that Fischer and Wicksell did not?', *Quarterly Journal of Economics*, **115**, 1375–409.

Blankart, Charles B. (1987), 'Review of: G. Radnitzky and P. Bernholz (eds), *Economic Imperialism: The Economic Method Applied Outside the Field of Economics*, (Paragon House, New York 1987)', *Zeitschrift für die Gesamte Staatswissenschaft (JITE)*, **143**, 669–73.

Bonus, Holger (1981), 'Das wissenschaftliche Gutachten in der Politik: Information, öffentliche Meinung, Verantwortung', in M. Timmermann (ed.), *Nationalökonomie morgen: Ansätze zur Weiterentwicklung wirtschaftswissenschaftlicher Forschung*, Stuttgart: Kohlhammer, pp. 263–98.

Brinkmann, G. (1970), 'Zur Wissenschaftstheorie der Ökonometrie', *Kyklos*, **23**, 205–25.

Buchanan, James M. (1987), 'The constitution of economic policy', *American Economic Review*, **77**, 243–59.

Buchanan, James M. (1987a), 'Constitutional Economics', in *The New Palgrave, A Dictionary of Economics*, Vol. 1, London: Macmillan, pp. 585–8.

Carter, John R. and Michael D. Irons (1991), 'Are economists different, and if so, why?', *Journal of Economic Perspectives*, **5** (2), 171–7.

Cooley, Tomas F. and Stephen F. LeRoy (1981), 'Identification and estimation of money demand', *American Economic Review*, **71**, 825–44.

Cooley, Tomas F. and Stephen F. LeRoy (1986), 'What will take the con out of econometrics', *American Economic Review*, **76**, 504–7.

Denton, Frank T. (1985), 'Data mining as an industry', *Review of Economics and Statistics*, **47**, 124–7.

Debreu, Gerard (1974), 'Excess demand functions', *Journal of Mathematical Economics*, **1**, 15–21.

Dewald, William G., Jerry G. Thursby and Richard G. Anderson (1986), 'Replication in empirical economics: The Journal of Money, Credit, and Banking Project', *American Economic Review*, **76**, 587–603.

Ericsson, Neil R. and John S. Irons (1995), 'The Lucas Critique in Practice: Theory Without Measurement', in K.D. Hoover (ed.), *Macroeconometrics: Developments, Tensions and Prospects*, Dordrecht: Kluwer, pp. 263–312.

Feyerabend, Paul K. [1975] (1993), *Against Method*, 3rd revised edition, London and New York: Verso.

Frey, Bruno S. and Stephan Meier (2003), 'Are political economists selfish and indoctrinated? Evidence from a Natural Experiment', *Economic Inquiry*, **41**, 448–62.

Friedman, Lee S. (1985), *Microeconomic Policy Analysis*, New York: McGraw-Hill.
Friedman, Milton (1953), 'The Methodology of Positive Economics', in M. Friedman, *Essays in Positive Economics*, Chicago: University of Chicago Press, pp. 3–43.
German Institute for Economic Research (ed.) (1994), *Wirtschaftliche Auswirkungen einer ökologischen Steuerreform*, Berlin: Duncker und Humblot.
Granger, Clive W. and Paul Newbold (1975), 'Economic Forecasting: The Atheist's Viewpoint', in G.A. Renton (ed.), *Modelling the Economy*, London: Heinemann, pp. 131–48.
Habermas, Jürgen (1983), *Moralbewusstsein und Kommunikatives Handeln*, Frankfurt: Suhrkamp; English translation: *Moral Consciousness and Communicative Action*, Cambridge, MA: MIT Press 1990.
Hendry, David F. (1980), 'Econometrics: alchemy or science?', *Economica*, **47**, 387–406.
Hesse, Helmut (1994), 'Als Wissenschaftler in der Politik?', in Universität Hannover (ed.), *Vorträge im Fachbereich Wirtschaftswissenschaften*, Vol. 20, Hannover, pp. 17–37.
Hildenbrand, Werner (1983), 'On the law of demand', *Econometrica*, **51**, 997–1019.
Ingrao, Bruna and Giorgio Israel (1987), *La mano invisibile*, Rome: Gius. Laterza et Figli Spa; English translation: *The Invisible Hand, Economic Equilibrium in the History of Science*, Cambridge, MA: MIT Press, 1990.
Kirchgässner, Gebhard (1991), *Homo Oeconomicus, Das Ökonomische Modell Individuellen Verhaltens und Seine Anwendung in den Wirtschafts- und Sozialwissenschaften*, Tübingen: J.B.C. Mohr (Paul Siebeck), 2nd edition 2000.
Kirchgässner, Gebhard (1992), 'Wissenschaftstheorie und Wissenschaftsbetrieb: Einige einführende Bemerkungen', Department of Economics, University of St. Gallen, Discussion Paper No. 68, November.
Kirchgässner, Gebhard (1992a), 'Towards a theory of low-cost decisions', *European Journal of Political Economy*, **8**, 305–20.
Kirchgässner, Gebhard (1996), 'Ideologie und Information in der Politikberatung: Einige Bemerkungen und ein Fallbeispiel', *Hamburger Jahrbuch für Wirtschafts- und Gesellschaftspolitik*, **41**, 9–41.
Kirchgässner, Gebhard (1999), 'On the Political Economy of Economic Policy Advice', in E. Mohr (ed.), *The Transfer of Economic Knowledge*, Cheltenham, UK and Northampton, MA, US: Edward Elgar, pp. 13–31.
Kirchgässner, Gebhard (2001), 'Ökonometrische Schätz- und Testergebnisse, empirisch gehaltvolle Aussagen über die Wirklichkeit und wirtschaftspolitische Beratung', *Konjunkturpolitik*, **47**, 103–38.
Kirchgässner, Gebhard (2001a), 'On Heroes and Average Moral Human Beings', Department of Economics, University of St. Gallen, Discussion Paper No. 2001-21, December.
Kirchgässner, Gebhard, Lars P. Feld and Marcel R. Savioz (1999), *Die Direkte Demokratie: Modern Erfolgreich, Entwicklungs- und Exportfähig*, Basel/München: Helbing und Lichtenhahn/Vahlen.
Krelle, Wilhelm (1979), 'Schlusswort', in C.C. von Weizsäcker (ed.), *Staat und Wirtschaft*, Berlin: Duncker und Humblot, pp. 851–5.

Lakatos, Imre (1970), 'Falsification and the Methodology of Scientific Research Programmes', in I. Lakatos and A. Musgrave (eds), *Criticism and the Growth of Knowledge*, Cambridge: Cambridge University Press, pp. 91–195.

Lechner, Michael (1998), *Training the East German Labour Force: Microeconometric Evaluations of Continuous Vocational Training after Unification*, Heidelberg/New York: Physika.

Lucas; Robert E. (1976), 'Econometric Policy Evaluation, A Critique', in K. Brunner and A.H. Seltzer (eds), *The Phillips Curve and Labor Markets, Carnegie-Rochester Conference Series on Public Policy*, Vol. 1, Amsterdam: North-Holland, pp. 19–46.

Mantel, R.R. (1974), 'On the characterization of aggregate excess demands', *Journal of Economic Theory*, **7**, 348–53.

Mas-Colell, A. (1977), 'On the equilibrium price set of an exchange economy', *Journal of Mathematical Economics*, **4**, 117–26.

OECD (1997), *Études économiques de l'OCDE 1996 – 1997: Suisse*, Paris.

Popper, Karl R. (1945), *The Open Society and Its Enemies, Vol. I: The Spell of Plato*, London: Routledge and Sons.

Popper, Karl R. (1962), 'Die Logik der Sozialwissenschaften', *Kölner Zeitschrift für Soziologie und Sozialpsychologie*, **14**, 233–248; quoted from the English translation: 'The Logic of the Social Sciences', in Th.W. Adorno et al., *The Positivist Dispute in German Sociology*, New York: Harper Torchbooks 1976, pp. 87–104.

Sachverständigenrat (1996), *Jahresgutachten 1996/97*, Bundestagsdrucksache No. 13/6200 of 18 November.

Samuelson, Paul A. (1948), 'Consumption theory in terms of revealed preference', *Economica*, **15**, 243–53.

Scholz, Christian M. and Frank Stähler (1999), *Unilateral Environmental Policy and International Competitiveness*, Tübingen: Mohr Siebeck.

Smith, Adam [1776] (1976), *An Inquiry into the Nature and Causes of the Wealth of Nations*, new edition, Oxford: Clarendon Press.

Sonnenschein, Hugo (1972), 'Market excess demand functions', *Econometrica*, **40**, 549–63.

Sonnenschein, Hugo (1973), 'Do Walras identity and continuity characterize the class of community excess demand functions?', *Journal of Economic Theory*, **6**, 345–54.

Weber, Max (1919), *Wissenschaft als Beruf*, München/Leipzig: Duncker und Humblot.

Weizsäcker, Carl Christian von (1976), 'Die Welt aus der Sicht der Ökonomen', in H. Körner u.a. (eds), *Wirtschaftspolitik: Wissenschaft und politische Aufgabe*, Bern: Haupt, pp. 67–83.

6. Philosophical Concepts of Truth in Economic Policy Advice

Martin Schürz

INTRODUCTION

This chapter tries to answer the question whether and how philosophical concepts of truth may play a role in justifying economic claims. It tries to trace implications of truth concepts for argumentation between economic policy advisors and economic policy-makers.

The first part surveys recent philosophical literature concerning the concept of truth with a particular focus on the pragmatist turn. We concentrate on divergent views within a coherence framework. In the second part the fairly abstract level of philosophical theories will be linked to the realm of economic policy advice.

Obviously, *truth* is a term hardly ever used in economic literature. After all, it is accepted that economics cannot provide true knowledge that rests on absolute certainty. There is no God's eye view from which we could judge an economic theory to be either true or false in an absolute sense. Models and theories are not claimed to be true but rather the best available description of the economy. Instead of *truth*, truth-related notions such as *knowledge, progress* and *explanation* are quite common. To avoid the use of *truth*, however, raises a number of complex questions and it may be unjustified to conclude that existing and broadly accepted standards to judge a theory at a particular point of time suffice to reject the quest for truth. To name two difficulties: what counts as an explanation will be relative to the specific interrogatory context, and the criteria for adequate knowledge depend on the questions we ask. As knowledge is always related to a purpose, it matters what counts as a problem. Our judgment about economic progress will be made in relation to our current beliefs about what reality is like. If these beliefs change we will also modify our evaluation of progress. To guide the process of knowledge evaluation of economics on the alternatives *better* and *worse* does not seem to be a viable proposition, because how should we use the terms knowledge or explanation without referring to what is believed to be true or false? Thus, the quest for the standards of such a judgment hints to open epistemological and methodological issues.

The concept of truth has a function for internal scientific reasons as a foundation or as a description of scientific practice or as a normative call for reflexivity. However, science is not the only domain for issues of truth and maybe not even the primary one. Truth also has a function for external reasons in argumentation. This refers to the distinction between *persuading* und *rationally convincing*. Persuasion can be understood as convincing someone rationally (*überzeugen*) or as persuading in the sense of *überreden*. In the former case it has to refer to the issue of truth; in the latter case it refers to resources of ideology and shared values.

Importance is a hard notion to argue about but we may say that the concept of truth is one concept we can use in describing human behavior. We will argue that differences in the truth concepts of economic policy advisors are particularly important for the external monitoring of economic science. The particular focus is on truth claims in the argumentation between economic science and economic policy. How economists argue concerning truth defines their form of accountability (Rehg 2004). Is it accountability vis-à-vis their economic peers or is it accountability towards reality? Is the mode of justifiedness of an economic theory 'to whom' or in the light of 'what'?

1. PHILOSOPHICAL CONCEPTS OF TRUTH

The concept of truth is a subject with a long history in philosophy. In semantics (the study of the relations between language and reality), epistemology (the study of the possibility of knowledge) and methodology (the study of the best means of knowledge-seeking) the concept of truth plays different roles.

In the framework of correspondence theory, the correspondence between thought and reality would account for truth. *Truth* and *Reality* are capitalized as they are Single Ones. A statement is true if it corresponds to facts.[1] The objectivity is ensured when the subject refers to the object in the right way. Correspondence theory is a realist theory as truth comes about independently from our interests and beliefs. What

---

[1] This refers to the Platonic distinction between what we believe and what we know.

makes a theory true is whether it reflects the causal structures of the world. And there are constraints of reality that make a statement false.[2]

Before Kant, almost all philosophers had a correspondence theory of truth. For Kant knowledge of the world is possible but it does not reach beyond experience. The transcendental conditions of objective experience are supposed to explain the truth of judgment of experience. We never know the thing as it is but the thing as represented. The representation is not a mere copy of the world but the result of our interaction with the external world.[3] There is a *thing in itself* and there are appearances.[4]

Today, a number of philosophers have given up on the correspondence theory of truth.[5] Critics argue there is no clear significance of the notions of *correspondence* and *fact* and many philosophers have dismissed as useless the traditional dichotomy between the world in itself and the concepts we use to think about it.[6] In the linguistic view the subjectivity of beliefs is checked not directly through confrontation with the world but rather through public agreement achieved in an *ideal speech situation* (Habermas 1984). Justification is done by supporting beliefs by other beliefs. In this sense, truth is a matter of coherence, and intersubjectivity replaces objectivity. As there is no way to get outside our beliefs and as truths do not come with a *mark* that distinguishes them from falsehoods there is no chance to test the truth of a proposition as corresponding to something in the world. The only test of truth is coherence.

Pragmatism is dominated by an instrumental notion of truth. For John Dewey, truth is what works in the solution of concrete problems and enhances human life. A theory is true if and when it promotes human affairs. Progress in this sense enables us to do things.[7] The paradigm of

---

[2] But theories are tested against other theories and not against some pre-theoretical foundation (Wendt 2002, p. 59).

[3] Post-Kantian philosophy argues that, when the world as we know it is influenced from our conceptual activity, what sense does it make to have *things in itself*.

[4] This Kantian distinction reappears in our analysis as the difference between truth and justification.

[5] They would be accused of Platonism and at the time of Popper, correspondence theory was so discredited that he gave it up for strategic reasons (Popper 1965, quoted in Hands 2001a, p. 223).

[6] See Rorty (1979).

[7] See Dewey 1948. A number of reasons may account for the renaissance of pragmatism (see Putnam 1985, Backhouse 1997, Rorty 2000, Hands 2001a). First, pragmatism seems to provide a way out of the dichotomy between foundationalist philosophy and relativism. Pragmatic theories relate concepts of truth to human concerns like language beliefs, thoughts and intentional actions. Second, pragmatism blurs the relationship between theory and practice. It lacks a rigid distinction between knowing and doing. Third, pragmatism is social. It does not start from the epistemic question of how beliefs reflect the world but

knowledge of objects is replaced by the paradigm of mutual understanding between subjects. Increased mutual understanding about what to believe and do among ever-increasing communities would be sufficient. The situated character of truth claims underlines that issues are practical rather than theoretical.

In the article 'How do make our ideas clear', Peirce (1878) defined truth as follows: 'The opinion which is fated to be ultimately agreed to by all who investigate is what we mean by the truth, and the object represented in this opinion is the real' (Peirce [1978] 1966, p. 407). Reality consists of facts that can be represented in true statements. It shall not be confused with the 'world' of objects about which these statements are. We presuppose the world to be the totality of objects rather than of facts. A fact about some object must be stated. The Peircean concept of reality as the totality of statable facts links the practice of stating facts to an orientation towards truth. Any scientific proposition whatsoever is always liable to be refuted. However this does not preclude attaining truth although we can never be absolutely sure. This orientation towards truth has a regulative function for fallible processes of justification. As Hilary Putnam underlines, 'before Karl Popper was even born, Peirce emphasized that very often ideas will not be falsified unless we go out and actively seek falsifying experiences. Ideas must be put under strain' (1985, p. 71).

Pragmatism detranscendentalizes objective knowledge and re-formulates it as discursive justification. Thus, Peirce defined *truth* as the limit of endless inquiry within a community using a scientific method. This concept of truth is explained epistemically in terms of progress toward truth. The meaning of truth is anticipated as a consensus that a scientific community would have to obtain under ideal epistemic conditions.[8] For Peirce, pragmatism was a part of logic. It was a way to clarify the meaning of terms and concepts. He argued that the idea of convergence towards truth is built into the presuppositions of discourse.[9]

The *epistemic concept of truth* in pragmatism assimilates truth towards *rational acceptability*. *Rational acceptability* means the idealization of the conditions of justification. What the scientific community can decide is the rational acceptability of propositions but not their truth.[10] Putnam

relates truth of beliefs to social processes. Fourth, the problem of theory-ladenness and underdetermination is considered by pragmatism (Hands 2001a, p. 215ff.).

[8] 'The unlimited ideal "community of investigators" constitutes the forum for the "highest court" of reason' (Habermas 2002, p. 19).

[9] Putnam and Habermas follow this argumentation.

[10] Dewey's technical term is *warranted assertibility*. The standards of *warranted assertibility* are historical products and reflect our interests and values. Whether a statement

understood truth as 'rational acceptability under ideal conditions' (1981, p. 55), 'some sort of ideal coherence of our beliefs with each other and with our experiences – as these experiences are themselves represented in our belief system' (ibid. p. 49).

Coherence theories are divided about the question what, if anything, is to be said about truth. The radical perspective of the neo-pragmatist Rorty is that there is nothing much to be said about truth. We should discard the notion of truth as an accurate representation and the idea of truth as one. Truth is a useless topic, and we should instead discuss how to increase the size of the relevant communities for justification is the radical point that the neo-pragmatist Rorty makes.

> Truth only sounds like the name of a goal if . . . progress towards truth is explicated by reference to a metaphysical picture . . . without that picture, to say that truth is our goal is merely to say something like 'we hope to justify our belief to as many and as large audiences as possible'. (Rorty 2000, p. 320)

Thus, he claims that 'we pragmatists deny that the search for objective truth is a search for correspondence to reality and urge that it be seen instead as a search for the widest possible intersubjective agreement'. Also Davidson states that 'truth as correspondence with reality may be an idea we are better off without' and only accepts a cautionary use 'justified but maybe not true' (Davidson 2000, p. 66). This indispensable function of the word 'true' is to caution by making gestures towards unpredictable situations (future audiences, other audiences).

The crucial premise of Rorty in his book *Philosophy and the Mirror of Nature* is that we understand knowledge when we understand the social justification of belief. Thus, we have no need to view it as accuracy of our representations. The only useful notion of truth is an extrapolation from beliefs and practices. The social justification is 'not a matter of a special relation between ideas (or words) and objects, but of conversation, of social practice' (Rorty 1980, p. 170).

In everyday practice we contrast less-informed with better-informed audiences or distinguish between past audiences and future audiences. In principle we can distinguish between what is held to be true and what is true. Habermas argues that languages offer the possibility of distinguishing between what is true and what we hold to be true. In his book *Truth and Justification* he underlines that the correspondence idea of truth takes account of the notion of unconditional validity, which – in

---

is warranted or not depends on whether the majority of one's cultural peers say it is warranted or unwarranted. Putnam states that the fact that our beliefs hang together – supposing they do – does not give an indication that they are true.

his eyes – is a fundamental meaning of the truth predicate.[11] Habermas states that '[w]hat we hold to be true has to be defendable on the basis of good reasons, not merely in a different context but in all possible contexts, that is at any time against anybody', but he continues; 'However, this does not mean that it is also true for this reason' (Habermas 2000, p. 46).

Thus, the truth of our beliefs about the world must be independent of our believing it. Understanding cannot be reached unless the discussants refer to a single objective world. The supposition of an objective world fulfils a functional requirement for our communication and coordination. Acting subjects have to cope with *the* world they cannot avoid, being realists in the context of their life world.[12] However, it is not a correct representation of the world but a supposition of a single world that is built into the communicative use of language (Habermas 2000, p. 41).[13]

This points to the difference between truth and justification. To contrast justification and truth is to say that a belief may be justified but not true. Thus, in the Habermasian understanding the explanation of truth needs a justification-transcendent element. Rorty and Davidson oppose this view and believe that there is a lot to be said about justification but only little about truth. In their view an inquiry never transcends social practice. The only goal of inquiry can be justification. We quote Davidson at length:

> We know many things, and will learn more; what we will never know for certain is which of the things we believe is true. Since it is neither a visible target nor recognizable, when achieved, there is no point in calling truth a goal. Truth is not a value, so the 'pursuit of truth' is an empty enterprise unless it means only that it is often worthwhile to increase our confidence in our beliefs, by collecting further evidence or checking our calculations.
> From the fact that we will never be able to tell which of our beliefs are true, pragmatists conclude that we may as well identify our best researched, most successful beliefs with the true ones, and give up the idea of objectivity. (Truth is objective if the truth of a belief or sentence is independent of whether it is justified by all our evidence . . .) But here we have a choice.

---

[11] 'Correspondence, while it is empty as a definition, does capture the thought that truth depends on how the world is and this should be enough to discredit most epistemic and pragmatic theories.' (Davidson 2000, p. 73)

[12] It is possible to have a belief only if one knows that beliefs may be true or false. I can believe that it is a cloudy day because I know that whether it is cloudy or not does not depend on my belief or that of others. It is up to nature. What is up to us is what we mean by our words.

[13] 'All languages offer the possibility of distinguishing between what is true and what we hold to be true. The supposition of a common objective world is built into the pragmatics of every single linguistic usage. And the dialogue roles of every speech situation enforce a symmetry in participant perspectives' (Habermas 2000).

Instead of giving up the traditional view that truth is objective, we can give up the equally traditional view (to which pragmatists adhere) that truth is a norm, something for which to strive. I agree with the pragmatists that we can't consistently take truth to be both objective and something to be pursued. But I think that they would have done better to cleave to a view that counts truth as objective, but pointless as a goal.' (Davidson quoted in Bilgrami 2000, p. 245).

Habermas (2002) does not support this claim. From his perspective justificatory practices are guided by an idea of truth that transcends the justificatory context in question. Thus, truth may not be assimilated to justified assertibility. Argumentation can lead only to a consensus when it is guided by truth in a context-independent way. Truth does not depend on how well a proposition can be justified. Justification is a context-relative notion as one justifies to a given audience and the same justification will not work to other audiences. Well-justified assertion can turn out to be false. Coherence depends on practices of justification. These practices are guided by standards that change from time to time.

2. CONCEPTS OF TRUTH RELATED TO ECONOMIC POLICY ADVICE

The idea of economic progress can be understood without a correspondence theory of truth. Thus, why should it matter whether economic policy advisors have a correspondent theory of truth, follow a coherent approach or a pragmatic understanding or neglect completely the philosophical issues? And is it relevant whether scientists consider justification within their community – or dominant parts thereof – as sufficient or whether they aim at a context-transcendent objective truth? After all, physicians disagree on the logical status of quarks and this does not influence their research.

First, in economics, scientists disagree on what their practice should look like and have often turned to philosophers for methodological guidance in the past (Wendt 2002, p. 48). Second, economists deal with social kinds that do not exist independently from human beings.[14] Third, the methods of natural science with their emphasis on causal mechanism must be replaced in economics – at least partially – with the methods of

---

[14] Social kinds are social functions such as money, social structures such as household, the state and the working class, institutions such as the central bank together with abstract kinds such as language and conventions.

interpretation (human behavior). Thus, the issue of truth cannot be avoided simply by shifting the debate to practical criteria.[15]

Even if the issue of truth cannot be avoided, maybe it can be reformulated. As Backhouse 1997 states:

> Though we may not be able to say whether economic knowledge is true, either the concept of truth cannot be tied down sufficiently tightly, or simply because the world is too complicated for such a goal to be feasible, we can ask whether economics is being pursued in a way that is likely to lead to progress. (Backhouse 1997, pp. 105–6)

Both the pragmatist and the Popperian tradition point toward progress as a kind of substitute for the concept of truth. Similar to Peirce, Popper locates scientific progress in methods and understands it as increasing truthlikeness.

One of the best known essays on methodology is the article from Milton Friedman on 'The Methodology of Positive Economics' (1953). Friedman wrote in this famous essay:

> [T]heory is to be judged by its predictive power for the class of phenomena which it is intended to 'explain'. Only factual evidence can show whether it is 'right' or 'wrong' or, better, tentatively 'accepted' as valid, or 'rejected' . . . [T]he only relevant test of the validity of a hypothesis is comparison of its prediction with experience. (Friedman 1953, pp. 8–9)

What counts is scientific progress measured as the 'development of a "theory" or "hypothesis" that yields valid and meaningful . . . predictions about phenomena not yet observed' (Friedman 1953, p. 7). However, the implicit assumption that success in the past ensures success in the future is obviously problematic. Otherwise predictive power is only an ex-post evaluation criterion. Theories may not even be intended as factual statements about reality. From an economist's point of view it may be sufficient to explain the methods of inquiry and theory selection, to explain what counts as success or progress in economic knowledge. In the approach of Friedman, where only predictions matter, the realism of the assumptions in economic models becomes entirely irrelevant.

But economists refer their claims not only to their internal reference group but also to audiences such as the media, the uninformed public and economic politicians. We do not follow the point of McCloskey (1985) that economists have two attitudes towards discourse, the explicit and the

---

[15] It seems to be a rather inner-methodological debate whether economics follows or should follow methodological rules (Hands 2000).

implicit, according to which explicitly, that is in official discourses, they refer to scientific rules, whereas implicitly they behave differently.[16] This is only an intuition and it needs to be verified empirically whether such a dichotomy exists in the behavior of economists.

For pragmatists and critical theories, theory and practice are not separate fields but rather interwoven. Rationality not so much pertains to the extent of knowledge one possesses but rather to 'how speaking and acting subjects acquire and use knowledge' (Habermas 1984, p. 11). Critical theory points to the necessity to focus on argumentation practices. The Habermasian idea is that it is important to draw a distinction between the perspective of *participants* and *observers* and that the concept of truth is Janus-faced as it plays two pragmatic roles in action contexts and in rational discourses (Habermas 1999). In action contexts, what dominates is behavioral certainty, but in rational discourses, what counts is discursively justified assertibility.

One has to avoid an exclusive participant point of view and an exclusive observer perspective. When we give up the concept of truth as a perspective from nowhere, 'we can do no better than move back and forth between different standpoints, playing one off against the other' (McCarthy and Hoy 1994, p. 81).

Economic science itself is a social activity. Scientific results have social consequences. For Dewey it was obvious that social sciences have failed to solve social problems because they have attempted to isolate problems similar to the ways in which physicists try to isolate a physical system. Mere understanding of reality is, for Dewey, never an end of inquiry (Putnam 1994). The problem he sees is the demand that science is value-free. As the data, hypotheses and problems of social sciences concern human behavior that distinction is untenable in science. When economists become policy advisors or advocate particular politics, the claim of Dewey to make explicit their underlying ideologies seems to be useful. Dewey argued in his *Logic of Inquiry* that without systematic formulation of ruling ideas, inquiry is kept in the domain of opinion and action in the realm of conflict.

---

[16] 'The word for it is Sprachethik, speech morality, the ethics of conversation. That the word comes from a hive of Marxist fuzzies in Frankfurt am Main should not be alarming, for it is liberalism incarnate: Don't lie; pay attention, don't sneer, cooperate. Don't shout; let other people talk; be open-minded; explain yourself when asked: don't resort to violence or conspiracy in aid of your idea' (McCloskey 1994, p. 99).

3. ACCOUNTABILITY

Logical positivists have argued for a sharp fact-value dichotomy: scientific economic statements are empirically verifiable, while values in economic policy are unverifiable. However, this assumes that there is a *method of verification*. Furthermore, epistemic values such as coherence and simplicity that are broadly accepted in economics cannot be reduced to physical notions and are not governed by precise rules. Putnam argues that 'we should recognize that all values, including the cognitive ones, derive their authority from our idea of human flourishing and our idea of reason' (1990, p. 141).

There exist different discourse communities that share particular beliefs and diverge on others. What kind of problems emerge when truth claims emerging in one community are justified vis-à-vis another discourse community?

When economists make their world views explicit and refer to the ontological connotations of their truth claims they can take realist or anti-realist positions.[17] Economic policy advisors may claim that their models are useful fictions or instruments for organizing their research but that they do not refer to real structures. This would weaken the strength of their policy suggestions. Or they may claim that their theoretical approaches are approximations to truth. A coherence theory will allow a number of further justification criteria. We may assess 'theories as to their usefulness, convenience, tractability, fruitfulness, applicability and efficiency rather than their truth and falsehood. In consequence, in an empirical test, one tests the usefulness and applicability of scientific theories, not their truth' (Mäki 1998, p. 254).

The social relationship between economists and economic politicians can be specified in epistemic terms in terms of the perspectives taken by the policy advisors and the economic politicians. These different standpoints cannot be resolved by expert information provided by economic policy advisors to an ignorant policy-maker but have to be dealt with practically in reflective practices. Pragmatism and critical social science argue that it is important to keep reflective practices open to the variety of possible perspectives (Bohman 2001). This practical turn avoids providing the single true approach that can be the basis for economic policy decisions. Technocratic approaches model the economist as an engineer who searches for truth and an optimal solution to a specific problem. This abstract model of economics in a closed

---

[17] Anti-realists in economics may well be common-sense realists.

setting does not work in a context of social relationships. Even truth-seeking economic politicians trying to see the world from the perspective of economic science have to do it in their own categories.

An alternative is to define the work of economic policy advisors through its social consequences. By making explicit the terms of social cooperation between economists and other social actors, the practice of economics would be reshaped. Rather than the search for an objective theoretical unification that explains the truth, the practical context would be the starting point for a debate on the agenda-setting of economic research. This creates a different context of social inquiry and should increase the reflective knowledge of all agents involved.

The economic politicians who ask for economic advice and do not have the formal skills of economists either have to trust the advice of economists or they have to make economic science accountable. The possibility to critically scrutinize the activities of economics arises from the indexicality of such an idea as truth (Rehg 2004).

The *fallibilism* of inquiry in economic science deals with controversial truth claims. However, fallibilism in economics might not be sufficient for the external evaluation of economic policy-makers. Also goals of research and the problem selection of economic scientists can be questioned. Furthermore, economists argue on all kinds of policy questions – not only the ones of their research field – and this implies a gap between their methodological pronouncements and their actual practice (McCloskey 1985).

What is the relevant context of justification? From the point of view of participants, standards for the rational acceptability of propositions may well be justified, while from the view of observers the distinction between economic convictions and economic theories might call for more caution. In the Habermasian concept of truth the idea of truth is something universal and context transcendent. Thus, an enhanced mutual understanding among an increased number of persons and groups would not be enough. We can never know that the agreement of all competent judges in economics operating under ideal epistemic conditions is something we have attained. Unknowability and unconditionality go hand in hand.

> While we have no standards of truth wholly independent of particular languages and practices, it remains that 'truth' serves as an idea of reason with respect to which we can criticize the standards we inherit and learn to see things in a different way. Neither the particularity of context-immanence nor the universality of context-transcendence of truth claims can be ignored without doing violence to our actual practices of truth. We can, and typically do, make contextually conditioned and fallible claims to objective truth. (McCarthy and Hoy 1994, p. 39)

Economists' justifications are often seen somehow intrinsically superior. Critical theory (for example McCarthy and Hoy 1994) undermines this epistemic privilege arguing that their modes of justification are context-dependent themselves. Truth claims are not separated from social practices of justification even though they cannot be reduced to any particular set thereof. There is a practical necessity to rely on what is held to be true for both groups, economic politicians and economists. Economic policy cannot function if it persistently falsifies explanations of economics and fundamentally questions advice of economists. Economic policies deal with the world in a rather direct way and have to rest on certainties and on an unqualified trust in the knowledge of people considered experts.

Only on the reflexive level of argumentation – where only arguments count – is this pragmatic certainty suspended. In argumentations discourse-participants who try to convince themselves of the justification of a truth claim have to suppose a single objective world.[18] As social kinds do not present themselves to the senses as observables in physics, conceptual analysis may be called for even more. Either policy-makers have their own context-dependent criteria of truth or they follow specific criteria of the economic community (coherency, empirical evidence, predictive power). The common sense attitude within the economic community that knowledge is fallible is no substitute for reflexivity in argumentation. Furthermore, the quest for truth may help economic politicians to recognize not only the interests and values of economists but also *bullshitting* from economists.[19]

CONCLUSION

Does a discussion of concepts of truth have any consequences for economics and or economic policy?

Our answer is ambiguous: in a particular way nothing would be changed. Neoclassical economists would continue to study rational agents, neo-Keynesian economists would include a few rigidities, post-Keynesian scientists stress the importance of uncertainty in their

---

[18] Mäki (2001) underlines that ontological convictions play a role in the theory choice of economists. Ontological core principles of economics define the boundaries of a research field and have social consequences.

[19] Someone who gets published in some academic journal just because he is prepared to use the jargon in the right way and not aiming to get things right (Bilgrami 2000).

analysis and heterodox economists would consider social kinds in their approaches. And economic politicians would be inclined to believe the advice of economists with whom they share values or an ideology.

But by making the truth claims and the standards of justification explicit, economic policy-makers would gain more criteria for evaluation. If economic policy-makers and the public want to evaluate the economic policy advice given by economists, the quest for truth might be helpful in order to distinguish between the economic suggestions. Since what economists and economic policy-makers see is conditioned by how they see it, their understanding of truth deserves attention.

Knowledge of the world views of economists and what role truth plays in their minds is of relevance for evaluating their policy suggestions as it is a decisive form of accountability.

First, making the concept of truth explicit might block *a priori* arguments against engaging in certain kinds of economic research. The quest to argue the concepts of truth in economics explicitly takes the argument for plurality of methods seriously. Second, the quest for the standards of truth claims might reveal patterns of domination and power behind enlightenment. Third, the difference between rational assertibility and truth in economic theory shows up in assertions that are not well-justified but relevant in economic policy. Also perspectives that are excluded from economic discourse, contributions that are suppressed, point to the difference between rational assertibility and truth.

In economic policy advice we cannot lose the regulative idea of truth, otherwise the practice of justifications of economic arguments would lose its point of orientation. The social norms of the scientific community of economists can be described from the perspective of a sociological observer or can be studied by rational choice approaches of the theory of science. However, this is not sufficient, because how would it be possible to distinguish between conventional practices and justified means? Without reference to truth, the justification standards would provide no possibility of self-corrections. They would be social facts, no more than that, and they could claim validity only for *us* – the relevant justification community – that is the neoclassical, the neo-Keynesian, the heterodox economists and the neoliberal or alternative economic politicians or whoever.

REFERENCES

Backhouse, R. (1997), *Truth and Progress in Economic Knowledge*, Cheltenham, UK and Lyme, US: Edward Elgar.

Bohman, J. (2001), 'Participants, Observers, and Critics: Practical Knowledge, Social Perspectives and Critical Pluralism', in W. Rehg and J. Bohman (eds), *Pluralism and the Pragmatic Turn*, Cambridge: MIT Press, pp. 87–114.

Bilgrami, A. (2000), 'Is Truth a Goal of Inquiry? Rorty and Davidson on Truth', in R.B. Brandom (ed.) (2000), *Rorty and His Critics*, pp. 242–62.

Brandom, R.B. (ed.) (2000), *Rorty and His Critics*, Oxford: Blackwell Publishers.

Davidson, D. (2000), 'Truth Rehabilitated', in R.B. Brandom (ed.) (2000), *Rorty and His Critics*, pp. 65–74.

Davis, J.B., D. Wade Hands and U. Mäki (eds) (1998), *The Handbook of Economic Methodology*, Cheltenham, UK and Northampton, MA, USA: Edward Elgar.

Dewey, J. (1948), *Reconstruction in Philosophy*, Boston: Enlarged Edition Press.

Dewey, J. (2002), *Die Theorie der Forschung*, Frankfurt am Main: Suhrkamp.

Friedman, M. (1953), 'The Methodology of Positive Economics', in *Essays in Positive Economics*, Chicago: University of Chicago Press, pp. 3-43.

Habermas, J. (1984), *The Theory of Communicative Action*, Vol. 1, translated by T. McCarthy (*Theorie des Kommunikativen Handelns*), Boston, USA: Beacon.

Habermas, J. (1999), *Wahrheit und Rechtfertigung*, Frankfurt am Main: Suhrkamp.

Habermas, J. (2000), 'Richard Rorty's Pragmatic Turn', in R.B. Brandom (ed.), *Rorty and His Critics*, pp. 31–56.

Habermas, J. (2001), 'From Kant's "Ideas" of Pure Reason to the "Idealizing" Presuppositions of Communicative Action: Reflections on the Detranscendentalized "Use of Reason"', in W. Rehg and J. Bohman (eds), *Pluralism and the Pragmatic Turn*, pp. 11–40.

Hands, D. Wade (2001a), *Reflections without Rules. Economic Methodology and Contemporary Science Theory*, Cambridge: Cambridge University Press.

Hands, D. Wade (2001b), 'Economic methodology is dead – long live economic methodology: thirteen theses on the new economic methodology', in *Journal of Economic Methodology*, **8** (1), 49–63.

Mäki, U. (1998), 'Instrumentalism', in J.B. Davis, D. Wade Hands and U. Mäki (eds), *The Handbook of Economic Methodology*, pp. 253–6.

Mäki, U. (2001), 'The Way the World Works (www): Towards an Ontology of Theory Choice', in U. Mäki (ed.) (2001), *The Economic World View*, Cambridge: Cambridge University Press pp. 369–90.

McCarthy, T. and D. Hoy (1994), *Critical Theory*, Oxford, UK: Blackwell.

McCloskey, N.D. (1985), *The Rhetoric of Economics*, Madison: University of Wisconsin Press.

McCloskey, N.D. (1994), *Knowledge and Persuasion in Economics*, Cambridge: Cambridge University Press.

Peirce, C.S. (1878), 'How to Make Our Ideas Clear', in P.P. Weiner (ed.) (1966), *Charles S. Peirce. Selected Writings*, Dover: New York.

Putnam, H. (1981), *Reason, Truth and History*, Cambridge: Cambridge University Press

Putnam, H. (1985), *Pragmatism. An Open Question*, Oxford: Blackwell Press.

Putnam, H. (1990), *Realism with a Human Face*, Boston: Harvard University Press.

Putnam, H. (1994), *Words & Life ed. James Conant*, Boston: Harvard University Press.

Rehg, W. and J. Bohman (eds) (2001), *Pluralism and the Pragmatic Turn. The Transformation of Critical Theory*, Boston: MIT Press.

Rehg, W. (2004), 'Communicative rationality as the basis of economic science: contextualist implications of the pragmatic turn in critical social theory' in P. Mooslechner, H. Schuberth and M. Schürz (eds), forthcoming in this volume, 62–83.

Rorty, R. (1979), *Philosophy and the Mirror of the Nature Princeton: Princeton University Press*

Rorty, R. (2000), 'Universality and Truth', in R.B. Brandom (ed.), *Rorty and His Critics*, pp. 1–31.

Wendt, A. (2002), 'Social Theory of International Politics', in *Cambridge Studies in International Relations.*

Wellmer, A. (1998), *Endgames: The Irreconcilable Nature of Modernity*, Cambridge, MA: MIT Press.

7. Macroeconomics, Pragmatism and Cognitive Scarcity: Keynes Should Have Read C.S. Peirce on Probability and Evolutionary Complexity

James R. Wible[*]

C.S. Peirce (whose maturer work Keynes does not cite), might be worthy of at least a bibliographic reference by an author who is setting up a category of probability. (Wilson 1923, pp. 436–7)

1. INTRODUCTION

Nearly seventy years have passed since John Maynard Keynes's 1936 founding treatise on macroeconomics, the *General Theory*, first appeared. Macroeconomics at seventy is a very different discipline than what it was when Keynes's work originally appeared. After nearly seventy years, we can again ask, How far have we come? Rather than focusing mostly on the question of the theoretical generality of that founding work of macroeconomics, our intellectual energies will be redirected to the question of scientific status. Did macroeconomics at any stage ever attain the status of a science? Alternatively, did Keynes or any of the various subsequent schools of macroeconomics including their policy implications reach the level of being scientific? Is this even the best way to conceptualize the scientific problems facing macroeconomics?

In answering the question regarding the scientific status of macroeconomics, several steps need to be taken. First, an overview of the history of the macroeconomics of the past seventy years is required. This history will show how pluralistic macroeconomics has always been as a

[*] Department of Economics, Whittemore School of Business and Economics, University of New Hampshire, Durham, New Hampshire, 03857. Please direct any comments to jrwible@cisunix.unh.edu.

discipline. Second, it will be argued that the persistent pluralism of macroeconomics is inconsistent with almost all varieties of positive economic methodology. To state it more strongly, one might argue on the basis of positive economic methodology of science that macroeconomics has failed as a scientific activity. Third, an alternative methodology and philosophy of science unfamiliar to most macroeconomists will be explored. This alternative view is the pragmatist conceptions of science and of an evolutionary world in the views of the American philosopher Charles Sanders Peirce. Fourth, E.B. Wilson's suggestion that Keynes should have considered Peirce's conception of evolutionary complexity will be set forth. The argument will be that Peirce's views, as recommended by Wilson, provide a much needed evolutionary framework for macroeconomics. Then an illustration of a scientific conflict in recent macroeconomics will be explored in the context of a Peircean vision of an evolving social and economic world. This conflict concerns the role of rational expectations in monetary models of the exchange rate. The argument will be that rational expectations as typically interpreted in mainstream macroeconomics is seriously flawed from a Peircean pragmatist conception of economic science.[1]

2. SEVENTY YEARS OF MACROECONOMICS: KEYNES AND THE CLASSICS ONCE MORE

Macroeconomics began with Keynes's famous claim that the economic circumstances of the Great Depression could not be addressed by the economic theory of his teachers. Keynes termed this view 'classical' even though the classical period in the history of economic thought had ended more than half a century earlier. Neoclassical economics as developed in the 1870s was a revolution in microeconomics but not in an overall perspective of how the whole economy functioned. Keynes claimed that the Great Depression was essentially an anomaly for the classical understanding of the economy requiring a fresh start from economic theorists. His *General Theory* was advanced as a totally new theory

---

[1] Readers should know that this chapter is a product of more than a decade-long conversation regarding macroeconomics and Peircean pragmatism with my colleague Michael Goldberg at the University of New Hampshire. Goldberg and his frequent co-author, Roman Frydman, have continually faced the limitations imposed by rational expectations in models of exchange rate patterns. Their area of research, monetary models of exchange rate dynamics, illustrates how a theoretical concept like rational expectations within the context of an outmoded conception of economic science can hamper scientific research in economics.

which relegated the classical view of the overall economy from his teachers to the status of a special case.

Without going into the theoretical details to a great degree, we now know that the first challenge to Keynes came from John Hicks. Within a year of the appearance of the *General Theory*, Hicks (1937) offered a framework which proposed a more general model from which to view both Keynes's theory and the classical views of his teachers. The now famous review by Hicks in *Econometrica* in 1937 created what came to be known as the IS/LM equilibrium framework. Using that model Hicks claimed that Keynes's work was no general theory. Hicks offered an equilibrium framework inspired by the mathematics of multiple equation systems and the mechanistic general equilibrium vision of Leon Walras. In Hicks's theory, the two equation, IS/LM version of an economy of three aggregate markets could be reduced to just two markets and two equations. Mathematically, this theoretical approach was more general than Keynes's theory. After Hicks, his insights about mathematical macro models led to a succession of ever more sophisticated versions of both classical and Keynesian theories of the economy. Indeed, much of the history of the past seventy years of macroeconomics can be reconstructed as an ever escalating mathematical and econometric arms race between successive versions of Keynesian and classical theories of macroeconomic performance. Even this perspective can be qualified by those who maintain that Keynes questioned the relevance of equilibrium theories in his *General Theory*. Keynes may have used equilibrium theory like a mathematician uses the idea of disproof. When a proof is impossible, perhaps a disproof of an opposing concept is the best that can be achieved. With this interpretation, Keynes's development of an equilibrium model in his *General Theory* should not be mistaken for the idea that he believed that patterns of macroeconomic phenomena in the real economy are in equilibrium. Here an equilibrium model couched within a theory of non-equilibrium patterns of evolving order would be used as a scientific benchmark which would be accompanied by additional theoretical claims regarding the limits of equilibrium macro theories for analyzing actual real world events.[2]

Meanwhile, macroeconomists of a classical bent took up the theoretical opportunity originally revealed by Hicks to look for flaws in

---

[2] Clearly the Keynesian and classical traditions were the dominant polarities in mainstream macroeconomics, but other intellectual currents were recognizable as well. On the left, often advocating a larger role for government in the economy, were the Post Keynesians with distinctly different versions in Britain and the United States. And on the right, criticizing a larger role for government, were the Austrians who have made something of a resurgence in recent decades.

the Keynesian theoretical apparatus. Hicks's multiple market, multiple equation approach provided an avenue of rebuttal for Keynes's critics. Hicks's more mathematically general model provided an opportunity for Keynes's classical adversaries to argue that depression-like features of an economy were special circumstances. Correction of such flaws could provide an opportunity to make a macro model function with classical rather than Keynesian properties. In this respect, Keynesian models could be intellectually hijacked and much of the Keynesian theory and econometric progress could be turned on its head to again argue that a classical view was more general. Shortly after Hicks, Pigou (1943) developed a wealth effect in the consumption function, later known as the Pigou effect, to show that an IS/LM economy in a depression experiencing deflation would self-adjust toward full employment. Pigou's core insight about the equilibrating consequences of the wealth effect on consumption was soon generalized to a classical model of the whole economy in Patinkin's (1965) *Money, Interest and Prices*. With wealth effects in the goods, money and bond markets, Patinkin offered a more generalized version of an IS/LM model that would be forced back to full employment as deflation increased the wealth of individuals participating in those markets. The clear implication of the Patinkin model was that Keynes's theory and model, as presented in the *General Theory*, was a special case of the Patinkin model of a classically functioning economy. Almost simultaneously with Patinkin, in the 1950s, Milton Friedman (1970) offered a contrasting vision of a classically functioning economy in providing a more general restatement of the Quantity Theory of Money, something that Keynes had tried but failed to do in his *Treatise on Money* authored a few years before his *General Theory*. Friedman also succeeded in arguing that the Keynesian theories of consumption, money demand and the Phillips Curve were not very general either. Because Friedman's theoretical critiques were accompanied by often massive amounts of historical statistics and reconstructed interpretations of economic history, Friedman's work advanced the argument that Keynesians were not very progressive empirically either.

From the 1950s through to the early 1970s, various versions of Keynesian economics were ascendant as their model of the economy grew from Samuelson's Keynesian cross, to the IS/LM model, to the AS/AD model, to the highly sophisticated FED-Penn-MIT macroeconometric model with hundreds of forecasting equations. In all of these models, Keynesians tended to take a conception of equilibrium as a state of rest in the patterns of movement of macroeconomic variables. They argued that recessions and depressions were special equilibria that did not occur very often. They also argued that fiscal and/or monetary policies could be used to ameliorate the worst aspects of recessions, crises in financial institutions and financial market panics. Until the late 1960s, Keynesian theories and policies were clearly ascendant in the field of macroeconomics taken as a whole. Critics like Patinkin and Friedman were tolerated more than accepted for their contributions. Much of this changed with three significant episodes of inflation and unemployment in the 1960s and 1970s. The economic consequences of the Vietnam War and two OPEC oil embargoes in the early and mid-1970s led to economic phenomena which the Keynesian models were ill-equipped to handle. As the Great Depression was advanced by Keynes as an anomaly for the classical theory of his Cambridge teachers, so these three episodes of inflation and unemployment were advanced by Friedman and other classically minded economists as anomalies for the extant Keynesian models of that era. While Keynesian theorists of that day were on the verge of advancing a disequilibrium interpretation of the *General Theory* as a way to save Keynes's reputation, classical macro views soon escalated beyond those of Friedman and other monetarists. Classically minded macroeconomists argued that Keynesian models could not accommodate the obvious inflationary dynamics that so dominated the American economy from the mid-1960s to the mid-1980s. It was Milton Friedman (1968) who led the critique by emphasizing the role of adaptive inflationary expectations in explaining the protracted adjustment process to a demand or supply shock to the economy. This was the debate surrounding the Friedman–Phelps expectations-augmented Phillips Curve with the Monetarists maintaining that the classical properties of the long-run Phillips Curve were more enduring than those of the Keynesian properties of the short-run Phillips Curve.

The next step was the shift from adaptive to rational expectations taken by a new, younger generation of macroeconomists who were led by the contributions of Robert Lucas and Thomas Sargent (1981a) and J.F. Muth (1961). At one point, Lucas and Sargent (1981b) thought that macroeconomics as a discipline was so bad that the whole discipline needed to start over and return to the classical ideas of Keynes's teachers in the 1930s. The macroeconomic ideas of Lucas and Sargent coalesced into a distinct school of macroeconomic thought by 1980 or so, a view called the 'New Classical' macroeconomics. There were other theoretical propositions in New Classical economics than rational expectations. They assumed a notion of market clearing and a view of aggregate supply often called the Lucas Supply Curve. The aggregate supply curve would be vertical giving the economy classical properties if the agents made no forecasting mistakes, otherwise the aggregate supply curve would be positively sloped as long as agents made errors. This had the effect of suggesting that Keynesian theory and models were focused on agents making patterns of systematic, irrational mistakes. Keynesian macro was portrayed as the economics of something akin to collective insanity. The New Classical macro was probably best known for its classical policy ineffectiveness propositions that publicly announced demand management policies would be completely offset by the utility and profit-maximizing responses of agents with rational expectations. Economic policies simply could not matter in a pure New Classical economy.

In spite of the extreme claims that New Classical macro theorists advanced in favor of their own vision of the economy and against Keynesian views, the New Classical school soon ran into its own difficulties. In the early years of that school, its proponents advanced an empirical claim for its theory and models. New Classicals claimed that econometric versions of their theoretical models would forecast better than the more elaborate, well-known Keynesian macroeconometric models of that era. Unfortunately, this prediction regarding the success of New Classical macroeconometric models failed. [3] Their models forecasted no better in aggregate with critics making even stronger negative claims. Soon one of the founders of New Classical macro, Robert Lucas, realized the inadequacy of their models. Lucas advocated shifting from monetary mistakes or misperceptions of economic agents as the main mechanism of cyclical macroeconomic phenomena to supply shocks. New Classicals had advanced the thesis that monetary misperceptions were sufficient to model the business cycle as observed in most industrial economies of the West. Criticized by Keynesians and others as being too weak, New Classicals later abandoned the monetary misperceptions rationale in favor of real shocks to the economy as an explanation of business cycles. This new version of classical macroeconomics became known as Real Business Cycle Theory.[4] In their models, supply shocks could set off chains of economic responses which implied fluctuations in economic activity on the order of magnitude of those observed in actual economic activity. Rather than performing econometric tests of these models, real business cycle theorists talked of calibration. Their aim was not to forecast business cycles, but rather to calibrate the parameters of their models so as to provide accurate simulations of the data in macroeconomic time series.

---

[3] Some of the issues of the empirical failures of New Classical macroeconomics are discussed by Snowdon, Vane and Wynarczyk (1994, p. 236).
[4] An overview of Real Business Cycle Theory can be found in Snowdon, Vane, and Wynarczyk (1994) and Romer (2001).

While the three successive versions of classical macroeconomics from the 1960s through the 1990s – Monetarism, New Classical and Real Business Cycle theories – often seemed to gain the upper hand, by the turn of the 21st century, another version of Keynesian economics seemed once again to gain ascendancy. It had become known as New Keynesian macroeconomics. [5] New Keynesians, like previous generations of Keynesians, thought the economy functioned in an adaptive manner with significant patterns of persistence in some of the most important macroeconomic time series variables. Rather than objecting to the theory of rational expectations, most New Keynesians simply accepted rational expectations as an econometric methodology for modeling expectations. In order to restore the adaptive functioning of the economy, New Keynesians needed to find other mechanisms or processes to slow down the speed of adjustment imagined by rational expectations theorists. Here the New Keynesians took a page from both the older micro foundations theorists and the younger rational expectations theorists. New Keynesians developed the thesis that agents in the economy found it in their self-interest to slow down market processes. As long as agents are free to make tacit or explicit mutually accommodating arrangements which restrain future decisions and behaviors, the macro economy does not need to function with the extreme classical properties of any of the classical visions of the economy. New Keynesians developed theories of implicit and explicit contracts in which workers and firms, borrowers and lenders, and consumers and retailers work out many mutual reciprocal patterns of behavioral interaction which are in the interest of both parties to an economic transaction. [6] By their very nature, such arrangements persist for significant periods of time, typically they are revised piecemeal rather than wholesale, and whenever wholesale instantaneous changes occur, they are viewed as breaches of trust and credibility. In the New Keynesian view, there are only a few pockets of the economy which function in a classical fashion. [7] Usually it is the financial and commodity markets where rational expectations and classical properties are thought to hold. Even this qualification needs to be amended with recent research

---

[5] For a collection of New Keynesian Essays see Mankiw and Romer (1991). Stiglitz and Weiss (1981) present a view in which imperfect information leads to credit rationing in the market for bank loans.

[6] For an analysis of some of the philosophical issues posed by the theories of implicit contracts and rational expectations see Wible (1990).

[7] Of course during episodes of significant inflation or in the very long run, even Keynesians maintain that the economy has important classical properties.

on behavioral theories of financial activity. [8] Classical aspects of economic activity are once again viewed as the special case.

More recently mainstream macro theory has turned to the question of long-run economic growth. Growth theory was mostly a complement to the mainstream macroeconomics of the 1950s and 1960s. Robert Solow's growth model making creative use of the time derivatives of a neoclassical production function mostly led to a dead end. Long-run economic growth could be described but largely not explained. The famous Solow residual, which identified that share of GDP growth which could not be attributed to the growth of capital and labor, was also itself largely unexplained. Furthermore, the Solow model implied that rich and poor nations would eventually converge to the same growth rate, an optimistic outcome if the most disadvantaged populations on our planet are to have genuine prospects for increasing their material standard of living. The failures of the Solovian model have given rise to the new endogenous growth models investigating other sources of economic growth such as knowledge and human capital. [9] While there have been successes, the new growth theories have not yet resolved the most important issues surrounding our understanding of long-run macro-economic growth.

Beyond the varieties of mainstream Keynesian and Classical versions of macroeconomic activity, the Post Keynesians mentioned previously continue to maintain that important central aspects of Keynes's vision of the economy have never been incorporated into either tradition. Post Keynesians contend that Keynes's concern about the central role of money in an advanced economy has never fully been incorporated into macroeconomics. [10] Much the same could be said for Keynes's conception of uncertainty and the vulnerability of financial markets and institutions to speculative waves of either optimism or pessimism. For Post Keynesians much of the problem is that a rigid, mechanistic equilibrium framework coupled with agents who are well endowed with knowledge about their present and future circumstances obviates the need for money, financial institutions and financial markets. Monetary and financial arrangements are part of the process by which the common sense knowledge of agents gets produced rather than just redistributed. Like Keynes, Post Keynesians emphasize the role of subjective factors in

---

[8] For an extensive survey of the literature on behavioral finance see Barberis and Thaler (2003). Akerlof's (2002) Nobel Prize lecture has recently applied these ideas arguing for a behavioral conception of macroeconomics.

[9] For an overview of recent growth theory see Romer (2001, Chaps 1–3).

[10] See Davidson's (1994) *Post Keynesian Macroeconomic Theory*, Chap. 6.

processes of economic decision making. Individuals are human beings with rational frameworks of description, cognition and analysis couched in contexts of uncertainty and subjective idiosyncrasies. Such individuals will mostly create a stable economic process, but there are interdependencies of information, interpretation and economic prosperity which create the opportunities for cumulative movements away from socially optimal macroeconomic outcomes. Such movements, while a break with the prior pattern of macroeconomic performance, may be orderly, catastrophically disruptive, or disingenuously unpredictable. Austrians, like the Post Keynesians, emphasize the significance of subjectively-minded agents in the economic process and the significant role of money and markets in creating economic knowledge. However, it is market processes rather than government interventionism which would most contribute to the stability of the economy in the Austrian view. They might also disagree that Keynes himself had an adequate conception of the role of subjective factors in economic processes.

3. MACROECONOMICS IS A SCIENTIFIC FAILURE IF YOUR CONCEPTION OF SCIENCE IS POSITIVE ECONOMIC METHODOLOGY

In the history of macroeconomics, there are many episodes where the theoretical debate appears to have moved forward in relation to historical or econometric evidence. There certainly is an appearance of progress in macro itself as schools ebb and flow in relation to rivals with some explaining economic events better than others. One might even fashion a hypothetical case that the overall clash between successive versions of Keynesian and classical theories of the economy has had an important empirical dimension. We can begin with the origin of macroeconomics. As an inaugurating episode of the discipline, the Great Depression can be interpreted as an unexplained macroeconomic event which created an opportunity for new developments in theoretical and applied macroeconomics – Keynes and Keynesian economics. The same could be said for the three episodes of inflation and unemployment in the 1960s and 1970s. Without those extraordinary events, Keynesian economics would have remained ascendant and the successive rise of three versions of classical economics – Monetarist, New Classical and Real Business Cycle theories – would not have occurred. In recent decades, the New Keynesian resurgence would not have been successful, if economic events of the late 1980s and 1990s had not occurred. A return to price stability and near-full employment seemed to restore domestic conditions more amenable to a Keynesian than a classical understanding of the economy.

To the overall rise and fall of macroeconomic schools in an apparent relation to the historical evidence one might also add seeming progress with microfoundations and macroeconometrics. Probably the most successful, classic clash and subsequent winnowing of theories from a scientific perspective was the consumption function research of the 1950s. More than any other episode in the growth of macroeconomic ideas, the creation and subsequent clash of rival theories of consumption mostly took place with newly discovered macroeconomic data in the background. Friedman's (1957) theory of the consumption function really seemed to explain the data better and it provided a more coherent microeconomic understanding of consumer behavior than the theory of Duesenberry. Then Modigliani's theory of the consumption function seemed to incorporate important aspects of Friedman's theory of both short- and long-run consumption.[11] And the theoretical advances were further confirmed by empirical results. A murkier macroeconomic episode than the research on consumption was the conflict over the stability of the money demand function. In the 1970s, dozens of dissertations and hundreds of articles were written on the stability of money demand. It turned out to be less stable than Friedman had contended, but not as unstable as Keynesians had imagined.[12] In hindsight, this result reminds us of the Phillips Curve debate. That debate resulted in the general conclusion that short-run patterns in the macro data have more plasticity and flexibility than long-run patterns which approach classical-like properties for the whole economy.

Another recent development in macroeconomics also might reinforce the view that macroeconomics has advanced in traditional, progressive empiricist fashion. In the past two decades or so, econometrics has created a sub-field mostly focused on empirical problems peculiar to macroeconomics.[13] Macro deals with time series data more than does microeconomics. Furthermore, it has been discovered that the appearance of certain patterns in macro time series data would lead to spurious results if traditional regression or other econometric tools were used. As the dynamic economy is moving through time, it is possible that the time series tracking significant economic variables might become unhinged. A

---

[11] The contributions of Duesenberry and Modigliani are reprinted in Williams and Huffnagle (1969, pp. 79–140).

[12] An interesting survey of the literature can be found in Ericsson (1998).

[13] For an introduction to time series methods, history and the literature see Charemza and Deadman (1997).

shock to the economy may change a previously established macroeconomic trend at a higher or lower level. What is known as a significant 'difference' in the data may appear from one period to the next. Time series techniques allow macroeconomists to search for such differences with what are called co-integration techniques. These new macroeconometric techniques really require the re-estimation of most macroeconomic equations and regressions particularly in the areas of monetary and financial research. In principle, one would hope that time series methods would be analogous to the launching of the Hubble telescope. Pre-time series macroeconometric methods, analogous to earth-based telescopes, seriously restricted the discipline's search for reliable empirical patterns in macroeconomic time series. In theory, the new time series methods, no longer clouded with distorting unrecognized differences in the macro data, should give us a sharper, more accurate picture of the dynamic movements of the most important variables affecting macroeconomic performance. Whether the performance fully matches the promise of the new techniques can be debated.[14]

Of all of the schools of macroeconomics surveyed, only one seems to have decisively disappeared for scientific reasons.[15] Only the New Classical macro theory as proposed around 1980 seems to have fallen off the map of macroeconomics. Its major classical implications and the theory of rational expectations have survived or been assimilated in a restricted way in Real Business Cycle Theory or within New Keynesian economics. But mainstream macroeconomics is much too pluralistic with too many schools to claim scientific status on the basis of conventional conceptions of either empiricism or positive economics. The Friedmanian and Lakatosian views of a dominant victorious school in macro-economics with rivals almost completely vanquished simply has not happened. While New Keynesian economics might appear to be the dominant school of mainstream macroeconomics in the first decade of the 21st century, almost all of the preceding versions of Keynesian and

---

[14] In a comment to this author, editor Helene Schuberth would qualify the optimism expressed regarding time series methods stating that structural vector autoregression techniques 'require strong identifying assumption[s] (e.g. long-run non-neutrality) that give strong priors to the dynamics modeled'. Identification problems are discussed in Bischoff and Belay (2001) and time series modeling problems are reviewed in Ericsson (1998). My own response is that the complexity of testing in time series econometrics has escalated dramatically relative to non-time series econometrics. Metaphorically, the data seems to have gotten the analytical equivalent of cancer since batteries of tests are made in applying time series techniques.

[15] This is apparent in the latest edition of David Romer's (2001) graduate macro theory text which contains a chapter on Real Business Cycle Theory but does not even mention New Classical macroeconomics.

classical economics are yet alive in the discipline including the non-mainstream alternatives of Austrian and Post Keynesian economics.[16]

At this point we can ask whether the overall pattern of the development of macroeconomic thought, theories, models and schools can be described as being scientific. Here, I would like to suggest that, if positive economic methodology is our point of reference, then macroeconomics has failed as a scientific enterprise. If macroeconomics is taken in total ranging over all of the views mentioned previously for the past seventy years including the microfoundations and the new time series macroeconometrics, then I reassert that it would be judged as a failure on scientific grounds. Again, those grounds would be the mostly widely accepted conception of science within the economics profession, Friedman's positive economic methodology. Fifty years ago, in an essay which is still the most famous single methodological piece, Milton Friedman presented the thesis that economics would advance based on a winnowing of theoretical ideas using empirical evidence. He asserted that the major differences among economists could be resolved with the advance of empirical inquiry:

> Positive economics is in principle independent of any particular ethical position or normative judgments . . . Its performance is to be judged by the precision, scope, and conformity with experience of the predictions it yields. In short, positive economics can be, an 'objective' science, in precisely the same sense as any physical science . . .
> I venture the judgment, however, that currently in the Western world, and especially in the United States, differences about economic policy among disinterested citizens derive predominantly from different predictions about the economic consequences of taking action – differences that in principle can be eliminated by the progress of positive economics – rather than from fundamental differences in basic values . . . (Friedman 1953, pp. 4–5)

But macroeconomics has not fully cooperated with the Friedmanian vision of scientific progress. Macroeconomic schools of thought during the past seven decades have advanced and retreated. However, like old soldiers, macroeconomic schools of theory, thought and policy mostly seem to never die – they just fade from view but remain in the background.[17] And some of them are resurrected by younger generations under the guise of a new, advanced level of mathematical or econometric

---

[16] The ideas of Austrian and Post Keynesian economists are not as well-known as they used to be. They seem to have less dialogue with mainstream macroeconomists than two or three decades ago.

[17] As remarked elsewhere in the chapter, the one exception seems to be New Classical macroeconomics which seems to no longer exist, but the assumption of rational expectations seems as entrenched as ever.

modeling. The problem is that macroeconomics has remained much too pluralistic in terms of theory and schools of inquiry to suggest that it has been a success scientifically if positive economics is taken as our benchmark conception of science. The role of evidence, while important in the discipline, has been much weaker than economists' positivistic conceptions of economic science would permit.[18]

The dominance of theory over evidence is not new in the history of economics. The name for this apparent imbalance throughout the past two centuries or so of economics has been termed the Ricardian vice.[19] Certainly there has been a Ricardian-like imbalance in macroeconomics during much of its history. The ebb and flow of macroeconomic schools seems to have been driven more by theoretical issues than the advance of theory in relation to empirical evidence. The complexity of theoretical and applied models has escalated dramatically in advance of macroeconometrics and the quality of the data. Applied empirical macroeconomics is no longer as valued an area of research as it once was. A young theorist wanting to make a first-rate reputation in macroeconomics would most likely put empirical applications at the bottom of his/her list of research priorities. Macroeconomic forecasting and testing is mostly left to economists in government agencies. Again, based on Friedman's criterion from his 'Essay on Positive Economics', macroeconomics as a discipline might be deemed a failure over the past seventy years.

A negative answer regarding the scientific status of macroeconomics cannot be fully resolved within the mainstream methodology of economic science. Every mainstream school of macroeconomics of either the Keynesian or classical varieties has adopted some version of a positive economic methodology of science. An alternative conception of science is needed which may help reframe the question of the scientific status of macroeconomics. This prompts one to ask: what is the problem with positive economics and other forms of empiricism? Almost all versions of positive economic science and empiricism have remained committed to the idea that one theory or point of view will achieve greater scientific status than its rival on the basis of best evidence available. One theory, research program, or school of inquiry ultimately will become the winner for an extended period of time. But this view has been questioned in the past few decades. Outside of economics and within the philosophy of science, the notion of a single dominating theory

---

[18] In spite of theoretical pluralism, there have been a number of scientific successes where macroeconomic theory has advanced in relation to significantly informative evidence.

[19] For interesting commentary on the Ricardian vice see Hutchison (1994, p. 109).

has been criticized and relinquished. Instead, an alternative has flourished. The idea that evidence will be insufficient so that no decisive choice can be made purely on empirical grounds between rival theories is known as the Duhem-Quine thesis.[20] In contrast to the Ricardian vice, the Duhem-Quine thesis results from the interrelatedness of theory and fact. What is taken as a fact varies somewhat from one scientific group to another. Evidence which is viewed as informative and potentially decisive in one research tradition may have lesser significance in another. Also, because of the complexity of the interrelationship among theory, fact, data collection and testing methodology, it is difficult to refute an important theoretical construct within its own research program.

Many of these ideas surrounding the Duhem-Quine thesis were incorporated in Imre Lakatos's (1978) conception of scientific research programs. His ideas were applied to macroeconomics more than two decades ago. In the 1970s, a conference was held to see if macroeconomics conformed to Lakatos's conception of scientific progress (Latsis 1976).[21] Progressive research programs were those that were advancing in response to evidence generated within the program while degenerating macroeconomic research programs left important anomalies and puzzles unexplained. However, Lakatos also left us with the notion that one research program ultimately would be viewed as ascendant over its rivals. Supporting evidence for one research program should count against a rival research program. In Lakatos's view it would be rational for a young scientist to choose a progressive macroeconomic research program over scientifically degenerating rivals. But what should the young scientist do if there is no clear winner or dominant school of macroeconomics? Lakatos's research program conception, while helpful in describing what has happened in macroeconomics over the past seventy years, has been unable to explain the persistence of so many alternative views in the discipline. From the vantage point of a Lakatosian embellished interpretation of positive economic methodology, the persistence of theoretical pluralism in macroeconomics would again suggest that macroeconomics has failed as a scientific enterprise.

Fortunately, there has been a great deal of new research on the nature of science. The older views of the methodology and philosophy of science which permeated economic methodology since the early decades of the 19th century have been mostly rejected. The two most dominant views of economic science were based either on British empiricism or

---

[20] For an excellent discussion of the Duhem-Quine thesis see Hands (2001, pp. 96ff.).

[21] One aspect of the conference was to consider whether the Keynesian Revolution was a scientific revolution. See Coats (1969) and Leijonhufvud (1976).

continental metaphysical philosophy. British empiricism was first and some believe best expressed in J.S. Mill's conception of economic theory as inductive generalizations which did not need a separate process of testing. With a continued Ricardian-like imbalance favoring theory over evidence in contemporary economics, there are those who believe that Mill's methodology is still the best conception of economic science. Shifting from Mill's empiricism to the continental philosophies of science, rationalist methodologies of science coming from Kant, Hegel, or other continental philosophers seemed to influence the German Historical School and the Austrians in economics.[22] These are economic perspectives which at best seemed more to function as complements rather than rivals of mainstream classical and neoclassical macroeconomic theories. The full story of the rejection of these two traditional philosophical lines of thinking about science is told by Wade Hands (2001) in his recent methodological treatise, *Reflection without Rules*. In Hands's view, the traditional methodologies of rationalism and empiricism and the more recent Popperian growth of knowledge literature have been superseded with new methodological views. Since scientists are people, one strand of new methodology is that the tools and methods of the social sciences need to be used for a more complete understanding of science as a social process. This has led to sub-fields such as the psychology, sociology, history, and even the economics of science. [23] This same trend has led to the reemergence of another philosophical framework which decades ago had been almost obliterated by the British analytical empiricism of the early and mid-20th century. American pragmatism is now resurgent along with the social science-based approaches to understanding science. Pragmatism will now be explored as a philosophical and methodological context for macroeconomics since Keynes.

4. PEIRCE'S CONCEPTIONS OF PRAGMATISM, INDETERMINISTIC EVOLUTIONARY COMPLEXITY, AND COGNITIVE SCARCITY

While macroeconomics has had significant advances in relation to evidence, it is still quite pluralistic. Many of the rival schools of

---

[22] Hands (2001, pp. 38ff.) provides a discussion of the German Historical School, Austrian economics and the influence of Kant.

[23] My own contributions to the economics of science literature can be found in Wible (1998b).

macroeconomics still claim success relative to an opposing school on the basis of evidence preferred by that theoretical school. However, no school has dominated its rivals for very long. Domination buttressed by supportive evidence is something which would be expected if either positive economic methodology or Lakatos's methodology of scientific research programs were robust conceptions of economic science.[24] But persistent theoretical pluralism is not the only anomaly with mainstream macroeconomics and its alternatives. Besides theoretical pluralism there is another anomaly. In comparison to the other social and natural sciences, economics seems to have an exceptionally rigid conception of reality. Virtually all schools of mainstream macroeconomics which have contributed to the 'Keynes versus the classics' debate have presumed a deterministic conception of economic phenomena. In economic terms, they seem to have assumed a mechanistic, equilibrium interpretation of the overall functioning of the economy and its markets. Even if given a stochastic twist, this largely remains what the philosophers call a deterministic conception of macroeconomic dynamics. The problem is that almost all of the other natural and social sciences and almost every other alternative philosophy of natural and social science has incorporated an evolutionary indeterministic conceptual context of the subject matter being investigated. Furthermore, many of the sciences have added a conception of complexity to the evolutionary indeterminism. The view is that our natural and social worlds have evolved multiple systems and layers of systems of natural and social phenomena which are changing dynamically at various rates of flux.[25] Only the most rigid and unchanging systems can be modeled with the theories and equations of mechanistic equilibrium systems.

While some may see the question of the conception of reality embedded in economic models as another version of the realism of assumptions debate, I would argue that this is not so. The reason is that an indeterministic conception of economic phenomena affects one of the most fundamental conceptions in all of economics. There is a profound difference between a deterministic, mechanistic conception of economic phenomena and one of indeterministic, evolutionary complexity. The problem is scarcity and in particular scarcity of knowledge. From the vantage point of indeterministic evolutionary complexity, existing

---

[24] The reader should know that in an attempt to find out what philosophical framework is most compatible with Friedman's essay, a book has been written claiming that Friedman's positive economics is a version of Dewey's instrumentalism. This would connect Friedman with pragmatism through Dewey. See Hirsch and De Marchi (1990).

[25] For an overview of the literature and conceptions of complexity and complexity in Peirce's writings see Wible (2000a, 2000b).

mainstream theorists including macro theorists have not assumed enough scarcity. In an economy which is assumed to be deterministic and mechanistic, sufficient stability exists in the order and pattern of economic events to assume that search is the most efficient way to increase knowledge. Knowledge is out there and all one has to do is expend resources to look for it. However, in an indeterministic evolutionary economy, a reliance on empiricist search procedures alone leads to a narrow focus on relatively plentiful, highly ordered mechanistic phenomena in a state of equilibrium. This leaves the problem of what can be known when economic phenomena are not so rigidly ordered. Thus information search as the only form of knowledge acquisition becomes *in*efficient in an indeterministic world. In an indeterministic world, machines and mechanistic phenomena are special cases, not general circumstances. Mostly, there is a scarcity of knowledge facing economic agents in an indeterministic economy, particularly when circumstances are so ill-structured that empirical search processes fail. In such circumstances, knowledge must be created rather than discovered. All of this suggests that standard neoclassical micro and mainstream macro have drastically limited the assumption of scarcity in essentially assuming that agents face the informationally rich circumstances of a mechanistic, equilibrium world. Mainstream economists have not assumed enough scarcity in relation to the social and economic world. They have mostly ignored the information summarized in the conceptions of the world and our universe which the other sciences have produced. It seems irrational to ignore so much knowledge about our world from other sciences and consequently to assume such a limited role for scarcity in that world. In contrast to the conceptions of economic phenomena implicit in mainstream macroeconomic models, there is an understanding of science which takes a conception of indeterministic, evolutionary complexity as a starting point for understanding the world. The idea of cognitive scarcity pervades this conception of science, not just material scarcity. Cognitive scarcity may be a more fundamental problem than material scarcity in this view. The conception of science which fits this description is American pragmatism, and most particularly the version of pragmatism created by its most senior founder, Charles Sanders Peirce.

Pragmatism as a distinct school of philosophy began when, in the early 1870s, the original pragmatists met in Cambridge, Massachusetts, in an intellectual seminar they called the Metaphysical Club – most likely in emulation of the Metaphysical Society of London. [26] The most prominent of the members of that club were William James, Charles Sanders Peirce, Chauncey Wright, Oliver Wendell Holmes, and perhaps as many as half a dozen lawyers. Of this group, Wright was the eldest, a philosopher, and he was well-informed on the philosophy of John Stuart Mill. James and Peirce were the ones with the most scientific training. Holmes went on to become one of America's best known jurists and a member of the US Supreme Court. Peirce also was probably the best trained in philosophy and mathematics. Peirce's father, Benjamin, was America's best mathematician, a professor at Harvard and a founder of the Harvard Observatory during the middle of the 19th century. Benjamin tutored Charles in Kantian philosophy and had him read Kant's *Critique of Pure Reason* while he was in high school. Charles was also tutored in logic sometimes until sunrise by his father. The relationship between father and son has been characterized as being similar to the one between James and John Stuart Mill. Like Mill the son, Charles Peirce apparently suffered several breakdowns during his adult life and never achieved the academic status his intellect would have suggested.

American pragmatism is an evolutionary philosophy of science. One of the most important aims of the Metaphysical Club was to integrate the evolutionary views of Darwin with either or both of the two traditional philosophies of science, British empiricism or continental metaphysical philosophy. Finding such an integration almost impossible, Charles Peirce began to synthesize a new philosophy of science. Peirce was the first member of the Metaphysical Club to attempt a written presentation of their emerging point of view. Fragmentary manuscripts remain from the early 1870s, but the most important early record of pragmatism is six now famous essays setting forth the main ideas of pragmatism in the *Popular Science Monthly* in 1878 and 1879.[27] The philosophers typically read the first two essays, the 'Fixation of Belief' and 'How to Make Our Ideas Clear'. These essays set forth a philosophical interpretation of Peirce's method of science. Scientific method is an exploration of conditionally and inferentially constructed conceptions and models of natural and social phenomena. If the conditions under which conceptions, theory and models are constructed closely approximate the conditions being observed in an external world, then an empirical investigation should provide evidence supporting the theory for scientific purposes. Beyond science, pragmatism in Peirce's view is a generalization of the

---

[26] Accounts of the Metaphysical Club can be found in Fisch (1986), Brent (1998), Menand (2001) and Wiener's (1949) *Evolution and the Founders of Pragmatism.*

[27] See the titles of the six articles as listed in the references at the end of this paper.

mind-set of the experimental scientific method to all of thought and life. The scientific method is preferred to other methods of establishing belief such as methods of tenacity, authority and *a priori* reasoning. Peirce uses the term belief rather than knowledge in part because of the broader philosophical implication of pragmatism as a philosophy of inquiry for more than just science.

Commentary on Peirce's essays on pragmatism would be incomplete without an awareness of his contemporaneous achievements in the natural sciences. Four of the essays on pragmatism deal with the methods of science which Peirce practiced first-hand in the 1870s and 1880s. He was part of the first great era of modern scientific investigation. During the same years in which the Metaphysical Club met and he authored the essays on pragmatism, Peirce also conducted world-class research in applied science. He conducted state-of-the-art investigations into the distributions of the stars and the shape of the Milky Way Galaxy and he led the gravity experiments for the US Coast Survey. As a side bar to these investigations, Peirce also conducted smaller studies regarding the accuracy of the instrumentation and the degree of error introduced by a human observer. He also wrote a pathbreaking paper on the theory of errors. The theoretical ideas for these scientific studies were formulated using a high level of advanced calculus and the evidence was collected with understandings of random sampling, statistical inference and the theory of least square errors. In summary, a close investigation of Peirce's applied scientific work in the 1870s shows many of the hallmarks of modern scientific inquiry: (1) applied mathematical models of the phenomena, (2) randomized experimental procedures with specialized instrumentation, (3) data collection and reduction of data, (4) considerations of inferential statistics, (5) use of the logic of hypothesis formation and testing, and (6) a conception of a community of inquirers doing similar research.

Combining an awareness of Peirce's applied science and philosophy in the 1870s suggests some of the most important features of his overall system of scientifically motivated pragmatism were:

1. World-class, state-of-the-art contributions in applied science in astronomy, geology, and statistics.
2. Pragmatism as a philosophical extension of the lessons of applied science to concerns about meaning and belief outside of natural science. Mostly this is contained in the first two essays on pragmatism mentioned above.
3. A general statement of the algebraic rules of probability and a sampling conjecture. The sampling conjecture asserts that random statistical sampling is an informative and reliable procedure for the

scientist as long as the future persists in being like the present and the past. These ideas are contained in the third and fourth essays of the series on pragmatism.

4. A broad statement of an evolutionary ontology in the fifth essay on pragmatism.
5. A consideration of the logic of drawing scientific inferences and falsification in the last essay.
6. An articulation of a convergence conception of truth in an evolutionary world. This is found in the first essay.

Peirce's convergence conception of truth is stated in the first essay on pragmatism, 'Fixation of Belief'. He defined truth as the final opinion which would be reached by a community of scholars over a very long period of time:

> On the other hand, all the followers of science are fully persuaded that the processes of investigation, if only pushed far enough, will give one certain solution to every question to which it can be applied . . . Different minds may set out with the most antagonistic views, but the progress of investigation carries them by a force outside of themselves to one and the same conclusion. This activity of thought by which we are carried, not where we wish, but to a foreordained goal, is like the operation of destiny. No modification of the point of view taken, no selection of other facts for study, no natural bent of mind even, can enable a man to escape the predestinate opinion. This great law is embodied in the conception of truth and reality. The opinion which is fated to be ultimately agreed to by all who investigate, is what is meant by the truth, and the object represented in this opinion is the real. That is the way I would explain reality. (Peirce 1878a, WP 3, p. 273)[28]

Peirce's long run was longer than the long run of classical economics which Keynes encapsulated in his remark, 'In the long run, we are all dead.' Peirce's long run could take centuries for groups of scientists to converge to the truth. Almost two and a half decades later, in a long manuscript on the history of science, Peirce remarks:[29]

> With science it is entirely different. A problem started today may not reach any scientific solution for generations. The man who begins the inquiry does not expect to learn, in this life, what conclusion it is to which his labors are tending. Strictly speaking, the inquiry never will be completely closed. Even

---

[28] For the Peirce quotations, the abbreviations CP, WP, and EP refer to the most common sources of his published writings. The letters stand for *Collected Papers*, *Writings of Peirce* and *Essential Peirce*. For full details, please review the note on bibliographic information which precedes the Peirce entries in the reference list at the end of this paper.

[29] For a lengthy discussion of the economic and philosophical issues in Peirce's (1901) essay see Wible (1998a).

without any logical method at all, the gradual accumulation of knowledge might probably ultimately bring a sufficient solution. Consequently, the object of a logical method is to bring about more speedily and at less expense the result which is destined, in any case, ultimately to be reached, but which, even with the best logic, will not probably come in our day. (Peirce 1901, EP 2, p. 85)

In the second essay, 'How to Make our Ideas Clear', Peirce offers the scientific method as the best process for clarifying the meaning of ideas. His often quoted pragmatic maxim suggests the hypothetical consideration of possible future consequences of our ideas as the most important part of the meaning of our conceptions of the world, both scientific and nonscientific:

> Consider what conceivable effects, which might conceivably have practical bearings, we conceive the object of our conception to have. Then, our conception of these effects is the whole of our conception of the object. (Peirce 1878a, WP 3, p. 266)

Having articulated his general philosophical ideas on pragmatism in the first two essays in the *Popular Science Series*, Peirce wrote four more essays on philosophy of science. He wrote two essays on the logic and philosophy of probability, one on the evolutionary order of nature, and the last on the logic of scientific inference. The essays on probability explore basic issues of sampling in relation to the techniques of science such as when probabilities are added or multiplied together. Beyond some basic rules of probability, Peirce also inquired about the validity of sampling in an evolutionary world. This has led to what I would like to call Peirce's 'sampling conjecture'. The lowest level of the sampling conjecture is the idea that a random sample will exhibit the same properties as the entire process generating the sample. Unless one is prepared to observe every outcome of the process, reliance on sampling will forever remain conjectural for the scientist. A higher level of interpretation for the sampling conjecture is also addressed by Peirce. He asks how we know that sampling will lead to reliable information about any processes under scientific investigation. His answer is that we only know that past processes of sampling have led to successful outcomes. The thesis that our universe can, in part, be known through the sampling techniques of modern science is a conjecture regarding the validity of those methods. For Peirce, the universe is not a mathematician's urn where all possible draws or outcomes are known in advance. Sampling, as a category of knowing, is an abductive guess:[30]

> The relative probability of this or that arrangement of Nature is something which we should have a right to talk about if universes were as plenty as blackberries, if we could put a quantity of them in a bag, shake them up, draw out a sample, and examine them to see what proportion of them had one arrangement and what proportion another. But, even in that case, a higher universe would contain us, in regard to whose arrangements the conception of probability could have no applicability. (Peirce 1878c, WP 3, pp. 300–301)

In the fifth essay on pragmatism, Peirce raises the issue of how an evolutionary universe is structured so that any kind of inductive knowledge is at all possible. Peirce rejects Kant's notion of synthetic, *a priori* knowledge, or genuine knowledge about our world possessed by our minds or embedded in our concepts prior to experience or scientific investigation. Instead, he articulates a hypothetical version of how inductive, empirical knowledge is possible. I shall call this the 'Peirce conjecture'. Peirce essentially asserts that human beings can have imperfect and incomplete knowledge of the patterns and orderings of natural and social phenomena. Such knowing is fallible, incomplete, and contingent. It is contingent on the circumstances which generated the pattern and whether they continue from the past and present into the future. Knowing is also contingent on how accurately human processes of conceptualization and representation model the changing patterns of evolutionary order. About a decade later in the late 1880s, Peirce (1887–88) articulated a more general version of his conception of the world. As Popper (1972, p. 213) recognized in one of his essays, Peirce may be the first philosophical, evolutionary indeterminist.

For Peirce the world began in a total state of chaos with natural order emerging as the world cools down from the initial moments of what we today call the 'big bang'. Order appears and grows for Peirce. The same is true for the social universe. Social order evolves, grows more complex, and some of it perhaps disappears. By the latter 1880s, Peirce began to portray the universe as an array of evolving natural and social processes. He developed a unique logic of the evolutionary process. Having read Kant at an early age and having challenged Hegel's dialectical logic in a series of articles in the late 1860s, Peirce created a logic of three aspects

---

[30] Abduction is the process of forming a guess suggested on the basis of known data. It goes beyond what the data might support scientifically. For Peirce, induction is the process of forming and testing a scientific hypothesis. Inferences are made deductively. Peirce's remarks on abduction can be found in his 'Logic . . ' (Peirce 1901, pp. 106–7).

or categories of evolutionary processes. In comparison to Hegel, Peirce's logic of the evolutionary process is triadic rather than dialectical. Before they unfold, Peirce imagines processes in an *ex ante* state. All alternative outcomes or processes are equally likely at some prior point in the history of an event or population. There is a uniform singularity of all possibilities before a process unfolds. Then something happens which alters circumstances so that order appears and a developmental path is taken. Quickly the process moves from simple, to dualistic, to complex patterns of relations which have triadic or greater complexity. When the growth process slows down, patterns of equilibria emerge and dualistic relations reappear on a relatively permanent basis. Facts and constraints are dualistic in terms of Peirce's logical categories of the evolutionary process. There is also a complex systems aspect to Peirce's portrayal of evolutionary processes. Systems have self-structuring characteristics and follow the triadic logic of the creative evolutionary process. Systems can also form hierarchies and be nested within other systems. For example, biological systems can be nested within physical systems and psychological systems can be nested both within biological and physical systems.

In the last essay on pragmatism, Peirce returns to themes regarding the logic of inference and explores a conception of falsification in some detail decades before Karl Popper did it in the 1930s. Peirce is certainly among the first generation of scientists to have a modern, inferential rather than a descriptive understanding of the logic of the process of scientific investigation.

5. E.B. WILSON: KEYNES SHOULD HAVE READ PEIRCE

In contrast to an appraisal premised on positive economic methodology, an appraisal of the seventy years of macroeconomics since Keynes from a Peircean perspective leads to a different conclusion. On the basis of a Peircean perspective of pragmatism and indeterministic evolutionary complexity, one might argue that macroeconomics has been scientific. But the argument is not as straightforward as one might expect. Within Peirce's science and philosophy is found the outlines of a conception of science itself as a complex evolutionary phenomenon which is engaged in the study of complex indeterministic, evolutionary phenomena as its subject matter. In a social world of complex phenomena, with as many systems and subsystems, processes and sub-processes, and cultures and sub-cultures as the pragmatist vision would allow, one would expect a proliferation of conceptual points of view. One should expect theoretical pluralism about complex social and economic phenomena. Since pragmatism envisions scientists as human agents with active, creative minds of the highest degree, those same considerations suggest that theories may always develop more expansively than they can be tested. Once a number of theories have been created, we should expect many of them to persistently endure because the evidence is weak in relation to each theory. Macroeconomics could be inherently pluralistic. Additionally, the complex systems aspects of Peirce's evolutionary indeterminism lead scientists to talk of patterns and hierarchies of patterns in various stages of dynamic evolutionary growth. Such patterns prevail for a time and at some point are replaced by new patterns of phenomena. Highly ordered patterns may be described with the concepts and terminology of machines, but the more fundamental conception is that of processes of order, some of which may be mechanistic, within the context of indeterministic evolutionary complexity.

Beyond the broad argument that macroeconomic events are better conceived from the vantage point of Peirce's pragmatism as indeterministic, evolutionary complex phenomena, one can ask if the point can be made more directly. Should Keynes and subsequent macroeconomists of all varieties have read Peirce and his conceptions of pragmatism and indeterministic evolutionary complexity? Certainly this is the major point of this chapter, but a version of this argument was made regarding Keynes before he had written any of the macroeconomics in the *General Theory*. In a more limited way, the argument had already been made eighty years ago. The argument was made by E.B. Wilson, a mathematician at MIT and then Harvard who taught mathematics to engineers, mathematicians, and occasionally to economists. Wilson's argument about Peirce and Keynes is made in his 1923 review of Keynes's *Treatise on Probability*.[31] Wilson specifically makes the point that Keynes should have read Peirce's views on probability. This would suggest that Keynes should have read Peirce's three essays on probability, sampling, and the logic of inference – the third, fourth, and sixth essays on pragmatism. Wilson also suggests reading an article by Josiah Royce which more expansively characterizes a broader criticism which Wilson would direct at Keynes. Royce's (1914) article essentially summarized Peirce's theory of evolutionary complexity and its relation to conceptions of probability and statistics. Peirce's views on evolutionary complexity are found in the fifth essay on pragmatism, 'Order of Nature',

---

[31] One issue that Wilson does not raise in his brief review is that Peirce adopted a relative frequentist view of probability and appears to have rejected a version of the subjectivist view that Keynes might have favored.

and his evolutionary writings of the late 1880s and the early 1890s. It should come as no surprise that Wilson's argument about Keynes reading Peirce's views of probability and evolutionary indeterminism can be more broadly raised with regard to Keynes's *General Theory* and subsequent macroeconomics.

At the beginning of this chapter, there is a brief truncated quotation of Wilson's regarding Keynes. That quotation states in the simplest and fewest words the argument that Keynes should have read Peirce. Just below is the complete quotation so that the reader may better judge the breadth of Wilson's suggestion for Keynes. Wilson comments on some of the limitations of Keynes's views on probability and suggests additional bibliographic sources which might have been useful. Specifically, Wilson suggests broadening the scope of Keynes's *Treatise* to include the philosophical views of Royce, Gibbs and C.S. Peirce:

> To the long bibliography [of Keynes's *Treatise on Probability*] one might add the essay of Royce on *The mechanical and the statistical* (italics in original), *Science*, April 17, 1914, pp. 551–566. There are points of philosophic import that seem not to have been covered by Keynes and might be worked into his system. Moreover some might feel that the *Statistical Mechanics* of Gibbs (1901), when viewed philosophically, particularly with respect to the meaning of equilibrium and of natural systems (whether physical or economic) and collated with the very general viewpoint of Royce and C.S. Peirce (whose maturer work Keynes does not cite), might be worthy of at least a bibliographic reference by an author who is setting up a category of probability. (Wilson 1923, pp. 436–7)

The material suggested by Wilson for Keynes from Royce and Gibbs would have led Keynes to Peirce's conceptions of evolutionary complexity. The latter part of the quotation seems to suggest that Keynes should read some of Peirce's writings on probability, at least the three of the six essays on pragmatism and his research on the theory of errors. Wilson was a student of Willard Gibbs at Yale and he also had an interest in the life and thought of Peirce.[32] Gibbs was a physicist and renowned for his work on thermodynamics. After finishing his doctorate under Gibbs, Wilson taught engineering and mathematics classes at both Harvard and MIT. In the 1930s he taught a seminar on mathematical economics which Paul Samuelson and a few others attended. Josiah Royce was a professor of philosophy at Harvard who seemed to understand Peirce's philosophical contributions as well as any contemporary. Although a narrow interpretation of the preceding quote

---

[32] A brief history of Wilson's professional life can be found in the National Academy of Sciences biography of Wilson by Hunsaker and Mac Lane (1973).

would suggest that Wilson's comment was nothing more than a bibliographic footnote for Keynes, a broader interpretation is possible. The broader view would suggest that Keynes had an incomplete view of the interrelationships of the conceptions of probability, evolution and thermodynamics. That broader view is found in Royce's interpretation of the philosophy of C.S. Peirce in Royce's (1914) article in *Science*.

The purpose of Royce's article is to suggest Peirce's evolutionary philosophy as an interpretative framework for the methodological views of a well-known scientist in the early 20th century, Clerk Maxwell. Maxwell was a highly regarded physicist with an interest in thermodynamics. H.S. Thayer (1968, p. 70) tells us that Peirce actually met Maxwell and they discussed how pendulums function in the early 1870s. From Royce we know that Maxwell had advanced the thesis that there are three methods by which anything is known – historical, mechanical and statistical methods. Historical methods deal with events in our personal and social lives. Scientists use mechanistic or statistical methods. Initially in his paper, Royce discusses Maxwell's more detailed views on science, statistics, electricity, and the kinetic theory of gases. Then Royce considers the widely accepted view in the early 20th century that statistical processes are exceptionally complex mechanical processes which are too difficult for direct computation. This view can be known as stochastic mechanism. He rejects the limitations of this view in favor of the thesis that statistical regularities are a really different way of talking about processes of evolution. The remaining third of Royce's paper outlines the view which he believes is the best alternative to stochastic mechanism as a conception of the world, the views of Charles Sanders Peirce. Royce essentially summarizes Peirce's view of the world as one of indeterministic evolutionary complexity. In a Peircean view, an evolutionary process may be so highly ordered that it may give the appearance of mechanism while remaining more fundamentally indeterministic:

> As Charles Peirce pointed out, you need not suppose the real world to be mechanical in order to define and to conceive this sort of evolution . . .
> Suppose these three tendencies (aggregation, selection and habit); suppose these three, and you can define a process of evolution, never mechanical and never merely expressive of any previously settled designs, either of gods or men. This process of evolution will then lead from mere chance towards the simulation of mechanism, from disorderly to a more orderly arrangement, not only of things and of individual events, but of the statistically definable laws of nature; that is, of the habits which nature gathers as she matures. (Royce 1914, p. 565)

Royce tells us that the views of Peirce which he is summarizing were expressed in a fragmentary way in three papers in the *Monist* in the 1890s, titled 'The Architecture of Theories', 'The Doctrine of Necessity Examined' and 'The Law of Mind'. It is interesting that in another paper in that same series titled 'Evolutionary Love', Peirce suggests that economic and evolutionary theories are interrelated:[33]

> The *Origin of Species* of Darwin merely extends politico-economico views of progress to the entire realm of animal and vegetable life. The vast majority of our contemporary naturalists hold the opinion that the true cause of those exquisite and marvelous adaptations of nature for which, when I was a boy, men used to extol the divine wisdom, is that creatures are so crowded together that those of them that happen to have the slightest advantage force those less pushing into situations unfavorable to multiplication or even kill them before the reach the age of reproduction. Among animals, the mere mechanical individualism is vastly reenforced as a power making for good by the animal's ruthless greed. (Peirce 1893, CP 6, p. 196)

Previously, in the same paper, Peirce had described the 19th century as an economic century:

> The nineteenth century is now fast sinking into the grave, and we all begin to review its doings and to think what character it is destined to bear as compared with other centuries in the minds of future historians. It will be called, I guess, the Economical Century; for political economy has more direct relations with all the branches of its activity than has any other science. (Peirce 1893, CP 6, p. 192)

Then Peirce criticizes the classical theory of economic motivation based on the utilitarian concepts of pleasure and pain. In these critiques, Peirce takes issue with the classical theory of greed as the motivator of individual behavior. Greed as a high-level principle of evolutionary motivation is rejected by Peirce:

> What I say, then, is that the great attention paid to economical questions during our century has induced an exaggeration of the beneficial effects of greed and of the unfortunate results of sentiment, until there has resulted a philosophy which comes unwittingly to this, that greed is the great agent in the elevation of the human race and in the evolution of the universe. (Peirce 1893, CP 6, p. 193)

From a general critique of 19th century political economy, Peirce then moves to considering views specifically expressed by Simon Newcomb

---

[33] The complete list of the five articles in *The Monist* series can be found in the references.

in his *Principles of Political Economy* (1886). Near the end of the *Principles*, Newcomb presents policy implications of economics. Peirce strongly objects to these policy implications and the conception of human nature on which they are based.

Peirce's critique of classical political economy in the 1890s was not his first extensive foray into economics. In the early 1870s, at approximately the same time that the Metaphysical Club was meeting, another intellectual seminar was held to discuss science and mathematics. It was called the Cambridge Scientific Club. That club read Cournot's (1838) *Researches* which contains the now famous model of duopoly. From correspondence with his father, we know that Charles Peirce (1871) worked through the equations of the duopoly model and essentially articulated what later became known as the Bertrand critique about ten years before Bertrand. In other manuscripts which survive from that period, Peirce was also extensively concerned with the economic theories of monopoly and competition. Peirce also met Stanley Jevons and wrote a utility model for allocating funds to alternative research projects. This paper is called the 'Note on the Theory of the Economy of Research' (Peirce 1879).[34] The mathematical model bears a remarkable similarity to the presentation of utility theory in Jevons's (1871) *Theory of Political Economy*. The resemblance is so strong that it is plausible to suggest that Peirce had Jevons's presentation in mind when he wrote his own equations for the model of the economy of research. The level of mathematics in Peirce's economic manuscripts of the early 1870s suggests that his command of mathematics equaled and probably exceeded that of any economist of that era. In one of his manuscripts, Peirce actually thought sufficiently about demand and utility theory to formulate the consumer axiom of transitivity:

> The dependence of demand on price arises from this fundamental proposition. The desire of a person for anything has a quantity of one dimension, and a person having a choice will take that alternative which gives him the greatest satisfaction. In other words if a person prefers A to B and B to C he also prefers A to C. This is the first axiom of Political Economy. (Peirce 1874, WP 3, p. 176)

These contributions are of sufficient quality that Peirce should be counted among the founders of the marginalist revolution in microeconomics. However, he forever remained a critic of economics on the basis of his philosophies of pragmatism and indeterministic evolutionary complexity.

---

[34] Wible (1994) discusses Peirce's model in greater detail.

At this point let us return to Wilson's main point that Keynes should have read Peirce on probability and indeterministic evolutionary complexity. Wilson's even broader point, that Keynes should have read Royce's more expansive interpretation of Peirce, coupled together with our awareness that Peirce was keenly interested in economics at several points in his life provide a basis for a more robust interpretation of the views of Wilson and Royce. Peirce's views on indeterministic, evolutionary complexity could help us understand Keynes's *General Theory* and many of the more substantive difficulties faced by the various schools of macroeconomics in their attempts to become more rigorous and scientific. Wilson recognized the inherently pragmatic views of Keynes (1921) in his *Treatise on Probability*. Wilson writes:

> Some of Keynes's comments on illustrious investigations and originations in probability might have been cast in far different language had he realized the essentially pragmatic, the unconsciously pragmatic, point of view of the scientific as compared with the philosophic investigator. (Wilson 1923, pp. 435)

In an earlier and then in a subsequent passage, Wilson had asserted the relevance of a pragmatic point of view to Keynes:

> Apparently our author [Keynes] little realizes that, stumbling in the dark, he has hit upon a very clever characterization of Poincare's real philosophic system – pragmatism . . . To the philosopher or economist who may rarely make a definite statement, and who from the nature of his work and interests perhaps cannot, the definite style of the scientist appears dogmatic, rather than pragmatic, and altogether damnable – but it is written; Judge not that ye be not judged. (Wilson 1923, pp. 435–6)

6. ASPECTS OF EVOLUTIONARY COMPLEXITY AND KEYNES'S *GENERAL THEORY*

According to Wilson, in the comments just made above, both Keynes and Poincare practiced a version of applied mathematical-scientific inquiry which Wilson labeled as pragmatism. Similarly, as Wilson observed of Keynes, many other scientists appear to practice science in the scientific analytical style of pragmatism developed by Peirce. This assessment would extend to macroeconomists. Almost every well-trained contemporary macroeconomist practices macroeconomics in the mathematical and statistical modeling style pioneered by Peirce and many other scientists who subsequently followed after him such as Wilson and Gibbs. However, hardly anyone in economics has conceptualized his/her scientific research in the context of the philosophical framework of evolutionary, indeterministic complexity such as was first articulated by Peirce. To remedy this deficiency, Wilson advocates Peirce's philosophical framework via Royce for Keynes. Naturally, it should come as no surprise to realize that after seventy years as a major sub-discipline within economics, perhaps macroeconomics should consider a conceptual framework of indeterministic evolutionary complexity.

Before proceeding further, it would be helpful to specify the most general characteristics of social phenomena in an evolutionary, indeterministic world. Much of what follows is derived from my interpretations of Peirce's many papers and writings on pragmatism, science and economics. Also, there are two other individuals whose views have had a significant influence on the list of characteristics articulated below. Other than Peirce, one view of an evolutionary economy which ranges over much of the same intellectual, scientific and economic terrain as Peirce is Nicholas Georgescu-Roegen's (1971) well-known work, *Entropy and the Economic Process*. Within economics, Georgescu-Roegen's *Entropy* may be the single work which is most compatible with a Peircean conception of the natural and social worlds. The other economist whose evolutionary views have had a significant impact are those of Friedrich Hayek. His essays on complex phenomena, competition as a discovery process, and the role of knowledge in the market process are found in his *Studies in Philosophy, Politics and Economics*.[35] His work on the evolutionary way knowledge is processed by humans beings can be found in his monograph, *The Sensory Order* (Hayek 1952). These writings and others have contributed significantly to my view of an evolutionary world.[36] A really detailed exploration of the main features of an evolutionary world as found in the works of Peirce, Hayek, Georgescu-Roegen and others would require nothing less than a short treatise. As an imperfect substitute, I would like just to list some of the most important features of an evolutionary world for economics. This list represents an expansion of Peirce's ideas that Wilson recommended to Keynes. A more detailed but general list of some of the most general properties of evolutionary indeterministic, complex phenomena would be as follows:

---

[35] The references to five of the best of Hayek's articles can be found in the references at the end of the paper.

[36] Another well-known work on evolutionary economics is Nelson and Winter (1982).

1. *Evolutionary indeterminism*: The cosmos originated in a genesis-like explosion suggesting chaos and indeterminacy are more fundamental than order and pattern in natural and social phenomena.
2. *Patterns of evolving order*: Many social and natural processes originate, grow, develop and dissipate in cognizable sequences of order.
3. *Complexity*: Entities exhibiting patterns of order replicate and aggregate into systems and hierarchies of systems of larger scale.
4. *Mechanism as a special case*: Mechanistic order is a special case of evolutionary order where the patterns of repetition have become exceptionally rigid.
5. *Stability*: Once established, patterns of natural and social order are stable for limited periods of duration.
6. *Punctuated changes in order*: Patterns of order are often quickly destroyed followed by new patterns of order and growth.
7. *Material scarcity*: The natural and material resources of our evolutionary world are finite.
8. *Intelligent individuals with active (abductive) cognitive creativity*: Human beings have been created as part of the evolutionary process. They have the capacity to precociously and actively structure abstract conceptions of the systems niche in which they and others live. This includes qualitative, verbal and mathematical models and the quantitative models of the applied sciences and statistics. Such abstract, abductive conceptions are constructed as general ideas which transcend specific events and experience.
9. *Nesting*: Individuals are nested within physical, social and cultural systems.
10. *Cognitive scarcity and localized knowledge*: Reliable knowledge about our natural and social worlds is always deficient and incomplete. Human individuals have localized knowledge of the array of evolutionary systems in which they live. Knowledge of more general circumstances beyond the localized niche of complex systems in which the individual functions is possible, but costly. Evolutionary processes may destroy the relevance of existing knowledge.
11. *Cognitive versus material scarcity*: In an evolutionary world, because most events are ill-structured and do not exhibit the highly ordered patterns of mechanistic equilibrium, cognitive scarcity is worse or poses more problems for people than material scarcity most of the time. Material scarcity is a sub-category of cognitive scarcity.
12. *Qualitative versus quantitative knowledge*: In the evolutionary process, qualitative knowledge typically precedes quantitative

knowledge. This sequencing is efficient and is a consequence of both cognitive and material scarcity.

13. *Time is first qualitative, then quantitative, then subjective*: Time first emerges qualitatively as mere succession, then it becomes quantitative as patterns of natural phenomena stabilize, then it becomes subjective, historical, and cultural after humans appear.[37]

14. *Mathematics as symbolic pattern construction*: Mathematics is a humanly created linguistic process for symbolically constructing the logic of abstract patterns of repetition. Such humanly constructed systems of abstract pattern construction can be used to approximate the patterns of phenomena that human agents observe in the social patterns and relations in which they are embedded.

15. *Science as active pattern testing*: Scientifically constructed models of external patterns of social and natural phenomena need to be tested against the less structured data from the external world with the methods of empirical inquiry and statistical inference.

16. *Ordinary experience as active pattern testing*: Intelligent individuals qualitatively test the pattern reliability of their cognitive conceptions continuously in order to survive and to prosper beyond the minimum of survivability.

17. *Institutions and moral values as rational responses to cognitive scarcity*: Markets, values and nonmarket institutions help to alleviate cognitive scarcity and localized knowledge in two ways: (a) by creating knowledge or proxies for knowledge, and (b) by constraining human interactions with and thereby constructing patterns of social order with contract, custom, law, and cultural norms.

18. *Knowing and learning*: Human agents are capable of progressively structuring more accurate pattern representations and interpretations of the phenomena in their domain of experience. Such representations are incomplete and may gradually decay in accuracy as orders of pattern are created, grow, and diminish.

19. *Pluralism in the present and future short run*: Creative human agents construct rival conceptual frameworks and models of personal, social, and scientific phenomena.

---

[37] As a corollary to the statement on time, time has been an issue in macroeconomics. Usually this takes the form of various conceptions such as momentary, short- and long-run time periods. Also, there is a difference between analytical time and the time index of dynamic models and calendar time that occurs in the real history of society and the economy. Post Keynesians and Austrians seem to be more sensitive to these distinctions than Keynesians and New Keynesians. Keynes and the old classicals thought more in terms of historical than analytical time.

20. *Truth in the long run*: Truth is a long-run judgment regarding the consensus of the community of scientists over multiple generations.

While this list may to some appear too long, the attempt to characterize a world of indeterministic evolutionary complexity should be acknowledged as incomplete. However, the philosophical perspective behind the list would provide a vastly different philosophical interpretation for macroeconomics of the past seventy years than the conventional mainstream interpretation of the 'Keynes and the classics' debate. Consider applying the above attributes to Keynes's *General Theory*.

Just imagine how differently one would interpret Keynes's *General Theory* if the postulates of pragmatic evolutionary indeterminism given above served as the intellectual context for that work.[38] The very clash between Keynes and his classical teachers might be conceived as a fundamental clash of alternative conceptions of the social world – a clash of evolutionary indeterminism versus stochastic mechanism. For example, the various classical theories of macroeconomic activity from Keynes's teachers through Friedman, Real Business Cycle Theory and the New Classical macroeconomics seem to presume a conception of the social world and the economy as an array of stochastic equilibria.[39] We need look no further than the Walrasian conception of a mechanistically coordinated economy found in all conceptions of Walrasian general equilibrium. Things are different in our alternative view. In an indeterministic, evolutionary economy there is no super individual, social process, or machine which is capable of achieving the high levels of equilibrium order which general equilibrium theory implies. Similarly, Keynes's claims that the classical theory of his teachers is a special case of his theory make more sense if we follow Wilson toward Peirce and interpret Keynes as an evolutionary indeterminist. Machines are special cases of evolutionary processes, so in this sense a mechanistic macro theory would be a special case of an evolutionary one.

Another conception which fits more coherently with a pragmatic conception of evolutionary indeterminism is Keynes's and even Frank Knight's conception of radical uncertainty. In an evolutionary world and economy, Keynesian uncertainty is an expression of the fundamental cognitive scarcity which is pervasive in a creatively evolving economy.

---

[38] This author offered an indeterministic interpretation of Keynes's *General Theory* in Wible (1995).

[39] The importance of the notion of equilibrium to Chicago School economics has been described by Reder (1982).

In this respect, Keynes seemed to be aware of the more pervasive relevance of cognitive scarcity in relation to material scarcity than his classical and neoclassical critics. Consider Keynes's comments on money. Keynes claims that money plays a central role in structuring our economy and the financial system. He also portrays the dynamic role of money as a cognitive connection actively linking the past and present with the economic future. These comments on money make more sense from a perspective of indeterministic, evolutionary complexity. Money is an institution which has been created to help alleviate cognitive scarcity, but once it has been created, its patterns and processes of order can be altered and broken in unexpected ways. The properties of monetary processes seem to mirror those of the patterns of creation, growth and decay of evolutionary natural and social processes studied by the many natural and social sciences. These comments about uncertainty and money suggest a broader interpretation. As Wilson suggested for Keynes's view of probability, the *General Theory* makes more sense when interpreted with a conception of Peirce's pragmatic evolutionary indeterminism in the background.

The preceding remarks should not be further interpreted to suggest that Peirce might have been a follower of Keynes or a Keynesian on policy questions. Had he lived for a few more decades, Peirce no doubt would have been interested in the development of applied mathematical models and methods in economics in macro, micro and econometrics. On the basis of his philosophical framework, he certainly would have been critical of the extreme equilibrium interpretations of those models. But Peirce was critical of both government and the economics profession. He criticized the inefficiency of government agencies and the philosophical narrow-mindedness of the economics profession in the late 19th century. My guess is that he would not have been as liberal on matters of economic policy as John Dewey nor as conservative as most classically minded economists of his time. But that is a topic for another day.

7. MACROECONOMISTS AS PRAGMATISTS: PHELPS, FRYDMAN AND GOLDBERG ON RATIONAL EXPECTATIONS

We could continue with an expansive extrapolation of Wilson's suggestion regarding Keynes and apply Peirce's conceptions of probability and evolutionary indeterminism to many other contributions to macroeconomics. However, at this point I would like to direct Wilson's suggestion to a more contemporary theoretical issue in macroeconomics. Other than the dominance of mechanism as a conception of order in macroeconomic equilibrium models of both the classical and Keynesian varieties, there is one other macroeconomic conception which requires some comment. That conception has played a pivotal role in macroeconomic theory and policy over the past three decades. That conception is none other than rational expectations. Rational expectations is the idea that economic agents use all available information in economic processes. As an expectations concept, rational expectations has been operationalized with the assertion that rational agents essentially have expectations which are the equivalent of the reduced form results from the equations of the economists' macroeconometric models. This means that individuals in economic processes are assumed to have attained the global knowledge of economic processes in the macroeconomists' econometric forecasting models. Rational expectations has also been advanced as a critique of adaptive expectations, the view of expectations which Keynes and others such as Friedman assumed. The essence of the critique is that it is irrational for economic agents to make partial and continuously adaptive use of new information over time if they have complete knowledge of a new macroeconomic trend and its consequences.

Since it first appeared in the macroeconomic literature around 1970, rational expectations has become one of the most entrenched of all macroeconomic theoretical ideas. It has become synonymous with the conceptions of rationality and science. The presumption was that this was the only way rational economic agents deal with information and thus equivalent to the only scientific approach on the use of knowledge in economic processes. In some interpretations, economic agents have been interpreted as mini-scientists possessing the same models and information that macroeconometric forecasters have. In a sense, this means that agents have solved their scientific problems by becoming the instrumental equivalent of the economist. No explanation of this extreme version of rational expectations is given, other than the instrumental justification that, if the idea leads to better forecasts, then that is all that matters. But intellectual context does matter. One can ask how the conception of rational expectations would be viewed from the perspective of evolutionary indeterminism.

While the concept of rational expectations may make some sense from a mechanistic view, from the perspective of a Peircean world of indeterministic, evolutionary complexity, the conception of rational expectations is absurd.[40] In a Peircean evolutionary world, individuals in

---

[40] The reader should peruse the story of the Santa Fe Institute which investigates complexity where the physicists responded with disbelief to presentations of some of the best

fact do make use of all available information. Peirce is sufficiently aware of the implications of Darwinian evolution implying that mere survival requires the most extensive use of existing information. However, in an economy characterized by evolutionary indeterminacy, cognitive scarcity is more fundamental than material scarcity. Creative agents will act not only to search for information about their world, but they will also enter into relationships and processes which serve to structure their lives. Their learning is active and they recognize the incompleteness of their own and economists' conceptions and models about their world. Also, they come to know that almost all knowledge is local and contingent rather than general and universal. They react adaptively to new information because its relevance to their specific economic circumstances needs interpretation. Creative agents require meta knowledge about knowledge as a framework for understanding. Such meta knowledge can also manifest itself as skepticism about macro forecasts and conceptions such as rational expectations premised on a stochastic, mechanistic view of the world. In an evolutionary world, it is not rational to believe in the conception of rational expectations as proposed by its strongest adherents. They have a mechanistic conception of the economy and the world which needs to be rejected as grossly inadequate in the context of the evolutionary conceptions of the world from the other sciences. Rational expectations theorists waste too much general scientific information about our universe and our economy.

At this point, I would like to consider an episode in macroeconomics which illustrates how important a conceptual framework of indeterministic evolutionary complexity can be in understanding the underlying macroeconomic events and the disputes among economists over rational expectations. The episode I have in mind is the attempt to understand movements in exchange rates over the past few decades using models with rational expectations. Foreign exchange markets are financial asset markets. Ever since Keynes considered the economic implications of the instability of the stock and bond markets in London and on Wall Street as contributing causes of the Great Depression, the interrelationship of expectations, financial markets, and economic activity has been a key aspect for understanding the overall dynamics of macroeconomic activity. Also the effectiveness of monetary policy clearly depends on the interrelationships of financial markets and the economy. The scientific problem of understanding foreign exchange markets is that almost all of the research using rational expectations

---

macroeconomists in the world at that time, such as Sargent and Summers. See Waldrop (1992, pp. 136–43).

models of the past twenty years or so has failed to explain the most fundamental empirical puzzles of the foreign exchange market. The anomalies of the foreign exchange literature involve the centrality of rational expectations as a theoretical lynch pin for that genre of macroeconomic models.

The issues surrounding macroeconomists' understanding of rational expectations in the foreign exchange markets are presented in a long article by Roman Frydman and Michael Goldberg (2003) in a volume of essays from a recent conference honoring the macroeconomic contributions of Edmund Phelps.[41] In that volume, Phelps himself has some interesting general remarks about the role of knowledge in economic processes and whether rational expectations was a plausible theoretical concept. At the end of the volume, Phelps makes some interesting comments about the ideas which drove his understanding of macroeconomics. He begins by confiding that:

> What bothered me in the mid-1960s lay at the heart of Keynes's theory of unemployment: Why would the monetary impact of a real or nominal shock, unobserved and, say permanent . . . cause an appreciable decrease of unemployment – and probably a protracted decrease? . . .
> The ideas I hoped would answer this question rested on imperfect information (data, costs, coordination obstacles) and, at places, imperfect knowledge (ambiguity, disagreement, uncertainty). Undoubtedly, Robertson, Hayek, and Keynes himself had pointed me the way. (Phelps 2003, p. 271)

Again, on a subsequent page, Phelps conceptualizes the individual and market dynamics of financial markets and capitalism:

> What got lost in monetary macroeconomics amid its considerable achievements in modeling imperfect information is the *imperfect knowledge*, or uncertainty in the sense of Knight, that pervades the more entrepreneurial of the market economies . . . The ongoing injection of new products, new methods, and new markets entails a *discovery* process of guesswork and sequential investigation by entrepreneurs and venture capitalists. The ensuing stream of such innovations, in creating new opportunities, generates *diffusion* processes of search and evaluation by potential adopters of recent innovations. Moreover, the adoption of innovations requires and stimulates a *learning* process by actual buyers and sellers. The participants in the economy are in the business of narrowing the gaps in their private knowledge. They cannot know fully the current structure within which they operate . . . By its nature then, then, no one could possibly know the current structure of this non-stationary economy as a whole. (Phelps 2003, p. 277)

---

[41] Previously these authors presented their work in Goldberg and Frydman (1996).

The preceding comments obviously make a great deal of sense if couched in the context of a Peircean conception of an indeterministic, evolutionary economy. Phelps's remarks regarding uncertainty, ambiguity, imperfect knowledge, learning and discovery parallel those of Keynes and are quite generally compatible with Peirce's view of an evolutionary social world characterized by cognitive scarcity. The last sentence in Phelps's quote immediately above suggests that rational expectations may not be very relevant to the evolving patterns of a non-stationary macro economy.

Returning to foreign exchange rate models, Roman Frydman and Michael Goldberg have argued that economic models using rational expectations have failed to explain the important movements in exchange rates since they began to float with the collapse of the Bretton Woods international monetary system in the early 1970s. This is tantamount to saying that the area of international monetary macroeconomics has failed using the standard criterion of positive economic science. Frydman and Goldberg begin with the widely used Dornbusch and Frankel model of exchange rate dynamics. That model consists of three equations: a money market equilibrium equation describing the relative interest rates in two countries, a foreign exchange market equilibrium condition, and a domestic price adjustment equation. Those equations are solved for a reduced form equation which yields the 'steady-state value of the exchange rate under RE' (Frydman and Goldberg 2003, p. 150). The scientific problem is that the values of the exchange rates do not closely follow the equilibrium path predicted by the Dornbusch and Frankel model which assumes rational expectations. The equilibrium path in the literature has been termed purchasing power parity or ppp which relates the relative prices of goods produced by nations involved in international trade. Actual exchange rates show significant and systematic departures from the ppp path for considerable periods of time. These are called long swings in the literature and they have lasted from 3 to 5 years during the 1980s and for shorter periods during the 1990s. Including the long swings puzzle, Frydman and Goldberg argue that the closely related puzzles in international finance are the following:

1. A long swings puzzle which means exchange rates persistently move away from ppp.[42]

---

[42] Another less complicated aspect of the long swings puzzle is the 'ppp puzzle' which asks why nominal exchange rates, even though their markets are in continuous momentary equilibrium, adjust more slowly around the ppp path than do goods prices in their markets.

2. An 'exchange rate disconnect puzzle' which means that movements in exchange rates seem to be unrelated to the fundamental dynamics of macroeconomic models and processes.
3. An 'excess returns puzzle' which concerns the inability of standard exchange rate theory to explain the failure of uncovered interest rate parity.

To deal with the preceding puzzles, Frydman and Goldberg develop an alternative framework based on imperfect knowledge. Their work has evolved from alternative conceptions of expectations which they have successively called 'Theories Consistent Expectations' (TCE), 'Imperfect Knowledge Expectations' (IKE), and now 'Imperfect Knowledge Forecasting' (IKF). Some important aspects of their approach are an emphasis on the priority of qualitative knowledge of transactors. Rather than assuming that agents have precise knowledge about the parameters in the macro forecast as a rational expectations theorist would require, Frydman and Goldberg assume that agents might have qualitative knowledge about the important parameters in a model of macroeconomic activity. Agents may know what the important variables are and the signs of the coefficients of those variables without having exact knowledge of parameter values or the confidence intervals associated with those parameters. In a more recent development, Frydman and Goldberg allow the economic agent to work with many models rather than just one. This means that decision makers assess the qualitative properties of several different models of foreign exchange rates in relation to each other. Agents are theoretically pluralistic:

> The TCE framework assumes that the extant stock of the *plurality* of economic models provides agents with *qualitative* knowledge about which variables to include in their individual forecast functions and the *signs* of the weights that should be attached to the included variables. Despite its qualitative specificity, the TCE framework does not determine which of the fundamental variables from the extant models should be included in individual and aggregate forecast functions. (Frydman and Goldberg 2003, p. 147)

In other comments, Frydman and Goldberg relate their conception of imperfect knowledge to Keynesian uncertainty. They assert that the imperfect knowledge part of both IKE and IKF corresponds to Knight's views on risk versus uncertainty and Keynes's remarks about the difficulty of forming expectations in interdependent financial markets:

> Beyond the promise to provide reasonable explanations of empirical regularities, especially in asset markets, and its compatibility with the postulate of individual rationality, the IKE framework appears to rest on solid

and plausible behavioral foundations . . . Knight for example, in his classic book, introduced the distinction between measurable uncertainty – which he called risk – and 'true uncertainty' . . . With his beauty contest example, Keynes underscored the role played by subjective guesses of the average opinion in the formation of individual expectations of asset prices. (Frydman and Goldberg 2003, p. 148)

One of the most difficult empirical features of actual exchange rates is the persistent but reversing swings of exchange rates around the ppp equilibrium value for considerable periods of time. Frydman and Goldberg intend their imperfect knowledge contributions to provide an explanation for such swings away from and back to ppp. In their model, they allow agents to revise their expectations discontinuously as well as continuously. Agents may behave in a rule-governed way for a certain period and rapidly alter their responses describable under another rule or equation modeling responses:

> . . . We allow for the updating of forecast functions to involve jumps in $\overset{\cdot}{\widetilde{s}}$ and $\widetilde{s}$ [TCE forecasts of the exchange rate and the rate of change of such forecasts] in addition to continuous movements of $\widetilde{s}$ over time. Since the REH and standard learning models do not admit such updating (independently of policy changes), we focus only on the updating of TCE and IKE functions . . . First, from an empirical standpoint, a turnaround in the time path of the exchange rate . . . requires jumps in expectations functions within the context of our modified model . . .
> A second reason for allowing expectations dynamics to involve jumps is that it is reasonable to suppose from a behavioral standpoint that agents update their expectations functions both continuously and discontinuously in a world of imperfect knowledge . . . Finally, . . . *rational* agents will not follow fixed rules for updating their expectations in a world of imperfect knowledge, that is, agents' expectations dynamics will involve discontinuous jumps in $\widetilde{s}$ and $\widetilde{s}$. (Frydman and Goldberg 2003, p. 169)

Frydman and Goldberg also have advanced epistemological arguments. They argue that the rational expectations hypothesis embeds conceptions of knowledge acquisition which are contrary to psychological and philosophical theories of knowing and learning. Furthermore, given the persistence and severity of the empirical anomalies of rational expectations models of foreign exchange rates, the epistemological problems of rational expectations acquire significant connotations of scientific validity. They argue that it is the theory of rational expectations which has stood in the way of further advances of the empirical movements of exchange rates:

> In this chapter we formulate an alternative model of individual expectations that recognizes the importance of imperfect knowledge and advance the argument that the standard REH assumption appears to be the primary reason

for the gross empirical failure of the monetary models of the exchange rate. (Frydman and Goldberg 2003, p. 146)

Frydman and Goldberg's argument that the assumption of rational expectations might be a cause of the failure of exchange rate models is certainly plausible from the perspective of Peircean, evolutionary indeterminism.[43] Frydman and Goldberg share many of the main features of the indeterministic view of the world that were enumerated in the previous section. They treat movements in economic data as patterns of evolving order rather than as mechanistic phenomena. They allow for punctuated changes in the patterns of order of market processes observed in foreign exchange markets. Frydman and Goldberg particularly challenge the mechanistic informational assumptions of rational expectations models. They allow agents to have active rather than passive cognitive capacities, they essentially assert that the economic knowledge of transactors is local and embedded, and they thus recognize that cognitive scarcity is a difficult problem for agents in the foreign exchange markets. Most recently, they have begun to incorporate the insights of behavioral finance into their response to rational expectations. What is probably most surprising in Frydman and Goldberg's paper is that they reverse the traditional empiricists ranking of quantitative knowledge as being more important than qualitative knowledge. In an evolutionary world, as Peirce and other evolutionary thinkers have recognized, human beings first apprehend the world qualitatively, then quantitatively. And quantitative results are always embedded within conceptual frameworks of more general qualitative ideas and theoretical relationships. On a similar note, Frydman and Goldberg's views of learning by economic agents are compatible with learning as a clash of alternative qualitative theoretical and conceptual frameworks with embedded quantitative content.

The preceding remarks suggest that we could view Phelps, Frydman and Goldberg as Wilson viewed Keynes. As Wilson recognized an inherent Peircean style of pragmatism in Keynes's *Treatise on Probability*, so we also can recognize that same style of pragmaticist inquiry in the macroeconomic research of Phelps, Frydman and Goldberg.[44] Peirce was one of the first applied scientists to practice

---

[43] Space limitations make it impossible to explore the contributions of macroeconomist Kevin Hoover who has been significantly influenced by Peirce and is critical of the conception of rational expectations. From among his many contributions, I would suggest Hoover (1994a, 1994b).

[44] Pragmaticism is the new name Peirce coined for his philosophical ideas after pragmatism acquired popular interpretations with which he disagreed. Pragmaticism requires rigorous

science coupling the applied tools of mathematical modeling with statistical inference and modern sampling techniques. He certainly was the first philosopher to offer a systematic philosophical interpretation of the tools of modern science. Wilson also recommends Peirce's evolutionary philosophical system as a context for understanding the scientist's conceptions of probability and the nature of the phenomena being investigated. Peirce was an evolutionary indeterminist and framed his interpretation of scientific inquiry, his theory of probability, and his interpretation of mathematics with that philosophy of evolutionary complexity. Although our review of their contributions has been fragmentary, it appears that Phelps, Frydman and Goldberg share many of Peirce's, Wilson's, and even Keynes's evolutionary philosophical instincts about science, the economy, and how individuals learn in an evolutionary world characterized by cognitive scarcity.[45]

8. CONCLUSIONS

How scientific has macroeconomics been over the seven decades of its history? If positive economics methodology is our conception of science, then macroeconomics has not been very scientific. The mainstream 'Keynes and the classics' debate as well as recent research on monetary models of exchange rates both lend themselves more toward an appraisal of scientific failure than success if positive economic methodology is our guide. However, positive economic methodology itself has failed according to the most recent research on economic methodology. Fortunately, an alternative conception of science which is quite amenable to macroeconomics has reappeared. This is a conception of science focused on patterns of complexity. If one adopts a pragmatist conception of science and an evolutionary view of the world as found in the papers and writings of C.S. Peirce, then an argument can be constructed that macroeconomics has been scientific. But even more importantly, an awareness of Peirce's views transforms our conception of the world and the economy. Peirce's view of the world is one of indeterministic, evolutionary complexity. Such a view implies that economic phenomena,

---

methods of logical and scientific inference which popularizers of pragmatism tended to ignore.

[45] This brief appraisal of the contributions of Phelps, Frydman and Goldberg relative to Peirce and the list of twenty or so characteristics of an indeterministic, evolutionary world of complex phenomena is obviously incomplete. One research idea would be to assess each of the schools of macroeconomics of the past seventy years against these characteristics. This task is obviously beyond the scope of this chapter.

including both micro and macroeconomic phenomena, are complex phenomena and typically non-stationary. Both economic agents and policy-makers function differently in an evolutionary world of complex phenomena than they do in a mechanistic economy. Cognitive scarcity is more pervasive and more fundamental than material scarcity. Pluralism for agents and for policy-makers is also a consequence of a conception of the economy as a complex phenomenon. Agents and policy-makers see the value of being aware of multiple theories and explanations of economic events in a world of incomplete, imperfect knowledge.

Two core concepts in mainstream economics since Keynes bear the brunt of the philosophical criticism from Peircean evolutionary perspective. Both general equilibrium and rational expectations, while possessing a grain of truth in some circumstances, need to be reconceived within the context of a pragmatist, evolutionary conception of science and the world. Both have significant limitations and drastically limit the way truly rational human beings deal with cognitive scarcity in real markets and financial processes. Since pragmatism makes for a broader use of what is known about our world and human knowledge of that world from the other sciences, pragmatism would seem to be the more efficient philosophical system from which to view the economy and the world than the theories of those trained narrowly in positive economic methodology and rational expectations. One can only hope that more macroeconomists and policy-makers will come to view the economy as Peirce might have, with a pragmaticist conception of indeterministic, evolutionary complexity with active, cognitively creative agents in the economic process.

REFERENCES

Akerlof, G.A. (2002), 'Behavioral macroeconomics and macroeconomic behavior', *American Economic Review*, **92** (3), 411–33.

Barberis, Nicholas and Richard Thaler (2003), 'A Survey of Behavioral Finance', in G.M. Constantinides and R. Stulz (eds), *Handbook of the Economics of Finance*, Elsevier Science B.V., pp. 1053–123.

Bischoff, Charles W. and Halefom Belay (2001), 'The problem of identification of the money demand function', *Journal of Money, Credit and Banking*, **33** (2) Part 1, 205–15.

Brent, Joseph (1998), *Charles Sanders Peirce: A Life*, 2nd ed., Bloomington, Ind.: Indiana University Press.

Charemza, W.W. and D.F. Deadman (1997), *New Directions in Econometric Practice*, Cheltenham, UK and Lyme, US: Edward Elgar.

Coats, A.W. (1969), 'Is there a "structure of scientific revolutions" in economics?', *Kyklos*, **22**, 289–94.

Cournot, Augustin [1838] (1929), *Researches into the Mathematical Principles of the Theory of Wealth*, trans. N.T. Bacon, New York: Macmillan.

Davidson, Paul (1994), *Post Keynesian Macroeconomic Theory: A Foundation For Successful Economic Policies For The Twenty-First Century*, Camberley, UK and Brookfield, US: Edward Elgar.

Ericsson, Neil R. (1998), 'Empirical modeling of money demand', *Empirical Economics*, **23**, 295–315.

Fisch, Max (1986), 'Introduction' in C.J.W. Kloesel, et al. (eds), *Writings of Charles S. Peirce: A Chronological Edition*, Vol. 3, 1872–1878, Bloomington, Ind.: Indiana University Press, pp. xxi–xxxvi.

Friedman, Milton (1953), 'The Methodology of Positive Economics', in M. Friedman, *Essays in Positive Economics*, Chicago: University of Chicago Press.

Friedman, Milton (1957), *A Theory of the Consumption Function*, Princeton: Princeton University Press.

Friedman, Milton (1968), 'The role of monetary policy', *American Economic Review*, **58**, March, 1–17.

Friedman, Milton (1970), 'A theoretical framework for monetary analysis', *Journal of Political Economy*, **LXVII** (2), 193–238.

Frydman, Roman and Michael Goldberg (2003) 'Imperfect Knowledge Expectations, Uncertainty-Adjusted Uncovered Interest Rate Parity and Exchange Rate Dynamics', in *Knowledge, Information, and Expectations in Modern Macroeconomics: In Honor of Edmund S. Phelps*, Princeton: Princeton University Press, pp. 145–87.

Georgescu-Roegen, Nicholas (1971), *The Entropy Law and the Economic Process*, Cambridge: Harvard University Press.

Goldberg, M.D. and Roman Frydman (1996), 'Imperfect knowledge and behavior in the foreign exchange market', *Economic Journal*, **106** (437), 869–93.

Hands, D. Wade (2001), *Reflection without Rules: Economic Methodology and Contemporary Science Theory*, Cambridge, UK: Cambridge University Press.

Hayek, F.A. (1948a) 'Economics and Knowledge', in F.A. Hayek, *Individualism and Economic Order*, Chicago: University of Chicago Press, pp. 33–56.

Hayek, F.A. (1948b), 'The Use of Knowledge in Society', in F.A. Hayek, *Individualism and Economic Order*, Chicago: University of Chicago Press, pp. 77–91.

Hayek, F.A. (1952), *The Sensory Order*, Chicago: University of Chicago Press.

Hayek, F.A. [1964] (1967), 'The Theory of Complex Phenomena', in *Studies in Philosophy, Politics and Economics*, Chicago: University of Chicago Press, pp. 22–42.

Hayek, F.A. [1968] (1978), 'Competition as a Discovery Procedure', in *New Studies in Philosophy, Politics, Economics and the History of Ideas*, Chicago: University of Chicago Press, pp. 179–90.

Hayek, F.A. (1969), 'The Primacy of the Abstract', in A. Koestler and J.R. Smythies (eds), *Beyond Reductionism: New Perspectives in the Life Sciences*, New York: Macmillan, pp. 309–33.

Hicks, John [1937] (1967), 'Mr Keynes and the "Classics"' originally published in *Econometrica*, **V**, April (1937), reprinted in *Critical Essays in Monetary Theory*, Oxford: Clarendon Press, pp. 126–42.

Hirsch, Abraham and Neil de Marchi (1990), *Milton Friedman: Economics in Theory and Practice*, Ann Arbor: University of Michigan Press.

Hoover, Kevin D. (1994a), 'Econometrics as observation: the Lucas critique and the nature of econometric inference', *Journal of Economic Methodology*, **1**, 65–80.

Hoover, Kevin D. (1994b), 'Pragmatism, Pragmaticism, and Economic Theory', in Roger Backhouse (ed.), *New Perspectives on Economic Methodology*, London: Routledge, pp. 286–315.

Hunsaker, Jerome and Saunders Mac Lane (1973), 'Edwin Bidwell Wilson', in *Biographical Memoirs*, **XLIII**, National Academy of Sciences of the United States of America, New York: Columbia University Press, pp. 285–320.

Hutchison, T.W. (1994), '"Ricardian Politics": Another Case of Ricardian Hagiography?' in T.W. Hutchison, *The Uses and Abuses of Economics: Contentious Essays on History and Method*, London: Routledge, pp. 107–26.

Jevons, W.S. [1871] (1957), *The Theory of Political Economy*, 5th ed., London: Macmillan.

Keynes, J.M. (1921), *A Treatise on Probability*, New York: Macmillan.

Keynes, J.M. (1936), *The General Theory of Employment, Interest and Money*, New York: Harcourt, Brace and World.

Lakatos, Imre (1978), 'Falsification and the Methodology of Scientific Research Programmes', in *Philosophical Papers*, Vol. 1, Cambridge: Cambridge University Press, pp. 8–101.

Latsis, S.J. (ed.) (1976); *Method and Appraisal in Economics*, Cambridge: Cambridge University Press.

Leijonhufvud, Axel (1976), 'Schools, "Revolutions", and Research Programmes in Economic Theory', in S.J. Latsis (ed.), *Method and Appraisal in Economics*, Cambridge: Cambridge University Press.

Lucas, R.E. and T.J. Sargent (1981a), *Rational Expectations and Econometric Practice*, Minneapolis: University of Minnesota Press.

Lucas, R.E. and T.J. Sargent (1981b), 'After Keynesian Macroeconomics, in Lucas and Sargent, *Rational Expectations and Econometic Practice*, pp. 295–320.

Mankiw, N. Gregory and David Romer (eds) (1991), *New Keynesian Economics*, Vol. 1, Cambridge: MIT Press.

Menand, Louis (2001), *The Metaphysical Club*, New York: Farrar, Straus and Giroux.

Muth, J F. (1961), 'Rational expectations and the theory of price movements', *Econometrica*, **29**, 315–35.

Nelson, R.R. and S.G. Winter (1982), *An Evolutionary Theory of Economic Change*, Cambridge: Harvard University Press.

Newcomb, Simon [1886] (1966), *Principles of Political Economy*, New York: A.M. Kelley.

Patinkin, Don (1965), *Money, Interest and Prices: An Integration of Monetary and Value Theory*, 2nd ed., New York: Harper and Row.

For the Peirce references and quotations, the abbreviations CP, WP and EP refer to the most common sources of his published writings. CP stands for *The Collected Papers of Charles Sanders Peirce*, 8 volumes published by Harvard University Press done in the 1930s and 1950s. WP stands for the *Writings of Charles S. Peirce: A Chronological Edition*, published by the Peirce Edition project in Indianapolis. Presently there are six volumes in print and more are planned. EP stands for *The Essential Peirce*, two volumes of Peirce's core philosophical writings for use in graduate and undergraduate level classes on philosophy and intellectual history.

Pcirce, Charles Sanders [1871] (1976), 'Letter to Benjamin Peirce', in Carolyn Eiselee, *The New Elements of Mathematics*, Atlantic Heights, NJ: Mouton Publishers, pp. 553–4.

Peirce, Charles Sanders [1874] (1982), 'On Political Economy', in C.J. Kloesel et al. (eds), *Writings of Charles S. Peirce: A Chronological Edition*, Vol. 3, 1872–1878, Indianapolis: Indiana University Press, pp. 173–6.

Popular Science Monthly Series: Illustrations of the Logic of Science. Six papers published in the *Popular Science Monthly* in 1877 and 1878 and reprinted in C.J. Kloesel et al. (eds), *Writings of Charles S. Peirce: A Chronological Edition*, Vol. 3, 1872–1878, Indianapolis: Indiana University Press, pp. 242–338.

Peirce, Charles Sanders (1877), 'The Fixation of Belief', WP, Vol. 3, pp. 242–57.

Peirce, Charles Sanders, (1878a), 'How to Make Our Ideas Clear', WP, Vol. 3, pp. 257–76.

Peirce, Charles Sanders (1878b), 'The Doctrine of Chances', WP, Vol. 3, pp. 276–89.

Peirce, Charles Sanders (1878c), 'The Probability of Induction', WP, Vol. 3, pp. 290–305.

Peirce, Charles Sanders (1878d), 'The Order of Nature', WP, Vol. 3, pp. 306–22.

Peirce, Charles Sanders (1878e), 'Deduction, Induction, and Hypothesis', WP, Vol. 3, pp. 323–38.

Peirce, Charles Sanders (1879), 'Note on the Theory of the Economy of Research', in *United States Coast Survey* for the fiscal year ending June 1876, US Government Printing Office, reprinted in *Operations Research*, XV (1967), pp. 642–8. Also reprinted in A.W. Burks (ed.) (1958), *The Collected Papers of Charles Sanders Peirce*, Vol. 7, Cambridge: Harvard University Press, pp. 76–83; and in C.J.W. Kloesel (ed.) (1986), *The Writings of Charles S. Peirce: A Chronological Edition*, Vol. 4, 1879–1884, Indianapolis: Indiana University Press, pp. 72–8.

Peirce, Charles Sanders (1887–88), *A Guess at the Riddle*, reprinted in Nathan Houser et al. (eds) (2000), *Writings of Charles S. Peirce: A Chronological Edition*, Vol. 6, 1886–1890, Indianapolis: Indiana University Press, pp. 168–210.

The Monist Series: Five papers published in *The Monist* from 1891 to 1893. They elaborate the ideas from 'A Guess at the Riddle'. They are reprinted in Nathan Houser and Christian Kloesel (eds) (1992), *The Essential Peirce*, Vol. 1, Bloomington: Indiana University Press, pp. 285–371.

Peirce, Charles Sanders (1891), 'The Architecture of Theories', EP, pp. 284–96.

Peirce, Charles Sanders (1892a), 'The Doctrine of Necessity Examined', EP, pp. 297–311.

Peirce, Charles Sanders (1892b), 'The Law of Mind', EP, pp. 312–33.

Peirce, Charles Sanders (1892c), 'Man's Glassy Essence', EP, pp. 334–51.

Peirce, Charles Sanders (1893), 'Evolutionary Love', EP, pp. 352–71.

Peirce, Charles Sanders [1901] (1958), 'On the Logic of Drawing History from Ancient Documents Especially from Testimonies', reprinted in Peirce Edition Project (eds) (1998), *The Essential Peirce*, Vol. 2, Bloomington: Indiana University Press, pp. 75–114, and in A.W. Burks (ed.) (1958), *The Collected*

Papers of Charles Sanders Peirce, Volume VII, Cambridge: Harvard University Press, pp. 89–164.

Phelps, E.S. (2003), 'Reflections on Parts I and II', in *Knowledge, Information, and Expectations in Modern Macroeconomics: In Honor of Edmund S. Phelps*, Princeton: Princeton University Press, pp. 271–81.

Pigou, A.C. (1943), 'The Classical Stationary State', *Economic Journal*, **53**, December, pp. 343–51.

Popper, Karl (1972), 'Of Clouds and Clocks: An Approach to the Problem of Rationality and the Freedom of Man', in K. Popper, *Objective Knowledge: An Evolutionary Approach*, Oxford: Oxford University Press.

Reder, M.W. (1982), 'Chicago economics: permanence and change', *Journal of Economic Literature*, **XX** (1), 1–38.

Romer, David (2001), *Advanced Macroeconomics*, 2nd ed., New York: McGraw-Hill.

Royce, Josiah (1914), 'The mechanical, the historical, and the statistical', *Science*, NS, **XXXIX** (1007), April 17, 551–66.

Stiglitz, J.E. and A. Weiss (1981), 'Credit rationing in markets with imperfect information', *American Economic Review*, **71** (3), 393–410.

Snowdon, Brian, Howard Vane and Peter Wynarczyk (1994), *A Modern Guide to Macroeconomics*, Camberley, UK and Brookfield, US: Edward Elgar.

Thayer, H.S. (1968), *Meaning and Action: A Critical History of Pragmatism*, New York: Bobbs-Merill Co.

Waldrop, M. Mitchell (1992), *Complexity: The Emerging Science at the Edge of Order and Chaos*, New York: Simon and Schuster.

Wible, James R. (1990), 'Implicit contracts, rational expectations, and theories of knowledge', *Review of the History of Economic Thought and Methodology*, **7**, 141–70.

Wible, James R. (1994), 'Charles Sanders Peirce's economy of research', *Journal of Economic Methodology*, **1**, 135–60.

Wible, James R. (1995), 'Of clouds and clocks and Keynes: conceptions of reality and the growth of knowledge function of money', *Review of Political Economy*, **7** (3), 308–37.

Wible, James R. (1998a), 'Peirce's Economic Reasoning in His Methodological Essay: "On the Logic of Drawing History from Ancient Documents Especially from Testimonies"', in Malcolm Rutherford (ed.), *Perspectives in the History of Economic Thought*, London: Routledge, pp. 233–57.

Wible, James R. (1998b), *The Economics of Science: Methodology and Epistemology as if Economics Really Mattered*, London: Routledge.

Wible, James R. (2000a), 'What is Complexity?', in David Colander (ed.), *Complexity in the History of Economic Thought, Perspectives in the History of Economic Thought*, London: Routledge, pp. 15–30.

Wible, James R. (2000b), 'Complexity in Peirce's Economics and Philosophy: An Exploration of His Critique of Simon Newcomb', in David Colander (ed.), *Complexity in the History of Economic Thought, Perspectives in the History of Economic Thought*, London: Routledge, pp. 74–103.

Wiener, Philip P. (1949), *Evolution and the Founders of Pragmatism*, Cambridge: Harvard University Press.

Williams, Harold R. and John D. Huffnagle (1969), *Macroeconomic Theory: Selected Readings*, New York: Appleton-Century-Crofts.

Wilson, E.B. [1923] (1998), 'Keynes on Probability', in *Bulletin of the American Mathematical Society*, **XXIX** (7), 319–22, reprinted in C.R. McCann, Jr (ed.),

John Maynard Keynes: Critical Responses, Vol. I, New York: Routledge, pp. 434–7.

8. Truth, Uncertainty, Morals: The Uneasy Relationship between Economic Advice and Politicians

Kurt W. Rothschild

In many law courts throughout the world witnesses are sworn in and expected to tell the 'truth, the whole truth and nothing but the truth'. Even when we neglect the sophisticated philosophical debates doubting whether such a thing as 'truth' actually exists it is easy to see that this is a very exacting demand indeed. To expect human beings to tell the *whole* truth about anything extending beyond some very simple factual relationships means to neglect the limitations of the human brain. To look through the entire network of complex and changing situations surpasses the capacities of individual thinking. If such analyses were easy, 'truth' could not only be gradually approached but could be fully established. Progress in knowledge and science would become superfluous. The admonition to tell 'nothing but the truth' is less demanding and could – at least in principle – be realized. But it would mean that one does not only refrain from telling lies but also avoids any indications of uncertain assumptions and possibilities which surround the subject under question, even when they may be helpful for coming to a decision.[1]

In spite of these obvious restrictions the above-mentioned formula does make sense. It provides a clear signal to the witness to stick to the truth as far as possible, to avoid lies at all costs, even when the truth may harm his interests, and to desist from mere hunches and speculations. Subjecting the witness to this legal and moral imperative serves a recognizable and generally accepted purpose. It provides the judge or the jury, who have the enormous power to send individuals to jail or even to the death chamber, with the necessary 'true' information so that they can come to a 'just' decision. At the same time it helps to prevent misuses of

---

[1] The legal rules in some countries (including the US) explicitly forbid the utterance and acceptance as evidence of mere assumptions or hearsay on the part of the witnesses.

legal power. The whole arrangement serves the more or less unanimous societal aim to punish criminal behavior in a correct and 'just' way for security and moral reasons.

This sketch of the witness–judge relation can serve as a useful background and contrasting example to the expert–politician connection which is the subject of this article. In one aspect one can regard the two cases as parallel specimens of a common situation. In both examples we have on the one side a person with the power and the will to act (judge, politician), and on the other side there is the knowledgeable 'expert' (witness, economist) who is supposed to provide the relevant 'true' information which is needed for a successful execution of the desired action. But on closer examination it turns out that in spite of this basic formal similarity, the underlying differences in situations and motives disturb the apparent analogy and let the policy-advice case appear in a different and more diffuse light than that of the law courts. In particular it will be seen that the maxim 'the truth, the whole truth and nothing but the truth' loses its simple character as the obvious and dominant guiding principle in the political environment.

To begin with one should point out a fundamental difference between the objective character of witness–judge and expert–politician relationships. In the law court we have a clear-cut division between the fact-providing witness and the decision–making judge ('not guilty' or 'guilty and punishment'). The witness provides facts about the past and is not concerned about the future and not involved in the judge's decision. *In principle* there exists the possibility for the witness to tell the truth and nothing but the truth. In policy advice in the public (and equally in the private) sphere the situation is different. Normally the expert is not (only) required to describe and analyze past facts but he or she is also asked to provide considered information about future consequences of planned or still to be determined actions of the politician.

Yet as the famous English economist Joan Robinson used to stress (and to remind fellow economists): 'The past is fixed and the future is uncertain.' This 'certainty' about future uncertainty may not matter very much when the advice concerns technical matters, like the 'required' strength of a new bridge. In such cases reliable and more or less unchanging 'natural laws' permit a neglect of the uncertainty element. But in the more complex social and economic fields where human actions and reactions have a decisive influence such neglect is not permissible. We are faced with 'non-ergodic' situations where the future cannot be 'scientifically' fully foreseen on the basis of presently available facts. The future is partly dependent on the way the present has been arrived at and partly on uncertain human actions and reactions to the ongoing dynamic process. Uncertainty is therefore an *unavoidable and inherent* element in most cases of policy advice. Since 'truth' and 'uncertainty' are not compatible and yet *considered* speculations about the future are essential for future-oriented actions it is obvious that a strict formulation of 'nothing but the truth' is not applicable in policy advice in general and in economic policy advice in particular.

In economics this problem tends to be overlooked because of a birthmark of the mainstream neoclassical theory. From the beginning it tried to copy methods of mechanical physics (Mirowski 1988) with their 'ergodic' assumptions (that is the existence of clear-cut and unique causal chains following from given circumstances). The fact that politicians are frequently not sufficiently aware of the unavoidable indeterminateness of social theories and ask for 'clear-cut' advice, which the conscientious expert cannot give, leads to irritations on both sides. They either create dissatisfied politicians who are faced with 'blurred' information or they induce experts to meet the demands of the politicians by providing 'precise' forecasts (for example 2.6 percent GDP growth in the coming year instead of a 'scientifically' defensible forecast of 2.1 to 2.9 percent), thereby sacrificing their aspiration to pronounce 'scientific truth'.

A similar but basically different source of such irritations is the existence of several, partly contradictory theories. Here again we have a situation that has its roots in objective circumstances which cannot be – if at all – easily overcome. In contrast to the *unavoidable* uncertainty connected with an open future the uncertainty caused by competitive theories could be removed by finding the one and only 'true' theory.[2] In practice, however, this seems – at least at present and quite apart from subjective factors to be discussed later – to be impossible because of the enormous complexity and dynamism of economic processes. No theory can be found which could be satisfactorily applied in all circumstances and in all places; and even the 'best' partial theories, tailored to some special problems, have only restricted validity. Thus, while the economist is certainly in a better position than the (non-economist) politician to survey and judge the applicability of alternative theories, he is nevertheless faced with uncertainties about the choice of relevant theoretical models in concrete situations.

As in the previous case of future-uncertainty we have here a conflict between a politician hoping for 'clear' and reliable explanations and an

---

[2] No theory can, of course, be 'true' in the strict sense of the word, that is offering a complete correspondence with all the elements of the real situation. On the contrary: theories are essentially *not* true in this sense because their task is to help – through *abstraction* from less relevant elements – to provide a *generally* (and uniquely?) applicable access to an explanation of a large class of real phenomena.

economist faced with theoretical uncertainty. As before, one of two possible consequences may follow. Either the economist lays before the politician not only his most favored theoretical model but also the competing approaches and thus leaves some uncertainty for the decision-making process. Or he neglects his 'the whole truth' imperative and bases his advice exclusively on his chosen model and thus meets the politician's preference for clear guidance. A mutually satisfactory solution is not possible.[3]

So far we have dealt with *objective* difficulties which are inherent in the expert–politician relationship. Added to these are a number of more or less subjective factors connected with different perspectives and interests of the agents on both sides. One difficulty arises from the already mentioned fact that in contrast to the law court with its sharp division between fact-providing witness and law-determined decision-making judge there is a considerable interdependence between the activities of the economic expert and the politician. The politician approaches the adviser not only with the wish to decide whether to say yes or no ('guilty or not guilty') but with the hope to obtain expert advice about the possibilities and the methods required in order to reach a given aim. Such advice can be in the form of proposing suitable actions or of critically judging the suitability and consequences of actions proposed by the politician. Advice is not needed for the choice of the policy aim, which is at least partly always a political choice, but is required because the economic aspects of achieving the aim and of judging its side-effects are too complex to be fully understood by the layman. 'Good' economic advice is therefore needed and should be helpful.

A problem arises because economic policy has many side-effects and consequences which affect numerous aspects of society and create winners and losers. Almost always a wider political problem is involved. In order to effectuate a chosen economic policy and to reach a desired aim in a democratic society it is not only necessary to know the economic mechanics and their immediate consequences. It is also essential to have sufficient public support for the necessary actions and an acceptance of the combined economic, political and social consequences. The purely economic mechanisms and consequences are often the most complicated elements in economic policy processes, but they are certainly not the only

---

[3] The irritations of politicians caused by the unavoidable 'fuzziness' of expert opinions are well illustrated by two well-known anecdotes (which I dare to repeat here because it is said that old jokes are the best jokes). Thus Churchill is said to have complained that if he asks five economists for advice he gets six different answers, two of them coming from Mr. Keynes. And Truman is reported to have asked for a one-handed economist because he is fed up from hearing his advisers always saying: 'On the one hand . on the other hand'.

important ones. The complexity of the 'purely' economic side leads to the frequency of special economic advice. But the extreme specialization of the social sciences often prevents even very good economists from seeing the economic policy project in its entirety, that is including public reactions and other non-economic elements which play an essential role in its ultimate implementation. That is, they overlook or neglect the fact that the problem for the politician, who wants political success (and needs it in order to act in the longer run), always touches questions not only of economics but also of political science, sociology, psychology, and so on. In these fields the politician needs less advice, since as far as they are concerned he is himself an experienced practitioner and to some extent an expert. But what is needed is to see the project as a whole, embedded in an interrelated political–economic–social environment.

One could of course say – and this is the opinion of some economists – that a clear division of labor between economic adviser and politician could solve this aspect of economic policy advice. The economist provides the 'purely' economic comments related to the desired policy and the politician adds his expert knowledge about feasibilities and socio-political side-effects. Taken together these two efforts should yield the necessary basis for policy action. In other words, in a composite undertaking, which an economic policy plan usually is, the 'half truth' of a virtual 'pure' economic world is combined with the 'half truth' of a 'pure' socio-political environment to deliver the 'whole truth' ('truth' here meant in the sense of approximation to reality) for handling the total situation. But this would only be correct if the 'partial truths' were 'additive'. And this is typically not the case when we have to deal – as is usual for economic policy processes – with parts which are interdependent and where one is faced – in the terminology of Gunnar Myrdal – with 'circular causation' (Myrdal 1957). The 'laws' of the economic world are not quite independent of the socio-political environment and the socio-political aspirations and policy formulations are not independent of the actual and perceived economic possibilities and limitations. Efficient advice approaching as far as possible the 'true' opportunities for political action in its entireness demands a give-and-take position between advice and action in which flexible economic alternatives face flexible policy arrangements which influence each other. The simple policy chain running from clearly stated aims over strict economic advice to satisfactory fulfillment of the given aims does not work.

There are, of course, other possibilities to take account of and to overcome this difficulty of 'relative' truth. Two alternative routes offer themselves. One is that the economist expands his basic 'pure' economic model and includes those sociological, psychological and country-specific elements that can facilitate judgments about the practical feasibility of a project and about wanted or unwanted side-effects. An interdisciplinary approach, which is in any case desirable in complex situations, becomes particularly relevant in practical policy applications. But as experience shows, interdisciplinary skill is not easily achieved and runs counter to the tendency of ever finer subdivisions and specializations in sophisticated research fields. The other possibility is to give up the simple one-track strategy of aim–advice–action and to acknowledge the interdependence of the several stages by an ongoing cooperation between economist and politician with each contributing his own specialized knowledge. In the course of such cooperation both aims and methods will develop in more realistic ways than could be planned or envisaged at the beginning of the process. But here again it should not be overlooked that time perspectives, methods, language and so on differ between economic theorists on the one hand and politicians (or political and psychological experts) on the other hand. This does not exactly help to make cooperation a success.[4] One of the basic difficulties is also that the economists and the politicians have different 'values' at the back of their minds which influence their perspectives and the way they 'construct' propositions and 'truth'. For economists 'allocational efficiency' is a prominent target, politicians have to care particularly for distributional and equity aspects.

Anyway, whether these problems of interdependence are overlooked or pushed aside in view of their additional requirements, the fact is that economic policy advice often follows the simple one-way route from specialized economist to specialized politician with the consequence that – because of the unavoidable shortcomings of this method[5] – both sides are disappointed. The economist complains that his careful economic analysis is not (fully) applied in policy action and the politician points out that the advice he obtains is too much removed from his action radius to make it useful as a blueprint.

So far we have dealt with objective and some semi-subjective problems which make it difficult to establish 'truth' (both in its hard and

---

[4] That interdisciplinary discussions can lead to dubious results when not properly prepared is shown by the recollections of the late Sir Alec Cairncross who as an economist was for many years actively engaged in advisory activities for the British government. He remembers discussions 'between economists, administrators, and ministers at which it (was) by no means uncommon for the economists to talk politics, the administrators to talk economics, and the ministers to discuss administrative problems' (Cairncross 1971, p. 203).

[5] 'Whether or not economists should take political constraints into account when forming policy advice is still a matter of debate among academic economists, but in the reality of political decision-making political constraints cannot be ignored' (Roland 2000, p. 26). An extensive treatment of the problems involved can be found in Funk (2000).

soft interpretations) in the economic policy advice process. But though uncertainty and methodological difficulties prevent a final arrival at 'truth', truth can still act as a target at which all participants in the process should aim. This is the 'ideal' vision behind the process and this is also what the onlooking public hopes for and – optimistically – expects. It wishes that the politicians openly declare what aims they want to achieve and what side-effects they want to include or avoid, and expects the economic advisers to provide the politician with all the relevant facts to the best of their knowledge. This can be done by presenting a unique 'model' which the adviser sincerely regards to be the best available, or – even better – by adding to his preferred proposition other serious alternatives in order to indicate the uncertain fringes of his 'truth'. If both sides are driven by such motives a transparent advice process can develop which will establish trust between the partners and between them and the public even when – unavoidably – things do not always turn out as planned or forecasted.

But 'truth' may be endangered not only because of the objective impediments to get behind its tricks and whims, but because one or the other partner (or both) are *intentionally* moving outside the 'truth' imperative. In other words there can be motivations on the subjective side to 'falsify' the advice procedure so that even the objectively attainable 'degree of truth' is not achieved. As far as the political side is concerned the political literature – both historical and analytical – has a long tradition of dealing with strategies of misinformation and deception in order to win elections and to gain political or economic power. As far as the advice process is concerned this means that politicians may – in order to display a serious endeavor – submit their populistic programs to expert advice without any intention to follow that advice (Peters and Barker 1993, p. 3). The expert who does not look through this maneuver will of course be disappointed when he sees that his advice is neglected or regarded as irrelevant.

But motivational factors undermining the search for 'truth' play also a part on the economist's side though this is a less frequently treated theme. It is a strange phenomenon that economists who rely in all their analyses of decision-making on the model of the homo oeconomicus, whose decisions are driven by the wish to maximize his own utilities, are often reluctant to apply the same perspective to their own actions (Peacock 1994). Thus, while they have no difficulty in charging politicians who talk of the 'common welfare' to aim in reality at maximizing votes and political power (the subject of the 'New Political Economy'), they are quite ready to assume that the guild of economists is always eager to give objective, 'true' advice. Yet economists may be driven by a desire for public recognition and possibly also (like other people) for additional sources of income and this may enter their utility-maximizing decisions (Kirchgässner 1999). Policy advice can then be attractive for the economist as a means to achieve such aims. This leads to a temptation to sacrifice a bit of the scientific morale to look for the 'whole truth and nothing but the truth' in order to improve the chances for obtaining advisory positions. A tendency develops to stress those elements which favor the desired policy aims and to suppress those which are disliked by the politician.[6] (This 'sin' against scientific morals must be distinguished from the different moral question how far a conscientious adviser can be expected or should agree to give objective advice for a successful policy which goes against his 'values' as a citizen. But this is a different story.)

Such behavior can have two consequences. Either the quality of the advice suffers (because the 'truth' was willingly distorted), leading to a loss of confidence in the advisory process in the longer run; or we have a situation – important in many fields of the social sciences – where forecasts, and particularly forecasts by well-known experts, become themselves elements which influence the uncertain future (self-fulfilling or self-destroying forecasts). When this is the case the economist ceases to be the independent expert. He turns – at least partly – into a political agent who supports or hinders the politician's plans. The question of 'truth' then recedes into the background because the activity of the adviser is at least partly guided by his values and biases which cannot have a scientific foundation. If the lack of impartiality is not openly admitted the disclosure of it in the course of time will again undermine public confidence in the advisory process. The 'anti-truth' tendency becomes of course particularly explosive when dishonest politics are combined with compliant experts.[7] Advisory processes can then become a mere supporting instrument for a given program.

In conclusion I want to stress that this account of the difficulties of economic policy advice and of irritations which follow from them is *not* meant as an argument against making use of this method, and even more use than is presently the case. As Schumpeter once said in reply to a natural scientist who criticized the shortcomings of economic theory: 'The theory may not be very good, but it is the best we have.' To make

---

[6] 'An adviser who repeatedly submits proposals in direct contradiction to the minister's known views or the government's publicly announced policies is likely to be ignored, dismissed or put into a position where he or she cannot be heard' (Coats 1999, p. 77).

[7] In a symposium on Economic Policy Advice an US Congressman complained: 'Unfortunately, we are more inclined to listen to those who are telling us what we want to hear, and an ample supply of economists are willing to meet this demand' (Hamilton 1992, p. 63).

use of the second- or even the third-best that economic theory has to offer is probably better than searching in the dark. Yet from what has been said it should be clear that one should maintain a critical and skeptical attitude towards the advisory process in order to watch out for unavoidable shortcomings and pitfalls. When the limitations of the process are known and efforts to improve it are taken, it can certainly play a useful role. In this sense I want to end this chapter with a few passages from an Introductory Address, dealing with this theme, held at the 1986 Annual Conference of the American Economic Association by its then acting President, the economist Alice Rivlin:

> Economists know that the economic system is incredibly complicated, and that increasing global interdependence and rapidly changing technologies and public attitudes are not making it easier to understand . . . Like the medical profession which also deals with an incredibly complex system, we economists just have to keep applying our imperfect knowledge as carefully as possible and learning from the results. Both doctors and economists need humility, but neither should abandon their patients to quacks. The objective of economists ought to be to raise the level of debate on economic policy . . . and to increase the chances of policy decisions to make the economy work better. Much of the time that means telling the public and politicians what they would rather not hear: hard choices must be made. We are stuck with being the dismal science. (Rivlin 1987, p. 8)

REFERENCES

Cairncross, Sir Alec (1971), *Essays in Economic Management*, London: George Allen & Unwin.

Coats, A.W. (1999), 'Economic Policy Advice: Opportunities and Limitations', in E. Mohr (ed.), *The Transfer of Economic Knowledge*, Cheltenham, UK and Northampton, MA, USA: Edward Elgar, pp. 74–89.

Funk, L. (2000), 'Wissenschaftliche Beratung der Wirtschaftspolitik: Ist Politikberatung Wirklich Obsolet?' in U. Albertshauser and H. Knödler (eds), *Ökonomie und Politikberatung im Spannungsfeld von Theorie und Praxis*, Berlin: Verlag für Wissenschaft und Forschung, pp. 75–108.

Hamilton, L.H. (1992), 'Economists as public policy advisers', *Journal of Economic Perspectives*, **6** (3), 61–4.

Kirchgässner, G. (1999), 'On the Political Economy of Economic Policy Advice', in E. Mohr (ed.), *The Transfer of Economic Knowledge*, Cheltenham, UK and Northampton, MA, USA: Edward Elgar, pp. 13–31.

Mirowski, P. (1988), *Against Mechanism: Protecting Economics from Science*, Totowa, NJ: Rowman and Littlefield.

Myrdal, G. (1957), *Economic Theory and Underdeveloped Regions*, London: Duckworth.

Peacock, A. (1994), 'The utility maximizing government economic adviser', *Public Choice*, **80** (1/2), 191–7.

Peters, B.G. and A. Barker (1993), *Advising West European Governments. Inquiries, Expertise and Public Policy*, Edinburgh: Edinburgh University Press.

Rivlin, A.M. (1987), 'Economists and the political process', *American Economic Review*, **77** (1), 1–10.

Roland, G. (2000), *Transition and Economics. Politics, Markets and Firms*, Cambridge, Mass.: Cambridge University Press.

9. Serving Two Masters: Economic Methodology between Philosophy and Practice

Roger E. Backhouse[*]

ABSTRACT

Economic methodology is caught between the competing demands of philosophy and economics, placing economic methodologists located in economics departments in an uncomfortable position. The chapter discusses the way in which methodologists have responded to this dilemma and argues that, although the gap between the two demands has narrowed considerably over the past decade, it remains substantial. It suggests that, in order to understand what economists are doing, it is important that methodology attends to the methodological agenda set by practicing economists, even if this implies a greater concern with the technical methods of economics than has become customary.

1. THE PLACE OF ECONOMIC METHODOLOGY

A defining feature of a discipline such as economic methodology is that it is caught between the competing demands of philosophy and practice. There is a sense in which economic methodology is simply a branch of philosophy – it is concerned with the principles of reasoning underlying economics and could thus be viewed as philosophy of science concerned with one specific science.[1] However, the field has been developed by

---

[*] R.E Backhouse@bham.ac.uk.
[1] Note that I do not say 'philosophy of science applied to a particular science', because that might be taken to imply a specific relationship between philosophy of science and methodology.

economists as well as philosophers.[2] These economists have brought to it their own concerns, which are not the same as those of philosophers. In particular, many economists use methodology to improve economics. Others use it as a weapon in battles with other economists.

Economic methodology is also caught between two masters in another sense. Its practitioners are divided, institutionally, between philosophy and economics departments.[3] Thus even if economic methodologists in economics departments communicate effectively with their colleagues in philosophy, doing work that is respected by philosophers, they face the task of defending what they do to their colleagues who are practitioners of economics. 'Live and let live' is one response. Economic methodologists need not communicate with practicing economists any more than specialists in forecasting speak to game theorists or economic historians. However, this response is neither ideal nor easy to sustain. In the modern academic world, publications have to be assessed. People in economics departments typically have to satisfy economists that their publications are of high quality and possibly that they contribute to economics.[4] This may take the form of pressure to abandon methodology in favor of contributions within economics or pressure to publish in 'general' journals (such as the *JPE*, *QJE* or *Econometrica*) rather than in journals where methodology is valued more highly.

More importantly, however, economic methodologists are often speaking about things on which economists have strong views that may go against ideas taken for granted in philosophy. For example, most philosophers and sociologists would take for granted the symmetry thesis – the idea that theories of science should explain the failures of science as well as its successes. Similarly, they would immediately reject the idea that 'correctness' of scientific ideas is enough to explain why those ideas prevailed. Yet to some economists, such ideas are incomprehensible. Economists are also prone to take for granted things that philosophers and economic methodologists want to question. Examples include the assumption of rationality and the idea that economics has been successful. When economic methodologists question such assumptions,

---

[2] Throughout this chapter, I am using the term 'philosophers' to encompass sociologists and others whose ideas have been brought to bear on economics. There are circumstances where it is important to separate these but this is not one of them.

[3] The qualification in Note 1 applies here too.

[4] In the UK, this takes the form of a national Research Assessment Exercise. In the RAE, work by economists will typically be submitted to the economics panel, where it is judged by a panel of economists. This applies to all economics departments that seek research funding. For those departments that form part of business schools, the same arguments apply, but with 'business studies' replacing 'economics'.

they are in danger of being seen by their economist colleagues to be 'knocking' the subject. Even where economists recognize that criticisms of economics are in order, they may take the view that it is better not to wash dirty linen in public.

The situation facing economic methodologists is made even harder by the fact that some economists do engage in methodology and some use explicit methodological critiques of their opponents to justify their own approaches to economics. This is largely, though not exclusively, a characteristic of heterodox economists – Austrians, institutionalists, post-Keynesians, critical realists and others – who use methodology to attack the neoclassical mainstream. Many such critics start from the assumption that neoclassical economics is fundamentally flawed. Because they are so critical of it, they fail to take neoclassical economics sufficiently seriously and attach what, to insiders, often seems a caricature of what is going on in the subject. This gets economic methodology a bad reputation within economics and contributes to the idea that it is, at best, a waste of time.[5]

Some economic methodologists in this situation are 'caught'.[6] Their training does not equip them for life in a philosophy department, for they earn their living by teaching economics. Others, however, would choose to stay in economics. This may be because methodology is only one of their passions and they are committed to research within economics that can be undertaken only within an economics department. A third group, overlapping with both the others, simply regards economics as the right disciplinary base from which to tackle economic methodology. Being caught between two masters may sometimes be uncomfortable, but it is nonetheless the right place to be.

2. TWO FACES OF THE METHODOLOGY LITERATURE

If we focus on the conventional canon of influential twentieth-century works on economic methodology, this literature was, for most of the century, written by economists and for economists.[7] This remark covers

---

[5] This attitude underlies Hahn (1992).

[6] Much of this paragraph reflects the arguments in Schabas (1992) and responds to these.

[7] This leaves aside nineteenth-century writing, for in this period the sociology of the economics profession and its relationship with philosophy were different. It was an age in which major economists, such as J.S. Mill, Henry Sidgwick and W.S. Jevons were also important philosophers. There are important stories to be told about this period but they lie beyond the scope of this chapter.

Robbins (1932), Friedman (1953), Koopmans (1957), Machlup's numerous writings, and Boland (1979). Such work drew, in varying degrees, on philosophy but it was driven by the concerns of economists, to whom it was addressed. The same is true of the heterodox methodological writing of Veblen (for example 1919), Myrdal (1938) and Dobb (1937). Even where the philosophical input was very great, as with Hutchison (1938), the result was a book by someone trained as an economist, addressed to economists.

The situation changed with the advent of a generation that approached economic methodology from the perspective of philosophy. There were at least two strands to this development. One involved the influx of philosophers who found in economic methodology a source of interesting questions (Hausman 1981; Rosenberg 1976). Though curious about economics, and though they passed judgments and offered what might be seen as advice to economists, their agenda was philosophical. Another strand involved historians of economic thought. These were, for the most part, scholars trained in economics, often engaging in research and teaching in economics. However, they approached the history of economic thought not as something directed primarily at economists, but as a subject in its own right, distancing themselves from economics. What turned such historical and sociological inquiry to methodology was, arguably, Kuhn's *Structure of Scientific Revolutions* (1962), particularly as mediated and developed in Lakatos's methodology of scientific research programs (1970). This is often presented as having shown how a historical dimension was required to the philosophy of science, but for historians of economic thought it showed that there could be a strong methodological dimension to their historical inquiries. The result was a body of people (for example Coats, Blaug, Hutchison, De Marchi) who, though economists, were to approach the subject primarily as philosophically-informed 'economist watchers'[8] rather than from the perspective of practicing economists.[9] McCloskey (1983, 1986), also highly influential, arguably falls into this category as well. Though an economist, McCloskey made the transition from having an agenda driven by economics to having one driven by ideas from outside the discipline. Though her message was very different from any of theirs, it falls squarely into the category of 'economist watching'.

---

[8] This is Coats's phrase.

[9] Hutchison appears twice in this account, in two roles. His first book was a philosophical analysis of economics, not involving history. After moving to LSE he took up the history of economic thought and adopted the perspective described in this sentence.

When, in the early 1980s, following the publication of Blaug's (1980) textbook, economic methodology began to emerge as an identifiable field in economics, it was dominated by this combination of historians of economic thought and philosophers interested in economics. Though the field remained distinct from philosophy, and though judgments were offered that it was thought economists should take notice of, the orientation was primarily philosophical. The result was a literature that did not engage with the practical problems with which most economists are concerned because it sought to address more general philosophical problems. Blaug (1980, p. xi) expressed this when he argued that economic methodology was concerned with 'how economists explain' (the subtitle of his book) and not with 'the technical procedures of [the] discipline'. Given the way that the term 'methodology' has come to be used indiscriminately as a longer and pretentious synonym for 'method',[10] this emphasis is not only understandable – it was necessary in order to show that there was something going beyond cookbooks of 'technical methods'. However, the result was unfortunate as it led to a focus on grand philosophical themes – falsificationism, paradigms, rhetoric, instrumentalism, prediction and so on. Economic methodology turned away from economists, inevitably concerned with the 'technical procedures' that Blaug said were not his concern.[11]

3. ECONOMISTS AND METHODOLOGISTS

Over the past decade or so, the situation has changed in that economic methodologists have moved towards greater concern with the details of economists' practices. In part, this reflects disillusion with the 'grand theories' about science that were pursued in the 1980s and the view that different, more 'local' questions need to be asked about what is happening in economics. Case studies have increasingly been used not simply to test general philosophical theories about science but to understand the peculiarities of economics, why economists do things as they do, and to explore concepts on which economics rests. Such work has the potential to interest both philosophers and economics and opens up the possibility of engagement between them. This is illustrated by the

---

[10] The Oxford English Dictionary offers one definition of methodology that is a synonym for method.

[11] It is worth noting that Blaug (1980) contains many case studies that could have formed the basis for a different approach. I conjecture, however, that the vast majority of people who have cited his book or used it in teaching have focused on the more general philosophical discussions.

results of a conference held at the University of Bergamo in 1996 (Backhouse et al., 1997) at which methodology case studies were discussed by both philosophers and economists.

However, although there was real engagement between these two groups, important differences remained. The nature of the engagement between philosophers and economists varied according to the nature of the case study. [12] Common ground was greatest when discussion concerned the meaning of fundamental theoretical concepts, such as individualism in game theory. It was least when historical case studies were involved (these included the evolution of the concepts of externalities and involuntary unemployment and the stabilization of demand theory). Economists were inclined to dismiss them as dealing with episodes in the history of economic thought that were of no relevance to contemporary economics. They were also much readier than were methodologists to see the truth of ideas as explaining why those ideas came to be accepted by economists.

This conference, however, did not bring out the full extent of the differences in perspective between economists and philosophers. The case studies were written by people who, even though some were primarily philosophers and others primarily economists, all had a prior commitment to methodology. The agenda was thus set by methodology. Economists might find the issues interesting, and even important, but they were not necessarily the issues that they would regard as most important. In addition, economists with no special interest in methodology were in a minority. There was little scope for disagreements to emerge between practicing economists.

A second conference held in Bergamo two years later (Backhouse and Salanti, 2000) brought out the differences much more clearly. The papers were written by practicing economists who were invited to reflect on methodological aspects of certain topics. Though some of the papers stuck closely to suggestions laid out in the invitation, many did not, with the result that the methodological agenda was set by practitioners, not by methodologists. In addition, for each topic two papers were commissioned[13] – typically one by an economic theorist and one by an econometrician. [14] Methodologists were chosen as discussants. These

---

[12] For a more detailed discussion, see Backhouse et al. (1997), pp. 439–42.

[13] This contrasts with the earlier conference where a call for papers was sent out, the papers being selected from those submitted.

[14] This characterization is a great oversimplification. A more accurate, though less concise, account would be to say that there is a spectrum ranging from 'pure' theorists at one end to 'pure' empiricists at the other. Contributors were chosen who could be placed at different points on this spectrum. See also the remarks made in Section 4 below.

selection criteria meant that practitioners were in a clear majority and were in sharp disagreement over practical methodological issues. Furthermore, because the topic of the conference was macroeconomics, it avoided areas such as rationality, where the interests of economists and philosophers have traditionally overlapped with each other. If the differences between economists and philosophers had converged, these differences in the way the conferences were organized should have had only a small effect. The outcome, however, was a completely different emphasis.

Invitations to contributors asked them to address the theme of 'theory and evidence in macroeconomics', suggesting several possible questions that could be tackled. There was, however, great variety in the way people responded. Some tackled the questions directly. Others presented what appeared to be the next paper in their research program. Others chose to make a methodological point that had a bearing on the questions asked, though without answering the questions explicitly. The result was that, despite the wording of the invitations, the conference focused much more on 'technical methods' than would be normal in the methodological literature. Much of the discussion was about how to do various things in macroeconomics in a way that would not have been the case had methodologists set the agenda or dominated the discussion. It would, however, be a mistake to conclude that the conference was not methodological in the sense in which most methodologists would use the term. Methodological issues were pervasive. Even where they were not raised explicitly in the papers, they became explicit during the discussion. [15] Becoming involved in discussions between practicing economists in this way has several consequences. It raises issues that might otherwise be overlooked. It guards against oversimplification and homogenization of the views of economists. It shows that substantive and methodological views cannot always be separated.

4.   ACADEMIC ECONOMICS AND POLICY-MAKING

Up to this point the discussion has treated practicing economists as a homogeneous group. In doing so it has ignored the potential divide between academic economists and policy-makers. To some extent there has been convergence. McCallum (2000, p. 117) has argued that it is now difficult to distinguish between macroeconomic articles written by

---

[15] The two volumes contain detailed reports of the discussion as well as the papers and formal discussants' comments.

economists in academic positions and by those working in policy-making institutions such as central banks and international organizations. He finds evidence for considerable convergence over the past few years. Others, perhaps because they look in different places, find a bigger gap. Maes (2000, 2002), for example, finds a significant gap between many of those working in the European Commission, who often have backgrounds in law, and their academic counterparts.[16] However, even if the gaps are narrowing in significant ways, there remains much academic work that is of little relevance to policy-making, either because it fails to address issues that are of concern to policy-makers, or because it fails to take account of what policy-makers see as practical realities.

The significance of this point for methodology is that, if methodologists are to engage the full range of economists, it is not enough to tackle issues that concern only what has been called 'highbrow' theory. It is necessary, as well, to consider the broader set of ideas and practices that are familiar to economists involved in the policy-making process. This may involve moving away from topics such as general equilibrium theory or game theory, to consider the less fashionable areas of the construction and use of statistics, or the way policy prescriptions derived from abstract theory get modified to take account of different institutional contexts. It is often assumed, implicitly if not explicitly, at least by academic economists, that there is a hierarchy ranging from abstract theory to policy. Abstract models such as general equilibrium theory or non-cooperative game theory that are too general to yield definite conclusions are used as the basis for more specialized 'applied' models. These models are then used to draw policy-relevant conclusions.[17] However, attractive as this hierarchy may sound, it may not be like that. The 'foundation' provided by abstract economic theory may in practice be of little consequence. The point is that unless the problem of how economic ideas are used in policy-making is investigated, we will not know what the situation is.

There are two ways to look at the implications of this problem for economic methodology. One is to observe that economic practice may be a more difficult master to serve than many methodologists have realized. It is not enough to engage economic theorists in issues such as the nature of rationality in game theory. It may be necessary to deal with ideas and

---

[16] See also Mayer (2000) who also discusses the issue, and the discussion of Mayer (2000) and Maes (2000) reported on pp. 276–81 of the same volume.

[17] This is the hierarchy expressed by Weintraub (1985) when he places general equilibrium theory within the 'hard core' of a neo-Walrasian research program. This location of general equilibrium theory is criticized in Backhouse (1993).

practices that are hard to characterize because they are less rigorous, less sharply differentiated from other disciplines, and much less clearly articulated. Not only are methodologists' loyalties split between philosophy and economics, but they are also torn between analyzing 'best-practice' methods and practices that many of their academic-economist colleagues may see, whether correctly or not, as hardly worth taking seriously. Against this, of course, the gap between academic and non-academic economics presents methodologists with an opportunity, for it is something to be investigated. It is even possible that methodologists might be able to help bridge this gap through helping economists understand better the processes whereby economic ideas are applied to policy. It is quite possible that there may be stronger rationales for 'lowbrow' theories and practices of non-academic policy-makers than is evident at first sight.

5. CONCLUSIONS

Economic methodology appears to have gone through a cycle. In the 1950s, it addressed the concerns of economists, tackling practical problems. Should theories be based on realistic assumptions? Is it legitimate to construct models that are not testable or are based on assumptions that are not testable? In the context of the 1950s, when Marshallian price theory was being displaced by more abstract model-building, these were of immediate concern to theorists. From the 1960s, under the influence of Lakatos and Kuhn, methodology, in a loose alliance with history of economic thought, turned towards philosophy. It moved away from the concerns of economists who, given the dominance of Walrasian general equilibrium theory, increasingly regarded fundamental methodological issues as having been solved. From around the late 1980s, methodology moved back towards a concern with the detailed practices of economists. This was partly in response to disillusion with Kuhn and Lakatos and partly in response to developments in philosophy and the related fields (sociology, discourse analysis, rhetoric) on which methodologists were increasingly drawing.

If this movement back to economics is to continue, it is not enough for methodologists to concern themselves with economists' practices. If they are to do this, it is necessary that methodology be undertaken in such a way as to involve practicing economists. This means opening up the subject to pay much more attention to applied economics and to the very practical questions about operational methods that concern economists.[18] Without this involvement, methodologists will not become sufficiently sensitive to the details of what is going on in economics. To return to the metaphor used at the beginning of this chapter, the uncomfortable boundary, institutionally as well as intellectually, between two masters is where economic methodology needs to be undertaken.

REFERENCES

Backhouse, Roger E. (1993), 'Lakatosian perspectives on general equilibrium analysis', *Economics and Philosophy*, **9** (2), 271–82, reprinted in Roger E. Backhouse (1998), *Explorations in Economic Methodology*, London: Routledge, pp. 56–70.

Backhouse, Roger E. and Jeff Biddle (2000), 'The Concept of Applied Economics: a History of Ambiguity and Multiple Meanings', in R.E. Backhouse and J. Biddle (eds), *Toward a History of Applied Economics*. (Annual Supplement to *History of Political Economy*, **32**), Durham, NC: Duke University Press, pp. 1–24.

Backhouse, Roger E. and Andrea Salanti (2000), *Macroeconomics and the Real World*, Volume 1: *Econometric Techniques and Macroeconomics*, Volume 2: *Keynesian Economics, Unemployment and Policy*, Oxford: Oxford University Press.

Backhouse, Roger E., Daniel M. Hausman, Uskali Mäki and Andrea Salanti (1997), *Economics and Methodology: Crossing Boundaries*, London: Macmillan for the International Economic Association.

Blaug, Mark (1980), *The Methodology of Economics: How Economists Explain*, Cambridge: Cambridge University Press.

Boland, Lawrence A. (1979), 'A critique of Friedman's critics', *Journal of Economic Literature*, **17** (2), 503–22.

Dobb, Maurice (1937), *Political Economy and Capitalism*, London: Routledge and Kegan Paul.

Friedman, Milton (1953), 'The Methodology of Positive Economics', in M. Friedman (ed.), *Essays on Positive Economics*, Chicago: Chicago University Press.

Hahn, Frank (1992), 'Reflections', *Royal Economic Society (RES) Newsletter*, 77, p. 5.

Hausman, Daniel M. (1981), *Capital, Profits and Prices: An Essay in the Philosophy of Economics*, New York: Columbia University Press.

Hutchison, Terence W. (1938), *The Significance and Basic Postulates of Economic Theory*, London: Macmillan.

Koopmans, Tjalling C. (1957), *Three Essays on the State of Economic Science*, New York: McGraw Hill.

---

[18] Though it is tangential to the present argument about methodology, it is worth noting that there has been a similar neglect of applied economics in the history of economic thought. See Backhouse and Biddle (2000).

Kuhn, Thomas S. (1962) *The Structure of Scientific Revolutions*, Chicago: University of Chicago Press.

Lakatos, Imre (1970), 'Falsification and the methodology of scientific research programmes', in I. Lakatos and A. Musgrave (eds), *Criticism and the Growth of Knowledge*, Cambridge: Cambridge University Press.

Machlup, Fritz (1963), *Essays on Economic Semantics*, Englewood Cliffs: McGraw Hill.

Maes, Ivo (2000), 'Macroeconomic Thought at the European Commission in the First Half of the 1980s', in Backhouse and Salanti (2000), Volume 2, pp. 251–68.

Maes, Ivo (2002), *Economic Thought and the Making of European Monetary Union*, Cheltenham, UK and Northampton, MA, USA: Edward Elgar.

Mayer, Thomas (2000), 'Using Government Documents to Assess the Influence of Academic Research on Economic Policy', in Backhouse and Salanti (2000), Volume 2, pp. 223–50.

McCallum, Bennett T. (2000), 'Recent Developments in Monetary Policy Analysis: the Roles of Theory and Evidence', in Backhouse and Salanti (2000), Volume 1, pp. 115–39.

McCloskey, D.N. (1983), 'The rhetoric of economics', *Journal of Economic Literature*, **21** (2), 434–61.

McCloskey, D.N. (1986), *The Rhetoric of Economics*, Brighton: Harvester Press.

Myrdal, Gunnar ([1938] 1953), *The Political Element in Economic Thought*. Translated by Paul Streeten, London: Routledge and Kegan Paul.

Robbins, Lionel (1932), 'The Nature and Significance of Economic Science', London: Macmillan.

Rosenberg, Alexander (1976), *Microeconomic Laws: A Philosophical Analysis*, Pittsburgh: Pittsburgh University Press.

Schabas, Margaret (1992), 'Breaking away: history of economics as history of science', *History of Political Economy*, **24** (1), 187–203.

Veblen, Thorstein B. (1919), *The Place of Science in Modern Civilization*, New York: Viking Press.

Weintraub, E. Roy (1985), *General Equilibrium Analysis: Studies in Appraisal*, Cambridge: Cambridge University Press.

10. The Issue of Uncertainty in Economics

Sheila C. Dow[*]

To teach how to live without certainty, and yet without being paralysed by hesitation, is perhaps the chief thing that philosophy, in our age, can still do for those who study it. (Russell 1946, p.14)

1. INTRODUCTION

Policy-makers are required to act, even if the action is a continuation of the status quo. The institutional structure within which monetary policy is made requires that a decision is taken at regular intervals as to the repo rate to be set by the central bank. This decision has to be taken on some grounds, and the focus here is on the grounds which economics provides.

It is clear that such decisions are not made under conditions of certainty. The Minutes of the Bank of England Monetary Policy Committee, for example, reveal that the arguments put forward by each member involve more or less uncertainty, but also that the arguments among all the members can be quite diverse. Indeed the Bank of England's inflation forecast is expressed in the form of a 'fan', whose amplitude is a measure of uncertainty surrounding the core forecast.

That this uncertainty should be made so explicit, and so public, is an interesting development in itself, contrasting with such periods as the 1980s when policy-making was made apparently with great confidence on the basis of large macro models. Experience showed that much of this confidence was misplaced.

But if we cannot be certain as to the outcome of policy actions, what is their justification? There is a long tradition of Austrian, or neo-Austrian, economics within which the scope for policy action is limited on the

* Department of Economics, University of Stirling, Stirling FK9 4LA, Scotland UK, s.c.dow@stir.ac.uk, August 2003. Presented to the Economic Methodology Workshop, Oesterreichische Nationalbank, Vienna, 18 October 2002.

grounds that the knowledge base of policy-makers is insufficient, relative to that of economic actors. Indeed the macroeconomic aggregates on which policy is designed to impinge are seen as having limited meaning.

The purpose of this chapter is to explore the concept of uncertainty and how it affects the foundations of policy-making in economics. We start by considering what we mean by uncertainty, and its source. We will consider first the distinction between uncertainty as a property of the real world, and uncertainty as a property of our knowledge about the real world. We then consider the distinction between uncertainty as a subjective concept and as an objective concept. Economic actors and their knowledge of the real world are the subject matter of economics; in the third section we consider their knowledge and uncertainty in relation to the knowledge and uncertainty of economists about them. We consider how both economists and economic actors can deal with uncertainty, introducing partial, provisional closures in order to construct knowledge about an open system. We conclude by taking further the explicit question of monetary policy-making under uncertainty.

2.   THE NATURE AND SOURCE OF UNCERTAINTY

The term 'uncertainty' is being used here with a much broader meaning than is often the case in economics. By uncertainty we mean here unquantifiable risk, although quantifiable risk is often referred to in economics as uncertainty. If risk is quantifiable, we can insure against it. It is of limited interest because it allows the focus to continue to be on the core prediction. Of course greater quantifiable risk is relevant to decision-making, when the potential loss arising from outlying outcomes is taken into account. Indeed much of the monetary policy literature dating from Brainard (1967) and Poole (1970) has focused on the significance of higher variance in the error terms of equations representing the transmission of monetary policy. But much of the macroeconomics which provides the foundation for policy advice has effectively ignored the size of error variance; as long as the error term has zero mean and is normally distributed, the stochastic nature of the system can effectively be ignored, and certainty equivalence assumed.

Quantifiable risk has been the main focus of economics, rather than unquantifiable risk, because of the attractions of mathematical formalism (see Backhouse 1998, for a modified advocacy of this position, and Blaug 1999, for a historical account). But the possibility of unquantifiable risk needs to be addressed, not least because its existence is evident. Keynes introduced his *Treatise on Probability* (where he treated degrees of certainty and degrees of probability as equivalent) as follows:

> In most branches of academic logic . . . all arguments aim at demonstrative certainty. They claim to be conclusive. But many other arguments are rational and claim some weight without pretending to be certain. In metaphysics, in science, and in conduct, most of the arguments, upon which we habitually base our rational beliefs, are admitted to be inconclusive in a greater or lesser degree. (Keynes [1921] 1973, p. 3, emphasis in original)

Considering the source and extent of uncertainty gets to the heart of economics and its philosophical foundations.

Uncertainty is a property of knowledge. But a distinction is drawn in the literature regarding the source of uncertainty, that is, between aleatory and epistemic uncertainty (see Lawson 1988, for a full discussion). The former is uncertainty which arises from the nature of the real world, while the latter arises from our capacity to have knowledge about the real world. If there is randomness in nature, for example, so that an economy experiences random real shocks, then our knowledge of these shocks is inevitably incomplete, and therefore our ability to predict is limited accordingly. Randomness however is measurable and entails certain knowledge that shocks are random, so that this representation of aleatory uncertainty in fact corresponds to quantifiable risk. Aleatory uncertainty in the broader sense of unquantifiable risk is much less easy to pin down; we may not have any basis for knowing that the real world conforms to a stochastic system.

Epistemic uncertainty arises from an inability to know the real world. In the monetary policy literature, epistemic uncertainty can arise because of lags in the availability of data, or because of an inability to measure variables such as potential output (see Goodhart 1999). More generally, epistemic uncertainty understood as bounded rationality refers to limitations on the human ability to compute. The presumption is that in principle the economic structure and the mechanism for the transmission of monetary policy are knowable, but in practice we cannot fully access this knowledge. The implication of much of the discussion in the theoretical literature is that it is simply a matter of time before impediments to knowledge are overcome (see for example Blanchard and Fischer 1989, p. 505). The policy literature is less sanguine. This type of epistemic uncertainty is less amenable to capturing in a random error term, so the (policy-focused) model uncertainty literature has addressed this type of uncertainty by considering policy rules which are robust across a range of possible representations of the real world (see for example Bray et al. 1995).

But it may be that the nature of the real world is so complex that we cannot have full knowledge of it, even in principle; this may be one way of understanding the human condition. Indeed David Hume's theory of human nature involved this inevitable limitation on knowledge; this was the source of his (commonly misunderstood) problem of induction (Dow 2002). Observation gives us clues to underlying causal mechanisms and we build knowledge as best we can, but we have no direct access to knowledge of these mechanisms.

Further, since human knowledge and action based on this knowledge are central to the real world of social systems, the distinction between aleatory and epistemic uncertainty becomes blurred. To pursue this idea, it is helpful to consider what the uncertainty is about. In most of the monetary policy literature the goal is to construct a model which represents the economic structure and the transmission of monetary policy within that structure. What cannot be pinned down is classified as uncertainty. If the structure the economist is trying to capture is stochastic, uncertainty is aleatory. If there are difficulties in pinning down the structure, uncertainty is epistemic. This classification presumes that the economic system is such that it can be captured in a model. If on the other hand the real world is complex and organic, with behavior and institutions evolving over time, sometimes gradually and sometimes with discrete shifts, then it cannot conceivably be fully captured in a model. Models will capture aspects of that complexity and thus add to knowledge. But that knowledge is inevitably partial and provisional. It is not just that there are limitations to human knowledge. These limitations are inevitable not only because of human failings, but also because of the nature of the real world about which we are trying to build up knowledge, and of which human nature is a central part. The creativity of individuals as well as the evolving social patterns of behavior mean that the economic structure changes in inevitably unpredictable ways.

It is helpful to recall Popper's (1982) three-way classification of the universe: world 1 is the physical world, world 2 the psychological world, and world 3 the product of the human mind. The first two constitute one of the conventional understandings of the subject matter of economics to which the concept of aleatory uncertainty may be applied. World 3 is the province of epistemic uncertainty. But, as Popper argues, the three worlds are all interdependent, with human constructions being both the product of worlds 1 and 2, and in turn affecting them. Popper concluded that, taken together, the three worlds produce an indeterminate whole. The indeterminacy is not stochasticness, but a more profound indeterminacy which means that the universe is an open system. Once we understand the universe as an open system, according to Popper, it cannot be represented by a deterministic (even if stochastic) model. It is therefore no longer appropriate to talk in terms of the 'true' model about which we are uncertain. There is no such thing (other than hypothetically, as something known by the deity). Epistemic uncertainty therefore follows from, and in turn contributes to, the openness of the real world.

A more appropriate distinction may then be between subjective uncertainty and objective uncertainty. Subjective uncertainty refers to the individual perceptions of the real world, and the different psychological states of different individuals. This can be distinguished from the degree of uncertainty which it is in some sense rational to hold with respect to a given body of knowledge. This distinction is important for the (neo-) Austrian approach to knowledge. Methodological individualism emphasizes the subjective. But the Austrian approach stems from a particular understanding of the nature of the real world as an open system (a particular ontology). It is therefore logically compatible with a less subjectivist approach which sees objective grounds for uncertainty arising from the openness of the economic system. There is a huge debate in the literature on this subject, not least about how to understand Keynes in relation to subjectivism and objectivism with respect to uncertainty (see for example Davis's 1994 account). But in fact the focus on duals (such as objective/subjective) is itself more compatible with a closed-system approach. By exploring an open systems approach here, we emphasize more the totality of uncertainty as arising from the openness of the real world, rather than dualistic categories (see further Dow 1990).

In order to function in this real world, individuals do build up knowledge, albeit uncertain knowledge. Indeed, it was central to Menger's (1963) contribution that institutional arrangements evolve in order to provide a reasonably stable foundation for knowledge. So the economic structure itself is conditioned by knowledge limitations and attempts to surmount them. Similarly, the project of science can be understood as an exercise in reducing uncertainty about the real world, and in turn impacts upon the real world. Epistemic uncertainty and efforts to address it become bound up with the real economic structure and thus with sources of aleatory uncertainty. In the next section we focus on the parallelism between the efforts of economic actors to reduce uncertainty and the efforts of economists (see Dow 2003, for a fuller account).

3. UNCERTAINTY OF ECONOMISTS AND UNCERTAINTY OF ECONOMIC ACTORS

As a social science, economics is concerned with individual and social action, within social structures. Economists therefore aim to build up knowledge about this action and these structures. This provides the basis for policy action and the design of economic structures. But knowledge in turn can be understood to be central to both action and structures within the economy, so that issues of uncertainty can be seen to impact both on the subject matter and on economic science. In the passage quoted above from Keynes's *Treatise on Probability*, he clearly sees the issues as applying to science and to conduct.

Knowledge has been even more central to the Austrian understanding of the economic process. Drawing on this tradition and the Marshallian tradition, there is a large modern literature which sees knowledge at the core of economic reality. A key contributor to this literature, Brian Loasby (2003), draws explicit parallels between the way in which knowledge is generated in the firm and in markets, and the way in which it is generated among economists (see for example Loasby 1999). He goes back (most recently in Loasby, forthcoming) to Smith in a way which resolves the objectivity/subjectivity dualism which has the potential to threaten a blending of the Austrian and Marshallian traditions. Drawing on Hume, Smith accepted that truth was not demonstrable. He turned therefore from a rational account of science to a psychological account, focusing on the motivation for science and the basis for reasoned persuasion to accept (provisionally) one account of reality over another. Although science was explained in psychological terms, it was not seen as subjective (as the dual of objective) since it was grounded first in a belief in the existence of the real, and second in practice (both scientific and non-scientific). Indeed, the methodological individualism of Austrian economics has accordingly recently been conditioned by its blending with evolutionary economics, such that individual behavior is seen as conditioned by pre-existing institutions (see for example Caldwell and Boehm 1992).

Loasby (2003) further explores the role of closed models in building up knowledge of an open reality. For firms, some closure is a necessary feature of knowledge as the basis for action; for example, planning requires some expectation as to the outcome of innovation (some closure in what we might think of as an inherently open process). The firm itself is a form of closure. Action is based, and institutions are designed, on the basis of the identification of patterns, of connections which are understood to be present as opposed to absent. The very notion of a system entails incomplete connectedness of reality. Similarly, as economists, we build theoretical systems on the basis of patterns which we understand to be present in nature.

A fixedly closed system precludes uncertainty (as opposed to quantifiable risk); it requires internal relations to be given, and external forces to be random. In reality a perpetually closed system is generally unsustainable; firms come and go, institutions evolve. Provisional closure is necessary for action, while perpetual attention to change from within and without leads to paralysis. Further, provisional closure itself reduces uncertainty for other actors. The existence of labor contracts, of posted product prices, of stable institutions all serve as a set of patterns within which action can be taken. Periods of crisis are those where familiar patterns break down, uncertainty is rife, and paralysis sets in.

Chick and Dow (2001) argue that the methodology of employing partial, provisional closures in order to build up knowledge of an open reality allows for generality. It reflects the generality of uncertainty, while allowing different partial closures to reflect different contexts. Further, this kind of pluralist analysis may simultaneously employ different closures, even when addressing a single context. Thus one part of the analysis may take the money supply as given, while another part explores the process which determines the money supply.

The provisional closures within which actors make decisions in the economy can be thought of as models. They are human constructs which facilitate the economic process. When actors are uncertain they can be thought of as being uncertain about whether there is good reason to continue with the models they provisionally employ as the basis for action. There is apparently a direct parallel with the model uncertainty of economists. The critical issue however is what the uncertainty is about. We need to distinguish between uncertainty as to which is 'the best model' and uncertainty as to which is 'the best collection of provisional, partial models', that is between monism and pluralism.

The model uncertainty literature in general avoids this parallelism between economists' knowledge and the knowledge of economic actors. The literature which assesses the relative merits of a given range of leading macroeconomic models makes no comment on the fact that these models depict individual economic actors as displaying no such uncertainty. Similarly, the Bank of England (1999), which in other respects is most outspoken on the need for pluralism as the basis for policy decisions, nevertheless employs models which presume certainty equivalence among economic actors. The major exception is work in which Sargent plays a leading part, such as Sargent (1999); he is concerned with symmetry of treatment between economist and agent. But to make agents' uncertainty and the uncertainty of economists tractable, it is depicted for both as a complex stochastic process which is subject to pre-defined limits. What is expressed as uncertainty is in fact risk with respect to knowledge of the true model of the economic structure.

Keynes (1921) explicitly addressed the question of how individuals (in the economy, or economists, or whatever) establish reasoned grounds for belief such as to provide a basis for action; this found an echo later (Keynes 1937) when he encapsulated a key element of the *General*

Theory, the theory of liquidity preference. In the absence of a true model which individuals or economists could aim to access, given the openness of the real world, no one best route to knowledge can be identified. Action, according to Keynes, is based on reason (understood as rational grounds for belief), subject to a psychological force (intuition, animal spirits, and so on). Classical logic alone is insufficient to justify action since we cannot be certain of the outcome of our actions, far less the environment within which they will be played out. For Keynes, reason is instead based on ordinary logic, or human logic, which does not require certainty as to the truth or falsity of premises.

Ordinary logic, for economic actors and for economists, consists of multiple strands of reasoning, drawing on a range of sources of direct knowledge. Both actors and economists employ a pluralist methodology. Recourse is made to convention. In the absence of adequate knowledge derived from individualistic rationality, conventional knowledge is built up at a societal level. When forming expectations under uncertainty, individuals use what individual knowledge they have, but also refer to expert sources and indicators of societal expectations. The framework within which knowledge is formed and action taken is a set of conventions and institutions built up over the years in response to the need to cope with uncertainty, ranging from the rule of law to conventional market behavior. But by the same token expectations, lacking a rationalistic foundation, are subject to periodic discrete shifts. A change in conventional understanding, due for example to a highly publicized event, or an expression of a new expectation by a leading pundit, can have widespread consequences for expectations, for the degree of uncertainty with which they are generally held, and for ensuing action.

The same is true of economists. One of the major insights of Kuhn's (1962) approach, taken forward by the sociology of scientific knowledge, or science studies, is that scientific communities' normal research is built on a conventional foundation shared by the members of the community. The modern rhetoric approach, echoing Smith's theory of rhetoric, focuses on what is conventionally persuasive in the presentation of new ideas. Further, these conventions are embedded in an institutional structure set up to provide a basis for scientific activity: journals, textbooks, conferences, and so on. Were scientific knowledge not subject to uncertainty then rationalistic arguments could compete in a world akin to perfect competition. But, just as that world is impractical for markets in general in a world of uncertainty – markets require conventional behavior and institutions in order to function – so too scientific communities require some underpinning. This introduces some closure which allows science to proceed. But there is an inevitable circularity in the conceptual framework conventionally adopted by a particular community or paradigm, the way it understands the economic system, and the way it understands arguments about that system (see Loasby 2002). A fixed closure is unsustainable and science is subject to paradigm shifts just as conventional expectations are subject to discrete shifts. Economic paradigms do evolve over time, responding to experience of reality which challenges a particular choice of closure.

Monetary policy provides an excellent example of such a challenge. We turn in the next section to consider where this discussion takes us in considering the methodological foundations for monetary policy.

4. UNCERTAINTY AND MONETARY POLICY

The conventional closure involved in basing policy on one large macro model, treated as the 'true' model, was confronted by the experience of predictive failure (see for example Clements and Hendry 1995). One response has been the Bank of England's (1999) professed embracing of pluralism (although there is still an emphasis on one core macro model).

The 1980s can be understood as a period in which policy was based on a form of humanism. There was optimism that the large macro models provided an adequate guide to policy action, which could be expected to yield the predicted outcomes. This optimism was gradually punctured when these expectations were confounded. The prevailing paradigm of New Classical Economics had relied on certainty equivalence on the part of economic actors and economists alike. Within this paradigm, there emerged the Lucas critique which challenged one of the closures within the model structure: that behavior was invariant in the face of policy action. Lucas (1976) argued that rational individuals in fact respond to policy action in such a way as to make it impotent. The conclusion was that policy action could only have an impact on the economy if it was random, that is there was no point in policy action.

This conclusion found support from a line of argument which took a very different starting-point. Far from individuals and economists knowing too much, the problem with policy action might derive from unknowability resulting from radical uncertainty. Thus Hayek, for example, expressed the radical uncertainty of the Austrian approach as grounds for an argument against humanism:

> If man is not to do more harm than good in his efforts to improve the social order, he will have to learn that . . . where essential complexity of an organised kind prevails, *he cannot acquire the full knowledge which would make mastery of the events possible.* He will therefore have to use what

knowledge he can achieve, not to shape the results as a craftsman shapes his handiwork, but rather to cultivate a growth by providing the appropriate environment, as the gardener does for his plants. (Hayek 1975, p. 42, emphasis in original)

This argument attracted support from a wide range of perspectives which were influenced by the emergence of postmodernism, which more generally challenged humanism. Thus for example, while starting from a closed-system theoretical perspective based on certainty-equivalence like Lucas, Hahn (1983) denied the empirical validity of the New Classical approach – the knowledge requirements could not in practice be met. Like those coming from a radical uncertainty perspective, Hahn therefore raised questions as to how policy intervention could be justified.

The Keynes uncertainty approach is aimed more at a middle ground (an argument developed in detail by O'Donnell 1989). Uncertainty itself justifies government intervention, since it can serve to provide an element of stability for economic actors. O'Donnell explains this role in terms of knowledge and institutions:

State activity was thus a precondition of successful individualism, improving the efficiency of resource utilisation and eliminating some of the hazards of pure laissez-faire. By attacking remediable sources of uncertainty, providing data banks and by reforming institutions, it could improve the environment in which individual rationality was exercised. (O'Donnell 1989, p. 303, emphasis in original)

The role is extended by the content of Keynesian fiscal and monetary policy – both are designed to provide a sound basis for investment; in the case of fiscal policy the government may actively intervene by engaging in its own capital projects to increase aggregate demand.

The implementation of this policy arguably was so successful that the relative stability of the 1950s and 1960s encouraged inattention to issues of uncertainty and expectations. The neo-classical synthesis of that period ignored these central features of Keynes's economic theory. This coincided with a high level of confidence in the capacity of the state to manage the economy and a continuation of closures in theorizing which became increasingly untenable, leading to the New Classical revolution.

There has been a dualistic swing away from humanism, but now a return to seek out some middle ground. Central banks, including the ECB, are addressing methodological issues as they grapple with the uncertainty of their knowledge in the face of the requirement to act. This is a time of rather uncomfortable transition, as old closures (such as certainty-equivalence on the part of economic agents) bump up against the actual uncertainty of policy-makers. The Bank of England has taken a lead by pointing to pluralism as the methodological route to follow. But much needs to be done to spell out what that entails for how the knowledge foundations of monetary policy are constructed.

5. CONCLUSION

We have addressed here the fundamental issues raised for economics by a consideration of uncertainty in its broadest sense. These issues get to the heart of what it is that we do as economists, as well as what we do as economic actors. There is a danger of falling into one or the other of two sharp categories with respect to knowledge: the certainty equivalence of closed-system models on the one hand and the radical uncertainty of completely open systems on the other. Both inhibit policy action. But by considering the middle ground where some closures are introduced (by individuals, by social institutions, by government, by theorists) in order to reduce uncertainty, we can see how social structures do manage to function in spite of uncertainty, and how actions to affect behavior and institutional design may serve to reduce uncertainty.

The methodological approach implied by this middle-ground is a form of pluralism – not 'anything goes', but a recourse to a range of methods and types of knowledge suited to the problem at hand and the type of economic structure within which it is understood to occur. This seems to be what central bankers tend to do anyway, being closer to the real world and more compelled to action than academic economists. But there is still an uncomfortable juxtaposition between this practice and the approach which is often professed by central bankers as well as academics: modeling which is closed-system in a fixed way, rather than in the partial, provisional way of the pluralist approach. A fundamental rethink at the methodological level is required to produce an approach to the knowledge base of policy which is philosophically consistent in a world profoundly colored by uncertainty.

REFERENCES

Backhouse, R.E. (1998), 'If mathematics is informal, then perhaps we should accept that economics must be informal too', *Economic Journal*, **108** (451), 1848–58.

Bank of England (1999), *Economic Models at the Bank of England*, London: Bank of England.

Blanchard, O. and S. Fischer (1989), *Lectures in Macroeconomics*, Cambridge, MA: MIT Press.

Blaug, M. (1999), 'The Formalist Revolution or What Happened to Orthodox Economics after World War II?', in R.E. Backhouse and J. Creedy (eds), *From Classical Economics to the Theory of the Firm: Essays in Honour of D.P. O'Brien*, Cheltenham, UK and Northampton, MA, USA: Edward Elgar, pp. 257–80.

Brainard, W. (1967), 'Uncertainty and the effectiveness of policy', *American Economic Review Papers and Proceedings*, **57**, 411–25.

Bray, J. S. Hall, A. Kuleshov, J. Nixon and P. Westaway (1995), 'The interfaces between policy-makers, markets and modellers', *Economic Journal*, **105** (431), 989–1000.

Caldwell, B.J. and S. Boehm (eds) (1992), *Austrian Economics: Tensions and New Directions*, Boston: Kluwer.

Chick, V. and S.C. Dow, (2001), 'Formalism, logic and reality: a Keynesian analysis', *Cambridge Journal of Economics*, **25** (6), 705–22.

Clements, M.P. and D. Hendry, (1995), 'Macroeconomic forecasting and modelling', *Economic Journal*, **105** (431), 1001–31.

Davis, J.B. (1994), *Keynes's Philosophical Development*, Cambridge: Cambridge University Press.

Dow, S.C. (1990), 'Beyond dualism', *Cambridge Journal of Economics*, **14** (2), 143–58.

Dow, S.C. (2002), *Economic Methodology: An Inquiry*, Oxford: Oxford University Press.

Dow, S.C. (2003), 'Probability, Uncertainty and Convention: Economists' Knowledge and the Knowledge of Economic Actors', in S. Mizuhara and J. Runde (eds), *Perspectives on the Philosophy of Keynes's Economics: Probability, Uncertainty and Convention*, London: Routledge.

Goodhart, C.A.E. (1999), 'Central bankers and uncertainty', *Bank of England Quarterly Bulletin*, February, 102–16.

Hahn, F.H. (1983), *Money and Inflation*, Cambridge, MA: MIT Press.

Hayek, F. von (1975), 'Full employment at any price', *Hobart Paper*, 45, London: I.E.A.

Keynes, J.M. (1921), *A Treatise on Probability*, reprinted in (1973), *Collected Writings*, Vol. VIII, London: Macmillan for the Royal Economic Society.

Keynes, J.M. (1936), *The General Theory of Employment, Interest and Money*, reprinted in (1973), *Collected Writings*, Vol. VII, London: Macmillan.

Keynes, J.M. (1937), 'The general theory of employment', *Quarterly Journal of Economics*, **51**, 209–23.

Kuhn, T.S. (1962), *The Structure of Scientific Revolutions*, Chicago: University of Chicago Press.

Lawson, T. (1988), 'Probability and uncertainty in economic analysis', *Journal of Post Keynesian Economics*, **11** (1), 38–65.

Loasby, B.J. (1999), *Knowledge, Institutions and Evolution in Economics: the Graz Schumpeter Lectures*, London: Routledge.

Loasby, B.J. (2002), 'Closed models and open systems', *Journal of Economic Methodology*.

Loasby, B.J. (2003), 'Closed models and open systems', *Journal of Economic Methodology*, 10(3), 285-306.

Lucas, R.E. Jr. (1976), 'Econometric Policy Evaluation: A Critique', in K. Brunner and A.H. Meltzer (eds), *The Phillips Curve and Labor Markets*, North-Holland, Amsterdam, and *Carnegie-Rochester Conference Series on*

Public Policy, Vol. 1, a supplementary series to the *Journal of Monetary Economics.*

Menger, C. (1963), *Problems of Economics and Sociology*, Urbana, ILL: University of Illinois Press.

O'Donnell, R.M. (1989), *Keynes: Philosophy, Economics and Politics: The Philosophical Foundations of Keynes's Thought and their Influence on his Economics and Politics*, London: Macmillan.

Poole, W. (1970), 'Optimal choice of monetary policy instruments in a simple stochastic macro model', *Quarterly Journal of Economics*, **84** (May), 197–216.

Popper, K. (1982), *The Open Universe: An Argument for Indeterminism*, London: Routledge.

Russell, B. (1946), *History of Western Philosophy*, London: George Allen and Unwin.

Sargent, T.J. (1999), 'Comment', in J. Taylor (ed.), *Monetary Policy Rules*, Chicago: University of Chicago Press, pp. 144–54.

11. Uncertainty in Econometrics: Evaluating Policy Counterfactuals

Julian Reiss and Nancy Cartwright[*]

1. INTRODUCTION

There is without question a great deal of uncertainty in planning and policy formation. Our starting point in approaching this uncertainty is that '[c]ounterfactuals are the very guide of life'.[1] For rational planning we need counterfactuals because we need to evaluate what would happen were each of the actions under consideration implemented. For this kind of deliberation there is always a vast amount we do not know – facts, laws, probabilities, people's reactions and so on. This chapter will focus on a more abstract source of ignorance that contributes to uncertainty in planning: we do not know how in principle to evaluate counterfactuals. There is a considerable literature in philosophy on the semantics of counterfactuals and recently contributions in economics itself. The bulk of this literature, we shall argue, puts the problems back to front. It attempts to use counterfactuals to evaluate causal claims; we argue instead that one must use causal claims to assess counterfactuals.[2] That said, there is as yet no general account of how to do so.

The reason the literature has the problems back to front is that parts of both philosophy and economics are still in the grip of the 'Hume problem'. Like David Hume, many philosophers and economists feel that causality is an illegitimate concept. Counterfactuals are called in to

[*] This chapter is part of our ongoing LSE research project *Causality: Metaphysics and Methods*. We are very grateful to the Arts and Humanities Research Board for funding. Nancy Cartwright would also like to thank the Latsis foundation for support. Corresponding address: CPNSS, LSE, Houghton St, London WC2A 2AE, philcent@lse.ac.uk.
[1] Paraphrased from the famous dictum, 'Probability is the very guide of life' See Kyburg and Thalos (2003).
[2] Apart from the work on causality and counterfactuals there is also a great deal of work on the logic of counterfactuals. (For a survey, see Edgington 1995.) But the semantics provided in this area is difficult to connect with economic problems. At any rate we shall not discuss it here.

secure legitimacy for it. As we shall argue, this skews the study of *genuine* policy counterfactuals – those counterfactuals that can be exploited for policy purposes. The Humean philosophers and economists study a different kind of counterfactuals – counterfactuals that could possibly stand in for causal concepts. But what we need for policy are counterfactuals that describe what would happen were our policies put into place. Unfortunately a semantics geared to the stand-ins for causal concepts fares badly at evaluating policy counterfactuals.

Section 2 will argue the case that we need causal models to answer the kinds of 'What if?' questions raised in policy and planning. We shall then point out in Section 3 a number of ways in which counterfactuals can be ambiguous. A first step in providing counterfactual hypotheses for use in policy and planning, we maintain, is to be clear exactly what counterfactual hypothesis is under consideration, and this requires explicit assumptions about how the counterfactual antecedent is to be implemented. Sections 4 and 5 will describe two attempts to do the job we urge. Section 4 will describe Judea Pearl's theory of causal models and counterfactuals, based on his work on Bayes nets. Section 5 will look at the work of James Heckman.

Both of the accounts we shall look at use counterfactuals to explicate causal notions. Neither, however, is engaged in a fully-fledged Hume program. For both begin, as we urge one must, with a causal model, a model that contains some set of causal principles. The notion of causality involved in the causal principles is left unanalyzed. The causal model is used to evaluate counterfactuals and then the causal concept of concern is defined in terms of the counterfactual. Even if this method does not provide a total elimination of causal concepts, if successful it can at least explicate more problematic causal notions in terms of less problematic ones. The cost, however, is in the hope to use the accounts to answer more general kinds of counterfactual questions. The attempt to capture the intended causal notions skews the accounts; whether or not they succeed at explicating the causal notions of concern, neither can double as a semantics for the 'What if?' counterfactuals required for policy formation.

2. THE NEED FOR CAUSAL MODELS TO EVALUATE POLICY COUNTERFACTUALS

Policy analysts are often interested in answers to questions with the structure 'What would have happened to Y (the 'target variable'), had X been x (the 'control variable' and its value, respectively)?' We want to call these questions *genuine* 'What if?' questions (and the corresponding policy counterfactuals, *genuine* policy counterfactuals) because although formally they refer to hypothetical scenarios, their answers prepare the policy-maker for a situation in which what he supposes actually happens.

How does one find answers to a genuine 'What if?' question? We contend that such questions are always answered against a causal model in which the control variable figures as a cause and the target variable as an effect.

Philosophers, and some economists, tend to regard priority the other way around. Many thinkers in the Humean tradition view counterfactuals as more fundamental and causal relations as derivative. David Lewis, for example, develops a counterfactual theory of causation that takes the following quote from Hume as starting point:

> We may define a cause to be an object followed by another, and where all the objects, similar to the first, are followed by objects similar to the second. Or, in other words where, if the first object had not been, the second never had existed. (quoted from Lewis [1973] 1993, p. 193)

Based on this underlying idea, Lewis develops a theory that defines causal relations in terms of 'chains of counterfactual dependence'. The details of his theory do not matter here. But in our view, it is peculiar to invoke Hume for this project. Hume was an empiricist of a particular brand. For him, a concept was meaningless unless associated with an idea which itself was a copy of a direct sense impression. Now, it is disputable whether we can have direct sense impressions of causal relations. Hume certainly believed that we cannot. But it is absurd to suppose that there is a sense impression from which we can copy the idea of the 'object that would never have existed'.

Hume's associationist theory of knowledge has long been out of fashion. In its stead, a contemporary empiricist will demand that our claims are made on the basis of the best evidence at hand. But from the evidential point of view, counterfactuals do not seem to fare any better. No (direct) evidence can be had for a statement that describes a state of affairs which is 'counter to the facts'. The usual strategy, then, is to translate the counterfactual into a different kind of statement, for example a statement about possible worlds or about laws of nature. Although theories of counterfactuals tend to focus on semantic rather than epistemological issues, eventually the problem of how to justify belief in counterfactuals must be addressed.

But now it seems that the theorist who regards counterfactuals as more fundamental than causal relations is in a dilemma. The statement into which the counterfactual is translated either does or does not involve causal concepts. If it does involve causal concepts, the theory is circular and counterfactuals have not been shown to be more fundamental than causal relations.[3] If, on the other hand, the statement does not involve causal concepts, the theory is likely to fall prey to one or more of the difficulties that agonize all reductive theories of causation. These difficulties include[4]:

- the problem of concomitant effects
- the problem of co-extensionality
- Simpson's paradox
- . . .

Of course, one cannot prove that all reductive theories, even future ones, will suffer difficulties like these. However, from the past record of failed attempts it seems a reasonable move to give up trying rather than keeping to fail.

Witness that our argument here against counterfactual theories of causation differs from the usual strategy employed when these theories are criticized. The usual strategy consists in choosing a particular formulation of a theory, finding a case where one would intuitively say that x causes y but where the theory yields a negative answer (or the other way around).

These criticisms are based on intuitions or ordinary language usage. The argument put forward here, by contrast, is based on evidential considerations. It maintains that the evidence in favor of a counterfactual can never be better than the evidence in favor of the associated statement about causal relations. Therefore, we reject the view that counterfactuals are more fundamental.

Thus far, conditional on the soundness of our argument, we can reject counterfactual theories of causation, but this does not give us a causal theory of counterfactuals. Why, then, believe that counterfactuals can only be analyzed in terms of causal models? The reasons for this are mainly pragmatic. There is a great variety of kinds of counterfactuals, and each kind demands its own mode of translation. Just consider a few stock philosophical examples:

---

[3] It is a different question whether the circularity is vicious or virtuous. Below, we will discuss a case where certain causal concepts are defined in terms of counterfactuals, which in turn are evaluated in a causal model. But knowledge about the causal concepts defined in this procedure is not required in the model construction. Thus new causal knowledge is extracted (among other things) from old causal knowledge. This kind of circularity is not vicious but it renders the counterfactual definition superfluous.

[4] For further discussion see Cartwright (1983, 1989).

- If Bizet and Verdi had been compatriots, Bizet would have been Italian.
- If God had had a daughter, her name would be Zarines.
- If the pressure in this container had been *p*, its temperature would have been *t*.
- If Nixon had pushed the button, there would have been a nuclear holocaust.

To answer whether the first counterfactual is true is a matter of logic and meaning. To be compatriots, Bizet and Verdi would have needed to live in the same country. This could have been Italy, France or any other country for that matter. Thus the truth value is indeterminate. But we do not need *causal* knowledge in order to evaluate it. Living in a country does not cause one to be someone else's compatriot. The second counterfactual is metaphorical. In order to answer it, we may want to ask whether the person mentioned has a number of characteristics we usually ascribe to Jesus, say, kind-heartedness and generosity. For the third one, we might invoke a model but (according to many) a purely associational model is sufficient. We do not need to know how the pressure value comes about or how it brings about the temperature. Only the fourth counterfactual seems to require causal knowledge, knowledge about the technological and sociological nexus Nixon lived in.

The point is that different kinds of counterfactuals require different kinds of translations. *A priori*, there is no primacy of translation into causal models. But the topic here is not counterfactuals *simpliciter* but counterfactuals relevant to policy-making. It seems thus safe to suppose that counterfactuals which can be addressed on the basis of logical or semantic relations, or which are metaphorical in nature, do not play an important role.

The matter is not so simple with respect to causal versus associational models. Laws of association (or the models that represent them) *can* be used to evaluate counterfactual claims. Just recall that the gas law – an associational law – was used above with reference to the third example. But in the context of policy-making in most cases the formulation of the question is at least partly causal in nature. Usually, we ask whether one can use a certain socio-economic variable as a kind of handle to control another variable – the money stock to control prices, investment in schooling to control education and the latter to influence income and inequality, interest rates to control economic activity. Causal models, then, are the appropriate tools to evaluate these kinds of policy counterfactuals.

What, then, is a causal model? That, we contend, is the central question. What characterizes a causal model depends on what one wants to do with the model. Both Pearl and Heckman provide explicit answers to the question of what constitutes a causal model and both give explicit rules for how to assess the truth values of counterfactuals given a causal model. Both use the counterfactuals they evaluate to define new causal notions. But neither is adequate in general for assessing genuine counterfactuals of direct use in planning and policy formation. That is why we urge that more work needs to be done.

An adequate account of how to evaluate counterfactuals from causal models will require

- A description of what a causal model consists in
- Rules for how to evaluate counterfactuals given the model
- An argument to show that the results are correct: the propositions thus evaluated really are the ones we are trying to assess.

Pearl provides all three ingredients, as a good formal account of counterfactuals and causal models should. Despite this, we shall argue, the counterfactuals he assesses are not in general the ones we need for policy and planning, though they may serve a variety of other purposes, including the definition of new causal notions. Heckman has an explicit proposal for the first two. As to the third, we shall show that, trivially, his characterization captures the concept of *causal contribution* when applied in linear systems, but it will not double as a semantics for the kinds of counterfactuals that can be put directly to use in planning and policy formation.

3. EXACTLY WHAT COUNTERFACTUAL QUESTION IS AT STAKE?

The question of 'implementing the antecedent' is hugely important for policy purposes. In the philosophy literature the topic is usually discussed under the heading of 'backtracking'. The dominant view is that counterfactuals have to be non-backtracking. That is, for the evaluation of a counterfactual it should not matter how the antecedent is brought about. However, in general the evaluation of the kinds of genuine counterfactuals of direct use for policy will be extremely sensitive to the methods of implementation. Consider a standard example from philosophy. Jack and Jim had a quarrel yesterday and Jack is still furious. The question is if had Jim asked Jack for a favor today, would Jack have obliged? One plausible answer is 'Yes', since for Jim to ask Jack for a favor, there would have had to have been no quarrel before.[5]

Implementation matters all the more for policy. Suppose the counterfactual question of interest is 'Had investment in schooling, I, been i (rather than $i^* < i$, the actual value), what would the income, Z, of the cohort have been?' In the real world, the additional money cannot be manna from heaven – it has to be raised somewhere. And it might matter whether it would have been taken from the defense budget or the social security budget. For in either case, it is very likely that the cohort would have been influenced by the loss (for example because some unemployed would have received less benefit or some recruits would not have been hired) but in an asymmetric way (it is plausible to assume, for instance, that the cohort would have been less influenced had the money come from the defense budget).

So to assess the truth value of any particular counterfactual that we hope to use in policy formation we will need to know what changes are supposed to happen, where often the exact details matter. Sometimes when we consider a policy we have a very definite idea in mind how it will be implemented. We shall call the related counterfactuals, 'implementation-specific'. At the other end of the scale, we might have no idea at all; the counterfactuals are 'implementation-neutral'. When we evaluate counterfactuals, we had better be clear what exactly we are presuming.

For counterfactuals that are totally implementation-specific, we know exactly what we are asking when we ask 'What would happen if . . .?'[6] For others there are a variety of different strategies we might adopt. For one, we can employ the usual devices for dealing with epistemic uncertainty. We might, for instance, assess the probabilities of the various possible methods of implementation and weight the probability of the counterfactual consequent accordingly. In the methodology of economics literature we find another alternative: Stephen LeRoy and Daniel Hausman focus on counterfactuals that would be true *regardless* of how they are implemented. We begin with LeRoy.

LeRoy's stated concern is with causal ordering among quantities, not with counterfactuals. But, it seems, he equates 'p causes q' with 'if p were to change, q would change as well' – so long as we give the 'right' reading to the counterfactual. It is his proposed reading for the

---

[6] Or rather, we know this relative to the factors included in the causal model. Presumably no causal model will be complete, so this remains as a source of ambiguity in our counterfactual claims.

counterfactual that matters here. It may help to present his brief discussion of a stock philosophical example before looking to more economic cases – the case of birth control pills and thrombosis.

Birth control pills cause thrombosis; they also prevent pregnancy, which is itself a cause of thrombosis. LeRoy assumes that whether a woman becomes pregnant depends on both her sexual activity and whether she takes pills. Now consider: 'What would happen vis-à-vis thrombosis were a particular woman to become pregnant?' That, LeRoy points out, is ambiguous – it depends on whether the change in pregnancy comes about because of a change in pill-taking or because of a change in sexual activity.

In his formal characterization LeRoy treats systems of linear deterministic 'reduced form equations': 'In current usage an economic model is a map from a space of exogenous variables – agents' characteristics and resource endowments, for example – to a space of endogenous variables – prices and allocations.' (LeRoy 2003, p. 1) LeRoy assumes that the equations are functionally correct and that variables designated as 'exogenous' are not caused by any of the remaining (endogenous) variables. Since they are functionally related to the endogenous variables, we may assume that either they are causes of some of the endogenous variables or are correlated with such causes. For LeRoy's purposes it seems we must suppose they are causes. He also supposes that the possible sources of implementation for a change in an endogenous variable are exactly the members of the minimal set of exogenous variables that will fix the value of the endogenous variable according to the economic model. Together these assumptions constitute a characterization of the causal model that will be used to evaluate counterfactuals.

For illustration of his semantics, LeRoy considers a familiar supply and demand model:

$$q_s = \alpha_s + \alpha_{sp}p + \alpha_{sw}w$$
$$q_d = \alpha_d + \alpha_{dp}p + \alpha_{di}i$$
$$q_s = q_d = q. \tag{3.1}$$

Here p is price; q, quantity; w, weather; i, income. LeRoy asks what the effect of a change in price would be on the equilibrium quantity. By the conventions just described, a change in price can come about through changes in weather, income or both, and nothing else. But, LeRoy notes, 'any of an infinite number of pairs of shifts in the exogenous variables "weather" and "income" could have caused the assumed changes in price, and these map onto different values of q' (ibid., p. 6). Thus the question has no definite answer – it all depends on how the change in p is brought about.

LeRoy contrasts this model with a different one:

$$q_s = \alpha_s + \alpha_{sw}w + \alpha_{sf}f$$
$$q_d = \alpha_d + \alpha_{dp}p + \alpha_{di}i$$
$$q_s = q_d = q, \qquad\qquad (3.2)$$

where f is fertilizer. Here fertilizer and weather can change the equilibrium quantity, and no matter how they do so, the change in price will be the same. In this case LeRoy is content that the counterfactual, 'If q were to change from taking the value Q to taking the value $Q + \Delta$, p would change from $P = (Q - \alpha_d - \alpha_{di}I)/\alpha_{dp}$ to $P = (Q + \Delta - \alpha_d - \alpha_{di}I)/\alpha_{dp}$,' is unambiguous (and true). The lesson he draws is the following (where we substitute counterfactual language for his causal language): '[Counterfactual] statements involving endogenous variables as [antecedents] are ambiguous except when all the interventions consistent with a given change in the [antecedent] map onto the same change in the [consequent]' (ibid., p. 6).

The statement as it stands is too strong. Some counterfactuals are, after all, either implicitly or explicitly implementation-specific. In (3.1) we could ask, for instance, what the value of q would have been had $p = P$ been brought about by $i = I$. What LeRoy offers instead is a semantics for counterfactuals that are, either implicitly or explicitly, implementation-neutral. In this case the consequent should obtain *no matter what possible change occurs to bring the antecedent about*.

Daniel Hausman seems to have distinguished between implementation-specific and implementation-neutral counterfactuals, too, as we do here, though he does not explicitly say so. He considers an example in which engineers designing a nuclear power plant ask, 'What would happen if the steam pipe were to burst?' (Hausman 1998, p. 122) The answer, he argues, depends on how it will burst. 'Responsible engineers', he argues, must look to the origins of the burst 'when the consequences of the pipe's bursting depend on what caused it to burst' (ibid.). That is, in these situations responsible engineers will ask implementation-specific 'What if?' questions.

On the other hand, when Hausman turns to providing some constraints that a general semantics for counterfactuals must satisfy if we are to use counterfactuals to establish causal order, he seems to be concerned with implementation-neutral counterfactuals. It is not worth going into the details here; the results are similar to LeRoy's. Any semantics that satisfies Hausman's constraints should give the same result as LeRoy's prescription when restricted to counterfactuals evaluated via what LeRoy calls an 'economic model'.

So we may have counterfactuals that are implementation-specific; we may have ones that assume some one or another of a range of possible implementations; and we may have implementation-neutral ones where we wish to find out what would happen no matter how the change in the antecedent is brought about. For thinking about policy we had better know which kind of counterfactual we are asserting and ensure that our semantics is appropriate to it.

4. HOW WE EVALUATE COUNTERFACTUALS: PEARL AND WHY THAT'S NOT GOOD ENOUGH

We begin the discussion of evaluating counterfactuals with Judea Pearl because his account is the most formal, the most complete and the most powerful of any methods currently available, allowing evaluations of complex counterfactuals and their probabilities. Pearl is famous for his work on artificial intelligence, causal search algorithms and reasoning under uncertainty. In his work on causality, he is an advocate of the so-called Bayes'-nets methods. Although Bayes' nets can be put to a large variety of uses, one prominent application lies in causal inference. Here, they function as a tool for learning causal relationships from conditional probabilities on the basis of assumptions about the system considered.

As tools for causal inference, Bayes' nets methods are part of what we have called the 'Hume program': the program that aims at replacing 'problematic' causal notions with 'unproblematic' ones. We must emphasize that Pearl himself is not a strict Humean. He does not want to eliminate causal talk altogether. But he too uses his system in order to explicate more problematic causal notions, for example those relating to singular causation, in terms of less problematic notions, for example that of a causal model. Pearl's semantics for counterfactuals plays a vital role in his explication of causal notions. Since one might be tempted to think it doubles as a semantics for genuine 'What if?' questions, let us examine his account in more detail here.

Pearl envisages counterfactual statements of the form 'The value that Y would have obtained, had X been x' (Pearl 2000, p. 204).[7] According to him, counterfactual statements are always evaluated within a causal model. A *probabilistic causal model* is defined as a quadruple $<U, V, F, P(u)>$, where:

---

[7] Def 7.1.5 'Counterfactual'

(i)   *U* is a set of variables that are determined by factors outside the model;

(ii)   *V* is a set of variables that are determined by variables in the model;

(iii)   *F* is a set of functions $\{f_1, f_2, ..., f_n\}$ such that each f_i is a mapping from $U \cap (V \setminus V_i)$ to V_i and such that the entire set *F* forms a mapping from *U* to *V*;

(iv) $P(u)$ is a probability function over the domain of U.[8]

Condition (iii) says that each f_i gives the value of V_i given the values of all other variables in $U \cap V$, which is unique in case the system is recursive or 'acyclic'.[9] Each f_i is supposed to be functionally correct in the situation modeled and the quantities on the right-hand side are supposed to be a complete set of 'direct causes' of the quantity on the left.[10]

An important notion in Pearl's system is that of a *submodel*. A submodel M_x of a model *M* is relative to realizations *x* of a set of variables *X*. It is formed by deleting all functions in *M* that have members of *X* as an effect and replacing it with the constant function $X = x$. The effect of action 'set *X* to *x*', in short $do(X = x)$, on *M* is given by the submodel M_x. Finally, a counterfactual of the form 'The value *Y* that would have obtained, had *X* been *x*' on *M* is defined as the solution of *M* for *Y* under the action $do(X = x)$, that is, of M_x. The counterfactual value Pearl also calls 'potential response' and abbreviates it with $Y_x(u)$.

Pearl introduces a theorem according to which a counterfactual can be evaluated using three steps.[11] (See Pearl 2000, p. 206) The theorem shows how to assess the conditional probability $P(B_A|e)$ of a counterfactual statement of the form 'If it were *A* then *B*', given evidence *e*:

1.   **Abduction** – Update $P(u)$ by the evidence *e* to obtain $P(u \mid e)$.
2.   **Action** – Modify *M* by the action $do(A)$, where *A* is the antecedent of the counterfactual to obtain the submodel M_A.
3.   **Prediction** – Use the modified model ... to compute the probability of *B*, the consequence of the counterfactual.

---

[8] This is actually a merger of two of Pearl's definitions. For the precise formulations, see Pearl (2000), pp. 204f (Definitions 7.1.1, 'Causal Model', and 7.1.6, 'Probabilistic Causal Model').

[9] 'Acyclic' is a term from graph theory which basically means that there are no loops in the system.

[10] A direct cause is a cause that makes a contribution to the effect that is not mediated via other variables represented in the model.

[11] Theorem 7.1.7.

Let us then examine one of Pearl's policy analysis examples so that we can understand the definitions. The example consists of two equations:[12]

$$q \ c= b_1 p + d_1 i + u_1, \tag{4.1}$$

$$p \ c= b_2 q + d_2 w + u_2, \tag{4.2}$$

where q is the quantity demanded for some good, p is its price, i is income, w is the wage rate and u_1 and u_2 are error terms. Given the modularity assumption – each equation represents an autonomous mechanism – (4.1) and (4.2) constitute a causal model with Q and P as endogenous and U_1, U_2, I and W as the exogenous variables ($M = <\{U_1, U_2, I, W\}, \{Q, P\}, \{(4.1), (4.2)\}, P(u)>$).

Pearl considers the policy question, 'Given that the observed price is $P = p_0$, what would be the expected value of the demand Q had we controlled the price to be $P = p_1$?'. The required probability, $P(Q_{P=p1} \mid P = p_0)$, can be evaluated as follows, using the three steps.

1. **Abduction** – Update $P(u_1)$ by the evidence $P = p_0$ as well as $I = i$, $W = w$ to obtain $P(u_1 \mid P = p_0, I = i, W = w)$.

2. **Action** – Modify M by the action $do(P = p_1)$. That is, formulate the submodel $M_{P=p1}$:

$$q \ c= b_1 p + d_1 i + u_1, \tag{4.1}$$

$$p = p_1. \tag{4.2'}$$

3. **Prediction** – Use the modified model to compute the probability of Q. This yields for the expected value of Q:

$$E(Q_{P=p1} \mid p_0, i, w) = b_1 p_1 + d_1 i + E(U_1 \mid p_0, i, w). \tag{4.3}$$

One of the advantages of Pearl's semantics is that it ties in very nicely with purely philosophical accounts. In particular, it can be shown that under certain conditions Pearl's and Lewis's semantics yield *the same* results (for recursive systems).[13] In order to achieve this equivalence, the

---

[12] pp. 215ff. The symbol 'c=' replaces Pearl's '=' and reads 'functionally equivalent and the variables on the right hand side cause the variables on the left hand side'

[13] Pearl (2000), pp. 238ff.

counterfactual $Y_x(u) = y$ Pearl's notation is equated with Lewis's A $\rightarrow$ B (and A with the proposition that $X = x$ holds and B with the proposition that $Y = y$ holds).

In Lewis's account, the counterfactual antecedent is brought about 'by miracle'. That is, the laws that are responsible for A to obtain are broken and A is brought about *ex nihilo*. Equivalently, Pearl explicitly breaks all causal laws that have X as an effect and replaces these laws with the constant $X = x$.

What seems to be an advantage from a philosophical point of view is detrimental from the point of view of the policy-maker. For Pearl's semantics to work, it is required that the law for each variable in the system (P and Q in the example) be separately manipulable, and he reads the counterfactuals as supposing that the implementations can be represented by changes in exactly the laws governing the antecedent and no others. To evaluate a counterfactual, we model the implementation in one special way: by destroying one set of causal laws – (4.2) in the example, replacing it with another set – (4.2′) in the example, and leaving the rest of the system intact – (4.1) in the example.[14]

Do all socio-economic systems of interest for policy-making behave like this? We believe not. We shall illustrate that by pointing to one large class of systems relevant for policy-making familiar in economics. These are systems where agents' expectations play a role in determining the relations between the control variable and the target variable (the well-known 'rational expectations' models represent a special case of these). Consider a simple model of the money market:

money demand:

$$m_t = p_t + y_t - \lambda i_t \tag{4.4}$$

money supply:

$$m_t = m^* + \gamma(y^* - y_{t-1}) + v_t, \tag{4.5}$$

where m = money, p = price level, y = real output, i = nominal interest rate, m^* = exogenous money supply, y^* = potential output and v = white noise. We omit the goods side of the economy, which contains the

---

[14] It is of course always possible to evaluate a counterfactual according to Pearl's method *assuming* the truth of a model with the right properties (as we have done in the example). Thus, whether or not real socio-economic systems have these properties does not matter. Pearl is explicit, however, that he understands causality and related notions to append to the world, rather than a model (or our language, say). Models represent real features of the world. For policy considerations, then, we want the model to be true of the world and therefore the system in the world, not just the model, must have the right properties.

expectations parameters here; the model is presented for expositional purposes only.

Let us consider the counterfactual question 'What would the value of the price level p have been, had the money supply been m_c?' How would we model that counterfactual à la Pearl? He asks us first to replace the feedback mechanism (4.5) with a constant law:

$$m_t = m_c, \qquad (4.6)$$

where the m_c defines some constant value of m. What would the agents in the economy make out of it? As far as we know, there is no uniform answer in the literature but here are a number of possible replies.

First and foremost, the reply will depend on what the agents know. It seems that the most natural reply to Pearl's question would be that despite the central bank's regime change, the agents would believe that (4.5) is still intact. Since m_c is a possible realization of (4.5), viz. in case

$$v_t = m_c - m^* - \gamma \, (y^* - y_{t-1}),$$

the agents might still use (4.4)–(4.5) in their decision making. The point is that Pearl wants us to model the shift from the actual to the counterfactual situation minimally. Thus he replaces one law in the system with another one. If that means that the agents' expectations remain the same the central bank can change as much as it wants, agents' expectations would be formulated on the basis of (4.4)–(4.5) rather than (4.6). In this case, we would have to formulate Pearl's question more precisely as 'What would the value of the price level p have been, had money supply been m_c due to a realization of the error term of $v_t = m_c - m^* - \gamma \, (y^* - y_{t-1})$?'. In order to evaluate this counterfactual, we would just update the agent's beliefs using (4.5)–(4.6) and the realization of v_t. Pearl's semantics would not apply.

Alternatively, we could mean the counterfactual to say that central bank policy has now changed (temporarily? permanently?) to a fixed-policy regime. Fixed-policy regimes, however, are usually not modeled as (4.6) but as a mix of a deterministic term plus a random component. Economic agents are usually not held to believe that the central bank can perfectly control the money supply. Thus we have, for example,

$$m_t = m_c + \varepsilon_t. \qquad (4.7)$$

This comes closest to Pearl's suggestion. It would answer the question 'What would the value of the price level p have been, had money supply been m_c due to (a) a credible switch of monetary policy to a fixed regime and (b) the realization of $\varepsilon_t = 0$?'

Another alternative is to have the agents believe that the central bank has changed its policy to a so-called regime-switching system. This could be represented by

$$m_t = \begin{array}{l} m^* + \gamma\, (y^* - y_{t-1}) + v_t \text{ with probability } q \\ m_c + \varepsilon_t \text{ with probability } (1 - q). \end{array} \qquad (4.8)$$

The counterfactual question we answer with this model would be very similar to the preceding one but we would have 'regime-switching system' instead of 'fixed-policy regime'.

None of the preceding models models the expectations formation process of the agents very deeply. In particular, one can assume that the agents realize that the central bank's decision to set the value for the money supply is itself an outcome of a rational procedure. For example, they might believe that the central bank aims at minimizing the following loss function:

$$L = E_{t-1}\,(p_t - z_{t-1})^2, \qquad (4.9)$$

where z is an exogenous target value. The central bank would then set the money supply m_c such that $E_{t-1}\,(p_t) = z_{t-1}$. A change in m_c, then, would imply that the target variable z has changed.

The moral of this story is that if expectations matter, Pearl's semantics might not be applicable. Pearl assumes that we can change each law on its own. However, if some laws in a system contain expectations, the *actual* changes may be of little relevance. What matters more is what agents can be made to believe. And in order to make them believe the right thing, many more things might have to change than the one law Pearl envisages.

This is not, however, a problem confined to cases of rational expectations but a general one for Pearl's account. Pearl evaluates one particular kind of implementation-specific counterfactual, where the counterfactual antecedent is brought about by a precise incision that changes exactly the laws governing the counterfactual antecedent and nothing else *at all* (except what follows causally from just that difference). When we consider implementing a policy, we want to know what would happen were the policy really set in place – and this may well involve a variety of changes beyond those Pearl admits.

The problem is not with implementations that involve complex changes each of which can be represented in the overall scheme as a change in the value of one of the variables. Although we have not described it here, Pearl offers a detailed account of how to deal both with cases where our actions are complex – they involve changes in a number of different variables at once, and also where our complex actions may be conditional in specified ways on the values that other variables take. The problem is rather with implementations that result in changes in some of the causal laws that describe the system.

We might most easily locate this problem in Pearl's characterization of a causal model. Recall, a causal model for Pearl contains a set of equations, one for each effect. The effect is to be written on the left-hand side; on the right is a full set of direct causes of that effect, where the values of these causal variables fix the value of the effect. Note first that this means that Pearl's scheme cannot be used to evaluate counterfactuals in systems where causes may act purely probabilistically. Nor can it deal with systems where the causal laws themselves may be affected by our policies, for instance, where the causal laws are tied together so that if one changes, so too will others, or so too probably will others.

This is a familiar phenomenon and we are not always out of our depths in dealing with it. Occasionally we understand what will happen to the laws of the system as we implement different kinds of change and can provide a scientific account of it. This is one of the central aims of rational expectations theory, which is why we have used a rational expectations case as an example. Rational expectations methods cannot be encompassed by Pearl's scheme. But this is only an example. The general problem with Pearl's scheme is that it provides no place to encode information that we might well have about how the changes we envisage will affect the causal laws by which the system operates. His characterization of what constitutes a causal model is too narrow.

We should note that there is one quick solution to this problem that will not do: simply add more causal laws to express the information needed. In its first preliminary form the answer will not do because we need information about how changes in causal laws are correlated with each other and it does not make sense to write down causal laws that take causal laws themselves as both antecedents and consequents.

A different version of the answer supposes that where these problems arise it must always be because we are focusing on the wrong set of causal laws, a set of causal laws at the 'wrong level'. This view takes as a paradigm the situation in which there is some set of fundamental laws that have no connections with each other: each can change separately. From these, given certain specified boundary conditions, some further less fundamental laws can be derived. Under this picture, if there is a change in some targeted derivative law (keeping the boundary conditions fixed), there must necessarily be a change in the fundamental laws; this in turn might well lead to changes in other derivative laws beyond the one targeted. In this kind of situation, so the answer goes, counterfactuals should be evaluated relative to a causal model that describes the fundamental laws, not one that employs the derivative.

There are a number of problems with this way of defending the universal applicability of Pearl's scheme. The first concerns what the character of economic laws really is. We agree that the story of two tiers of causal laws, one more fundamental than the other, does show how correlations among laws can come about. But we have no reason to think that it is the only way. Moreover, whether there is one tier or many, it does not seem likely – no matter how far 'down' we go – that the principles for economic systems need ever have the kind of independence from each other that Pearl's scheme demands.[15]

The second set of problems concern the more realistic issues of how best to deploy what we know. Even if the two-tier story is the right account for why changes in certain economic principles occur in tandem, it is very often much harder to learn about the 'more fundamental' tier given even our best methods for empirical inference in economics. Nor do we need to know the principles at this level to evaluate our counterfactuals. What we need to know and to encode in our causal models is how the principles we propose using to make counterfactual judgments are likely to change given our envisaged implementations, and that is something we often come to learn, or to have good bets about, without having to calculate it from a 'more fundamental' theory.

Last, we should notice that rational expectations theory itself does not fit Pearl's scheme. Notoriously the theory does offer a two-tier account of why certain 'observational' regularities may well not be stable as we try to use them to implement policy. The observational regularities are supposed to be a consequence of the behavior of rational agents and those agents will – because they are rational – change their mode of behavior if they foresee that a new policy will be implemented. Thus the observational regularities that arise under the older modes of behavior may well no longer obtain were the policy to be implemented (or were agents to expect it to be implemented).

Nevertheless the methods suggested by rational expectations theory for calculating what would happen were a new policy undertaken are more complex than those proposed by Pearl. We do not just replace the law for the policy variable with a new one setting the value at the proposed level, then deduce from the 'fundamental' laws in their original unchanged form with parameters fixed what the values of the target

---

[15] See for example Estrella and Fuhrer (1999).

variables will be. For there is an interaction envisaged between the two tiers – a 'self-consistency' requirement is invoked. The variables that appear in the 'fundamental' laws include expectations (in the sense of beliefs and predictions) that the agents have about macro variables; the values of these are supposed to match the expectations (in the statistical average sense) of those macro variables in the less fundamental laws. This provides a method – albeit not formalized – for calculating simple (non-complex, non-conditional) counterfactuals. But so far as we can see, it cannot be fitted into Pearl's scheme.

Why does Pearl focus on this one kind of implementation, where variables change as the counterfactual antecedent is implemented, but no laws, excepting those governing the counterfactual antecedent? One reason is to resolve the problems of ambiguity. As we discussed in Section 3 ordinary language counterfactuals are open. They have different truth values depending on how they are supposed to be implemented. We have advocated disambiguating the counterfactual before trying to evaluate it; so too does Pearl. His detailed work on how to assess counterfactuals with complex and conditional antecedents is testimony to that.

Pearl is also worried about the problems of ambiguity that arise if laws can change. His solution here is to treat all counterfactuals the same. He insists that the laws of a causal model can be changed one at a time and that the right reading of the counterfactual is the one that supposes that that is just what happens: the laws governing the antecedent change and only those laws. This will work sometimes, but, as we have argued, it does not allow us to answer all the 'What if?' questions we want to ask. On the other hand, Pearl's is the most complete and well-developed formal apparatus available for assessing counterfactuals in science. This is why we are keen to bring this issue to the fore.

One of the tasks that Pearl's particular semantics undertakes is that recommended by the Hume program, that is, the elimination of 'problematic' causal notions in favor of non-causal ones. For example, Pearl defines *the causal effect* of one variable on another in terms of counterfactuals and then shows how to calculate the causal effect from the probabilities of propositions that employ neither causal nor counterfactual notions. As we noted, this is just the kind of program that philosophers have been heavily engaged in; in particular Pearl's account is very similar to that of David Lewis.[16] Pearl's account like Lewis's is skewed towards the job of evaluating counterfactuals that can deliver the

---

[16] See Lewis (1973, 1979 and 1986).

right verdicts on the targeted causal concepts. Correlatively it fails to provide the right answers to large numbers of genuine 'What if?' questions we want to ask.

Pearl's scheme can serve as a model for what is needed. It has the three requisite ingredients for a semantics for counterfactuals and it is both rich in detail and formally set up to allow for the proof of a variety of important and interesting results.[17] But it itself does not do the job of providing a semantics for genuine 'What if?' counterfactuals.

5. INPUT COUNTERFACTUALS AND OUTPUT COUNTERFACTUALS: JAMES HECKMAN

Counterfactuals are an important topic also in economic methodology today, especially since they have been championed by Nobel prize winner James Heckman.[18] Superficially the way the counterfactuals are pictured to work by Heckman is much as we have urged. A causal model is postulated and rules are supplied for how to calculate answers to specific 'What if?' questions from the model. But when it comes to setting counterfactuals to use there is a big difference. For the counterfactual analysis provided by Heckman cannot in general answer genuine 'What if?' questions. Nor does Heckman claim that it can. The analysis is offered, rather, as in the philosophy literature, as a causal surrogate. We wish to underline the fact that the two jobs are different. We cannot assume that what serves for the one job will serve for the other.

This does not mean, however, that the causal-surrogate counterfactuals are irrelevant for policy and planning. We shall point out that they can serve as *inputs* for constructing the causal models employed in generating the genuine policy counterfactuals needed for planning as outputs. This will require, however, a weaker interpretation than that put on the causal-surrogate counterfactuals.

As in the philosophy literature, Heckman's counterfactuals are offered as a way of defining causal concepts in terms of presumably less problematic non-causal concepts. We propose to view them instead as a way for finding out about independently understood causal relations in special situations. Entirely separate sets of considerations may then tell us whether we can export knowledge about these causal relations to new

---

[17] Cf. Reiss and Cartwright (2003) for a discussion of the third ingredient – an argument that the rules give correct results – which we had to omit here due to space limitations.
[18] Heckman (2000, 2001).

situations, for which we need to construct causal models and generate counterfactual outputs.

What kinds of considerations are required? The distinction between internal and external validity is of use here. A causal claim is internally valid if it is correct for the experimental system in which it was established. By contrast, the claim is externally valid if in addition it is correct for (possibly non-experimental) situations outside the original system. There is no systematic answer available to the question of how to establish external validity. We make only one small contribution here. The counterfactuals that are on offer as causal surrogates have little external validity when they are conceived as counterfactuals. Indeed they very often do not even make sense in the new situation. They only become relevant if they can be taken as measures of causal relations that hold in the situations in which the causal-surrogate counterfactuals are evaluated and that might (or might not) hold in the target situation.

We have talked about the importance of counterfactuals to questions of policy. Similarly when we want evaluate the effectiveness of a trial program we need answers to counterfactual questions: What if the program had not existed? Or had existed in some other form? Or were set up more widely without the trial controls? These are just the kinds of questions Heckman considers in his applied work on the evaluation of labor market programs, where he is at pains to point out that the question itself must be carefully formulated.

We have stressed the ambiguity in ordinary counterfactuals about how the antecedent will be implemented. Heckman points out other sources of ambiguity. We may for instance want to know what the wages of workers in the population at large would have been had the program not existed; more commonly we end up asking what the wages of workers *in the program* would have been. Or we may want to know what the GDP would have been without the program. We also need to take care about the contrast class: do we want to know the difference between the results of the program and those that would have occurred had no alternatives been present or the difference compared to other programs, real or envisaged?

Heckman begins his treatment with *causal functions*. As with LeRoy's starting point, causal functions are a special kind of sparse causal model. The models describe special kinds of systems, systems that mimic experiments: 'Causal functions are . . . derived from conceptual experiments where exogenously specified generating variables are varied . . . The specification of these hypothetical variations is a crucial part of model specification and lies at the heart of any rigorous definition of causality' (Heckman 2001, p. 14).

Heckman tells us three things about causal functions: (i) They 'describe how each possible vector of generating variables is mapped into a resulting outcome', where the generating variables 'completely determine' the outcome (ibid., p. 12). (ii) They 'derive from' – or better, we think, 'describe' – conceptual experiments. (iii) Touching on questions of realism and of model choice, models involving causal functions are always underdetermined by evidence; hence, as Heckman sees it, causality is just 'in the head' since the models relative to which it is defined are just in the head. From this we take it that causal functions represent (a probably proper subset of) the causal principles under which these special experiment-like systems operate, where the right-hand side variables – the ones Heckman calls the 'generating variables' – form a minimal complete set of causes of the quantity represented on the left[19] and where each cause can each vary independently of the others; that is they are variation-free.[20] This is why we say that Heckman's starting point is a causal model.

Imagine that the causal function for an outcome y is given by

$$y \mathbin{c=} g\,(x_1, \ldots , x_n). \tag{5.1}$$

The *causal* or *counterfactual effect* (Heckman seems to use the terms 'causal effect' and 'counterfactual effect' interchangeably) of x_j on y fixing the remaining factors in the causal function is defined thus:

Causal effect of x_j on y:

$$[\Delta y/\Delta x_j = x'_j - x''_j] =_{\mathrm{df}} g\,(x_1, \ldots , x'_j, \ldots x_n) - g\,(x_1, \ldots , x''_j, \ldots x_n). \tag{5.2}$$

Read in terms of counterfactuals we have here the evaluation, relative to a specific assignment of values to all x_j, $j \neq i$, of the difference between the value y would have were $x_1 = x_i'$ and the value y would have were $x_1 = x_1''$.

As Heckman insists, in order for this definition 'to be meaningful requires that the x_j can be independently varied when the other variables are fixed so that there are no functional restrictions connecting the arguments . . . it is thus required that these variables be variation-free'. (Heckman 2001, p. 18) We shall call the counterfactual effect as thus defined a *Galilean effect* since it is just the kind of effect we look for in a

---

[19] Or, keeping in mind Heckman's view that causality is only relative to a model, the right-hand side variables record what the model designates as causes.
[20] Formally, a set of variables $(x_1, x_2, \ldots, x_n)$ is variation-free if $(x_1, x_2, \ldots, x_n) \in X_1 \times X_2 \times \ldots \times X_n$ (where the capital letters denote the support of the variables).

Galilean experiment, where a single cause is varied controling for all other relevant features in order to observe the effect of that cause 'acting alone'.

Heckman considers simultaneous supply and demand equations as an example. For simplicity we can look at the specific equations that we have already considered in discussing LeRoy, where we have added the additional equilibrium constraint on price:

$$q_s = \alpha_s + \alpha_{sp}p_s + \alpha_{sw}w$$
$$q_d = \alpha_d + \alpha_{dp}p_d + \alpha_{di}i$$
$$q_s = q_d = q$$
$$p_s = p_d = p. \tag{5.3}$$

Heckman points out that these equations do not fit Pearl's scheme since they are not recursive and hence Pearl's method for assessing counterfactuals will not apply. This fits with familiar remarks about these kinds of systems: p and q are determined jointly by exogenous factors. It seems then that it makes no sense to ask about how much a change in p will affect a change in q. To the contrary, Heckman points out. We can still assess causal efficacy using his definition – so long as certain 'exclusion' conditions are met.

Say we want to assess the causal/counterfactual effect of demand price on quantity demanded. We first look to the reduced form equations:

$$q = (z_d, z_s)$$
$$p = (z_d, z_s), \tag{5.4}$$

where z_d is the vector of exogenous variables in the demand equations and z_s, those in the supply equations. In LeRoy's equations (5.3), $z_d = i$ and $z_s = w$. Heckman takes these to be causal functions, otherwise the causal model has not properly specified the 'exogenous' variables. That means that the exogenous variables are 'generating variables' for p and q and that they are variation free. Now the task is easy: 'Assuming that some components of $[z_d]$ do not appear in $[z_s]$, that some components of $[z_s]$ do not appear in $[z_d]$, and that those components have a non-zero impact on price, one can use the variation in the excluded variables to vary $[p_d$ or p_s in the reduced form equations] while holding the other arguments of those equations fixed' (Heckman 2001, p. 36). The result (using the equality of p_d and p_s and of q_d and q_s) is

$$\partial q_d/\partial p_d - [\partial q/\partial z_s(e)]/[\partial p/\partial z_s(e)], \tag{5.5}$$

where $z_s(e)$ is a variable in z_s that is excluded from z_d and that, as he puts it, 'has an impact on' p_d. In (5.3) this job can be done by w; the causal effect thus calculated of p_d on q_d is α_{dp}.

Notice how much causality is involved here. By definition we are supposed to be evaluating the change in q_d holding fixed all the factors in a causal function for q_d except p_d. What we actually do is hold fixed z_d while z_s varies. Presumably this is okay because z_s is a cause of p_d that can produce variations in p_d while z_d is fixed; and z_d being fixed matters because z_d constitutes, along with p_d, a minimal full set of causes of q_d. So when the exclusion condition is satisfied, the demand equation is a causal function and the counterfactual definition of causal effect is meaningful.

Now consider a slightly altered set of equations:

$$q_s = \alpha_s + \alpha_{sp}p_s + \alpha_{sw}w + \alpha_{si}i$$
$$q_d = \alpha_d + \alpha_{dp}p_d + \alpha_{di}i + \alpha_{dw}w$$
$$q_s = q_d = q$$
$$p_s = p_d = p. \tag{5.3'}$$

In this model the demand equation cannot be treated as a causal function and the question of the causal effect of demand price on quantity demanded is meaningless. This is true despite the fact that α_{dp} still appears in the equation and it still represents something – something much the same one would suppose – about the bearing of p_d on q_d. The intermediate case seems even stranger. Imagine that $\alpha_{sw} = 0$. Now α_{sp} measures a Galilean effect but α_{dp} does not.

We propose an alternative interpretation of what is going on. We begin with causal principles. A causal principle is just like a causal function but without the restriction that the causes (or 'generating variables') are variation-free. We shall continue to restrict attention to linear causal models of the kind both LeRoy and Heckman use for illustration. Then define for any linear causal model, *the contribution a cause x_c makes to an effect x_e =* def the coefficient of x_c in any causal principle for x_e in the model.[21] It is trivial to show for any linear causal model that where Heckman's measure for the causal/counterfactual effect of x_c on x_e applies, it has the same value as the contribution x_c makes to x_e.

Given this characterization the contribution of p_d to q_d is the same in

---

[21] This supposes that all principles in the model with x_c on the right-hand side and x_e on the left will have the same coefficient. This will be the case given a proper statement of 'transitivity' and the definitions for the form of causal principles sketched in Cartwright (2003).

(5.3) and (5.3'). What is different is that in (5.3) we have a particular way to find out about it that is not available in (5.3'). (5.3) is what we call *an epistemically convenient system*:[22] having an epistemically convenient system implies among other things that it is possible to find out what a cause, x_c, contributes to an effect, x_e, in one particular simple way – hold fixed all the other contributions that add up to make the effect the size it is; then vary the cause and see how much x_e varies. Any difference has to be exactly the contribution that x_c adds. This does not mean, however, that for systems where this independent variation is not possible, all is lost. There are hosts of other legitimate ways of defending claims about the size of causal contributions that apply both in systems with independent variation and in ones without.

There are two advantages to the account that takes Heckman's causal surrogate counterfactuals as measures of causal contributions rather than as mere counterfactuals.

First, few systems we confront are governed by principles in which the causes are variation-free. The vast majority are not. In these systems Heckman's counterfactuals are irrelevant.

Second, even if we are studying a system where the causes are variation-free, there is a puzzle about why we should wish to ask just these implementation-specific questions. If we are thinking of setting policy or evaluating the success of some program in the system, then these, with their special method of implementation, might be relevant sometimes. But there is no necessity to implement policies in the single way highlighted by Heckman; generally we would want to consider a variety of different methods of implementation and frequently to assess implementation-neutral counterfactuals as well. Even where causes are variation-free, the counterfactual changes that Heckman studies generally have no privileged role.

There are two familiar enterprises where they do have a special role. The first is in trying to determine if, and to what degree, one factor contributes causally to another. In an epistemically convenient system we can ask Galilean-type counterfactual questions; and the answers we obtain will double as answers to our causal questions. They are a tool for finding out answers to our causal questions. But note that they are only a tool for finding out about causes in special epistemically convenient systems. For other systems we cannot even ask these counterfactual questions, let alone let the answers to them supply our causal answers as well.

---

[22] For a definition see (Cartwright 2003).

The other is in Heckman's own field, evaluation. In setting up new programs, we might try to set them up in such a way that the causal contribution they make to the result can be readily disentangled from the contribution of other factors. Of particular concern are other factors that might both contribute to the effect independently of the program and also make it more likely that an individual entered (or failed to enter) the program. If we can arrange the set-up of our program so that it is epistemically convenient, then again we can ask Galilean counterfactual questions – 'What difference would there be in outcome with the program present versus the program absent, holding fixed all other contributions to the outcome?' And again these counterfactual questions will tell us the contribution the program makes, since in these circumstances the difference in outcome between when the program is present and when it is absent must be exactly the contribution the program makes. So we can use information about Galilean effects to learn about the causal contributions of the program we set up. Still, all we learn is about that program in those special epistemically convenient circumstances.

In either case, whether it be experimental systems or program set-ups that we engineer to make the measurement of causal contributions easy, we need to ask, why should we be interested in causal contributions in these special – and rare – kinds of systems? The answer is clear. Generally we want this information because we hope it will tell us something about causal contributions in other systems. But we confront here the familiar problem of internal and external validity. In an epistemically convenient (linear) system, using counterfactual differences as a measure of causal contributions is provably valid: internal to the situation this method is bound to give us correct results about the question of interest. But nothing said in this discussion bears on external validity: when will the results that we can be sure are correct in an epistemically convenient system hold elsewhere?

So how do these odd Galilean counterfactuals bear on more useful 'What if?' counterfactuals? In a very indirect way, it seems. We can use Galilean counterfactuals to tell us about causal contributions in Galilean experiments. Then, to the extent that we can expect the facts about causal contributions to remain stable across situations of interest, we can use the information about causal contributions in Galilean experiments to help build causal models for new non-Galilean situations. And we can use the causal models so constructed for these new situations to answer real 'What if?' questions that we want to ask about these new situations. Galilean counterfactuals are one of many inputs in a multi-step process that yields as outputs counterfactuals of immediate use in policy and planning. Figure 11.1 lays out this picture.

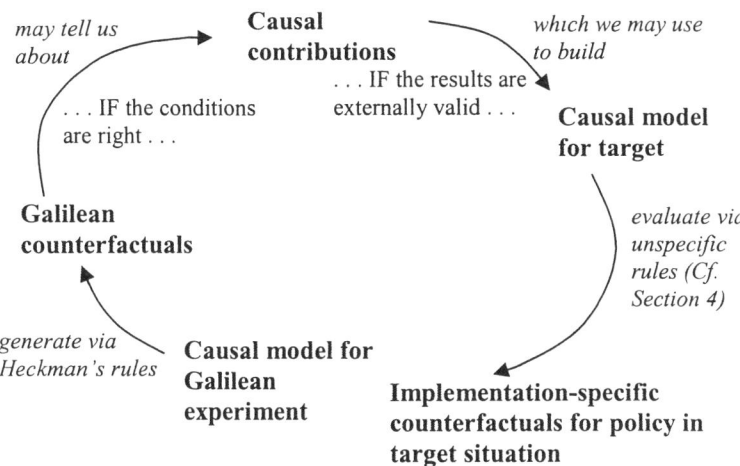

Figure 11.1 How counterfactuals relate to causal models

It is important to stress, however, that assumptions about when information about causal contributions learned in one setting will obtain in others are not justified by anything we have discussed so far, and in particular not by any information about counterfactuals of the kinds we have explored. Showing that results on causal contributions have external validity – and how far and of what kind – requires a different methodology altogether. This is one of the reason we have been at pains to distinguish input counterfactuals from output counterfactuals.

Recent work in economics like that of LeRoy and Heckman provides some clear formal characterizations of how to evaluate special counterfactuals with very particular assumptions about their methods of implementation. But they leave us a long way from any characterization of counterfactuals whose implementations are the ones we are generally interested in. For we have no good rules for how to judge external validity; that is, for when we can export what we learn from a Galilean effect to build a causal model for a non-Galilean situation. And then, as we saw in discussing Pearl, we have only a thin start on how to use a causal model to answer the 'What if?' questions we ask for planning and policy.

6. CONCLUSION: DISAMBIGUATE BEFORE YOU EVALUATE

The lesson we want to draw from the preceding discussion can be captured by the slogan 'Disambiguate before you evaluate'. All three accounts we have been looking at – LeRoy, Pearl and Heckman – provide unambiguous semantics for counterfactuals. But they do so at the cost of seriously constraining the range of admissible counterfactual questions. More importantly, they often provide semantics for counterfactuals that have no relevance for policy analysis whatsoever. What we urge instead is to disambiguate the question first and subsequently use semantics that are tied closely to precisely that kind of question.

First and foremost, we will need to know whether the counterfactual at stake is a Heckman-style Galilean counterfactual of the kind we have discussed in Section 5 or a genuine policy counterfactual as discussed in Sections 2–4. A Galilean counterfactual helps us to evaluate the contribution of a causal factor to a quantity of interest in very specific – that is, epistemically convenient – systems. Without further tests, the results of this evaluation tell us nothing beyond the experimental system at hand. But we may be lucky and find that test results are exportable or 'externally valid'. In this case, we can use the knowledge gained in one particular system as a building block for the evaluation of a genuine policy counterfactual.

Let us assume that we have knowledge of all causal laws governing a particular socio-economic system. If we now want to evaluate a genuine policy counterfactual, we have to decide whether it is meant in an implementation-specific or -neutral sense. Implementation-neutral counterfactuals are true no matter how the antecedent is brought about. These come in particularly handy in case we don't know how to implement the antecedent. But this kind of epistemic uncertainty is neither necessary nor sufficient for evaluating counterfactuals in an implementation-neutral way. On the one hand, we might just want to know what the answer to our counterfactual question was in case it didn't matter how we implemented the antecedent. On the other hand, there are other strategies available for situations of epistemic uncertainty. And these are important if the causal structure of the socio-economic system that we contemplate does not lend itself to implementation-neutral evaluation (recall for instance that there was no answer to LeRoy's question for system (3.1), where the price variable appeared in both equations).

Turning to implementation-specific counterfactuals, finally, once more both metaphysics and epistemology matter. For systems which are characterized by the axioms of Pearl's formalism, we can use his semantics and implement the antecedent without disturbing any other relationship in the system. But for many socio-economic systems that will not do, so we may have to use the more involved (and less formal) modeling strategies of, say, rational expectations economics. In both cases we assume that we have a clear idea of how the antecedent is to be brought about.

If we do not have a clear idea, we must fall back on alternative strategies to deal with epistemic uncertainty. Though we may not know for sure where the money for the new schooling program comes from, we may know that it is far more likely to be raised by a tax increase than by cutting defense. Thus we can use our best guess as to the probability of each possible implementation and weigh the results accordingly.

The main message of our musings about the use of counterfactuals in policy advice is, then, to make the underlying assumptions as transparent as possible. Answering a counterfactual question can amount to a myriad of things. We believe we had better be clear about precisely what issues are involved and give answers that are tailored to the specific case at hand, rather than provide a semantics that yields results across the board but in so doing fails to resolve the question we are in fact interested in.

REFERENCES

Cartwright, Nancy (1983), *How the Laws of Physics Lie*, Oxford: OUP.

Cartwright, Nancy (1989), *Nature's Capacities and Their Measurement*, Oxford: OUP.

Cartwright, Nancy (2003), 'Two theorems on invariance and causality', *Philosophy of Science*, **70** (1), 203–24.

Edgington, Dorothy (1995), 'On conditionals', *Mind*, **104**, 235–329.

Estrella, Arturo and Jeffrey Fuhrer (1999), 'Are "deep" parameters stable? The Lucas critique as an empirical hypothesis', *Federal Reserve Bank of Boston Working Paper*, 99–4.

Hausman, Daniel (1998), *Causal Asymmetries*, Cambridge: CUP.

Heckman, James (2000), 'Causal parameters and policy analysis in economics: A twentieth century retrospective', *Quarterly Journal of Economics*, **115**:1, 45–97.

Heckman, James (2001), 'Econometrics Counterfactuals and Causal Models', Keynote Address *International Statistical Institute*, Seoul, South Korea.

Kyburg, Henry and Mariam Thalos (2003), *Probability Is the Very Guide of Life*, Chicago and La Salle, Ill.: Open Court.

LeRoy, Stephen (2003), 'Causality in Economics', MS, University of California, Santa Barbara.

Lewis, David (1973), 'Causation', *Journal of Philosophy*, **70**, 223–67, reprinted in Ernest Sosa and Michael Tooley (1993), *Causation*, Oxford: OUP, pp. 193–204.

Lewis, David (1979), 'Counterfactual dependence and time's arrow', *Noûs*, **13**:4,

455–76.

Lewis, David (1986), 'Postscripts to "Causation"', *Philosophical Papers*, Vol. 2, Oxford: OUP, pp. 172–213.

Pearl, Judea (2000), *Causation: Models, Reasoning and Inference*, Cambridge: CUP.

Reiss, Julian and Nancy Cartwright (2003), 'Uncertainty in econometrics: evaluating policy counterfactuals', *Causality: Metaphysics and Methods Technical Reports*, 11/03, CPNSS, LSE.

12. Uncertainty and Monetary Policy

Paul Davidson[*]

Since the breakdown of the original Bretton Woods fixed exchange rate system in 1973, the world has witnessed increasing volatility in many financial markets. In fact, after the Far Eastern currency crises of 1997 and the Russian debt default of 1998, financial markets around the world seemed on the brink of collapse. Why is there so much volatility since 1973? Are financial markets *inherently* destabilizing and fragile or is today's financial fragility the result of the global movement towards independent central banks and/or the market 'liberalization' policy decisions taken since the 1970s?

1. EFFICIENCY VS. LIQUIDITY

Peter L. Bernstein is the author of the best-selling book *Against The Gods* (1996), a treatise on risk management, probability theory and financial markets. Bernstein noted that since World War II 'the number of stock markets around the world has grown from 50 to just over 125 – even the Chinese, nominally still socialists, have seen fit to establish stock markets on their territory' (Bernstein 1998, p. 16). Accordingly, one might ask, if financial markets are, as Minsky (1982) suggests, so fragile and destabilizing, why are so many emerging economies developing them?

How one responds to these queries depends on the underlying economic theory that one explicitly, or implicitly, utilizes to explain the role of financial markets in an entrepreneurial economy. There are two alternative (and non-compatible) economic theories regarding the role of financial markets in the economy: the classical efficient market theory and Keynes's liquidity preference theory. Each theory has different implications for monetary policy.

---

[*] Editor, *Journal of Post Keynesian Economics.*

The efficient market theory assumes that data on economic fundamentals permits financial market participants to reliably (in a statistical sense) forecast the future. Market prices of financial assets accurately reflect the present value of the 'known' future stream of money receipts that will accrue to the asset holder. Efficient market theory is the backbone of conventional economic wisdom whose mantra is 'the market knows best' how to optimally allocate scarce capital resources and promote maximum economic growth.

This efficient market theory view is succinctly epitomized in former US Treasury Secretary Lawrence Summer's (1989, p. 166) statement: 'the ultimate social functions [of financial markets are] spreading risks, guiding the investment of scarce capital, and processing and disseminating the information possessed by diverse traders . . . prices will always reflect fundamental values . . . The logic of efficient markets is compelling.' Logically consistent proponents of efficient market theory should urge a policy of liberalizing financial markets whenever there exists any governmental or central bank regulation or interference of financial flows. In efficient market theory there is little or no discretionary role for central bankers and for monetary policy in general. The primary role of the Monetary Authority is to increase the supply of money in line with the growth of real GDP.

In contrast, there is Keynes's liquidity preference analysis where the existence of an uncertainty (nonergodic) future can create the potential for devastating effects on financial markets that can spill over onto the real economy. In such an analytical framework, the role of the Monetary Authority is significantly different than under the efficient market theory. The liquidity preference approach suggests the need for vigilant oversight, regulation and, if necessary, intervention in financial markets by the Monetary Authority so that society can affect the behavior of financial market participants in a socially desirable way.

In the liquidity preference approach, the primary function of financial markets is to provide liquidity for asset holders and entrepreneurs. Since a liquid market must be an *orderly* one, rules, institutions and policies must be developed to guarantee orderliness. Central bankers, as the creators of domestic liquidity in a modern economy, are the best situated of existing institutions to guarantee orderliness – if they understand their job![1] If Keynes's liquidity preference theory of orderly financial markets

---

[1] For as Keynes suggested (1930 ii, p. 220) bank 'credit is the pavement along which production travels, and the bankers if they knew their duty, would provide the transport facilities to just the extent that is required in order that the productive powers of the community can be employed at their full capacity'

is relevant to real world economies, then liberalized financial markets can not be expected to deliver, in either the short or long run, the market efficiency promised by efficient market proponents. *In today's global economy, efficient markets are not liquid and liquid markets are not efficient.*

Bernstein has argued that efficient market theory is *not* the relevant theory for the 21st century entrepreneurial world in which we live. Bernstein (1999, p. 132) states 'The fatal flaw in the efficient market hypothesis is *that there is no such thing as an [efficient] equilibrium price* . . . [and] a market can never be efficient unless equilibrium prices exist *and are known*'. If the future could be reliably predicted using probability measures of risk, then self-interested market recipients would 'know' with actuarial certainty what the equilibrium spot and forward market price structure is and would immediately establish such a price structure in a free market place. There would be no need for central bankers to intervene in either domestic or international financial markets. The ability of market participants to reliably predict the future is the essential element supporting the efficient market theory.

If, however, future economic events are generated by what statisticians call a nonergodic stochastic process, then statistically reliable forecasts can not be made from existing market data, that is necessary information about the future does *not* exist today. The future, therefore, cannot be discovered by studying today's market data (fundamentals). Instead the future is created by entrepreneurial and household spending and liquidity preference decisions in tandem with governmental fiscal and central bank monetary policies – often in ways that are not anticipated by the decision makers. Bernstein recognizes that the entrepreneurial system in which we live involves an uncertain, nonergodic world. Consequently, Bernstein endorses Keynes's liquidity preference theory as the relevant explanation of the operation and growth of global financial markets when Bernstein (1998, p. 23) argues 'a stock market without liquidity ceases to be a market'.

2. TAXING VOLATILITY: THEORY VS. THE FACTS

New Keynesians Joseph Stiglitz (1989) and Lawrence Summers (Summers and Summers, 1989), following the lead of Old Keynesian James Tobin (1974), have argued that an ad valorem tax on all financial market transactions is socially desirable in that it will reduce the observed volatility in our 'super-efficient financial markets'. They also indicate that Keynes initiated the recommendation for a universal financial transactions tax as a socially desirable policy.

In contrast to classical efficient market theory where speculation is stabilizing,[2] Keynes (1936, p. 159) did argue that speculation can destabilize and have severe adverse effects on real economic outcomes. Keynes suggested that public access to financial markets should be, like access to casinos, inaccessible and expensive. After the collapse of the Wall Street stock market in the 1930s, Keynes (1936, p. 160, emphasis added) suggested that the 'introduction of a *substantial* Government transfer tax on all transactions might prove the most serviceable reform available, with a view to mitigating the dominance of speculation over enterprise in the United States' that is especially likely to occur when 'a large number of ignorant individuals' (Keynes 1936, p. 154) are allowed to play the market.

An empirical study by Jones and Seguin (1997), however, appears to conflict with this 'Keynesian' claim that transaction taxes reduce volatility. This study notes that on 1 May 1975, fixed commissions on the New York Stock Exchange (NYSE) and American Stock Exchange (AMEX) were uniformly changed (that is lowered[3]) to negotiated commissions, while the commission structure on all over-the-counter (OTC) transactions in the United States was unchanged. Using daily data for one year before and one year after the change in commission basis, Jones and Seguin examined daily volatility in five sample portfolios sorted by size.[4] A total of 1872 securities traded on NYSE and AMEX and the OTC were studied and the OTC portfolios were used as a 'control sample'. Jones and Seguin (1997, p. 729) calculated cross-sectional mean market values for each portfolio and daily return standard deviations (their measure of volatility). Jones and Seguin (1997, p. 729) concluded that the 'empirical evidence uniformly rejects the hypothesis that the abolition of [higher] fixed commissions increases volatility . . . we find a reduction in transactions costs is associated with a decline in . . . volatility'.[5]

We may ask 'How can such eminent economic theorists as Tobin, Stiglitz and Summers, and even the old, original Keynesian, J.M. Keynes, apparently be so wrong?' The apparent difference between Jones and

---

[2] Traditional classical theory conflates speculation with arbitrage.

[3] The introduction of negotiated commissions on the NYSE and AMEX 'instigated a permanent decline in commissions – regardless of the metric used commissions on institutions fell between 31% and 42% . . . [and for individuals] between 2% and 47% while volume increased substantially' (Jones and Seguin 1997, p. 750).

[4] Each sample portfolio was based on outstanding market value of common equity (size) with sample 1 being largest size stocks and sample 5 being smallest size.

[5] Using Swedish data, S.P. Umlauf (1995, pp. 227–40) also demonstrated that variance increased as a financial transactions tax rate increased.

Seguin's empirical results and the claims that transaction taxes reduce volatility requires an investigation into how economists explain the existence of speculative activity on financial markets.

3.   EFFICIENT MARKETS AND NOISE TRADERS

In efficient market theory agents analyze fundamentals that provide 'information' about future events to form rational expectations. These rational expectations invoke market participants to take actions that move market prices to a level that accurately reflects the present value of the 'known' future income stream. Logical consistency, therefore, requires any observed market volatility to be explained as due to random shocks that push the system away from the 'proper' present value and long-term growth rate. Accordingly, the role of monetary policy is to 'lean against the wind' by maintaining a preannounced money supply growth rate so as to aid the system in its dampening down the volatility.

The ergodic axiom is a necessary logical building block for efficient market theorists to claim that there exist real 'market fundamentals' that immutably determine future outcomes and an optimum economic long-run growth path. If the economic system is an ergodic process, then active government fiscal policies and/or interventionist central bank policies will merely disrupt the real economy's movement towards its immutable full employment real growth path. This is the philosophy behind the simple-minded Monetarist view that independent central bankers are necessary to prevent politicians, who are desirous of re-election, forcing an easy monetary policy on central bankers even during the boom of a business cycle. Efficient market theory logic indicates that there is a need for an 'independent central bank' that typically raises interest rates as a cure for a market boom that raises real output and growth rates above the historical secular trend.

This view of the role of an independent central bank is diametrically opposed to Keynes's conclusion that 'the remedy for a boom is not a higher rate of interest but a lower rate of interest! For that may enable the so-called boom to last. The right remedy for the trade cycle is not to be found in abolishing booms and thus keeping us permanently in a semi-slump; but in abolishing slumps and thus keeping us permanently in a quasi-boom' (Keynes 1936, p. 322). Experience has shown that independent central bankers have not followed Keynes's dictum as most post-World War II recessions have been deliberately created by central bankers raising interest rates in a boom to fight inflation by creating slack markets that reduce the bargaining power of workers and business firms.

In the last half of the 20th century, tight monetary policies were the 'incomes policy' of choice of independent central bankers.

While not abandoning the efficient market hypothesis, Stiglitz has tried to explain the role of uncertainty in generating observable persistent market volatility by his asymmetric information analysis. Stiglitz argues that, even if one assumes efficient markets, gathering and analyzing fundamentals to generate information about the future is costly. Consequently, there can be private return incentives for each market participant to outrace all others in calculating the actuarially reliable future and thereby beat the rest of the market participants by having information that others have not yet obtained. In his asymmetric information theory of financial markets, Stiglitz (1989, p. 103) states that beating the market 'affects how the pie is divided, but does not affect the size of the pie'. In other words, the size of the market payoff 'pie' is fixed and determined by 'real' immutable parameters or 'fundamentals' and will not, in the long run, be changed by discretionary fiscal or monetary policy decisions or speculative activity by market participants.

Stiglitz's assertion (1989, p. 103) that 'production, in every state of nature, in every contingency, is precisely what it would have been had the information not been available' implies that the future path of the economy (and hence tomorrow's financial market prices) have already been predetermined. Stiglitz is, therefore, assuming that information about the future exists today even if (some, all?) humans are not clever enough (and rich enough to spend the resources) to decipher the existing evidence regarding the pre-programmed future outcomes. The asymmetric information hypothesis presumes that the future is willing to reveal itself to those willing to spend sufficient resources in the short run; and the future inevitably reveals itself (at least in the long run) via the observed secular trend of financial prices determined in a free market. This condition, that is that evidence regarding a pre-programmed and immutable future exists today, requires the fundamental assertion that the economic system be ergodic [6] (that is probabilistically risky but not uncertain). Information embedded in today's fundamentals provides a statistically reliable indicator of future events, even if only a few market participants can pay the resource cost of making these actuarial calculations.

The logically inevitable conclusion therefore is (Stiglitz 1989, pp. 102–3) that the most 'important social function of financial markets is to *correctly* allocate real capital among industries in accordance with

---

[6] Samuelson (1970) insists that the 'ergodic hypothesis' is an essential presupposition of those who claim that economics is a 'science'.

reliable information about future rates of return determined by fundamentals'. If Stiglitz's policy recommendations are to be logically consistent with his asymmetric information theory, then the only role for bank monetary policy (or the World Bank's lending policy) is to (1) encourage increased 'transparency' about current and past market transactions so the cost of analyzing this data is reduced, and (2) World Bank loans should be made in accordance with the actuarial calculations developed from this increased transparency.[7] If, however, the economic system is not an ergodic stochastic process, then it is impossible to have a transparent window on the uncertain (nonergodic) future no matter how readily available past data on market transactions are made to the public. Transparency *per se* will not do the job of promoting the orderliness in financial markets that will help us achieve a permanent state of 'quasi-boom'.

4. CAN A TOBIN TAX FISCAL POLICY CREATE THE ORDERLINESS THAT MONETARY POLICY HAS FAILED TO PRODUCE?

Instead of monetary policy to maintain orderliness, Keynesians such as Tobin, Stiglitz, Summers and others advocate fiscal policy in terms of a small transactions tax to reduce volatility especially in international financial markets. This 'Tobin tax', it is claimed, creates a strong deterrent effect primarily on short-term speculators.[8] The tax will not be a deterrent to long-term asset holders who are rational[9] market participants who 'base their trading on fundamentals . . . and are willing to wait a long time to realize a return' (Stiglitz 1989, p. 105). Long-term asset holders are displaying optimal behavior.

Short-term traders consist of essentially two groups: '[t]he noise traders and those who live off them' (Stiglitz 1989, p. 106). In other words, observed volatile financial market prices are movements – *away* from fundamentals determined values. This volatility is attributed

---

[7] This suggests that Stiglitz's break with his former employer, the World Bank, and his subsequent criticisms of World Bank lending policies did not logically follow from his asymmetric information framework. Instead his criticisms came from Stiglitz's common sense.

[8] If asset holders are presumed to be wealth maximizers, then, as I have demonstrated (Davidson 1997) this claimed differential impact of a transactions tax on short-term holders vis-à-vis long-term asset holders can be demonstrated to be mathematically incorrect. Also see Hicks (1935) and Kahn (1954) who demonstrate that the effects of any change in transactions costs is independent of the holding time of an asset.

[9] Note that the term rational only makes sense in an ergodic world.

primarily to the existence of 'noise traders', that is speculators who mistakenly believe they know how the stock market works and therefore do not have to acquire the (presumed to exist) information regarding future outcomes from the fundamentals. Noise traders 'are betting that they can do better than the market . . . based on the mistaken belief that (all!) speculators can do better than the average'[10] (Stiglitz 1989, p. 106). Stiglitz's explanation of the horrendous speculative volatility that we observe in our world is the 'mistaken belief of all speculators' that they can do better than the market by ignoring fundamentals (Stiglitz 1989, p. 106). Since 'the turnover tax primarily affects the short-term [noise trader] speculator' (Stiglitz 1989, p. 105) who, in this analysis, is the creator of excessive volatility, a tax on such foolish speculators will save them from their own folly and save resources for society and is therefore socially desirable.

Stiglitz and Summers argue that some rational market participants become short-term traders feeding on the foolish noise traders and thereby ultimately returning the market to its fundamental trend value. If financial markets are efficient, and immutable market fundamentals are the determinants of the future returns, then those irrational noise traders who make persistent errors become either extinct via some Darwinian economic process such as the rational traders feeding upon them, or they survive only by learning how not to make persistent mistakes.[11] After a single generation, this 'survival of the fittest' efficiency principle should assure that the foolish noise trader will be an extinct species. Those too impatient to wait for Darwinism to take its single generation evolutionary toll urge (1) the Monetary Authority to raise the margin requirement to 100 per cent to prevent using borrowed money to speculate in financial markets, (2) the central bank to regulate the highly leveraged hedge funds and (3) the regulation of the use of derivatives. But central bankers such as Alan Greenspan do not want to impose such regulations because they believe these financial activities help investors spread the risk – just as efficient market theory would suggest.

The pragmatist Stiglitz recognizes that after several centuries of significant volume of daily trades on financial markets – and daily trading volume has increased dramatically in the last two decades –

---

[10] In most empirical studies the *ex post* moving average of what actually happens in the markets is presumed to be the best estimate of the statistical average (over time) that the fundamentals of an ergodic world has predetermined. The fact that econometric analysis of time series market data always reveals a reversion to the mean is merely, as Basil Moore often says, an arithmetic necessity of calculation of time series moving averages.

[11] Moreover, there is no reason to have a public policy to rescue specific individual market participants from the error of their ways.

speculation continues to exist and even increase. How can theorists who believe in super-efficient financial markets explain the centuries-long persistence of speculation and volatility in real world financial markets? How can generations of persistently mistaken 'noise traders' continue to exist in an efficient market system where rational traders can feed off of these fools?

For volatility to persist over more than a single generation, Stiglitz assumes there is a never-ending stream of new noise traders who constantly replace those old noise traders who can not survive in a free market. Stiglitz appeals to authority – the ultimate free market authority and successful circus impresario – P.T. Barnum. Stiglitz misquotes Barnum's dictum 'There's a sucker born every minute'[12] as 'There is a fool born every moment' (Stiglitz 1989, p. 106). Stiglitz's appeal to Barnum's authority implies that society continues to produce, even in the long run, fools who irrationally believe they can beat the market.

Stiglitz buttresses his argument that 'irrationality is pervasive' and perpetual by appealing to the fact that this ubiquitous, persistent irrationality exists even among Stiglitz's brightest economics students.[13] If students at our most prestigious universities are such irrational dolts, then what can one expect of the average financial market participant bereft of exposure to any efficient market analysis?

Stiglitz either does not realize, or else he ignores the idea, that if centuries-long 'pervasive irrationality' is necessary for his explanation of financial market volatility, then logical consistency requires him to admit that irrationality can persist not only in financial markets but 'irrationality' may be pervasive in all product markets.[14] If Barnum's homily that there is a sucker born every minute is a necessary condition for one's market model, then one must reject the orthodox argument that every market involves efficient Darwinian processes that, at least in the long run, eradicate persistent error-making fools. If Barnum is correct (and he certainly understood the circus market), then orthodox theory cannot claim that laissez-faire markets are efficient and will maximize the welfare of the community, even in the long run. Pareto efficiency becomes a tale on a par with Aesop's fables. To provide an analysis of

---

[12] See *The Oxford Dictionary of Quotations* (1959), p. 35.

[13] 'This kind of irrationality is pervasive. Three-fourths of my students believe they are in the top half of the class' (Stiglitz 1989, p. 106).

[14] Especially durable goods where the expected stream of utility will be yielded at many dates far into the future.

speculation and volatility, Stiglitz is throwing away both the classical bath water and the classical baby.[15]

Stiglitz's problem in particular, and orthodox theorists' problem in general, is that they confuse the logic of efficient financial market behavior in a presumed ergodic system with real-world financial and real investment market behavior when real-world decision makers 'know' they are dealing with an uncertain (nonergodic) future.[16] For, as Hahn has noted, when one claims that real world markets are efficient, a

> [q]uick way of disposing with the claim is to note that an Arrow-Debreu equilibrium must be an assumption he is making for the economy and then to show why the economy can not be in this state. The argument will here turn on . . . the inadequate treatment of time and uncertainty. This negative role of Arrow-Debreu equilibrium I consider almost a sufficient justification for it, since practical men and ill-trained theorists everywhere in the world do not understand what they are claiming . . . when they claim a beneficent and coherent role for the invisible hand. (Hahn 1973, pp. 14–16)

Stiglitz, however, is not alone in making these logical errors. Using the same micro-foundations as Stiglitz to explain financial market volatility, Summers (Summers and Summers 1989, p. 170) argues that exacerbating this impact of noise traders on market values is the trading strategy by rational traders who see their self-interest is to go with the flow. They trade often in the short term (using strategies like stop-loss orders) to insure themselves of short-term gains rather than swimming

---

[15] Finally, it should be noted that Stiglitz initially argued that it is the rush to be the first to obtain reliable information in a world of asymmetric information that wastes society resources. Nevertheless in laying the blame for volatility on 'noise traders' who do not try to find *reliable* information about fundamentals (Stiglitz 1989, p. 105), Stiglitz's argument that a transactions tax will reduce the waste of resources seeking to beat the crowd by obtaining reliable information first is irrelevant. A transaction tax, according to Stiglitz, will not affect rational traders seeking reliable information. Rational information seekers in a world of asymmetric information will still have an incentive to beat the rest of the crowd of rational traders in a feeding frenzy on noise traders as long as the tax is less than the hypothesized social return.

[16] Moreover, in developing his noise trader-as-fool argument, Stiglitz has cornered himself in to another logical inconsistency that requires him to use a contradiction to try to extricate himself. Implicit in Stiglitz's model is the notion that there is something strange and different about financial markets vis-à-vis product markets. Stiglitz accepts the argument that the imposition of a transaction tax in any product market will *distort* the Pareto-efficient price structure. Stiglitz argues that a similar tax in the financial markets, however, does not have such a deleterious effect but rather 'such a tax may be beneficial' Short-run speculation trading is attributed primarily to the action of fools (noise traders) who interfere with the efficient capital allocation function of financial markets. A transaction tax, by making it more costly for fools to engage in short-run financial market activity, therefore improves the efficiency of financial markets.

against the tide to make the inevitable long-run arbitrage profit resulting when spot prices move away from 'fundamental values'. Summers (Summers and Summers 1989, pp. 165–6) therefore claims that there 'are strong economic efficiency arguments in support of some kind of [transactions tax] . . . that throws "sand into the gears" to use Tobin's phrase, of our excessive well-functioning [super-efficient?] financial markets. The efficiency benefits from curbing speculation are likely to exceed any costs of reduced liquidity or increased costs of capital. . . . Excessive speculation that increases volatility . . . create[s] rather than reduce[s] risk, distort[s] the allocation of investment, and limit[s] information contents of asset prices'.

Finally, perhaps the best-known advocate of financial transaction taxes is James Tobin (1974). In 1995, Eichengreen et al. (1995, p. 164) forcefully argued that short-term volatility in foreign exchange markets due to speculation can have 'real economic consequences devastating for particular sectors and whole economies'. To constrain speculative behavior they propose a global transaction tax to discourage short-term round tripping, thereby putting 'grains of sand' into the operation of what they called 'super *efficient* financial markets'.[17] Or as Sargent suggests:

> Rational expectations . . . impute to the people inside the model much more knowledge about the system they are operating in than is available to the economist or econometrician who is using model to try to understand their behavior. In particular, an econometrician faces the problem of estimating probability distributions and laws of motion that the agents in the model are assumed to know. Further, the formal estimation and inference procedures of rational expectations econometrics assumes that the agents in the model already know many of the objects the econometrician is estimating. (Sargent 1993, p. 21)[18]

In the neoclassical Walrasian microfoundations that Samuelson synthesized with Keynes's macroeconomics, all producible goods are readily resalable at the equilibrium price vector that encompasses all spot

---

[17] For those who proclaim the efficiency of financial markets, logical consistency requires them to claim that the 'observed' secular trend of financial market prices (typically measured by a moving average) are determined by immutable (ergodic) real sector fundamentals.

[18] Presumably these fundamentals are 'dynamic' in the sense of Sargent that the probability 'of how likely it is' to have a future regime change, that is a change in the fundamentals, must be already encapsulated in the information existing at the initial instant for rational expectations to be formed (Sargent 1993, pp. 26–7). If one does not presume that every possible future regime change is already nested in existing probabilistic information about every contingency in every state of the world, then financial markets cannot be claimed to be efficient as today's real capital allocations can result in unforeseen and unforeseeable future possible egregious costly errors.

and forward prices determined at the initial instant for all future times. In such an equational system, there is no separation of the market value of underlying real asset and market value of corresponding financial assets – for money and hence nominal financial asset prices are presumed neutral. Liquidity therefore is not a primary function of only financial markets. The $n + m-1$ markets for all new and pre-existing goods assure that every good in every time period has the property of liquidity since anyone can be either a buyer or a seller in any of these myriad of markets. In an ergodic world, therefore, it is not possible to experience any drastic reevaluations of the price of assets that are predetermined by real fundamentals[19] (see Eichengreen et al. 1995, p.164). I have discussed why the Tobin tax does not have a greater disincentive to short-term round tripping elsewhere (Davidson 1997).

The Tobin tax is just the wrong policy for the job. Proponents of a Tobin tax have conflated the concept of volume with that of volatility. Of course, any increase in transactions costs, *ceteris paribus*, will lower market volume – but not necessarily volatility. It is this confusion of volume with volatility that makes Tobin tax proponents claim that increased transactions costs will lower volatility inconsistent with the empirical findings that lowering transaction costs will lower the measured volatility of financial markets.

Reducing transactions costs is equivalent to lowering the price of admission to potential market participants. The entry of more traders increases the breadth of the market. In statistical terms, this implies that lower transactions costs increase the size of the sample. It is a mathematical property of sampling from a homogeneous population that as the size of the sample increases, the variance decreases. It should not be surprising, therefore, that Jones and Seguin found their measure of volatility, the variance around the daily mean, decreased when transactions costs were lowered on the NYSE and AMEX compared to the unchanged transactions costs on the OTC market in New York. Their finding of a reduction in 'measured velocity' had nothing to do with the speculative behavior of market participants. It was merely a reflection of the property of a larger sample size.

The Jones and Seguin empirical findings, therefore, are consistent with Keynes's liquidity preference analysis where the larger the sample

---

[19] By claiming that financial markets are not only efficient but are super-efficient, Tobin and the New Keynesians are accepting the ergodic axiom in spades. Consequently, the measured daily variance around the statistical time series (moving) average that is determined by fundamentals can only be attributed to random 'white noise' (and hence the name 'noise traders').

(that is the number of market participants with differing opinions), *ceteris paribus*, the less the measure of volatility (the sample variance) of the market price of traded liquid assets. The more stable the price in financial markets, the greater the degree of liquidity of the asset.[20]

Tobin, Summers and Stiglitz are excellent econometricians and should have recognized that their acceptance of the logic of efficient market theory and the use of a white noise analogy implies that raising transactions costs must, *ceteris paribus*, increase variance by reducing the size of the sample (volume) at any point of time.

5. SPECULATION AND LIQUID FINANCIAL MARKETS

Keynes's liquidity preference explanation of the persistent existence of speculative activity and market volatility requires rejecting the restrictive classical ergodic axiom. At any point of time, the future is uncertain in the sense that the actuarial profit or a reliable mathematically based expectation of gain calculated in accordance with existing probabilities *cannot* be obtained from any existing data set (Keynes 1936, pp. 161–3). In 1937, Keynes emphasized the difference between his 'general theory' and classical orthodoxy. In classical theory

> [f]acts and expectations were assumed to be given in a definite form; and risks . . . were supposed to be capable of an exact actuarial computation. The calculus of probability . . . was supposedly capable of reducing uncertainty to the same calculable state as that of certainty itself. . . . I accuse the classical economic theory of being itself one of these pretty, polite techniques which tries to deal with the present by abstracting from the fact that we know very little about the future. . . . [A classical economist] has overlooked the precise nature of the difference which his abstraction makes between theory and practice, and the character of the fallacies into which he is likely to be led. (Keynes 1937a, pp. 112–15)

In other words, even if 'fundamentals' exist today and even if a data set permits one to estimate today's (presumed to exist) objective conditional probability distribution, such calculations do not form a *reliable* base for

---

[20] Only in the nonergodic world that is our entrepreneurial economic system is it sensible to organize complex and lengthy production and exchange processes via the use of nominal contracts (Davidson 1994). In such a world, the primary function of organized financial markets is to provide liquidity by permitting the resale of assets in an orderly market. Only secondarily do modern super-efficient financial markets affect the allocation of new capital amongst industries and to the extent it apportions capital, this distribution is not predetermined by some long-run immutable real economic fundamentals.

forecasting the future. *Today's conditional objective probabilities are not reliable actuarial guides to the future.*

Keynes's description of uncertainty matches technically what mathematical statisticians call a nonergodic stochastic system. In a nonergodic system, calculations of the mean, standard deviation, and so on from either existing cross-sectional or time series data cannot provide reliable statistical estimates of the probability distribution that will exist at any future date. In other words, in nonergodic circumstances, one can never expect today's data set to provide a *reliable* statistical guide to future outcomes. In a nonergodic world, because the future is uncertain and reliable probability estimates of future outcomes cannot be made, markets cannot be efficient. Accordingly, *the primary function of real world financial markets is to provide liquidity* not efficiency.

This liquidity function involves the ability of each individual to buy and resell assets in a well-organized, orderly market in order to obtain the medium of contractual settlement as needed to meet one's future nominal contractual liabilities when they come due.

Liquidity is a double-edged sword. The good cutting edge provides an orderly, well-organized market where financial assets can be readily resold for cash. Liquid financial markets encourage savers to provide funding to entrepreneurs for the purpose of purchasing expensive, durable investments. Liquid markets encourage financial asset holders to believe they can have a fast exit strategy that enables them to easily liquidate their position the moment they are dissatisfied with the way matters are developing. This fast exit strategy is not a problem as long as those exercising their fast exit plan approximately equal those wanting to enter. Only when most asset holders attempt to exercise their fast exit scheme at the same time is there a calamity in the making (see Davidson 2002).

Nevertheless without the existence of liquid financial markets for debts and equities, the risk of funding investments as a minority owner would be intolerable. Savers would *not* be willing to furnish funding if their investment in financial assets was illiquid.

The ability to maintain one's liquidity position is important to all decision makers in the real world in which we live, but it would not be an important function *if markets were efficient.*[21] Logical consistency for

---

[21] Stiglitz recognizes that market participants may want liquidity, that is may want to exchange money for securities or vice versa, and that such financial market exchanges (free of tax) are Pareto-efficient (Stiglitz 1989, p. 104). With asymmetric information however, those possessing less information about the future are (by definition) trading 'based on *incorrect expectations*'. Consequently, Stiglitz suggests, it is not obvious that a transactions tax that will make trading on incorrect expectations more expensive lowers social welfare.

those claiming financial market efficiency requires the presumption that people can also plan all their future contractual spending on goods and services efficiently by buying financial assets whose maturity date matches the individual's life-cycle spending pattern stream (for example as assumed in overlapping generation models). Sudden liquidity needs to meet uncertain, unpredictable future contractual obligations when they come due, or cases where issuers of financial assets cannot meet their contractual obligation to pay interest or redeem the security at its maturity date, have no role to play in efficient market theory.

If, however, agents in one's model believe their world is uncertain (nonergodic), as Keynes and later Hicks (1979, p. vii) claim, then decision makers 'know' that what others call today's 'fundamentals' do not provide a statistically reliable guide to the future. In such a world, protecting the value of one's liquid portfolio against unforeseen and unforeseeable changes in financial market values becomes an important economic activity. Accordingly, portfolio fund managers must, in an instant, conjecture how other market players will interpret a news event occurring anywhere in the world.

In a nonergodic system, one is always uncertain about future market valuations.

> . . . [A] practical theory of the future [market valuation is] . . . based on a flimsy foundation. It is subject to sudden and violent changes. The practice of calmness and immobility, of certainty and security, suddenly breaks down. New fears and hopes will, without warning, take charge of human conduct. The forces of disillusion may suddenly impose a new conventional basis of valuation. (Keynes 1936, pp. 150–51)

In today's world of instant global communication, any event occurring in the world can set off rapid changes in subjective evaluation of the market value of one's portfolio. Speculation about the psychology of other market players can result in lemming-like behavior which can become self-reinforcing and self-justifying. In a nonergodic system, if enough agents possess the same 'incorrect' expectations (to use Stiglitz's phrase), the result can be that these faulty expectations actually create future outcomes. The first 'irrational' lemmings to hit the ocean of liquidity may not drown. They may survive and even thrive to have more irrational expectations and lead more lemming-leaps into liquidity in the future.

6. MARKET MAKERS AND LIQUID FINANCIAL MARKETS

In an uncertain (nonergodic) world, financial markets furnish liquidity by providing an orderly, well-organized environment where financial assets can be readily resold for cash while the essential properties of the underlying real capital assets prevent them from producing the attribute of liquidity.[22] In so doing, financial markets promote the separation of ownership and management.[23] In the absence of a liquid financial market '[t]here is no object in frequently attempting to revalue an investment to which we are committed' (Keynes 1936, p. 151). If capital markets were completely illiquid, then there would be no separation of ownership and control. The purchase of an investment would be 'permanent and indissoluble, like marriage, except by reason of death or other grave cause' (Keynes 1936, p. 160). Once some volume of real investment was committed, the owners would have an incentive to use the existing facilities in the best possible way no matter what unforeseen circumstances might arise over the life of plant and equipment, rather than, say, follow the 1990s business plan of the Enron Corporation. Perhaps then illiquid capital markets might behave more like the efficient markets of mainstream theory.

When bullish sentiment dominates liquid financial markets, savers will be encouraged to readily provide the funding that induces entrepreneurial investors to spend vast sums on new investment projects that far exceed their current incomes. On the other hand, when the bear position is overriding, savers can develop an excessive desire to maintain a fully liquid position. This liquidity demand will impede funding of new investment projects even when real resources are idle and therefore readily available to produce new capital goods. Too great a demand for liquidity can prevent 'saved' (that is unutilized) real resources from being employed in the production of investment goods.

Keynes explicitly recognized that the introduction of sand in the wheels of liquidity-providing financial markets via a transactions tax is a double-edged sword. He noted that a financial transactions tax 'brings us up against a dilemma, and shows us how the liquidity of investment markets often facilitates, though it sometimes impedes, the course of new investment' (Keynes 1936, p. 160).

Stability in financial markets is 'dependent on the existence of a variety of opinion about what is uncertain. Best of all that we should know the future. But if not, then, if we are to control the activity of the economic system . . . it is important that opinions differ' (Keynes 1936,

---

[22] Keynes (1936, p. 241n) argues that the 'attribute of liquidity' is by no means independent of the presence of two essential properties, namely that the asset is not reproducible via the employment of labor and it is not substitutable for the producible output of industry.

[23] See Keynes (1936), pp. 150–51; Davidson (1972); Bernstein (1998), pp. 17–18.

p. 172). In other words, the 'best of all' possible worlds for financial market stability would be an ergodic system where the future can be known with statistical reliability – that is the hypothetical world of classical economics. Then the future can be reduced to actuarial certainty, that is 'we should know the future' and market efficiency would be assured as long as agents operated in their 'known' self-interest.

Unfortunately, the world of experience is not an ergodic system. Consequently the rational risk spreading that Summers and Stiglitz speak of is impossible, and *the guaranteeing of orderly financial markets to always provide liquidity for private sector financial asset holders should be the primary monetary policy goal of central bankers.*

In a nonergodic environment, the expectations of either the bulls or the bears cannot be described as either rational (in the Lucas sense) or *ex ante* correct. Relatively free liquid financial markets require a substantial number of market participants who hold continuously *differing* expectations about the future so that any small upward change in the market price brings about a significant bear reaction, while any slight downturn induces a bullish reaction. The result will be spot financial market (resale) price trend stability over time while the market maintains a high degree of liquidity based on private sector actions and reactions. Market stability, therefore, requires a continuous (and dense) spectrum of both bull and bear expectations simultaneously. The more participants in this bull–bear spectrum, the less, *ceteris paribus*, volatility. Ultimately, an important support over time for this dense spectrum of bull and bear expectations requires a credible market maker who assures the public that, no matter what happens, orderliness will be maintained. In this era where less government intervention is presumed to be better, liquid markets utilize private market makers to try to establish orderliness. Unfortunately, private market makers often tend to act like the rational traders in Summers's noise trader models and go with the flow rather than maintain strict orderliness. Although public information on these private market makers activities are not readily available, from time to time evidence[24] arises that suggests some private market makers use trading strategies arising from their unique position that limit the possibilities of short-term losses while increasing the possibility of volatility. Accordingly there can be the necessity of the Monetary

---

[24] In the spring of 2003, there were media reports that 'specialists' (the market makers on the New York Stock Exchange) were 'penny chasers', that is enhancing their income by making profits by intervening between buyers and sellers to increase the value of their asset holdings.

Authority to insert itself in financial markets (either directly or indirectly) more actively to support the function of orderly market making.

7.   SPECULATIVE WHIRLPOOLS AND BANDWAGONS

Although Keynes did not employ the ergodic–nonergodic taxonomy,[25] he implicitly utilized this classification when he claimed that Tinbergen's (econometric) Method 'was invalid [because] . . . the economic environment is not homogeneous over a period of time (perhaps because non-statistical factors are relevant)' (Keynes 1937b, p. 308), and economic time series are non-stationary. Since non-stationarity is a sufficient condition for nonergodicity, Keynes's concept of financial and economic uncertainty implies nonergodicity. More recently, Robert Solow has endorsed Keynes's position. Solow (1985, p. 385) wrote that 'much of what we observe cannot be treated as the realization of a stationary stochastic process without straining credulity'.[26] Solow's statement recognizes that important economic data, that some call the fundamentals, are not generated by ergodic stochastic systems. Consequently data regarding these 'fundamentals' provides no guide to the 'correct' equilibrium price of financial assets over time.

With his emphasis on uncertainty as the major force explaining the speculative demand for liquidity, Keynes had to reject the classical ergodic axiom of efficient market theory to explain market behavior. Consequently, using efficient market theory to explain speculation is, to Keynes and Post Keynesians, equivalent to relying on the axiom of parallel lines in a non-Euclidean world to explain why 'in experience, straight lines apparently parallel often meet' (Keynes 1936, p. 16). Rebuking these apparently parallel lines for crashing into each other is similar to relying on persistent irrational behavior of noise traders to explain market volatility. Both are useless homilies.

Liquidity requires market broadness to permit each individual to sleep easily assured that savings vehicles are good stores of general purchasing power. Jones and Seguin's empirical analysis merely demonstrates that by reducing transaction costs one enhances daily liquidity and stability

---

[25] The theory of ergodic stochastic processes was just being developed by the Moscow School of Probabilities in the mid 1930s. It is not surprising that Keynes did not know the ergodic–nonergodic terminology.

[26] In a personal letter to me (dated 21 May 1985) Solow wrote 'I have always admired the article of yours on non-ergodic processes, and thought it was right on the button'

provided certain conditions are met. These conditions are (1) both the bulls and bears are widely represented among the additional participants and (2) within each of these categories there are a continuum of divergent views among individuals as to when to change from the bull to bear position and vice versa. To the extent that a reduction in transactions costs increases the number of participants in both the bull and bear positions, then, *ceteris paribus*, there is more likely to be a denser continuum and therefore less moment by moment or daily variability. In such circumstances, as Keynes (1936, p. 159) noted, speculation can become mere bubbles on the steady stream of enterprise.

If, at any point of time, however, there is a sudden swing to a bandwagon consensus, that is there is an abrupt lack of broad market participants with differing (not rational) expectations about the future, then there can be a rapid swing in market prices. A bandwagon effect occurs when a consensus view suddenly congeals regarding the possibility of a severe change in the future spot market price of financial assets. The bandwagon concept implies that suddenly a preponderance of participants appear only on one side of the market (whether it be in the bull or bear position). What is required orderliness in the face of a potential development of a bandwagon mentality is a 'market maker' institution with sufficient resources to prevent instability resulting from actions of private individuals all attempting to jump on the bandwagon at once. The market maker must announce that it will swim against any developing bandwagon consensus view regarding a change in market psychology. This announcement by the market maker must be deemed credible by market participants. In order for this credibility to be assured, the market maker must either be the Monetary Authority or have a recognized position of support and preferred access to the Monetary Authority.

For example, the events in New York on 11 September 2001 created great uncertainty about the future of financial markets in the United States. The potential for a massive fast exit of market participants existed. Despite its ideological bias for the efficient market theory, the pragmatic side of the Federal Reserve management flooded the financial system with liquidity immediately after the 11 September 2001 terrorist attacks on the World Trade Center and the Pentagon. In the two days following the attack, the Federal Reserve pumped $45 billion into the banking system. Simultaneously, 'to ease cash concerns among primary dealers in bonds – which include investment banks that aren't able to borrow money directly from the Fed – the Fed on Thursday [13 September 2001] snapped up all the government securities offered by dealers, $70.2 billion worth. On Friday it poured even more into the system, buying a record

$81.25 billion of government securities' (*Wall Street Journal*, 18 October 2001, p. 1).

In effect, these virtually unlimited open market purchase actions of the Federal Reserve removed securities from the general public by making liquidity available to financial intermediaries who would purchase securities from those members of the general public who wanted to make a fast exit.

The *Wall Street Journal* also reported that just before the stock market opened the following Monday for the first time since the terrorist attack, investment banker Goldman Sachs, loaded with liquidity due to Fed activities, phoned the chief investment officer of a large mutual fund group to tell him that Goldman was willing to buy any stocks the mutual fund managers wanted to sell. Similarly, the *Journal* notes that corporations 'also jumped in, taking advantage of regulators' newly relaxed stock buyback rules' (*Wall Street Journal*, 18 October 2001, p. 1). These corporations bought back securities that the general public had held, thereby propping up the price of their securities.

The post–11 September 2001 activities of the Federal Reserve flooding the banking and financial system with liquidity vividly demonstrate that the Monetary Authority can either directly or indirectly make the market orderly when the public has a fast exit propensity. The result was that the terrorist attack did not exacerbate the mild economic recession that the United States had entered in the spring of 2000.

The Federal Reserve's policy actions meant that the public could satisfy its increased bearishness tendencies by increasing its money holdings without depressing the spot market price for financial assets in a disorderly manner. Until, and unless, the public's increase in bearishness recedes, the Monetary Authority and the banking and financial intermediaries can hold that portion of the total titles to the underlying real capital of enterprises that the public does not want to own.

Although the public shifted its portfolio holdings from titles to real capital goods and ownership of debt contracts toward money and other safe haven financial assets after the terrorist attack, the community could not alter its holdings of aggregate real capital at all in the short run. Accordingly, the total market value of titles to capital goods held by the public at any point of time does not necessarily bear any particular unique relationship to the total stock of capital goods in the economy despite the claims of some financial market 'experts' that there is a long-run fundamental price–earnings ratio.[27] At any point of time, the actual

---

[27] Thus Kaldor's (and others') use of the valuation ratio as a determinant of long-run equilibrium growth is highly misleading since there is no necessary relationship between

market value of securities depends on (1) the historical accidents of the past needs of firms to externally fund investment expenditures, (2) the net buy-back of securities by enterprise, (3) the current sentiment of the wealth-holding public, and (4) the behavior of the Monetary Authority, the banking system and financial intermediaries acting as market makers in response to changes in the bull–bear sentiment of the public.

In an economy where the major form of money is bank deposits, portfolio decisions in combination with the operations of the financial system will determine what proportion of the community's total of real wealth is owned by households and what proportion is owned or looked after by the banking and financial system.

In the absence of a market maker with sufficient financial asset resources to stem the bandwagon tide, 'enterprise becomes the bubble on a whirlpool of speculation' (Keynes 1936, p. 159). It is 'bandwagon' movements in financial markets and not daily white noise variance that causes 'volatility' problems in financial markets. The resultant change in the secular trend of financial market prices due to bandwagons can have 'real economic consequences devastating for particular sectors and whole economies' (Eichengreen et al. 1995, p. 164).

8. A POLICY IMPLICATION: BUFFERING CONVENTIONAL WISDOM

In a nonergodic world, Keynes insisted the conventional wisdom is that market participants believe that the existing market valuation is correct. The market 'knows' that

> . . . the existing state of affairs will continue indefinitely, except in so far as we have specific reasons to expect a change . . . We are assuming, in effect, that the existing market valuation, however arrived at, is uniquely correct in relation to our existing knowledge . . . though, philosophically speaking, it cannot be uniquely correct, since our existing knowledge does not provide a sufficient basis for a calculated mathematical expectation. (Keynes 1936, p. 152)

In the world of experience, the conventional wisdom is that as long as it is expected that the psychology of the market is not changing there will

the market value of the outstanding stock of titles in the hands of the public relative to the value of the net finance committed to the purchase of capital goods until both the marginal propensity to buy placements out of household savings and the actions of the Monetary Authority and the financial intermediaries who 'make' spot security markets are specified. Cf. N. Kaldor (1966) and J. Robinson (1954, p. 230).

be an inertia in market valuations. It then follows that any good monetary policy involves reducing if not eliminating the possibility of disruptive speculation in financial markets by building institutions and, when necessary, taking direct intervening actions that assure market participants that the 'correct' market psychology is a belief in a persistent, stable (moving average) trend in market prices over time.[28]

If, for example, the market participants believe that there exists a market maker who can guarantee an unchanging spot market price (or changing over time only within very small boundaries that move at an annual rate that does not exceed the rate of interest), then the existence of this creditable market maker will provide an anchor for 'market psychology'. For participants to believe in the market maker's ability to maintain the target spot (resale) price, however, the market maker must have a 'sufficient' inventory of a recognized fully liquid asset (money) and that financial asset that is being sold in the relevant market. In our current foreign exchange market system, for example, this implies that the domestic Monetary Authority[29] has creditability (and a sufficient inventory of foreign reserves or easy access to additional reserves). If the Monetary Authority announces that it will use its foreign reserves to maintain an orderly market at the 'proper' exchange rate[30] then market psychology will provide orderliness provided the buffer stock of foreign reserves remains sufficient.

To prevent all disruptive speculation in any specific market therefore requires a buffer stock policy[31] practiced either by the central bank or a

---

[28] In fact, all markets in liquid assets require the institution of one or more credible 'market makers' who follow some preannounced rules of the game to assure orderliness in the market. The more orderly the market maker keeps the market, the less the moment-to-moment volatility. It is only when market makers fail in their responsibility to maintain orderly markets that volatility becomes disorderly and speculation can have real disruptive effects.

[29] In the global economy of the 21st century, however, no national Monetary Authority is likely to always have sufficient credibility under all circumstances. Accordingly, we will require a cooperative international monetary payments system, an International Monetary Clearing Unit system that has specific rules for a buffer stock policy that assure exchange rate stability.

[30] That is the explanation of why currency boards with reserves equal to the domestic money supply can fix the exchange rate (often at the expense of the domestic credit market).

[31] Use of buffer stocks as a public policy solution to stabilize prices over time is as old as the biblical story of Joseph and the Pharaoh's dream of seven fat cows followed by seven lean cows. Joseph – the economic forecaster of his day – interpreted the Pharaoh's dream as portending seven good harvests where production would be much above normal followed by seven lean harvests where annual production would not provide enough food to go around. Joseph's civilized policy proposal was for the government to store up a *buffer stock* of grain during the good years and release the grain to market, without profit, during the bad years. This would maintain a stable price over the fourteen harvests and avoiding sky-

private market maker who has either direct (or indirect) privileged access to the central bank in times of dire stress in financial markets. If the majority of market participants believe in the market maker's buffer stock approach, the only speculators that could exist would then be fools, that is a small group of offsetting bulls and bears who disagree with the vast majority of market participants but whose actions cannot detrimentally affect market price movements. Provided there is an effective buffer stock market maker who recognizes when to act before disaster strikes, there should be no disruptive speculation and enterprise can continue at its current steady stream toward an unknown future.

9. MAINTAINING LIQUIDITY IN INTERNATIONAL FINANCIAL MARKETS

A problem arises as to what to do in international capital markets if the market maker in the foreign exchange market runs out of his buffer stock of foreign reserves. The answer to that question lies in developing a new international financial architecture. Keynes's Bretton Woods plan was to develop a supranational central bank that operated to provide all the international liquidity necessary for employment growth. From a political standpoint, an agreement among sovereign nations on a supranational central bank was impossible then and remains impossible today. In its stead I have suggested an international clearing union agreement that can achieve the same objective. My proposal has been developed in detail elsewhere (Davidson 1992–93, 1994, 2002). The essential aspect of my IMCU proposal is to develop a clearing union institution whose members are national central banks who can always act as credible market makers to ensure the orderliness of foreign exchange transactions. The main provisos of my clearing union institutional proposal are:

1. The unit of account and ultimate reserve asset for international liquidity is the International Money Clearing Unit (IMCU). All IMCUs are held *only* by central banks, not by the public. Consequently, they can never become objects for speculation.
2. Each nation's central bank is committed to guarantee one-way convertibility from IMCU deposits at the clearing union to its domestic money. Each central bank will set its own rules regarding

---

rocketing prices and speculative hoarding in the bad years and depressing prices and dumping inventories in the good years. The Bible records that this civilized buffer stock policy was a resounding economic success.

making available foreign monies (through IMCU clearing transactions) to its own bankers and private sector residents [32]. Ultimately, all major private international transactions clear between central banks' accounts in the books of the international clearing institution.

3. The exchange rate between the domestic currency and the IMCU is set *initially* by each nation – just as it would be if one instituted an international gold standard.

4. Contracts between private individuals will continue to be denominated into what ever domestic currency permitted by local laws and agreed upon by the contracting parties.

5. An overdraft system to make available short-term unused creditor balances at the clearing house to finance the productive international transactions of others who need short-term credit. The terms will be determined by the *pro bono publico* clearing house managers.

6. A trigger mechanism to encourage a creditor nation to spend what is deemed (in advance) by agreement of the international community to be *'excessive' credit balances accumulated by running current account surpluses*. These excessive credits can be spent in three ways: (1) on the products of any other member of the clearing union, (2) on new direct foreign investment projects, and/or (3) to provide unilateral transfers (foreign aid) to deficit members.

7. A system to stabilize the long-term purchasing power of the IMCU (in terms of each member nation's domestically produced market basket of goods) can be developed. This requires a system of fixed exchange rates between the local currency and the IMCU that changes only to reflect permanent increases in efficiency wages.[33] This assures each

---

[32] Correspondent banking will have to operate through the International Clearing Agency, with each central bank regulating the international relations and operations of its domestic banking firms. Small-scale smuggling of currency across borders, and so on, can never be completely eliminated. But such movements are merely a flea on a dog's back – a minor, but not debilitating, irritation. If, however, most of the residents of a nation hold and use (in violation of legal tender laws) a foreign currency for domestic transactions and as a store of value, then this is evidence that the residents are not civil law-abiding and have a lack of confidence in the government and its Monetary Authority. Unless confidence is restored and residents become law-abiding, all attempts to restore economic prosperity will fail.

[33] The efficiency wage is related to the money wage divided by the average product of labor, it is the unit labor cost modified by the profit mark-up in domestic money terms of domestically produced GNP. At this preliminary stage of this proposal, it would serve no useful purpose to decide whether the domestic market basket should include both tradable and non-tradable goods and services. (With the growth of tourism more and more non-tradable goods become potentially tradable.) I personally prefer the wider concept of the domestic market basket, but it is not obvious that any essential principle is lost if a tradable only concept is used, or if some nations use the wider concept while others the narrower one.

central bank that its holdings of IMCUs as the nation's foreign reserves will never lose purchasing power in terms of foreign produced goods, even if a foreign government permits wage–price inflation to occur within its borders.

8. If a country is at *full employment* and still has a tendency towards persistent international deficits on its current account, then this is *prima facie* evidence that it does not possess the productive capacity to maintain its current standard of living. If the deficit nation is a poor one, then surely there is a case for the richer nations who are in surplus to transfer some of their excess credit balances to support the poor nation.[34] If it is a relatively rich country, then the deficit nation must alter its standard of living by reducing the relative terms of trade with major trading partners. If the payment deficit persists despite a continuous positive balance of trade in goods and services, then there is evidence that the deficit nation might be carrying too heavy an international debt service obligation. The *pro bono* officials of the clearing union should bring the debtor and creditors into negotiations to reduce annual debt service payments by [1] lengthening the payments period, [2] reducing the interest charges, and/or [3] debt forgiveness.[35]

It should be noted that proviso #2 permits capital controls. Proviso #6 embodies Keynes's innovative idea that whenever there is a persistent (and/or large) imbalance in current account flows due to persistent trade imbalances, there must be a built-in mechanism that induces the surplus nation(s) to bear a major responsibility for eliminating the imbalance. The surplus nation must accept this burden for it has the wherewithal to resolve the problem.

In the absence of #6, under any conventional system, whether it has fixed or flexible exchange rates and/or capital controls, there will ultimately be an international liquidity crisis (as any persistent current account deficit can deplete a nation's foreign reserves) that unleashes global depressionary forces. Thus, proviso #6 is necessary to assure that the international payments system will not have a built-in depressionary bias. Ultimately, then, it is in the self-interest of the surplus nation to accept this responsibility, for its actions will create conditions for global

---

[34] This is equivalent to a negative income tax for poor fully employed families within a nation.

[35] The actual program adopted for debt service reduction will depend on many parameters including: the relative income and wealth of the debtor vis-à-vis the creditor, the ability of the debtor to increase its per capita real income, and so on.

economic expansion, some of which must redound to its own residents. Failure to act, on the other hand, will promote global depressionary forces which will have some negative impact on its own residents.

Some think that my specific clearing union plan, like Keynes's bancor plan, a half century earlier, is Utopian. But if we start with the defeatist attitude that it is too difficult to change the awkward system in which we are trapped, then no progress will be made. Global depression does not have to happen again if our policy-makers have sufficient vision to develop this post-Keynesian approach. The health of the world's economic system will simply not permit us to muddle through.

10. CONCLUSION

The message of this analysis is that in the real world in which we live, the primary function of financial markets is to provide liquidity. Moreover, a liquid market can *never* be efficient.

Orthodox economics, whether it be of the New Classical or New Keynesian variety, is founded on the premise that *all* markets are efficient. The theoretical characteristics of efficient markets require the absence of false trades (that is trades at the non-equilibrium price) or if a false trade has been made, then the trade is subject to *recontracting without penalty* at the equilibrium price. Since in the real world human agents are fallible and the future is uncertain, agents are continuously entering into contracts some of which – especially in financial markets – will involve contractually commitments at a non-equilibrium price as the contracting parties make errors of foresight. Since real world legal financial market contracts do not permit recontracting without penalty, then it should be obvious that real world financial markets are not, and cannot be, efficient – even in the long run.

This chapter has also demonstrated that New Keynesian scholars, for example Stiglitz, Summers, and so on, share the New Classical theoretical belief in efficient financial markets. The main difference between these schools of thought is that classical scholars see no constraints on free markets achieving an efficient equilibrium while New Keynesians argue that short-run price fixities in product and exchange rate markets and/or other short-run constraints (for example noise traders in financial markets) prevent markets from achieving the efficient equilibrium position immediately. Yet this is a distinction without a theoretical difference – at least in the long run when markets are ruled by efficient equilibrium fundamentals in both Classical and New Keynesian models.

Thus this short-run distinction between New Keynesians and New Classical scholars disappears in the long run. To describe this difference between New Keynesians and New Classical views of financial markets we can paraphrase Keynes's distinction between the major orthodox schools of thought in his time as: Old and New Classical economists offer us the 'supreme intellectual achievement, unattainable by weaker spirits [that is New Keynesians] of adopting a hypothetical world remote from experience and then living in it consistently. With . . . [weaker spirited New Keynesians, however,] common sense cannot help breaking in – with injury to their logical consistency' (cf. Keynes 1936, p. 192).

The New Keynesians, by emphasizing the short-run noise traders, contractual commitments in financial markets as simply the equivalent of random sampling errors (that is white noise) around a stable population average value, encourage the view that, in the long run, monetary policy-makers cannot affect market values based on 'real' fundamentals and therefore central bankers should not actively intervene in financial markets. This view endorses, if not encourages, the belief in the desirability of independent central bankers who 'know' that the 'proper' monetary policy is one that does not waiver in the face of economic setbacks and dislocations that might force weaker spirited politicians to encourage changes in monetary and fiscal policies to mitigate the dislocations and to create jobs and profit opportunities for domestic industries. Unfortunately in the New Keynesian long run, there is the distinct possibility that we shall all be dead.

REFERENCES

Bernstein, P.L. (1996), *Against The Gods*, New York: Wiley.

Bernstein, P.L. (1998), 'Stock market risk in a post Keynesian world', *Journal of Post Keynesian Economics*, **21**, Fall No. 1.

Bernstein, P.L. (1999), 'Why the efficient market offers hope to active management', *Journal of Applied Corporate Finance*, **12** (2).

Davidson, P. (1972), *Money and The Real World*, London: Macmillan.

Davidson, P. (1992–93), 'Reforming the world's money', *Journal of Post Keynesian Economics*, **15**, Winter No. 2.

Davidson, P. (1994), *Post Keynesian Macroeconomic Theory; A Foundation for Successful Economic Policies in the Twenty-first Century*, Camberley, UK and Brookfield, US: Edward Elgar.

Davidson, P. (1997), 'Are grains of sand in the wheels of international finance sufficient to do the job when boulders are often required?', *The Economic Journal*, **107**, September No. 3.

Davidson, P. (2002), *Financial Markets, Money and the Real World*, Cheltenham, UK and Northampton, MA, USA: Edward Elgar.

Eichengreen, B., J. Tobin and C. Wyplosz (1995), 'The case for sand in the wheels of international finance', *The Economic Journal*, **105**, March No. 1.

Hahn, F.H. (1973), *On The Notion of Equilibrium in Economics*, London: Cambridge University Press.

Hicks, J.R. (1935), 'A suggestion for simplifying the theory of money', *Economica*, **2** (1).

Hicks, J.R. (1979), *Causality in Economics*, New York: Basic Books.

Jones, C.M. and P.J. Seguin (1997), 'Transactions costs and price variability: evidence from Commission deregulation', *American Economic Review*, **87**, September No. 3.

Kahn, R.F. (1954), 'Some notes on liquidity preference', *Manchester School*, **2** (1).

Kaldor, N. (1966), 'Marginal productivity and the macroeconomic theories of distribution', *Review of Economic Studies*, 35.

Keynes, J.M. (1930), *A Treatise on Money*, 2, Macmillan, London.

Keynes, J.M. (1936), *The General Theory of Employment, Interest and Money*, New York: Harcourt, Brace.

Keynes, J.M. (1937a), 'The General Theory', in *Quarterly Journal of Economics*, reprinted in D. Moggridge (ed.), *The Collected Writings of John Maynard Keynes*, **14**, London: Macmillan. All page references are to the reprint.

Keynes, J.M. (1937b), 'On Mr. Tinbergen's Method', in *The Economic Journal*, 47, reprinted in D. Moggridge (ed.), *The Collected Writings of John Maynard Keynes*, 14, London: Macmillan. All page references are to the reprint.

Minsky, H.P. (1982), *Can It Happen Again?*, Armonk: M.E. Sharpe.

Oxford Dictionary of Quotations (1959), 2nd Edition, Oxford: Oxford University Press.

Robinson, J. (1954), *The Accumulation of Capital*, London: Macmillan.

Samuelson, P.A. (1970),'Classical and Neoclassical Monetary Theory', in R.W. Clower (ed.), *Monetary Theory*, Hammondsworth: Penguin.

Sargent, T. (1993), *Bounded Rationality in Macroeconomics*, Oxford: Oxford University Press.

Solow, R.M. (1985), 'Economic history and economics', *American Economic Review Papers and Proceedings*, **75**, May No. 1.

Stiglitz, J. (1989), 'Using tax policy to curb short term trading', *Journal of Financial Services*, **3** (1).

Summers, L.H. and V.P. Summers (1989), 'When financial markets work too well: a cautious case for a securities transactions tax', *Journal of Financial Services*, **3** (1).

Tobin, J. (1974), 'The New Economics One Decade Older', *The Janeway Lectures on Historical Economics*, Princeton: Princeton University Press.

Umlauf, S.P. (1995), 'Transactions taxes and the behavior of the Swedish stock market', *Journal of Financial Economics*, **23** (1).

13. Knightian Uncertainty, Accountability and Economic Policy Rules

Helene Schuberth

1. INTRODUCTION AND SUMMARY

Uncertainty that arises from both the nature of the real world (aleatory uncertainty) and our limited ability to know the real world (epistemic uncertainty) seriously impairs the process of inquiring into truth. Economic policy rules in monetary and fiscal policy seem to even further interfere with the truth-finding process. Uncertainty and our incapability of modeling it lead many to reject economic policy rules per se: in light of uncertainty, adherence to a rule would be costly since it does not allow for a flexible reaction to unforeseen events, the Stability and Growth Pact being an eminent case in point. On the other hand, the lack of accountability of economic policy institutions, whose activities do not depend on majority voting, lead many to become advocates of rules, despite the unresolved problem of uncertainty. By committing to a rule which is assumed to maximize overall welfare, so the argument goes, institutions that are not democratically legitimized become accountable to the public. Accountability consists, in this case, of observing and sanctioning deviations of economic policy outcomes from target values. In this line of reasoning, the judgment and discretion of economic policy-makers develop a negative connotation as a part of overall secrecy policy.[1]

* The views expressed in this chapter are those of the author and do not necessary reflect the views of Oesterreichische Nationalbank. The author is grateful to Daniel Eckert, Peter Mooslechner, Vanessa Redak, Stefan Schmitz and Martin Schürz for helpful comments on an earlier version of this chapter.
[1] Judgment and discretion of central bankers are usually justified by uncertainty. 'It is precisely that lack of knowledge that makes mechanical policy rules incredible . . . Perhaps one of the strongest arguments for delegating decisions on interest rates to an independent central bank is that, whereas democratically elected politicians do not often receive praise

Against the growing trend of delegating important policy-making powers to independent expert agencies, the traditional 'rules-versus-discretion' debate of the economics profession has been adapted by constructing a trade-off along different lines: control mechanisms, such as policy rules, are argued to strengthen democratic legitimacy and thereby reconcile accountability and independent agencies, but such mechanisms inadequately take into account uncertainty and thus, in substance, even weaken considerations of truth concepts. This has evolved implicitly as an influential view among some economists and political scientists who position themselves along this trade-off frontier (for example Svensson 1997). We will argue that the construction of this trade-off is flawed. It rests on the assumption that the prevalent property is measurable uncertainty (risk) which can be thought of as uncertainty characterized by a unique probability distribution. Past observations of the distribution of outcomes are viewed as a good guide for the distribution of outcomes that can be expected in the future. If we introduce unmeasurable uncertainty in the sense of Knight (1921), where no objective probability distribution exists, accountability of independent agencies cannot easily be accomplished by policy rules, as agency losses increase with the degree of Knightian uncertainty: given data, model and goal uncertainty that cannot be characterized by a unique probability distribution, the decision makers dispose over a high amount of discretion in following a rule. Data, model and goal uncertainty are major issues in both monetary and fiscal policy; in the latter case there is even uncertainty about the sign of the growth effect of a fiscal impulse, which makes the recent proposal of delegating fiscal policy to an independent authority of experts most problematic.

We contrast the literature on policy rules with procedures of economic policy-making currently in place. The literature on monetary policy rules constructs an ideal case of 'optimal' policy. This pretension to optimality is founded on the claim that the rule is defined as a technical procedure that minimizes a loss function; in other words, the 'optimal' rule is supposed to maximize society's welfare. Uncertainty is introduced by modeling specific kinds of quantifiable risks and by analyzing how these kinds of risks modify the 'optimal' rule. Knightian uncertainty, in particular uncertainty about the goals of monetary policy, is by and large ignored. A major gap between the notion of a welfare-maximizing rule

---

when they say 'I don't know', those words should be ever present on the tongues of central bankers. And, in a state of ignorance, it is important for the central bank to be transparent about both what it thinks it understands and what it knows it does not understand' (Mervyn King 1999, p. 32).

and actual policy is that neither the agent (central banks) nor the principal (general public) has so far announced an explicit loss function that includes the relative weight of output gap and inflation stabilization, which would only now make evaluation of monetary policy more tractable. The literature on fiscal policy rules, where uncertainty is not a central theme, does not even allege that rules are derived from welfare considerations by minimizing loss functions – hence the rules are better referred to as formal fiscal restraints aimed at limiting the discretion of politicians subject to deficit bias – but they are generally claimed to improve welfare.

We argue that the role of the policy rules literature is to refine the theoretical foundation of shielding economic policies from the democratic process by spreading illusions about the optimality of technocratic decision-making processes that supposedly serve society's welfare best. In this view, rules symbolizing the collective wisdom of society represent the best alternative for governance. Therefore, policy rules are discussed as substitutes for democracy grounded on the notion that the participation of a broad range of societal groups would lead to policy outcomes that are viewed as inefficient by the economics profession. We consider this concept of accountability crucially different from the democratic legitimacy of institutions.

The chapter is structured as follows: Section 2 reviews the literature on economic policy rules under uncertainty and discusses its implications for the 'optimal' rule. The growing body of literature on 'monetary policy rules under uncertainty' analyzes the impact of various kinds of risk for the degree of attenuation in monetary policy. So far, the practical use of this literature for policy is limited, mainly for three reasons. First, Knightian uncertainty is the kind of uncertainty central bankers are typically facing, given that complexity and time variation of the economic structure make an assignment of probability distributions to parameters of models impossible. The recent literature studying Knightian uncertainty actually models risk (quantifiable uncertainty) that is a consequence of the fact that unquantifiable uncertainty cannot be modeled satisfactorily. Most importantly, potential measurement errors of main variables, such as the output gap, that are a major source of Knightian uncertainty, are categorized as risk. Hence, the literature focuses on structured forms of uncertainty, while Knightian uncertainty has to be viewed as unstructured. Second, various kinds of risk and uncertainty arise simultaneously, leading to ambiguous policy implications: there may be uncertainty in some of the parameters that are assumed to have a known distribution (Brainard uncertainty), as well as model uncertainty, that is uncertainty about the structure of the economy, at the same time. The latter kind of uncertainty would, for most of the cases studied so far, require a more aggressive setting of interest rates, while Brainard uncertainty necessitates caution. Third, an issue which has been neglected in this literature is uncertainty about society's loss function, which gives information about the goals of monetary policy (goal uncertainty): how much weight to put on the goal of price stability versus the goal of employment? The cases studied presume still controversial specifics of the loss function which, in almost all of the cases, has a standard linear-quadratic form. It follows, for example, that positive output gaps are as costly as negative output gaps, or inflation above target is as welfare-reducing as inflation below target. Optimal policy thus requires the minimization of deviation from the steady state in a symmetric way, while it is far from clear whether the empirically unobservable steady state is optimal. We conclude that uncertainty literature focuses on some minor causes of risk and uncertainty while neglecting major sources such as uncertainty about the medium and long-run effects of monetary policies. In reviewing this literature we furthermore show that a specific class of rule, such as inflation targeting, does not exclude judgment and the use of extra-model information; hence, in following a rule, the decision maker disposes over a high degree of discretion to act according to wise men's beliefs. Discretion is especially high against the background of goal uncertainty: in the case of trade-offs between the objectives of output stabilization and low inflation, the central bank may decide which variable to stabilize at the expense of increased volatility of the other variable.

Contrary to the monetary policy rules literature, fiscal rules have not been formally derived by maximizing a welfare function. Hence, they effectively deviate from the theoretical conception of 'optimal' rules. In addition, the question as to how the introduction of uncertainty modifies the respective fiscal rule has not been a central theme in fiscal policy rules literature. However, the fiscal rule's design largely reflects different views on the fiscal transmission mechanism and the fiscal policy objectives. While in monetary policy there is a broad consensus about the sign of the short-term effects of a change in the interest rate on output and employment, and controversy arises over the main sources, distributional consequences and the aggregate size of this effect, there is even uncertainty about the sign of the impact of a fiscal impulse reflecting different priors concerning the 'true model' of the fiscal transmission mechanism. There is much more dispersion of beliefs among economists on the effects of fiscal policy than on the effects of monetary policies.

Given model, data and goal uncertainty, different policy prescriptions coexist for any policy problem (Section 3). Respective 'optimal' solutions adopted by experts can be derived for many different mental and cognitive constructions of economic causalities and priorities regarding economic policy objectives. Delegating policy to independent agencies staffed with experts is thus associated with high agency costs that cannot be reduced by policy rules, as the respective agent will – with or without a rule – act according to the wise men's belief. As democratic legitimacy and independence of agencies cannot be reconciled by policy rules, we argue that in a world of Knightian uncertainty the principal–agent setting does not seem to be appropriate for the conduct of fiscal and monetary policy, and alternative procedures of democratic accountability have to be developed.

2. ECONOMIC POLICY RULES AND UNCERTAINTY

Uncertainty in the Monetary Policy Rules Literature

Monetary policy rules
The literature on monetary policy rules draws on two different concepts of rules. With an *instrument rule*, the short-term interest rate, that is the central bank's instrument, is expressed as an explicit function of information available to the central bank. The best-known simple instrument rule is the Taylor rule, where the instrument rate responds only to the inflation and output gap. Hereby, monetary policy is represented by mechanical-reaction functions with no room for judgment. Generally, a change in the rule accounting for the arrival of new information about the transmission mechanism, the variability of shocks, or the source of shocks is not foreseen. Even if deviations are allowed, there is no rule for when these deviations are appropriate. Within the framework of a *targeting rule*, well-known examples are a money supply or an inflation targeting rule, target variables with their relative weights reflecting preferences aggregated across individuals enter a loss function that increases with the distance of the target variables from prescribed target levels. In a simple setting, the output and the inflation gap enter the loss function, which has a quadratic form. The loss function is then minimized subject to equations describing the structure of the economy, that is the central bank's information about the state of the economy and its view of the transmission mechanism. Since current monetary policy affects inflation and output only with lags, and the total effects are spread out over several quarters, forecasting targeting rules are usually considered an adequate characterization of the practice of inflation targeting. Here, forecasts of the target variables enter the intertemporal loss function. The decision-making process in a central bank involves making qualified forecasts of inflation and the output gap, conditional on

different paths of the interest rate. Then, the interest rate for which the corresponding qualified forecasts minimize the intertemporal loss function is chosen. If, for instance, the inflation forecast is too high (low) relative to its target, the interest rate has to be raised (lowered). Targeting rules allow for an immediate reaction to new information by updating the forecasts and the interest rate path. Contrary to an instrument rule, a targeting rule does not exclude extra-model information and judgment. Targeting rules are labeled 'optimal' by their proponents, since they involve the minimization of a loss function.

The role of uncertainty in monetary policy rules

Since the late 1990s the literature on monetary policy rules has incorporated risk and – with direct reference to Knight – uncertainty.[2] In this growing body of literature on 'monetary policy rules under uncertainty', the term uncertainty is used for quantifiable and, in a few cases, unquantifiable, uncertainty. The main conclusion of this literature is that different kinds of risks and uncertainty (additive, parameter and model uncertainty) require different kinds of policy responses (no response, caution (or conservatism), aggressiveness and/or experimentation). This analytical distinction between various risk categories is useful as it demonstrates what the current prevailing procedure does: so-called optimal policy rules are derived by adapting standard methods of optimization from control theory, that is optimal feedback coefficients based on econometric models that only take account of one specific kind of risk, namely additive uncertainty. In this certainty equivalence case, policy-makers can effectively ignore such risk and act as if they knew for certain. The policy responses related to all other kinds of risk are then formulated against this special case. The literature on robust decision theory, however, following its introduction into monetary economics by Hansen and Sargent (2000), is a special case since it resorts to Knightian uncertainty. However, as Dow (2004) has noted, this literature claims to model uncertainty in the Knightian sense even when it actually models risk: for the derivation of the robust decision rule, literature sets quantitative limits on that uncertainty.

Additive and multiplicative uncertainty: For a quadratic loss function and a linear model of the transmission mechanism where future target variables depend linearly on the current state of the economy and the instrument rate, certainty equivalence is a standard result in optimal control theory (additive uncertainty). Here, uncertainty only exists in the

---

[2] For an overview of the monetary policy rules literature and uncertainty, see Table 13.1.

form of additive shocks, which give information about the variance from the actual value that the dependent variable can take. Since the shocks follow a Gaussian distribution with zero mean, accounting for this kind of risk has no impact on central bank policy. Certainty equivalence assumes that

a)   policy-makers have exact knowledge of the parameter values in use,
b)   the variables are measured correctly, and, finally,
c)   the functional form of the economy is known with certainty.

As those three assumptions are hardly ever met, modifications of the 'optimal' rule have been studied in order to relax these assumptions.

A case where certainty equivalence breaks down was first studied by Brainard (1967): multiplicative, or Brainard uncertainty refers to uncertainty about the coefficient on variables in the transmission mechanisms (impact parameters). It is categorized as measurable uncertainty (risk) as it is assumed that policy-makers know the variance of the uncertain parameter. Parameter uncertainty might reflect structural changes in the economy or imprecise estimates of the parameters. In contrast to uncertainty generated by additive shocks, this implies that the larger the change in the variable, the greater the uncertainty about its effect on the economy. It further implies that policy-makers typically moderate the changes in the interest rate in response to a given change of a variable about whose parameter there is great uncertainty. For instance, if there is uncertainty about the interest elasticity of aggregate demand, then the central bank would be reluctant to move interest rates too sharply in response to shocks. The empirical observation that the 'optimal' interest rate under additive uncertainty is more volatile than the central bank's historical interest rate is often attributed to an interest-rate-smoothing behavior resulting from parameter uncertainty (Blinder 1998, Batini and Haldane 1999, Goodhart 1999, Sack and Wieland 1999). However, as Srour (2001) has noted, parameter uncertainty does not necessarily imply caution with regard to interest rate variations. Uncertainty about the response of future inflation to current inflation should cause policy-makers to strengthen their response to the output gap and the deviation of inflation from the target, as stronger action will minimize the potential for inflation to move away from its target.

A major source of uncertainty, ignored by the cases of additive and Brainard uncertainty, is data uncertainty. It especially aggravates the central bank's capability of identifying shocks correctly. Special attention has been devoted to measurement errors in the output gap and in inflation (Rudebusch 2001, Smets 2002). In these studies, optimal coefficients are calculated for inflation and output gap in the Taylor rule, conditional on a model that assumes no measurement error, and then the coefficients are recalculated allowing for measurement error. The studies conclude that uncertainty regarding the size of the output gap or inflation will contribute to reducing the optimal coefficients.

Model uncertainty: Parameter uncertainty is measured by the variance of the uncertain parameter derived from historical data, so the policy-makers know exactly how uncertain they are. Similarly, data uncertainty is categorized as risk (quantifiable uncertainty) as it is analyzed under the presumption that the variance of any measuremet error is known. Hence, not only additive but also parameter and data uncertainty are treated as hypothetical cases of quantifiable uncertainty (risk), while a more realistic assumption is that Knightian, unquantifiable uncertainty is the kind of uncertainty central bankers are typically facing: given complexity and time variation of the economic structure, they cannot posit any prior distribution on parameters of the model, they do not dispose over accurate information on the variance of measurement errors, and they are uncertain about society's preferences regarding monetary policy's objectives and about the 'true' model of the transmission mechanism.

Given 'model uncertainty', economists have designed robust decision rules that perform well across a set of alternative models that are regarded as plausible and not just a single linear model, as in the certainty equivalence case (Levin et al. 1999, 2001; Gerdesmeier et al. 2002). The basic idea is to search for a safe policy which guarantees stable performance under a prespecified set of potential misspecifications. From a Bayesian perspective, this approach corresponds to the adoption of uniform priors about which model describes the 'true' structure of the economy. Robust decision rules, put forward as an alternative to standard Bayesian decision theory in macroeconomics which suggests that uncertainty can be captured in subjective probabilities, do not make judgment redundant. One has to bear in mind that the alternative models representing the structure of the economy are created in line with the major propositions of standard models (for example long-run neutrality of money) that are usually not questioned. Relaxing any one of these major propositions can yield quite different results with regard to policy recommendations. Models may represent strong beliefs, priors or ideology. An output gap model relating inflation dynamics to deviations of output from its potential level reflects different beliefs than a P-star model that assigns monetary developments a crucial role in inflation dynamics. Almost all of the models employed assume monetary neutrality in the long run, despite the lack of overwhelming empirical evidence in the neutrality hypothesis (Espinosa-Vega 1998). [3] The arbitrary choice of models still involves a high degree of unquantifiable uncertainty.

Recently, the engineering literature on robust control has been applied to monetary policy under uncertainty.[4] It analyzes the incorporation of uncertainty into one reference model that is considered to be only approximately good but reflects the best estimate of the believed law of motion of the economy. Thus, utility loss from inconsistency in the target variable is minimized. Starting from the premise that uncertainty aversion implies preference ordering which corresponds to Wald's (1950) min-max type of decision rules, Hansen and Sargent (2002) started to apply the min-max approach of decision theory to model uncertainty. Some of the cases that have been studied within this framework recommend more aggressive policy responses; hence, caution is not always an adequate reaction to uncertainty. The intuition behind non-attenuation can be exemplified by the case of uncertainty regarding deflation. In the certainty equivalence case, such extreme events should be taken into account by the mean size of the event, that is, the probability-weighted size of the shock. Since deflation has not occurred in the recent past, it is not observable in the data, so the probability-weighted size of the deflation shock is zero. Defining probabilities of unique or never-observed events is an impossible task. The inability to characterize uncertainty in probability terms compels the monetary authority to protect against losses for worst-case outcomes. Robust monetary control involves the definition of a worst-case scenario (for example deflation). Against this worst-case scenario, the policy-maker then chooses a monetary response that leads to the best outcome in this scenario (minimal loss). If policy-makers want to forestall future consequences of events where no probability distribution can be attached, policy is adjusted (relative to standard control theory) in such a way as to provide insurance against the worst-case outcome.[5] Hansen and Sargent (2000)

---

[3] Monetary policy can also have, and has frequently had, longer-run effects when it contributes to violent swings in the economy that result in the destruction of physical and human capital that would otherwise have contributed to continuing real growth.

[4] Robust control theory has been introduced to monetary economics by, for instance, Onatski (1999), Tetlow and von zur Muhlen (2000), Hansen and Sargent (2002) and Onatski and Stock (2002).

[5] There are historical examples of situations in which central banks changed interest rates aggressively in order to maximize the chance of heading off the possibility that financial instability may endanger price stability: following the stock market crises in 1987, the Federal Reserve dropped the Federal Funds rate by 125 basis points despite robust growth and potential inflationary pressures. Other examples are the cuts in policy rates in the

explicitly refer to Knightian uncertainty. As Dow (2004) has noted, the initial choice of the model, the representation of uncertainty as, for instance, a particular specification of the error process, as well as the quantitative limits that are arbitrarily set to that uncertainty, are necessary for quantification, but involve constraints so that unquantifiable uncertainty remains. A new strand of literature, distinguishing between uncertain factors that are unknowable when setting interest rates and others that can be learned through experience (Wieland 2000, Rosal and Spagat 2002), argues that uncertainty about structural parameters can be reduced through experimentation. One might make the case that US monetary policy from the mid- to late 1990s was experimenting with lower interest rates to test whether the short-term Philips curve had changed (Ball and Moffitt 2001). Whether epistemic uncertainty can be reduced through learning, as shown in dynamic simulations, is still open to debate, given that, for example, a change in policy itself might change the model structure in an unpredictable way. The recommendation of some degree of experimentation under a wide range of initial beliefs about the unknown parameters challenges the view put forward by recent uncertainty literature that monetary policy rules just have to be modified to effectively account for uncertainty. The role of priors and beliefs of decision makers becomes crucial.

Goal uncertainty: Beliefs are even more imperative when considering the loss functions usually specified in the monetary policy rules literature. Monetary policy objectives are arbitrarily set and kept simple for technical convenience to allow for tractable solutions. Loss functions range from the precept of society's welfare depending only on the inflation gap, the deviation of inflation from target (strict inflation targeting) to loss functions that also depend on deviations of output relative to its potential level (flexible inflation targeting) (Svensson 2002), and, in some cases, they include interest-rate smoothing as an important objective. There is a high degree of uncertainty as to (a) whether deviations from target should be minimized in a symmetric way, (b) what the appropriate monetary policy objectives are and (c) how much weight should be attached to each of these objectives.

The standard linear quadratic loss function assumes that increases in the level of output above potential are as undesirable as decreases below the so-called steady state level, and increases of inflation above target are as costly as decreases below target. Optimal policy thus requires the minimization of the deviation from the steady state in a symmetric way.

United States following the difficulties at Long-Term Capital Management in September 1998, or in many countries the week after 11 September 2001.

The optimality of this technical procedure can be seriously doubted. One could assume negative output gaps to be more costly to society than positive gaps. Another argument for the institution of asymmetry in the welfare function might be that inflation below target is more harmful to society than higher inflation if, for instance, the grease effects establishing the beneficial effects of price increases dominate over the sand effects of inflation.[6] While the public's distaste can be viewed as firm enough to prevent inflation from running out of control, there is great uncertainty regarding monetary policy's power to control deflationary spirals, especially in an institutional setting where monetary and fiscal authorities are legally prohibited from coordinating their policies ex ante. Our understanding of the dynamics that generate deflation is far from perfect.

One important element in generating deflation might be financial instability, as the probability of a credit crunch rises with the overall debt burden. This is closely related to the issue of determining appropriate monetary policy objectives. Financial stability, a key objective for central banks, is viewed more often as a constraint on monetary policy than as a separate target variable in the loss function (Svensson 2002, Bean 2003). In this view, it is sufficient to consider the impact of financial imbalances on the target variables in the objective function. But does it affect aggregate supply and demand linearly or non-linearly? In the latter, more realistic case, the reaction function becomes non-linear and certainty equivalence breaks down. The objective of financial stability, if not accounted for in the loss function, is thus not always easily reconciled with flexible inflation targeting. In a situation of financial stress, not usually immediately reflected in the price mechanism, measured by the consumer price index, the unwinding of cumulative financial imbalances may cause a severe fall in aggregate demand. To offset this shock, a reduction in the interest rate may be required. The standard loss function for flexible inflation targeting with output and inflation gap as its arguments, however, would recommend constancy of rates, or even monetary tightening, if inflation is persistently above target and inflation expectations do not anticipate a probable increase in negative output gaps. Hence, the trade-off between output and inflation affected by this

---

[6] The sand effects that are commonly stated in the literature include the distortions of the relative price mechanism, inflation risk premia on interest rates, show leather costs of inflation and distortions due to the nominal tax system (Feldstein 1997). The more recent literature has stressed benefits of inflation, associated with the notion that a moderate level of inflation greases the wheels of the price and wage setting processes. See Akerlof et al. (1996 and 2000), Groshen and Schweitzer (2000) and Holden (2002).

shock requires a high degree of judgment and any mechanical adjustment to asset prices would be misplaced.[7]

Financial stability has only recently been proposed as an important objective of central banks, while low inflation, as well as high employment and growth have been considered the main monetary policy objectives throughout the history of economic thought, although the goals have been weighted differently in line with the respective predominant paradigms. Presently, a consensus among mainstream economists has emerged, according to which the objective function should include the deviation of output from its potential level to account for the stabilization objective of a central bank (Svensson 2002, Clarida et al. 1998) in addition to the deviation of inflation from target. Due to rigidities and information asymmetries, anticipated (systematic) as well as unanticipated (unsystematic) monetary policy shocks are generating short-term real effects on employment and output growth, but these effects fade out in the long run. This 'New Neo-Classical Synthesis', which extends the optimizing behavior underlying the Real Business Cycle literature to include the frictions considered by New Keynesian Economics, has come to dominate policy evaluation in central banks (Taylor 1999). The exclusion of an employment or output growth objective from the objection function is theoretically underpinned by long-run monetary neutrality assumptions: monetary policy is incapable of impacting the long run, and policy instruments other than monetary policies, such as structural policies, should be used to stimulate potential output growth. In the long run, only nominal variables are subject to monetary influences. But our knowledge of the long run is a 'black box'. Theoretical models of the Keynesian school and neo-classical models have been built that deliver long-run non-neutralities with different signs of the impact of monetary policies on long-run output growth.[8] Even if those effects are not large or permanent, they might be important. Furthermore, there is uncertainty about the appropriate inflation target. An inflation target that is set too low might increase the probability of hitting the zero lower bound on nominal interest rates if an extreme shock occurs, thereby losing its potential to stimulate the economy.

Even if the arguments in the loss function are known for certain, the relative weights attached to the targets have to be defined. Mainly due to

---

[7] There is controversy as to what extent a central bank should take account of asset prices and, in particular, potential asset-price bubbles, as it is difficult to judge whether an asset price movement reflects expectations about fundamentals or a bubble, and whether there are repercussions on inflation and growth.

[8] For an overview, see Espinosa-Vega (1998).

the existence of supply shocks, there is a trade-off between inflation and output gap variability – both cannot be minimized at the same time. Because of this trade-off, unpredictable shocks, uncertainty and, unavoidably, imperfect controls, there will always be some variability in both inflation and the output gap. The weight set for output gap relative to inflation gap stabilization becomes crucial for the decision whether to accommodate a supply-side-driven projected increase in inflation, thereby keeping output close to potential (flexible inflation targeting) or to keep inflation close to target at the cost of an increase in unemployment (strict inflation target). [9] As the weights are neither defined by the general public nor officially announced by the central bank, the latter is given discretion to choose whether inflation or output should bear the strain of the initial impact of any shock.

Mainstream economists have reached a consensus regarding the view that central banks maximize society's welfare best if the relative weight on output gap stabilization is less than society's. This idea of the need for a conservative central banker not only theoretically underpins a high degree of independence for central banks, it also supports the need for a loss function being defined by the (conservative) central banker and not by the general public – the latter being prone to inflation bias, the classic argument for weight conservatism in Rogoff (1985), or, as discussed more recently, to stabilization bias (Gaspar and Smets 2002). Both biases are model-dependent and are selective choices from among other biases that could be considered. The need for a higher relative weight for inflation stabilization is further emphasized by the literature investigating implications of uncertainty regarding the estimation of the output gap, suggesting a more cautious response to changes in output (Rudebusch 2001).

The loss function is thus viewed as the private objective function of the decision maker who – according to this paternalistic attitude – still maximizes welfare of society, the latter being prone to inferior knowledge and overall welfare-reducing incentives. The alternative interprets the loss function as an approximation of social welfare, assigned to the central bank by society or political authorities as in a principal–agent situation. To avoid agency losses, a well-known side effect of delegation, an explicit contract between the principal and the agent, including a clear objective, well-defined standards of performance, ex ante incentives and ex post sanctions, is suggested. Designed for the certainty equivalent case, this is the preferred model of those who want to

---

[9] A high relative weight on inflation gap minimization is equivalent to choosing a shorter horizon over which to bring inflation back to target.

make independent central banks more accountable to the public. But how is this model reconciled with uncertainty about society's monetary policy objective function? How is a contract established between the agent and the principal in light of uncertainty about how individual preferences regarding monetary policy objectives can be aggregated and whether it is reasonable to simply condense them to two? This makes the proposal of letting the general public define the objectives and their weights a difficult task.

Although the loss function plays a crucial role in the policy rules literature, its empirical and theoretical foundation is far from clear. The formalization of monetary policy's objective function involves a major source of Knightian uncertainty. In general, the uncertainty literature focuses on some minor causes of risk and uncertainty, but neglects major sources, such as uncertainty about the functional form of the objective function, the appropriate monetary policy targets and their relative weights. Furthermore it is far from clear whether the empirically unobservable non-inflationary steady state is optimal.

Monetary rules and practice of monetary policy

Research on monetary policy rules and the practice of monetary policy diverge. Although different from case to case, the procedure in decision making deviates from the mode of 'optimal welfare-maximizing policy-making' related to optimal control theory and its modifications implied by Brainard and model uncertainty. In general, instrument and targeting rules play the role of guiding monetary policy conduct rather than strictly adhering to it. If monetary policy rules literature is only partially reflected in actual policy-making, two issues remain open. First, should we be concerned about an inadequate account of uncertainty in the literature if this literature has no direct impact on policy per se? Second, what is the role of policy rules literature in general? The answers to both questions are closely interlinked. So far, most of the studies have only considered very specific and tightly-defined forms of risk. Disentangling different kinds of risks and analyzing the respective policy implications are of limited practical use to policy for various reasons. We are unsure about the kind of uncertainty we are facing, and we need to deal with various kinds of uncertainty, structured and unstructured, simultaneously (Dow 2004). While practical policy-making is not as rigid or rule-based, models are used in the policy-making process to at least generate forecasts and for scenario analysis. In general, these models only account for additive uncertainty.

A major gap between the notion of a welfare-maximizing rule and actual policy arises from the different treatment of the loss function in literature and in policy-making. While the 'optimal' policy rule is derived from minimizing a loss function, presumably reflecting society's preferences, no political authority or central bank has so far announced an explicit loss function.[10] Furthermore, the legislative mandates that differ widely across countries abstain from numerically defining the weights attached to inflation and, for some countries, to growth objectives. This gives the central banks a high degree of discretion concerning the employment or growth objective and inhibits a ready evaluation of the performance of the central banks. In the case of the Eurosystem, Article 105 of the Treaty of Maastricht stipulates that the primary goal of monetary policy is price stability, but that the ECB shall also take into account the goals set in Article 2 and 3a of the Treaty, which might be interpreted as output stabilization goals (Svensson 1997). It can be argued that keeping inflation stable also stabilizes output and employment, so there is no need for an explicit primary employment objective. However, this precept only holds in the case of demand shocks, and supply shocks of the cost-push would increase output volatility if the central bank were to keep inflation stable. In the case of supply shocks, where output and inflation move in opposite directions in the short run, the mandate does not give a clear directive as to which variable to stabilize (at the expense of increased volatility of the other variable), but implicitly leaves this decision to the ECB.[11] Contrary to the ranking of monetary policy objectives in the mandate of the Eurosystem, prevailing legislation in the United States compels the Federal Reserve to conduct monetary policy 'so as to promote effectively the goals of maximum employment [and] stable prices', among other objectives (Judd and Rudebusch 1999). But again, the mandate does not foresee relative weighting of the goals in cases involving trade-offs, which makes an evaluation nearly impossible. The accountability of central banks is most far-reaching in countries applying a strict inflation-targeting strategy that

---

[10] To improve transparency and accountability via better external monitoring and evaluation of monetary policy, Svensson (2002) has recommended that central banks specify a loss function where the members of the Monetary Policy Committee should vote on the relative weight of the output gap versus the inflation gap.

[11] Whether there is scope for stabilization policies depends on the time horizon of the inflation target. In the case of the euro area the inflation objective of below 2 percent has to be achieved in the medium term: '...by maintaining price stability over the medium term, the single monetary policy makes the best contribution it can to achieving a high level of output and employment, thereby supporting the general economic policies of the Community, as required by the Treaty.' Speech by Otmar Issing, 'How to achieve a durable macro-economic policy mix favorable to growth and employment?', contribution to the conference on 'Growth and Employment in EMU', organized by the European Commission, Brussels Economic Forum, Brussels, 4 and 5 May 2000.

is implicitly equivalent to a short (say 1-year) horizon in the inflation target.

Fiscal Rules and Uncertainty

As demonstrated in the case of monetary policy, a rule is regarded as 'optimal' if it is obtained from welfare considerations by minimizing a loss function that is defined in some respects. The literature on fiscal policy rules largely refrains from formally deriving an 'optimal' rule and does not even claim to be properly founded on a welfare function derived from society's preferences.[12] The fiscal rules analyzed herewith, such as the Stability and Growth Pact (SGP), are better referred to as formal fiscal restraints. Intergenerational equity (fair distribution of the burden of public spending across generations), low inflation (avoidance of negative externalities of excessive deficit) and growth (due to the declared existence of non-Keynesian effects of fiscal consolidation) are stated as the main objectives of disciplining fiscal restraints. These rules are considered to limit the discretion of politicians seeking re-election, as they are biased toward excessive deficits, and, in guaranteeing fiscal discipline, should contribute to efficient macroeconomic outcomes. Different views of the transmission mechanism of fiscal policy largely determine the rule's design. By restricting stabilization to the use of automatic stabilizers, the SGP rests on the view that discretion in fiscal policy is harmful, as so-called non-Keynesian effects may materialize.[13] A higher degree of discretion is allowed within the golden rule currently employed in the United Kingdom. This discretion allows a net deficit within the size of public investment over the business cycle (Emmerson et al. 2003). Even if the rules are not formally welfare-based, an underlying welfare function can be implicitly derived from the design of the fiscal rules discussed.[14]

---

[12] For an exception, see Buti and Giudice (2002) who derive a fiscal reaction function from the loss function with output gap and net deficit stabilization as its main arguments.

[13] For a review of the literature, see European Commission (2001).

[14] Contrary to the monetary policy rules literature, fiscal rules have not been formally derived by maximizing a welfare function. Only the design of the specific rule implicitly facilitates getting a hold of underlying welfare considerations. The design of the Stability and Growth Pact (SGP) allows the conclusion that output gap stabilization plays a minor role; stabilization of the business cycle is mainly restricted to the operation of automatic stabilizers. Price stability is a major concern. The provision of budgetary balances being close to zero or in surplus in the medium term had implied, in case of a permanent period of validity of the pact, that debt would virtually disappear and end up below a socially desired level determined by considerations of intergenerational justice and liquidity constraints.

As in monetary policy, time inconsistency, that is the temptation for governments to announce one policy now and follow another one later, has been a central argument for fiscal rules. To overcome this time inconsistency, some economists have suggested transferring the authority of designing the general lines of fiscal policy to an independent authority as an alternative to rules.[15] While so far limited to academic debate, an independent fiscal authority has also been suggested by the Swedish Government's Committee for stabilization policy in EMU (2002).

Fiscal rules in theory
While the Keynesian tradition, referring to market failures and the prevalence of non-Ricardian effects, would justify a strong and discretionary role for the government, neo-classical and monetarist authors have contrasted market failures with even greater government failures. The rationale for fiscal rules is derived from a combination of different theoretical approaches that hinge on the presumption of failure on the side of the government. Applying the logic of microeconomic principles to politics, political models of fiscal deficits, such as the application of public choice theory to fiscal policy, assume that politicians behave to maximize their votes and budgets. This results in a suboptimal oversupply of public goods and a deficit bias, as governments do not take full account of the costs future tax payers must pay due to deficit financing. Without a credible, that is discretion-removing, commitment to an ex ante optimal plan, policy-makers will always find it rational to deviate from their announced course. Through various transmission channels, a deficit bias results in higher inflation. In the view of the unpleasant monetarist arithmetic of Sargent and Wallace (1981), an undisciplined fiscal policy may exert pressures on the monetary authority to monetize the deficit by lowering interest rates, which will result in an increase in inflation. In the even more unpleasant view of the fiscal theory of the price level (Woodford 2001), price stability implies not only commitment to a monetary policy rule strictly applied by an independent central bank, but also an appropriate fiscal rule. The main channel for transmitting effects from fiscal policy to prices is through fiscally-induced shocks to private sector budget constraints, which in turn affect aggregate demand and inflation. In Woodford's model, even the expectation of a deteriorating fiscal balance can cause the price level to rise. Due to the quite restrictive assumptions and the empirically hard-to-verify postulates of the fiscal policy rules

---

[15] See Eichengreen et al. (1999), Wyplosz (2002), von Hagen (2003).

literature, the necessity of binding fiscal restraints is viewed in a critical light by many. Starting with the seminal work of Buiter et al. (1993), academic economics debate focused mainly on the discussion of economic reasoning for binding fiscal limits per se and the Maastricht deficit criteria in particular. Even if the postulates of the political models of fiscal deficits mentioned above were convincing, the need for fiscal restraints was rejected, as financial markets would sanction excessive deficits with higher risk premia on public debt.

The proponents of fiscal rules shifted attention to the discussion of the 'optimal fiscal rule'. Among the advocates of fiscal rules there is controversy about whether the rule should allow for discretion ('rules with discretion') by providing for a flexible reaction to projected output gap variations, or if it should rule out discretion by and large and simply let automatic stabilizers operate along the business cycle ('rules versus discretion') with only a limited smoothing impact on the cycle (Mélitz 2000). The different views regarding which is the appropriate rule reflect different priors concerning the 'true model' of the fiscal transmission mechanism. Model uncertainty is thus a major issue in fiscal policy. While in monetary policy the mainstream New Neo-Classical Consensus assumes at least short-term effects of changes in the instrument (Clarida et al. 1998) on output and employment, and controversy emerges over the main causes and the size of this effect, in fiscal policy literature there is even uncertainty about the sign of the effect of a fiscal impulse, reflecting strong and deep-seated divergent beliefs about the nature of fiscal policy. Thus there is much more dispersion of beliefs among economists on the effects of fiscal policy than on the effects of monetary policy. The Keynesian view, for instance, supports a strong stabilization role of fiscal policies, as in these models a fiscal contraction creates an economic downturn and vice versa. This was challenged – in line with the rational expectation hypothesis – by the so-called 'Ricardian equivalence-theorem', which states that fiscal contraction might even be expansionary: when spending cuts are perceived as permanent, consumers, insofar as they have rational expectations, anticipate a reduction in the tax burden and a permanent increase in lifetime income. Thus, in contrast with the Keynesian view, this wealth effect predicts that consumption increases when government spending is cut. A second source of expansionary effects of fiscal contractions is the credibility argument on interest rates. In reducing risk premia on interest rates, a fiscal consolidation can bring about a reduction in real interest rates and a boost in investment. Both sources of 'non-Keynesian' expansionary effects of fiscal contraction developed in theoretical models have been given some empirical relevance in a few extraordinary situations of high or previously rapidly increasing public debt (Alesina and Ardagna 1998,

European Commission 2003). However, in a recent contribution, van Aarle and Garretsen (2003) show that for a panel of 14 EU countries, in the transition period to EMU, the empirical evidence for non-Keynesian effects is limited. In specifying a structural vector auto-regression model for budgetary revenue and expenditure categories of the US, Blanchard and Perotti (2002) find evidence for both the neo-classical and the Keynesian view: government spending has a positive effect on private consumption, which supports the Keynesian model, but a strong negative impact in private investment. This latter 'non-Keynesian effect' was also found by Alesina et al. (2002) for a panel of OECD countries. One has to bear in mind that the methodological set-up of the empirical specification and the choice of the variables strongly reflect one's theoretical priors. Structural vector auto-regressions work by identifying restrictions derived from the respectively believed theoretical model, and, most importantly, only measure, if correctly identified, the unexpected exogenous policy action (Rudebusch 1995). Panel data techniques predominantly used for the empirical verification of multiplier effects of fiscal impulses have not been adequately solved for the simultaneity problems involved. While the empirical relevance of non-Keynesian effects is, at least, inconclusive and probably restricted to some rare events, the view that fiscal policy should abstain from discretion seems to be the dominant view in fiscal policy coordination in the euro area. Hence, fiscal policy-making in the euro area seems to have embarked on one theoretical model by largely disregarding the weak empirical justification for this view.

Controversy exists not only in regard to the stabilization properties of fiscal policy, but also arises with respect to the long-run growth impact of fiscal impulses. While exogenous growth models predict a permanent increase in the level of per capita output but a leveling off of this effect on the growth rate in the long run, endogenous growth models expect fiscal policy variables to impact growth rates as well. The empirical evidence supports the consideration of public finances as a source of endogenous growth with considerable uncertainty concerning the size of this effect.[16]

Independent fiscal institutions

Due to lack of enforceability of rules, it is suggested that fiscal policy be transferred to an independent authority, first in Latin America and later in

---

[16] For an overview, see Lamo and Strauch (2002).

euro area countries.[17] Among the numerous reform proposals for the SGP, the proposal for a politically independent fiscal body in different institutional settings is the most far-reaching device. Following the wise men approach, the authority of the independent body, an idea borrowed from the literature on central bank independence, ranges from the function of surveillance of budgetary procedures to the competence of setting targets for the size of the deficit and hereby, implicitly, for the debt. It has been proposed that the fiscal council be set up at the national level or at the EU level. The most far-reaching suggestion to equip the ECB with this competence was advanced by von Hagen (2003). Fiscal policies should be shielded from the democratic process, which yields undesirable outcomes: 'A [further] complicating factor is that fiscal policy is subject to democratic oversight. Every action has to be approved by parliament. This result is a high degree of politicization which naturally involves differences of opinion but also opens the door to lobbying by a myriad of interest groups that care little for the common public good' (Wyplosz 2002).

Concerns over the violation of fundamental principles of democracy by removing major fiscal issues from the participatory procedures established at the national level are countered by the proclamation that it is just the size of the deficit that is subject to decisions by the independent authority. The elected bodies might still agree on the size of the government or the composition of government spending. Numerous problems arise with this interpretation. The size of the deficit is not independent of society's preferences, for example the socially desired debt ratio which is related to specific intergenerational equity considerations, or the preferences for stabilization policies.

As one of the explicitly mentioned tasks of the fiscal council (in a softer version) is to monitor the fiscal process and to rely on the 'pressure of informed public opinion to discipline national governments' (Crockett et al. 2003), this activity also involves giving recommendations for the expenditure and the revenue sides of the budget if the deficit limit is breached. Hence, the violation of the prerogatives of the politicians would be much greater than envisaged by the architects of this proposal. Furthermore, the deficit is an imperfectly controllable, endogenous variable, mainly comprised of a structural and a cyclical component, and disentangling both involves a high degree of uncertainty. If the target is missed in an economic downturn, major conflicts between the elected

---

[17] See Eichengreen et al. (1999) on the proposal for the creation of independent national fiscal councils for Latin American countries, and Wyplosz (2002), Crockett et al. (2003) and von Hagen (2003) for the European Union.

bodies and the independent authority may arise regarding the relative magnitude of the components. Why should we believe that the independent authority possesses superior knowledge of how to estimate structural deficits in comparison with the staff of ministries or trade unions? In addition, the 'optimal' size of the deficit is related to one's view on the fiscal transmission mechanism, as outlined above. In the situation of a projected recession, for instance, proponents of the view of a predominance of non-Keynesian effects would prefer fiscal tightening as opposed to the fiscal expansion suggested by Keynesians. Most importantly, the proposals on the table so far, though difficult to interpret as they lack precision, resemble an inverse principal–agent model where, most strikingly, the independent council is endowed with the role of the principal. But even in a proper principal–agent setting in which the contract endows the elected bodies with the duty of setting the targets that have to be met by the agent (independent authority), agency losses, the noncompliance by the agent with the expressed preferences of the principal, might be quite severe as model uncertainty, symbolized in the divergent beliefs about how the objectives should be achieved, is a major issue in fiscal policy. Furthermore, noncompliance might result from a conflict of goals. If, for instance, the main, broad objectives of the principal are fiscal sustainability and stabilization policies, short-term trade-offs give the agent a high degree of discretion to act according to the wise men's preferences. Similar to trade-offs between monetary policy's objectives, an agency loss resulting from this source can hardly be overcome by a more precise contract between the agent and the principal.

3. POLICY RULES AND AGENCY INDEPENDENCE

Majone (1997) identifies the conditions under which the delegation of economic policy to independent institutions is legitimate in a democracy. The first justifiable condition is the existence of a set of control mechanisms by which accountability can be enforced. Within this set of mechanisms, policy rules are discussed as sufficient substitutes for democracy. Second, when the goal is to find a solution capable of improving the conditions of all individuals and groups in society, then the task of policy is a 'technical one of finding the optimal solution, and this is a task for experts' (Majone 1997, p. 153). Herewith, accountability by results provides satisfactory legitimacy for efficiency-oriented policies and institutions. On the other hand, any policy with redistributive consequences can only be legitimated by voters or their elected representatives. At this point, both conditions of democratic legitimacy are critically evaluated for the fiscal and monetary policy case.

Two prescriptions coexist to isolate economic policy [18] from the temptations and corruptions of the political process. One solution to the time inconsistency problem identified by economists, which is responsible for an inflation and stabilization bias in monetary policy and a deficit bias on the fiscal side, is to delegate economic policy to an independent institution staffed with 'neutral' experts and exempted from the need for democratic legitimacy, as they are not directly accountable to voters and do not depend on majority voting. The other prescription is to tie the hands of economic policy-makers by policy rules, which makes policy-makers accountable, as deviations from the rule can be sanctioned by elected politicians and voters who monitor adherence to the rule. In an attempt to make these two apparently irreconcilable prescriptions – agency independence and accountability – compatible and mutually reinforcing, a combination of control mechanisms has been suggested (Majone 1997). Such *control mechanisms* include: (a) statutory objectives should be clearly defined, (b) transparency requirements of independent institutions should facilitate public review and (c) strict procedures to justify agency decisions in cost–effectiveness and cost–benefit terms have to be implemented. This latter mechanism has been specified by the economics literature: to strengthen accountability, independent agencies should follow a rule designed to maximize economic policy goals (Svensson 1997). Within this concept of accountability one important agency cost of delegation, the potential loss of democratic legitimacy, can be reduced by combining independence with policy rules that are part of a variety of clearly designed substantive and procedural means.

As demonstrated for the monetary and fiscal policy case, even if the necessary control mechanisms as described above are in place, this concept of accountability breaks down in the presence of Knightian uncertainty. Hence, the problem of regulatory illegitimacy of independent agencies is not solved by policy rules, even in an ideal construction, but will persist. Major agency losses arise from the fact that the agent, in being compelled to follow a rule in an environment of deep uncertainty, still disposes over a high degree of discretion in choosing the believed-correct model of the policy transmission mechanism among a set of alternative models (model uncertainty). Against the lack of consensus of the appropriate economic model, the agent acts according to the wise

---

[18] In the following, though the rationale and implementation of policy rules differ widely between fiscal and monetary policy, both policy fields are treated equivalently.

men's beliefs. A continuous responsibility of the agent is to identify unforeseen events that necessitate deviations from the rule and to act in situations in which economic analysis can hardly offer any guideline on how to react to shocks of an unknown nature. The use of judgment to bridge the gap between the naivety of available models and real-world complexity is usually referred to as the 'art of central banking' (Blinder 1998). Accountability is supposed to be achieved by evaluating the deviations of the agent's policy outcomes from target. However, its effectivity is limited by the fact that the agent's discretion is also high in choosing the relative weights of conflicting policy objectives, even if they are clearly defined (goal uncertainty). This is an issue which is broadly ignored by the policy rules literature under uncertainty. Consequently, the first condition for democratic legitimacy of independent agencies, namely the implementation of a set of control mechanisms, cannot enforce indirect accountability, as agency losses are positively related to the degree of uncertainty.

Whether monetary or fiscal policies are neutral with respect to distributional effects – the second justifying condition of agency independence – and therefore can be conducted by efficiency-oriented experts is not the case for fiscal policies and controversial for monetary policies, depending on the respectively believed model of the monetary transmission mechanism (Romer and Romer 1998). Economists tend to perceive the beliefs of political actors as obstacles to rational, overall welfare-maximizing policies. But economic experts themselves acquire and act according to beliefs – they live in a world of Knightian uncertainty that requires them to form mental models, conscious *and* cognitive constructions of real life causalities that differ from people's beliefs. These systematic belief differences mainly seem to reflect ideological bias, economic training and education (Caplan 2002). Beliefs are at the center of economic policy-making by economic experts.

4. CONCLUSIONS

In the current policy debate the words democratic legitimacy and accountability are by and large used synonymously, with the substance of the often-used word 'accountability' ranging from describing procedures of giving information ex post to the principal (for example hearings of the ECB president at the European Parliament) and denoting transparency requirements to covering deliberative forms of democracy (for example the involvement of a broad range of societal groups in the goal formation process and the possibility to sanction the agent in the event that the goals are missed). Democratic legitimacy and accountability are interlinked but not identical. While accountability refers to a principal–agent relationship, where the principal delegates policies to an agent, legitimacy concerns the participatory quality of the decision making process. According to Scharpf (1999) democratic legitimacy requires that both input and output legitimacy be fulfilled. Applied to the principal–agent situation in monetary policy input legitimacy entails the incorporation of those who are affected by policies into the rule-making process (internal and external accountability) which involves the setting of targets and a procedure for achieving them. Output legitimacy relates to the effectiveness of policies, that is, to the ability to minimize deviations of policy outcomes from targets. In the current policy debate the quest for strengthening the accountability of independent agencies usually refers to output legitimacy only; for instance, a central bank is considered accountable if it effectively follows a policy rule, for example if inflation (and growth) turns out to be close to target. Input legitimacy, the participation of the principal (for example government, internal accountability) and other stakeholders (for example social partners, external accountability) in the rule-making process however is rather weak. It would imply for instance that the monetary policy rules are formulated and set by the principal and other stakeholders and not by the agent. But even if input legitimacy were to be strengthened, democratic legitimacy cannot easily be achieved as the agent still disposes over a high degree of discretion: given data, model and goal uncertainty the agent will – with or without a rule – act according to the wise men's belief. We have shown that agency losses increase with the degree of Knightian uncertainty. Hence, the principal–agent setting does not seem to be appropriate for the conduct of fiscal and monetary policy as it lacks democratic legitimacy. Given the widespread existence of these settings however, at least in monetary policy, how can legitimacy of independent institutions be strengthened?

Deliberative democracy might be a remedy for the legitimacy gap. It requires the active involvement of the stakeholders in a deliberative process of mutual persuasion. Not only are the mechanisms to control the agent strengthened and might potential policy errors of experts be corrected, but as the efficiency of economic policy hinges on the economic behavior of those who are affected by those policies, the public's incorporation into the policy process would contribute to the support of the policies and hereby contribute to the reduction of uncertainty about behavioral relationships. Designing institutions and deliberative procedures that serve this purpose is subject to future research.

However, deliberative democracy rests on the belief that citizens can be empowered to participate in the deliberative process of economic policy-making, a view that is not shared by those who believe they are equipped with superior knowledge.

REFERENCES

Akerlof, George A., William T. Dickens and George L. Perry (1996), 'The macroeconomics of low inflation', *Brookings Papers on Economic Activity*, **1996** (1), 1–75.

Akerlof, George A., William T. Dickens and George L. Perry (2000), 'Near rational wage and price setting and the long run Phillips curve', *Brookings Papers on Economic Activity*, **2000** (1), 1–60.

Alesina, Alberto and Silvia Ardagna (1998), 'Fiscal adjustments. why they can be expansionary', *Economic Policy*, **13** (27), 487–545.

Alesina, Alberto, Silvia Ardagna, Roberto Perotti and Fabio Schiantarelli (2002), 'Fiscal policy, profits, and investment', *American Economic Review*, **92** (3), 571–89.

Ball, Laurence and Robert Moffitt (2001), 'Productivity Growth and the Phillips Curve', in Alan B. Krueger and Robert Solow (eds), *The Roaring Nineties: Can Full Employment Be Sustained?*, New York: Russell Sage Foundation; New York: Century Foundation Press, pp. 61–90.

Batini, Nicoletta and Andrew Haldane (1999), 'Forward-Looking Rules for Monetary Policy', in John B. Taylor (ed.), *Monetary Policy Rules*, Chicago: University of Chicago Press, pp. 127–54.

Bean, Charles (2003), 'Asset prices, financial imbalances and monetary policy: are inflation targets enough?', BIS Working Paper, No. 140 (September).

Blanchard, Oliver and Roberto Perotti (2002), 'An empirical characterization of the dynamic effects of changes in government spending and taxes on output', *The Quarterly Journal of Economics*, **117** (4), 1329–68.

Blinder, Alan (1998), *Central Banking in Theory and Practice*, Cambridge: MIT Press.

Brainard, W. (1967), 'Uncertainty and the effectiveness of policy', *American Economic Review*, **57** (2), Papers and Proceedings of the Seventy-ninth Annual Meeting of the American Economic Association, May 1967, 411–25.

Buiter, Willem, Giancarlo Corsetti and Nouriel Roubini (1993), 'Excessive deficits: sense and nonsense of the Treaty of Maastricht', *Economic Policy*, **16** (1).

Buti, Marco and Gabriele Giudice (2002), 'EMU's Fiscal Rules: What Can and Cannot Be Exported', paper presented at the IMF–World Bank Conference on 'Rules-Based Macroeconomic Policies in Emerging Market Economies', Oaxaca, Mexico, 14–16 February, 2002.

Caplan, Brian (2002), 'Systematically biased beliefs about economics: robust evidence of judgmental anomalies from the survey of Americans and economists on the economy', *The Economic Journal*, **112** (479), 433–58.

Clarida, Richard, Gali Jordi and Mark Gertler (1998), 'Monetary policy rules in practice: some international evidence', *European Economics Review*, **42** (6), 1033–68.

Dow, Sheila (2004), 'Uncertainty and monetary policy', *Oxford Economic Papers*, forthcoming.

Eichengreen, Barry, Ricardo Hausmann and Jürgen von Hagen (1999), 'Reforming budgetary institutions in Latin America: the case for a national fiscal council', *Open Economies Review*, **10** (4), 415–42.

Emmerson, Carl, Chris Frayne and Sarah Love (2003), 'The government's fiscal rules', Institute for Fiscal Studies, Briefing Note No. 16.

Espinosa-Vega, Marco (1998), 'How powerful is monetary policy in the long run?', *Federal Reserve Bank of Atlanta Economic Review*, **83** (3), 12–31.

European Commission (2001), 'Public finances in EMU – 2001', *European Economy – Reports and Studies* No. 3.

European Commission (2003), 'Public finances in EMU – 2003', *European Economy* No. 3.

Fatás, Antonio, Andrew Hughes Hallett, Anne Sibert, Rolf Strauch and Jürgen von Hagen (2003), *Stability and Growth in Europe: Towards a Better Pact, Monitoring European Integration,* 13, London: Centre for Economic Policy Research.

Feldstein, Martin (1997), 'The welfare cost of permanent inflation and optimal short-run economic Policy', *Journal of Political Economy*, **87** (4), 749–68.

Gaspar, Victor and Frank Smets (2002), 'Monetary policy, price stability and output gap stabilisation', *International Finance*, **5** (2), 193–211.

Gerdesmeier, Dieter, Roberto Motto and Huw Pill (2002), 'Paradigm Uncertainty and the Role of Monetary Developments in Monetary Policy Rules', Paper presented at the ECB Workshop 'The Role of Policy Rules in the Conduct of Monetary Policy', Frankfurt, March 2002.

Goodhart, Charles (1999), 'Central bankers and uncertainty', *Bank of England Quarterly Bulletin*, **39** (1), 102–16.

Groshen, Erica L. and Marc E. Schweitzer (2000), *The effects of inflation on wage adjustments in firm-level data: Grease or sand?*, Mimeo, Federal Reserve Bank of New York.

Hansen, Lars. P. and Thomas J. Sargent (2000), 'Wanting robustness in economics', Chicago and Stanford Universities, mimeo.

Hansen, Lars P. and Thomas. Sargent (2002), *Elements of Robust Control and Filtering for Macroeconomics*, Manuscript, University of Chicago, Stanford University and Hoover Institution.

Hansen, Lars. P, Sargent, Thomas. J. and Thomas D. Tallarini (1999), 'Robust permanent income and pricing', *Review of Economic Studies*, **66**, 873–907.

Holden, Steinar (2002), 'The costs of price stability – downward nominal wage rigidity in Europe', NBER Working Paper, No. 8865.

Judd, John P. and Glenn D. Rudebusch (1999), 'The goals of U.S. monetary policy', FRBSF Economic Letter, 29 January 1999.

King, Mervyn (1999), 'Challenges for Monetary Policy: New and Old', in *New Challenges for Monetary Policy*, Proceedings of a symposium sponsored by the Federal Reserve Bank of Kansas City, Jackson Hole, Wyoming, August 26–28, 1999, Kansas City, pp. 11–57.

Knight, Frank H. (1921), *Risk, Uncertainty, and Profit*, Boston: Houghton Mifflin Company.

Lamo Ana and Rolf Strauch (2002), 'The Contribution of Public Finances to the European Growth Strategy', in *The Impact of Fiscal Policy*, Rome: Banca d'Italia, pp. 485–525.

Levin, Andrew, Volker Wieland and John C. Williams (1999). 'Robustness of Simple Monetary Policy Rules under Model Uncertainty', in J.B. Taylor (ed.), *Monetary Policy Rules*, Chicago: University of Chicago Press, pp. 263–99.

Levin, Andrew, Volker Wieland and John C. Williams (2001), *The robustness of forecast-based rules for monetary policy*, mimeo, Federal Reserve Board of Governors.

Majone, Giandomenico (1997), 'Independent Agencies and the Delegation Problem: Theoretical and Normative Dimensions', in Bernard Steunenberg and Frans van Vught (eds), *Political Institutions and Public Policy. Perspectives on European Decision Making*, Dordrecht: Kluwer Academic Publishers, pp. 139–56.

Mélitz, Jaques (2000), 'Some cross-country evidence about fiscal policy behaviour and consequences for EMU', *European Economy*, No. 2, 3–21.

Onatski, Alexei (1999), 'Minimax Monetary Policy: Comparison to Bayesian Approach. Worst Cases, and Exact Minimax Rules', forthcoming in *Robust Decision Theory in Economics and Finance*, Cambridge University Press.

Onatski, Alexei and James H. Stock (2002), 'Robust monetary policy under model uncertainty in a small model of the U.S. economy', *Macroeconomic Dynamics*, 2002 (6), 85–110.

Rogoff, Kenneth (1985), 'The optimal degree of commitment to a monetary target', *Quarterly Journal of Economics*, **100** (4), 1169–90.

Romer, Christina D. and David H. Romer (1998), 'Monetary Policy and the Well-Being of the Poor', in *Income Inequality and Policy Options*, Proceedings of a symposium sponsored by the Federal Reserve Bank of Kansas City, Jackson Hole, Wyoming, August 27–29, 1998, Kansas City, pp. 159–201.

Rosal, Joao M. and Michael Spagat (2002), 'Structural Uncertainty and Central Bank Conservatism: The Ignorant should shut their Eyes', CEPR Discussion Paper, No. 3568.

Rudebusch, Glenn D. (1995), *Do Measures of Monetary Policy in a VAR Make Sense?*, Federal Reserve Bank of San Francisco.

Rudebusch, Glenn D. (2001), 'Is the Fed too timid? Monetary policy in an uncertain world', *The Review of Economics and Statistics*, 83, 203–17.

Sack, Brian and Volker Wieland (1999), 'Interest-rate smoothing and optimal monetary policy: A review of recent empirical evidence', Board of Governors of the Federal Reserve System, *Finance and Economics Discussion Series*, No. 1999-39.

Sargent, Thomas and Neil Wallace (1981), 'Some unpleasant monetarist arithmetic', *Federal Reserve Bank of Minneapolis Quarterly Review*, No. 5.

Scharpf, Fritz (1999), *Governing in Europe: Effective and Democratic?* Oxford. Oxford University Press.

Smets, Frank (2002), 'Output gap uncertainty. Does it matter for the Taylor rule?', *Empirical Economics*, **27** (1), 113–29.

Söderström, Ulf (2002), 'Monetary policy with uncertain parameters', *Scandinavian Journal of Economics*, **104** (1), 125-45.

Srour, Gabriel (2001), 'Why Do Central Banks Smooth Interest Rates?', Bank of Canada Working Paper, No. 2001-17.

Svensson, Lars (1997), 'Inflation forecast targeting: Implementing and Monitoring inflation targets', *European Economic Review*, **41** (6), 1111–46.

Svensson, Lars (1999), 'Inflation targeting: Some extensions', *Scandinavian Journal of Economics*, **101** (3), 337–61.

Svensson, Lars (2002), 'Monetary Policy and Real Stabilization', in *Rethinking Stabilization Policy*, Proceedings of a symposium sponsored by the Federal Reserve Bank of Kansas City, Jackson Hole, Wyoming, 29–31 August 2002, Kansas City, pp. 261–312.

Svensson, Lars (2003), 'Optimal Policy with Low-Probability Extreme Events', in *Macroeconomics, Monetary Policy, and Financial Stability – A Festschrift for Charles Freedman*, Ottawa: Bank of Canada, forthcoming.

Swedish Government's Committee for Stabilisation Policy in EMU (2002), 'Stabilisation Policy in the Monetary Union', March.

Taylor, John (1999), *Monetary Policy Rules*, National Bureau of Economic Research Studies in Business Cycles, Chicago: Chicago University Press.

Tetlow, Robert J. and Peter von zur Mühlen (2000), 'Robust monetary policy with misspecified models: does model uncertainty always call for attenuated policy?', Board of Governors of the Federal Reserve System, *Finance and Economics Discussion Series*, No. 2000-28.

van Aarle, Bas and Harry Garretsen (2003), 'Keynesian, Non-Keynesian or no effects of fiscal policy changes? The EMU case', *Journal of Macroeconomics*, **25** (2) (June), 213–40.

von Hagen, Jürgen (2003), 'Fiscal Discipline and Growth in Euroland: Experiences with the Stability and Growth Pact', ZEI Working Paper, B 06 2003.

Wald, Abraham (1950), *Statistical Decision Functions*, John Wiley and Sons, New York.

Wieland, Volker (2000), 'Monetary policy, parameter uncertainty and optimal learning', *Journal of Monetary Economics*, **46** (1), 199–228.

Woodford, Michael (2001), 'Fiscal requirements for price stability', *Journal of Money, Credit and Banking*, **33** (3), 669–728.

Wyplosz, Charles (2002), 'Fiscal Discipline in Emerging Market Countries: How to go about it?', Paper prepared for conference on 'Financial Stability and Development in Emerging Economies: Step Forward for Bankers and Financial Authorities', organized by The Forum on Debt and Development (FONDAD) in Amsterdam, 3–4 June 2002.

Table 13.1. Monetary policy rules literature and uncertainty

Kind of uncertainty	Definition	Policy response in the setting of interest rates
Additive uncertainty	Random errors with zero mean	**No response** (certainty equivalence theorem)
Brainard (multiplicative) **uncertainty** (Brainard 1967)	Uncertainty about the transmission of policy to a target variable (uncertainty about the impact parameter); *these parameters are assumed to have known distribution*	**Caution** (Brainard conservatism)
Brainard uncertainty when only inflation enters the loss function (Svensson 1999)	Uncertainty in **some** of the parameters	**Caution** (Brainard conservatism)
Brainard uncertainty when inflation and output enter the loss function	2 cases: Uncertainty about persistence of inflation (Srour 1999, Söderström 2002) Uncertainty about the other parameters (Söderström 2002)	**Aggressiveness** **Caution**
Data uncertainty	Mis-measurement of data (that is output gap, inflation) *Variance of any measurement error is known* (Rudebusch 2001)	**Caution**
Model uncertainty (Hansen and Sargent 2000)	Uncertainty about the basic form of the true model	
Structured model uncertainty (Onatski and Stock, 2002)	Uncertainty located in one or more specific parameters of the model, *no probability distribution over parameters* (e.g. one-time shift in parameters)	**Caution**
Unstructured model uncertainty (Hansen et al. 1999)	*Location of uncertainty unknown* (e.g. arbitrarily serially correlated shock processes on top of the model's stochastic disturbances)	Backward looking models: **Aggressiveness** (to avoid worst-case scenario) Forwards looking models: **Caution** (Tetlow and von zur Mühlen 2000) **Experimentation** (Wieland 2000)
Goal uncertainty	*Arguments in the loss function unknown* Uncertainty about the relative weights of parameters in the loss function Uncertainty about the functional form of the loss function (Svensson 2003)	

289

14. In Between Popper and Kuhn: Some Reflections on How Economists Create Economic Reality and the Reality of Economic Policy

Peter Mooslechner[*]

1. INTRODUCTION: THE RENAISSANCE AS THE BASIS OF MODERN SCIENCE

With the Renaissance, the perception of reality, which determines the action of agents and which is in turn determined by their behaviour, changed almost completely in many different fields.[1] Generally, the closed medieval universe ceased to be the only accepted frame of reference. Contrary to what seems to be common wisdom, the decisive factor for this essential change was not the re-orientation towards the ancient world of Greek and Roman theoretical models but the opening up of completely new horizons. Illustrated in an oversimplified picture, in the medieval world knowledge was produced only vertically, with everything to be known about the world typically mirroring the rationality of a superior plan. The Renaissance, in contrast, introduced a horizontal approach, opening the width of the world and the universe to

---

[*] The views expressed in this chapter are those of the author and do not necessarily reflect the views of the Oesterreichische Nationalbank. The author is grateful to Markus Knell, Helene Schuberth and Martin Schuerz for helpful comments on an earlier version of this chapter and to Sheila Dow and Uskali Mäki for stimulating discussions during a workshop on this issue.
[1] See Burke (1998) for a comprehensive account of the Renaissance world. Garin (1996) provides an impressive overview of the rise of individualism, including differentiation, in Renaissance times.

the initiative of mankind – the creation of knowledge became an active and concrete process of discovery, realization and insight.[2]

Individualism and science, both interacting in a very specific way, were central to this development, which completely transformed the way people were thinking and understood the world until the beginning of the 17th century. Individualism, including individual independence and self-confidence, set the personal precondition by prompting people to understand the world in a completely new way. Objective science provided such individualism with a new institutional background, where reality and truth were considered independent elements, independent of the previous decisive layer of theological qualification.

In this historical context, a specific concept of knowledge appeared on the scene. This concept was very much related to the newly emerging process of discovering existing reality, the surface of the earth and the laws of causality. At the same time, this specific historical context also created the fundamental dilemma of how to organize this truth-seeking process under preconditions that (i) ask for the highest possible degree of individualism and independence while (ii) producing the most objective and general form of knowledge beyond all subjectivism.

Empiricism and rationalism – two concepts that had actually appeared earlier in history but gained importance only in the 19th century (Feyerabend, 1965) – were developed as the two main approaches to deal with reality (and in fact remain the two basic ways of thinking about reality today, although they can by no means be regarded as sufficient to cope with the complexity and interdependence of this issue). In the knowledge field, the establishment of modern universities and the networking of scientists on an international level, laid the foundations for what today we call scientific community.

The notion of economics as a science did not evolve until the late 18th century. The evolution of economic reasoning was triggered by the publication of Adam Smith's 'The Wealth of Nations' in 1776 – coincidentally the year when the United States declared its independence, thus changing the political map of the world. Of course, both practical economics and a basic theoretical underpinning had existed well before Adam Smith's comprehensive study.[3] To some extent, the establishment

---

[2] A stimulating perspective illustrating this point, comparing the work and life of Dante and Petrarca, is developed in Stierle (2003).

[3] Significant partial contributions can be traced back to Plato and Aristotle and many other philosophers, but one who should be mentioned particularly is Francois Quesnay (1694 – 1774) for his discovery and presentation of the circular flow of economic transactions ('Tableau Economique'). See Spiegel (1991) for a detailed treatment of the history of

of economics as a science immediately implied a separation between empiricism and rationalism,[4] a separation that has significantly shaped the development of economics ever since. As a starting point to be developed further in the following sections, both the distinction between economic policy and economic theory and the distinction between empirical or applied economics and theoretical economics can be used as simple models to illustrate the problem discussed here.

2. ECONOMICS AND ECONOMIC POLICY EMBEDDED IN REALITY: A TANGLED INTERDEPENDENCE

The interaction between economic theory and economic policy, both embedded in and part of economic reality, is one of the most complex and most important issues economists face. This is most likely the reason why questions and problems resulting from this interdependence are cut out of the discussion most of the time. Many, if not all, economists would claim that we have come a long way in understanding how modern market economies work and in identifying the driving forces behind the most important developments over the last decades. At the same time, the gap between economists' results and proposals on the one hand and the reality of economic problems and economic policy on the other hand has widened significantly.

This situation may also be held responsible for an often marked gap between public expectations about the capacity of policy to solve economic problems and what economic policy is actually able to deliver. A simple model illustrating this problem may help structure the case.

Let us think of a stylized policy advice process consisting of two parts: (i) an economic policy part containing all the relevant institutions and procedures for economic policy-making, and (ii) a theoretical part including all persons and institutions engaged in the production of theoretical economic knowledge and forming the scientific community that shapes our minds with regard to how the economy works. Both parts are embedded in economic reality, which contains all economic agents, their preferences, behavioural structures and the relevant economic events

---

economic ideas. A second important source for a historical perspective on economics is Blaug (1997).

[4] For the sake of clarity: neither 'empiricism' nor 'rationalism' claim to be mutually exclusive or that progress in knowledge can be created by concentrating on one approach only.

and shocks. Varying across countries and over time, economic reality also encloses a system of economic policy goals deriving from general political goals of how society should function and be organized.

Let us take this simple structure as given and, in particular, neglect the complex processes certainly present within these areas and concentrate on the interdependencies between them, thus illustrating some of the fundamental problems of how these parts interact. A hypothetical map of interactions could be drawn as follows:

(i)   Driven by the behaviour of agents, coordination failures and/or external shocks, substantial deviations between economic reality and economic policy goals may develop.

(ii)   Under these circumstances economic policy is expected to take appropriate measures to close the gap identified between economic reality and economic policy goals, preferably in the very short term.

(iii) Ideally, economic policy is able to rely on well-defined and agreed theoretical wisdom to understand the relevant causalities.

(iv)   Then, the necessary and successful policy measures can easily be identified and any rational and utility-maximizing policy-maker will follow the proposed recipes from theory, take the right measures and change economic reality so that it corresponds with the defined policy objectives.

There is no doubt that this hypothetical example describes the ideal case, which hardly ever appears in the reality of economic policy-making. Nevertheless, it is important because it clarifies the expectations of a considerable part of the public and certainly of the majority of the media regarding economic policy efficiency. These expectations are typically based on the belief that there exist simple and definite solutions for economic problems. The general public expects economists and policy-makers to know the solutions and to come up with the right measures for implementing them. Wrong interpretations and wrong action are mainly regarded as political inefficiency and/or result from the influence of (hidden) self or group interests present in the political process. If this model reasonably captures the dominant public view of economic policy issues, it neatly illustrates the pitfalls of giving economic policy advice.

To show the substantial imperfections of the ideal model some simple qualifications can be pointed out:

(i)   An appropriate reaction of economic policy requires that the policy-maker is able to realize and identify the problem virtually right away and in the right way. Otherwise his/her policy reaction may come too late or the wrong measures will be taken because of imperfect information.

(ii) Even if the policy-maker is able to correctly identify the problem and takes the right measures, lags in implementation, considerable uncertainty concerning the behaviour of agents and ineffective implementation may cause long-lasting deviations from the desired outcome.

(iii) More fundamentally, the assumption that economic policy-making can rely on generally accepted theoretical models to give immediate and definite advice is flawed in several respects (Selody, 2001). Economic theory is by no means a homogenous, universally agreed upon set of models. The theoretical community cannot be expected to propose the one and only solution to the problem at stake. On the contrary, policy-makers will find themselves confronted with a (large) number of suggestions of how to tackle the problem, some of which will be clearly contradictory.

(iv) Finally, economic reality contains an unavoidable historical time dimension. After all, problems tend to change over time and even if they hardly change at all, approved measures may turn out to be ineffective because relevant framework conditions or the behaviour of economic agents have changed. Therefore, it may take considerable time until economic theory can understand a new situation and offer appropriate instruments and policy measures for dealing with the new situation.

These points illustrate that expectations of a correctly identified and effectively implemented policy should be moderate. Interaction between theory and practice is always extremely complex and the process of effectively gaining knowledge of how to improve a situation should be the main concern. When we put all the pieces together the unavoidable interdependence seems very clear: policy needs to be firmly based on theory, whereas theory needs to be derived from real world problems. We need to understand what the appropriate model of the real world is and which instruments and measures should be used and may be expected to be efficient. Obviously, there is no clear ranking, no precedence or subordination of elements in this process. What is important for economic policy and economic policy advice to work is that the problems at hand are grasped in a reasonably simultaneous manner. In reality this can only be achieved by a certain degree of pragmatism, flexibility and experience in policy-making. The next question is how economists deal with this unavoidable and ever present challenge and what institutions they have created to overcome this challenge. But let us first focus on a number of other important elements before amalgamating them for a tentative understanding of the issue.

3. SHORT-TERMISM, LONG-TERM PARADISE AND THE CREATION OF REALITY IN ECONOMICS

One of the most fundamental questions for understanding the relationship between policy challenges and the subsequent policy reactions is how economists in their specific roles as policy advisors or academic economic theorists have adapted to this complex environment.

Of course, many influences may have had a potential impact on modern economics and on the behaviour of economists as a social group. The elements or 'stylized facts' selected in this context will be referred to as (i) 'short-termism' and (ii) 'long-term paradise'. Together they contribute to a specific reality created by economists, that is a kind of scientific development or strategy which opens up a considerable gap between the models used in policy advice and the real world problems to be tackled. Short-termism[5] refers to a significant shift in interest towards shorter time-horizons of economic development and explanations, thus putting much more weight on current events and on quick and preliminary answers and views. 'Long-term paradise' should be understood as a short-cut for delaying final benefits of proposed recipes and measures to the very long run, thus accepting and justifying short- and medium-term costs or disadvantages of proposed strategies and measures.

Before illustrating and discussing some of the consequences of these elements considered to be important, it should be stressed that they are by no means meant to be one-dimensional and originating from economics and economists alone. In contrast, a considerable number of these stylized facts reflect developments in economic reality and society as a whole, interacting with factors within academics but also due to effects on policies created by policy advice. Here these developments are presented mainly from the perspective of how they are mirrored in economic policy and the economics profession.

---

[5] Economist.com defines short-termism in the following way: 'Doing things that make you better off in the short-run but worse off in the end' and 'During the bubble, it was claimed, investors had become too focused on short-term profits and changes in share prices, and failed to probe deeply enough into long-term performance.' Hayes, Cuthbertson and Nitzsche (1997) provide a clear manifestation of this for the UK stock market.

'Short-Termism'

What is referred to as short-termism in this context cannot be traced back to a single cause or development and is by no means restricted to economics and economic policy-making. Short-termism is rather part of a more general social tendency which is present in many areas of society and which has a special impact on the economy. Many aspects of our modern world may be expected to have at least contributed to a situation in which short-term orientation has become more important for individual behaviour and policy challenges.[6] Let us think, for example, of the so-called 'revolutions' in communication and transport technologies which have speeded up the flow of information and shortened distances around the globe in terms of travel time.

At the same time, the general 'patience' of people would appear to have changed, from both a political and a policy perspective. In the 'new world' problems are expected to be solved in a significantly shorter time horizon, and benefits or profits are expected to be realized very fast. Obviously, if this is indeed the case, it puts the whole political system under considerable time pressure to deliver policy action very quickly – given the limited time-span left until the next election date – and to claim that the short-term solution provided is the best and only one.[7]

When a problem occurs in reality, it will take some time until people actually become aware of the problem; and only if it turns out to be big and important enough to call for policy action will policy-makers eventually react. When the structure of reality has changed in a way that the speed of shocks turning into a policy problem or, with similar consequences, the probability of global diffusion of shocks emerging elsewhere has increased, then the 'reaction lag' for policy is significantly shorter from both sides: from problems arising much more quickly and from the pressure to deliver solutions almost immediately.

There are two ways out of this situation, which are however quite uncomfortable solutions from an economist's perspective: The first one can be called the 'action-oriented' solution, a term often used in newspaper language and by far the most important type of policy reaction. Fast policy reactions may appear to be always preferable because they advertise that policy takes the problem seriously and is

---

[6] See Sennet (1998) for an account of the consequences this development has on the situation of the individual and on individual behaviour.

[7] Margaret Thatcher's famous TINA argumentation ('there is no alternative') has since that time become more or less common to all governments irrespective of their political position and, even more worrying, it seems to have become accepted by a vast majority of people as well.

indeed taking action and because the real proof whether such action will have effectively tackled the problems lies somewhere in the distant future. Because of the extremely short decision lag unavoidable in this model the 'theoretical basis' for the measures taken is likely to be an ideological and/or public relation-oriented one.

The second solution is to 'pass on' the time pressure weighing on policy to specialists or theoreticians. This is basically the way the model should work. Yet for several reasons the model can at best only be expected to provide third or lower best solutions. These reasons include the fact that under time pressure theoreticians may come up with problematic quick responses in view of additional factors that determine their behaviour as a social group.[8] The more fundamental point in this respect is that in economics, a science dependent both on the behaviour of economic agents and on historical development, there may be no agreed solution for tackling newly emerging problems and for providing adequate policy advice. Under these circumstances only a very cautious treatment of the situation based on several methods and models on the one hand and historical experience on the other hand may be feasible, which will most probably not meet the preference of policy-makers for unambiguous policy advice. Given this outcome, most policy-makers may be expected to rely on fast solutions rather than admitting to the public that a general solution is not available and that some policy experimentation and further research are necessary.

Perhaps the most appropriate example illustrating several aspects of 'short-termism' is financial market development. In the field of financial markets it is widely accepted that a significant shift towards short-term orientation has created a number of fundamental problems (Strange, 1986; Shiller, 2000) which put new pressure on economic policy in several respects. Without going into details which are discussed elsewhere,[9] financial market behaviour and the changing structure of financial markets have eventually led to a situation in which the risk of financial market crises constitutes an essential element. This asks for an effective and appropriate policy response whenever a crisis appears imminent. At the same time, it has to be recalled that economists as well as politicians have contributed to this situation by proposing substantial changes in financial market structures on the one hand and by underlining the economic benefits of this new world on the other hand (Edey and Hviding, 1995). Both groups find themselves confronted with

---

[8] See Section 5 for more on how economists as a social group have reacted to this situation.

[9] See, for example, Shleifer (2000) and Mooslechner (2003) for a detailed account of empirical facts and theoretical problems.

significant new policy challenges for areas such as financial stability (Poole, 2002), financial market supervision and monetary policy[10] with only limited answers available, sometimes even on a theoretical level.

'Long-Term Paradise'

The second element to be mentioned here shall be called 'long-term paradise'. This strategy has always been an essential element of the history of economic thought. Nevertheless, compared with the mainstream of textbook economics published in the decades after World War II, a significant change has taken place, which today puts much more weight on 'long-term paradise' arguments, at least in the economic policy-making of continental Europe.

Buiter (1980) in 'The Macroeconomics of Dr. Pangloss' was among the first to criticize this approach when it was imported from the US to Europe. The typical elements of 'long-term paradise' economics are twofold: first, a clear tendency to use long-term-oriented models and a particular set of specific assumptions, as a result of which these types of model tend to be very much oriented towards equilibrium solutions, although it is well known that these types of model and assumptions do not capture much of real world reality and focus almost exclusively on the implicitly assumed return of an economy to an equilibrium path. Typical examples of models like these are those predominant in 'New Classical Macroeconomics' (Klamer, 1984) or the more recent branch of all kinds of 'General Equilibrium Models' concentrating on allocation and substitution, leaving aside possible aspects of disequilibria.

The second important point Buiter stresses is the non-existence of sensible macroeconomic policies in these models. With very few exemptions, in these models macroeconomic policies appear as a kind of disturbance on their smooth way (back) to general equilibrium. Policy is considered useless as it provokes countervailing actions by relevant economic agents or because it hampers necessary adjustment and therefore delays the way back to 'long-term paradise'. The general policy message implicit in these models is that without policy interference reality would show a strong underlying tendency towards (full employment) equilibrium, given an appropriate institutional structure of the economy as well as sufficient flexibility of economic agents to appropriately adapt to external shocks. If any kind of policy response is

---

[10] For a comprehensive overview of the subject with a particular focus on monetary policy see the papers of a workshop 'Asset Prices and Monetary Policy' organized by the ECB, recently published on the ECB website (www.ecb.int).

needed it would be a policy that adjusts the institutional structure of the economy to these requirements.

What seems particularly interesting is that this fundamental model of thinking, although originating from the US, nowadays forms the core of European policy-making, whereas it has lost much, if not all, of its appeal in the US.

A particular illustrative example in this respect is the long-run neutrality of money, which has a long history in economic thought based, for example, on the specific interpretation the 'Quantity Theory of Money' provides in this respect.[11] Although the short- and medium-term impact of monetary policy on growth and inflation has been evidenced by many transmission mechanism studies, practical policy-making mostly acts as if neutrality of money was a dominant feature of modern market type economies even in the short run. In reality, this understanding leads to a significant downgrading of cyclical policies because they are assumed to be ineffective.[12] Taking into consideration the difficulties to execute appropriate policy under all circumstances the 'no policy' option seems to be the preferred solution in many situations.

All these elements contribute to a tendency which may be called 'creation of reality'. In this particular context and under the circumstances already described economists tend to construct their own type of reality and to base economic policy advice on it, irrespective of a considerable gap between reality created and real world problems. Regarding policy advice, they are accused of asking for adaption of the structures of reality to the assumptions of their abstract models. Obviously, this is very much interdependent on both factors as mentioned above. It can be understood as an overall summing-up of behavioural elements that make economists substantially deviate from real world issues (Zamora Bonilla, 2002). This is also confirmed when we closely examine how most of the influential contributions from philosophy of science for economics were integrated and transformed into economics by the scientific community.

---

[11] See Blaug (1997) and Spiegel (1991) for a comprehensive account of historical thought on the issue.
[12] For a fundamental criticism of this view see Espinosa-Vega (1998). Hetzel (2002a, 2002b) as well as Mankiw (2001) and McCallum (2002) give an account of the determinants of monetary policy-making in historical perspective.

4. THE POPPER–KUHN CONNECTION: HOW THESE TWO THEORISTS CONTRIBUTED TO MAKE THINGS EVEN MORE COMPLICATED

Among philosophers of science, Karl R. Popper and Thomas S. Kuhn, have had the biggest impact on social sciences and economics since the end of World War II.[13] Surprisingly enough, the Popper–Kuhn debate evolved without any direct interchange between the two original proponents.[14]

Kuhn hardly mentioned Popper in his challenging study, except for a short critical paragraph telling the reader that Popper's theory of falsification can be expected to run into the same troubles as any kind of verification approach. And in his postscript of 1969 Kuhn mentions Popper's essay in the Lakatos and Musgrave (1970) volume only to reject his position as being subjectivist or irrational. In a similar way, Popper's autobiography of 1976 does not mention Kuhn in the index of names and he is also neglected in the revised German edition of 1982. The same is true for Miller's reader of 1983 and later editions, including its latest German edition of 2000. At the same time Popper extensively referred to Lakatos in his late work.

Why is this the case and how can this be understood? The key to this – somewhat surprising – lack of connection between Popper and Kuhn can be found in the fact that they were very much interested in completely different questions of scientific progress.

Kuhn focused his analysis on the historical dimension of scientific progress, expressed in detail in the introduction to his famous study (Kuhn, 1962, chapter I). He was mainly interested in identifying important changes in scientific history as well as in the particular reasons for such 'paradigm shifts': how can a paradigm shift be identified, what are the necessary preconditions to make it happen and how can its particular role in the process of scientific development be described? Kuhn refers to the 'non-paradigm shift' of science as 'normal science', which can be best understood as a process of 'solving puzzles', dealing

---

[13] Popper's 'Logik der Forschung (The Logic of Scientific Discovery)' was first published (in German) in 1934, Kuhn's 'The Structure of Scientific Revolutions' in 1962. But World War II and Popper's emigration to New Zealand between 1937 and 1946 delayed the full reception of Popper's ideas until he finally returned to England in 1946 to teach at the London School of Economics. Popper's 'The Logic of Scientific Discovery' was first published in English only in 1959.

[14] Fuller's (2003) book is mainly based on the one important exception to this, a session organized by Lakatos, a friend of both, at the London School of Economics in 1965 chaired by Popper at which Kuhn spoke. Despite Fuller's in depth account the outcome remains somewhat in the dark.

with small additions to existing knowledge and questioning again and again tiny elements of common scientific knowledge. Only under very specific and rare circumstances can the process of normal science develop into a 'paradigm shift', which is a kind of scientific revolution in a given field. The conditions to make this happen depend on issues within the scientific community as well as on conditions that develop in the real world. In a nutshell, only if the degree of tension between the explanatory power of a specific theory and reality exceeds a certain level, can the preconditions for a 'paradigm shift' develop – assuming, in addition, that a better theory than the present one is already available.

In contrast, Popper almost exclusively concentrates on the very process of 'normal science'. He started from a specific point of the scientific process, the point where it is expected that theories or parts of theories can be proved to be true in one or the other way. Popper rejects this view and turns the mechanism into falsification by identifying wrong scientific statements or hypotheses.

The problems for the ongoing scientific work in economics identified by Popper and Kuhn are easily understood. First, Kuhn's 'paradigm shifts' are seldom by definition. Second, they are very much an ex-post concept and oriented towards the historical understanding of how radical changes in economic thought and their successful implementation in economic policy have occurred. Of course, situations that can be referred to as 'paradigm shifts' develop from time to time and when they bring about a change in thought, they have extremely significant effects. Examples for such shifts may be the 'Keynesian revolution', the systematic introduction of (rational) expectations, or the end of monetarism in the US (Hafer and Wheelock, 2001). Although groups of economists are working on certain 'paradigm shifts'[15] it is hard to say whether or how they may pin down such phenomena.

The enormous success of Popper's idea of falsification in economics[16] is traceable to three specific elements:

First, falsification is a typical concept well-suited for the 'normal science' part of the exploratory process in economics. Therefore, it could be implemented and understood as something that all economists can and should always use and that promises immediate return. Compared with

---

[15] Recent examples may be 'Behavioural Economics' (Rabin, 2002) and 'Experimental Economics' (Fehr and Falk, 2002), two disciplines which both won Nobel Memorial Prizes recently

[16] On the dominance of Popperianism as a methodological position in economics see Dow (2001).

this work on a definite 'paradigm shift' it is obviously a rather uncertain exercise with unknown rewards in a distant future.

Second, the Popper approach includes a certain type of incentive for scientific activism. It explicitly asks for investigating hypotheses and findings of others to point out their invalidity. Interpreted in a very strict and narrow sense there is no need for coming up with a competing and better theory. In practice, the scientific community is mostly satisfied with merely questioning the results of others. Evidently, with this approach researchers can collect the benefits of their work much earlier and more easily.

Third, all these obvious benefits of the Popper approach would have been less influential in economics if they had not been combined with a significant other strand of development in the profession, namely the development of econometrics into the dominant tool for dealing with reality. Econometrics turned out to be the kind of tool needed to do what economists thought Popper meant by falsification; at any rate it became the dominant and perhaps only accepted way to decide between 'true' and 'false' – thus developing into an instrument that 'creates' or 'defines' 'truth' in a simple and transparent way. Whoever wanted to participate in the game would be able to learn the 'rules' and to start producing results, implicitly acquiring the power to divide the world (of economics) into 'good' and 'bad'.

Despite substantial criticism on the role econometrics has acquired in the profession and how it is applied in practice,[17] econometrics has become almost the only standard of progress in economics. Given a considerably high degree of uncertainty in measurement and data production, econometric results need to be interpreted very cautiously. In addition, the way in which the use of econometrics has evolved over time has led to something quite different and far removed from what might have been the original intention of Popper. What is usually presented in the journals of applied economics are highly significant estimates for a limited number of particular hypotheses. Quite contrary to Popper, positive significance seems to be the main point to be made by econometrics, leaving aside the hundreds or thousands of estimates conducted that turned out to be less significant than the few estimates that were finally published. Indeed, from this approach it is a very small further step to pure data mining, which makes use of the now almost unlimited computerial calculation capacities (Sala-i-Martin, 1997; Rehmer, 2002).

---

[17] An impressive example in this respect is Leamer (1983).

In conclusion, it turned out that Kuhn's 'paradigm shift' model, although fascinating and important in many respects, was accepted by the scientific community in economics only as an extreme case, mainly useful and helpful for a better understanding of developments in the history of economic thought ex post. In contrast, economists developed Popper's ideas of the logic of scientific discovery into the dominant tool for defining progress, although it could be questioned whether the actual use of this tool had in fact something to do with Popper's original thought. This suggests that the economics profession was really very successful in developing and establishing a specific methodological approach to decide how 'significance' and 'progress' is created.[18]

5. HOW ECONOMISTS DEAL WITH THIS SITUATION IN THE REALITY OF ECONOMIC POLICY ADVICE

The consequences of all the above-mentioned aspects are not only reflected within the scientific community of economists but they have a considerable impact on economic policy advice and they are also transparent for the public. Perhaps the easiest way to illustrate this is to point out the different types of economists who have emerged under these circumstances:

Everybody is aware of 'short-term' economists – or, even worse, financial commentators – who almost immediately know and advertise answers to each and every kind of economic problem (and sometimes even a large number of problems in other areas as well). They are well known to the public because they tend to offer their advice mainly on TV or through other public media channels. They will typically reappear on TV the very next day with a new and only solution for the next problem at stake, sometimes even at the cost of some inconsistency in argumentation.

A second type of policy advice often heard in the public discussion of economic policy issues is of a 'once and forever' nature: Whatever the problem is, the right solution seems to be the same one as last time, as any time or at least of the same pattern as in the past. Similarly, changes in reality seem to be of limited or no relevance for the recipes suggested.

A third and more general way of how some groups of economists deal with the situation seems to be that they are less engaged in policy advice.

---

[18] Mäki's excellent introduction to his book (Mäki, 2002) with the euphonic title 'The dismal queen of the social sciences', albeit from a somewhat different perspective, argues along the same lines.

One good reason for this may be that they are very much aware of the risks and limitations of giving policy advice, in particular because much of the business is already occupied by 'short-term' economists. Therefore it has become a very difficult task for an economist to be heard and to get an argument accepted. Of course, the most negative consequence of this is that a considerable number of economists have ceased to give policy advice or to discuss their ideas in public.

Finally, there are economists who more or less right from the beginning of their work completely withdraw from the 'real life' component of economics and engage in theoretical exercises with only limited (direct) importance for economic policy. Some of them give policy advice, some of them do not. But common to all of them seems to be the limited interest in the features, the development and the variety of phenomena of the real world. They address the world of their models instead, which they believe to contain the essential core of real world issues (Tichy, 2003).

How far the situation has already developed, in particular with regard to the separation between theoretical economics and economic policy advice, may be stressed by several examples taken from recent history: on the one hand, recently we have seen a surprising number of outstanding members of the scientific community in economics – ranging from Joseph Stiglitz to Kenneth Rogoff and Paul DeGrauwe – treated with a high degree of scepticism by policy institutions because of certain policy positions they have argued for.[19] On the other hand, there were several cases, especially in Europe, where highly qualified economists more or less explicitly denied accepting positions in the field of policy advice (for example German research institutes). Vice versa, institutions engaged in economic policy advice have received very critical, if not unfair, evaluations based on rigorous academic standards.

Of course, the exact reasons for all these cases would have to be explored in detail. But what remains in any case and what has been taken up by the media is a certain feeling that the gap between the outcome of the scientific community and its application in economic policy has widened to a considerable extent. There is no particular group to be blamed alone for this separation, but one gets the impression, as in daily life, that many faults and mistakes from all sides have in the end led to this uncomfortable result.

---

[19] Blinder (1997) reports on his two years of experience as vice-chairman of the Board of Governors of the Federal Reserve; the discussion seems to continue along these lines with Ben Bernanke (see 'Free thinker pushing the envelope at the Fed', *Financial Times*, 9 March 2004).

In a recent interview,[20] Orley Ashenfelter, a labour market economist from Princeton University, stressed the fear of many economists that critical thoughts and contributions are no longer welcome once they are engaged in institutional policy advice. Julio Rotemberg (Harvard and CEPR) focused on the popularity issue, which is very important for policy-makers but less so for economists, who will not have to succeed in the next election.[21]

The series of interviews of economists with different professional backgrounds which have been published in *Financial Times Deutschland* since July 2002 ('Der Montagsökonom') on an almost weekly basis reveals a number of interesting elements in this respect which can be summarized as follows: economists who engage in academics tend to be rather critical of politicians and the political process and most of them refuse to engage in policy advice or in the political arena. Economists who work in or close to politics stress that there is no need for additional or even better theories; what is needed from their point of view is a better implementation of policies and that the public has to be convinced that policy measures are necessary. Finally, it is remarkable that both groups seem to disagree substantially on which kind of theory and policy would be urgently needed to improve policy-making.

The main conclusion to be drawn from this selection of behavioural reactions to the situation seems to be that we cannot deal with the questions at stake without adding aspects like economists behaving as a social group and what incentives and common rules are relevant for and within the scientific community of economics.[22] From this perspective the concept of 'truth' and how 'truth' is created in the scientific community is quite different from what usually comes to one's mind on the issue.

6. ANY CONCLUSIONS?

This chapter, which is very historical in its orientation, refers back to the Renaissance as the basis for modern science, as the time when the

---

[20] *Financial Times Deutschland*, 22 September, 2003.

[21] *Financial Times Deutschland*, 1 March, 2004.

[22] See the relevant contributions in Mäki (2002), in particular Hargreaves Heap (2002), Tuomela and Balzer (2002) and Zamora Bonilla (2002); a completely different but by no means less revealing – and much more amusing – way of dealing with the issue is presented in a novel by J.K. Galbraith (2001) and in a tetralogy of 'science in fiction' novels by C. Djerassi, the most impressive one being 'Cantor's Dilemma' (1989). Of course, the classic piece in this respect is Flaubert (1976).

institutional foundations were laid for what today is called scientific community. It discusses three main factors held relevant for modern economic thought: (i) philosophy of science as an essential background to everything economists do, (ii) the development of economic theory in its historical context and (iii) the evolution of economic reality and the challenges created for and from economic policy-making.

The main intention, of course, was to shed some light on the role and function of today's economists, in particular on how they behave and what kind of institutions they create and use to 'discover' the appropriate rationale for giving economic policy advice. However, 'truth' in the sense of a well-defined and stable concept could not be identified in this context. In contrast, it mainly seems to emerge from this analysis, from putting some historical, theoretical and social pieces together, that 'truth' is not a very helpful concept when we have to deal with real world issues in an economic policy context.

Are there any general conclusions to be drawn from this line of thinking? From a very personal point of view there are at least three conclusions that are worth mentioning and which ask for further consideration: first, economists seem to have been very successful in creating their own methodological basis of economics and economic policy advice. The transformation of Popper's ideas into a very narrow applied concept made the history of economics a science over the last decades, at the same time basically ignoring the important historical and social dimension Kuhn's work concentrates on. Second, many of the developments visible in economics and, in particular, economic policy advice can only be understood if the scientific community of economists is analyzed from the perspective of a social group. These determinants have eventually led to a situation where a widening of the gap between economics and real world problems seems to be clearly visible; therefore, economic policy advice has become less effective in several respects and for a number of different reasons. Third, and most importantly, it has to be taken into consideration that economics and economic policy are embedded into a reality which is very much characterized by an essential historical dimension as well as considerable uncertainties, for example regarding changes in behavioural reactions of economic agents. To become effective under these difficult preconditions a certain degree of pragmatism, flexibility and experience seems unavoidable to tackle real world challenges.

REFERENCES

Blaug, M. (1997), *Economic Theory in Retrospect*, Cambridge: Cambridge University Press.

Blinder, A. (1997), 'What central bankers could learn from academics – and vice versa', *Journal of Economic Perspectives*, **11** (2), 3–19.

Buiter, W. (1980), 'The macroeconomics of Dr. Pangloss: A critical survey of the new classical macroeconomics', *Economic Journal*, **90** (357), 34–50.

Burke, P. (1998), *The European Renaissance: Centres and Peripheries*, Oxford: Blackwell Press.

Djerassi, C. (1989), *Cantor's Dilemma*, New York: Penguin Books.

Dow, S. (2001), 'Methodology in a pluralist environment', *Journal of Economic Methodology*, **8** (1), 33–40.

Dow, S. (2002), *Economic Methodology: An Inquiry*, Oxford: Oxford University Press.

Edey, M. and K. Hviding (1995), 'An assessment of financial reform in OECD countries', *OECD Economic Studies*, No. 25, 1995/II.

Espinosa-Vega, M. (1998), How Powerful is Monetary Policy in the Long Run? Federal Reserve Bank of Atlanta Economic Review **83** (3) 12–31.

Fehr, E. and A. Falk (2002), 'Psychological foundations of incentives', *European Economic Review*, **46** (4/5), 687–724.

Feyerabend, P. (1965), 'Problems of Empiricism I', in R. Colodny (ed.), *Beyond the Edge of Certainty*, Englewood Cliffs: Prentice Hall.

Feyerabend, P. (1975), *Against Method*, London: NLB (Revised German editions 1976 and 1983).

Flaubert, G. (1976), *Bouvard and Pécuchet*, Harmondsworth: Penguin Books.

Fleck, L. (1980), *Entstehung und Entwicklung einer Wissenschaftlichen Tatsache*, Frankfurt am Main: Suhrkamp.

Fuller, St. (2003), *Kuhn vs. Popper: The Struggle for the Soul of Science*, Cambridge: Icon Books.

Galbraith, J.K. (2001), *A Tenured Professor: A Novel*, Boston: Houghton Mifflin.

Garin, E. (1996), *Der Mensch der Renaissance*, Frankfurt am Main: Fischer.

Hafer, R. and D. Wheelock (2001), 'The rise and fall of a policy rule: Monetarism at the St. Louis Fed 1968–1986', *The Federal Reserve Bank of St. Louis Review*, **83** (1), 1–24.

Hargreaves Heap, S. (2002), *The Reality of Common Cultures*, in U. Mäki (ed.), *Fact and Fiction in Economics: Models, Realism and Social Construction*, Cambridge: Cambridge University Press, pp. 257–68.

Hayes, S., K. Cuthbertson and D. Nitzsche (1997), 'The behaviour of UK stock prices and returns: Is the market efficient?', *The Economic Journal*, **107** (443), 986–1008.

Hetzel, R. (2002a), 'German monetary policy in the first half of the twentieth century', *Federal Reserve Bank of Richmond Economic Quarterly*, **88** (1), 1–35.

Hetzel, R. (2002b), 'German monetary policy in the second half of the twentieth century: From the Deutsche Mark to the Euro', *Federal Reserve Bank of Richmond Economic Quarterly*, **88** (2), 29–64.

Klamer, A. (1984), *The New Classical Macroeconomics*, Brighton: Wheatsheaf Books.

Kuhn, Th. (1962), *The Structure of Scientific Revolutions*, Chicago: University of

Chicago Press.

Lakatos, I. and A. Musgrave (eds) (1970), *Criticism and the Growth of Knowledge*, London: Cambridge University Press.

Leamer, E. (1983), 'Let's take the con out of econometrics', *American Economic Review,* **73** (1), 31–43.

Mäki, U. (ed.) (2002), *Fact and Fiction in Economics: Models, Realism and Social Construction*, Cambridge: Cambridge University Press.

Mankiw, G. (2001), 'US Monetary Policy During the 1990s', NBER Working Paper, No. 8471.

Mayer, Th. (1999), 'Some Practical Aspects of Pluralism in Economics', University of California, Davis, Working Paper Series No. 99-05.

McCallum, B. (2002), 'Recent developments in monetary policy analysis: The roles of theory and evidence', *Federal Reserve Bank of Richmond Economic Quarterly*, **88** (1), 1–22.

McClosky, Donald (1983), 'The rhetoric of economics', *Journal of Economic Literature*, **21** (2), 481–517.

McClosky, Deirdre N. (2002), *The Secret Sins of Economics*, Chicago: Prickly Paradigm.

Miller, D. (ed.) (1983), *A Pocket Popper*, London: Fontana.

Mooslechner, P. (2003), 'Finance for growth, finance and growth, finance or growth . . . ? Three perspectives on the interaction of financial markets and the real economy', *Focus on Austria,* No. 1, Vienna: Oesterreichische Nationalbank,. 76–94.

Nola, R. and H. Sankey (eds) (2000), *After Popper, Kuhn and Feyerabend: Recent Issues in Theories of Scientific Method*, Dordrecht: Kluwer Academic Publishers.

Poole, W. (2002), 'Financial stability', *Federal Reserve Bank of St. Louis Review*, **84** (5), 1–8.

Popper, K. (1976), *Unended Quest: An Intellectual Autobiography*, London and Glasgow: Fontana/William Collins Sons & Co. Ltd. (in German: revised edition 1982).

Popper, K. (1992), *The Logic of Scientific Discovery*, London: Routledge.

Rabin, M. (2002), 'A perspective on psychology and economics', *European Economic Review*, **46** (4/5), 657-85.

Rehmer, G. (2002), 'Why Run a Million Regressions. Endogenous Policy and Cross-Country Growth Empirics.', *Royal Economic Society Annual Conference 2002,* Working Paper Series, No. 157.

Robinson, J. (1971), *Economic Heresies*, New York: Basic Books.

Sala-i-Martin, X. (1997), 'I just ran two million regressions', *American Economic Review*, **87** (2), *Papers and Proceedings of the Hundred and Fourth Annual Meeting of the American Economic Association*, May 1997, 178–83.

Selody, J. (2001), 'Principles for building models of the monetary policy transmission mechanism', *Focus on Austria,* No. 3–4, Vienna: Oesterreichische Nationalbank, 202–17.

Sennet, R. (1998), *The Corrosion of Character*, New York: W.W. Norton.

Shiller, R. (2000), *Irrational Exuberance*, Princeton: Princeton University Press.

Shiller, R. (2002), 'From Efficient Market Theory to Behavioral Finance', Cowles Foundation Discussion Paper 1385, October.

Shleifer, A. (2000), *Inefficient Markets*, Oxford: Oxford University Press.

Spiegel, H. (1991), *The Growth of Economic Thought*, Durham: Duke University Press.

Stierle, K. (2003), *Francesco Petrarca*, München: Hanser.

Strange, S. (1986), *Casino Capitalism*, Oxford: Blackwells.

Thaler, R. (1994), *The Winner's Curse: Paradoxes and Anomalies of Economic Life*, Princeton: Princeton University Press.

Tichy, G. (2003), *Der Volkswirt als Politikberater*, in G. Chaloupek, A. Guger, E. Nowotny and G. Schwödiauer (eds), *Ökonomie in Theorie und Praxis*, Berlin, Heidelberg: Springer, pp. 359–77.

Tuomela, R. and W. Balzer (2002), 'Collective Acceptance and Collective Attitudes: On the Social Construction of Social Reality', in U. Mäki (ed.), *Fact and Fiction in Economics. Models, Realism and Social Construction*, Cambridge: Cambridge University Press, pp. 269–84.

Zamora Bonilla, J. (2002), 'Economists: Truth-seekers or Rent-seekers?', in U. Mäki (ed.), *Fact and Fiction in Economics. Models, Realism and Social Construction*, Cambridge: Cambridge University Press, pp. 356–75.

Zwiebel, J. (2002), 'Review of Shleifer's inefficient markets', *Journal of Economic Literature*, **40** (4), 1215–20.

Index